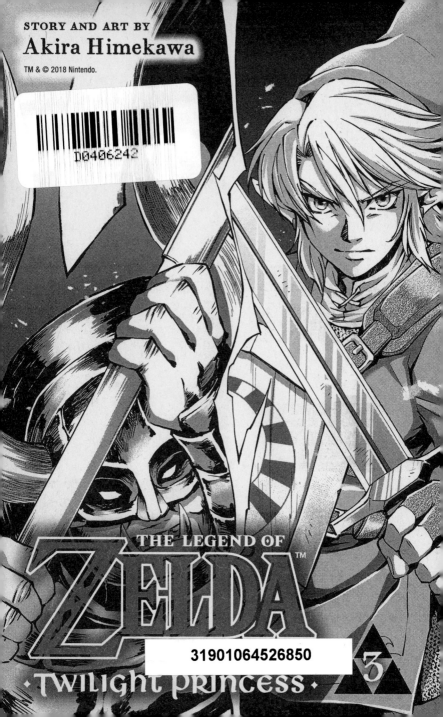

STORY AND ART BY
Akira Himekawa

TM & © 2018 Nintendo.

D0406242

THE LEGEND OF
ZELDA™

twilight princess

3

THE LEGEND OF ZELDA™

ZELDA

·TWILIGHT PRINCESS·

3

CONTENTS

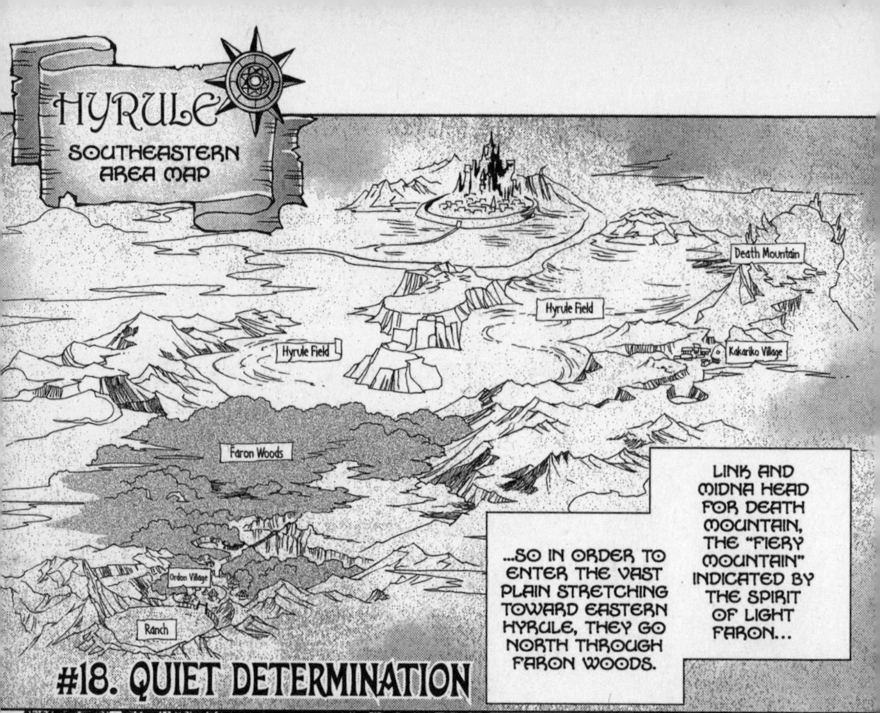
HYRULE
SOUTHEASTERN AREA MAP
Death Mountain
Hyrule Field
Hyrule Field
Kakariko Village
Faron Woods
Ordon Village
Ranch
LINK AND MIDNA HEAD FOR DEATH MOUNTAIN, THE "FIERY MOUNTAIN" INDICATED BY THE SPIRIT OF LIGHT FARON...
...SO IN ORDER TO ENTER THE VAST PLAIN STRETCHING TOWARD EASTERN HYRULE, THEY GO NORTH THROUGH FARON WOODS.
#18. QUIET DETERMINATION

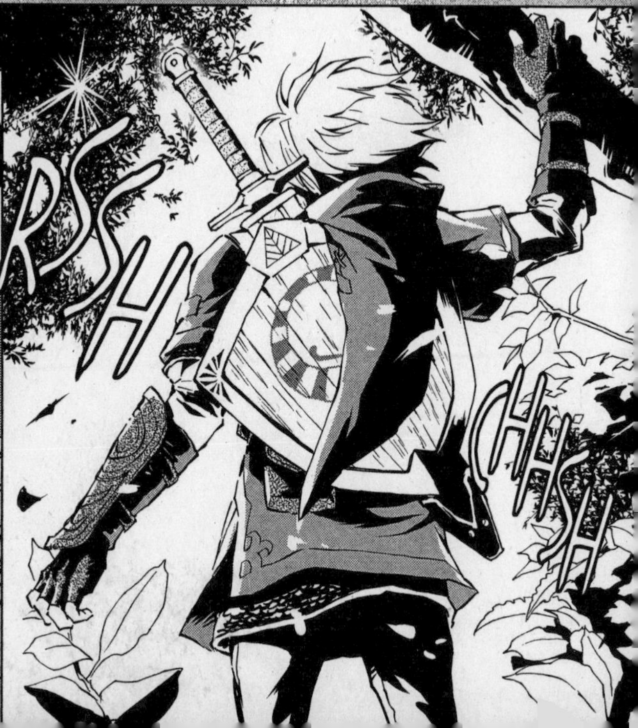
RSSH
CHISH

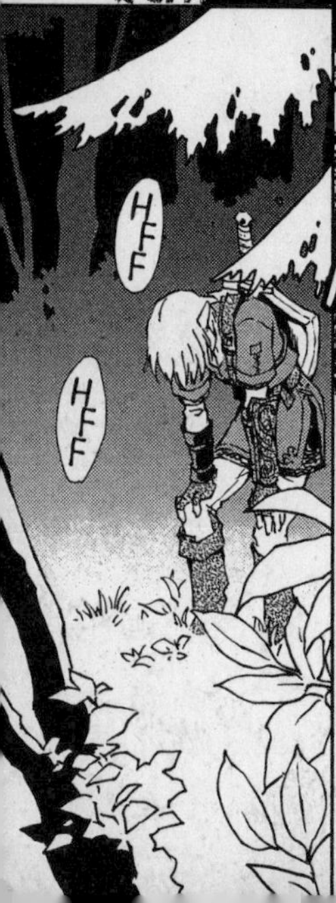
HFF
HFF

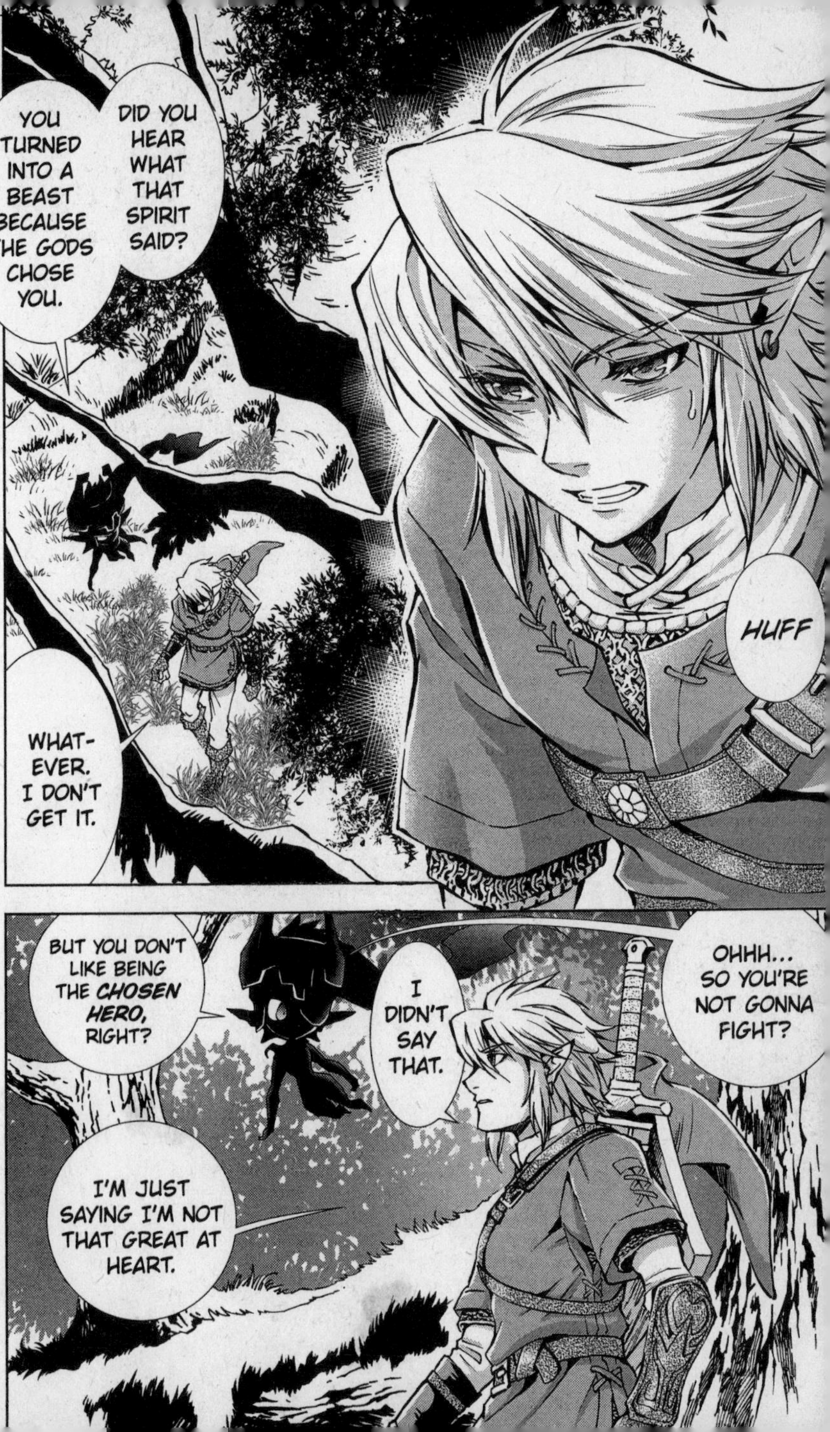
DID YOU HEAR WHAT THAT SPIRIT SAID?
YOU TURNED INTO A BEAST BECAUSE THE GODS CHOSE YOU.
HUFF
WHAT-EVER. I DON'T GET IT.
OHHH... SO YOU'RE NOT GONNA FIGHT?
I DIDN'T SAY THAT.
BUT YOU DON'T LIKE BEING THE *CHOSEN HERO,* RIGHT?
I'M JUST SAYING I'M NOT THAT GREAT AT HEART.

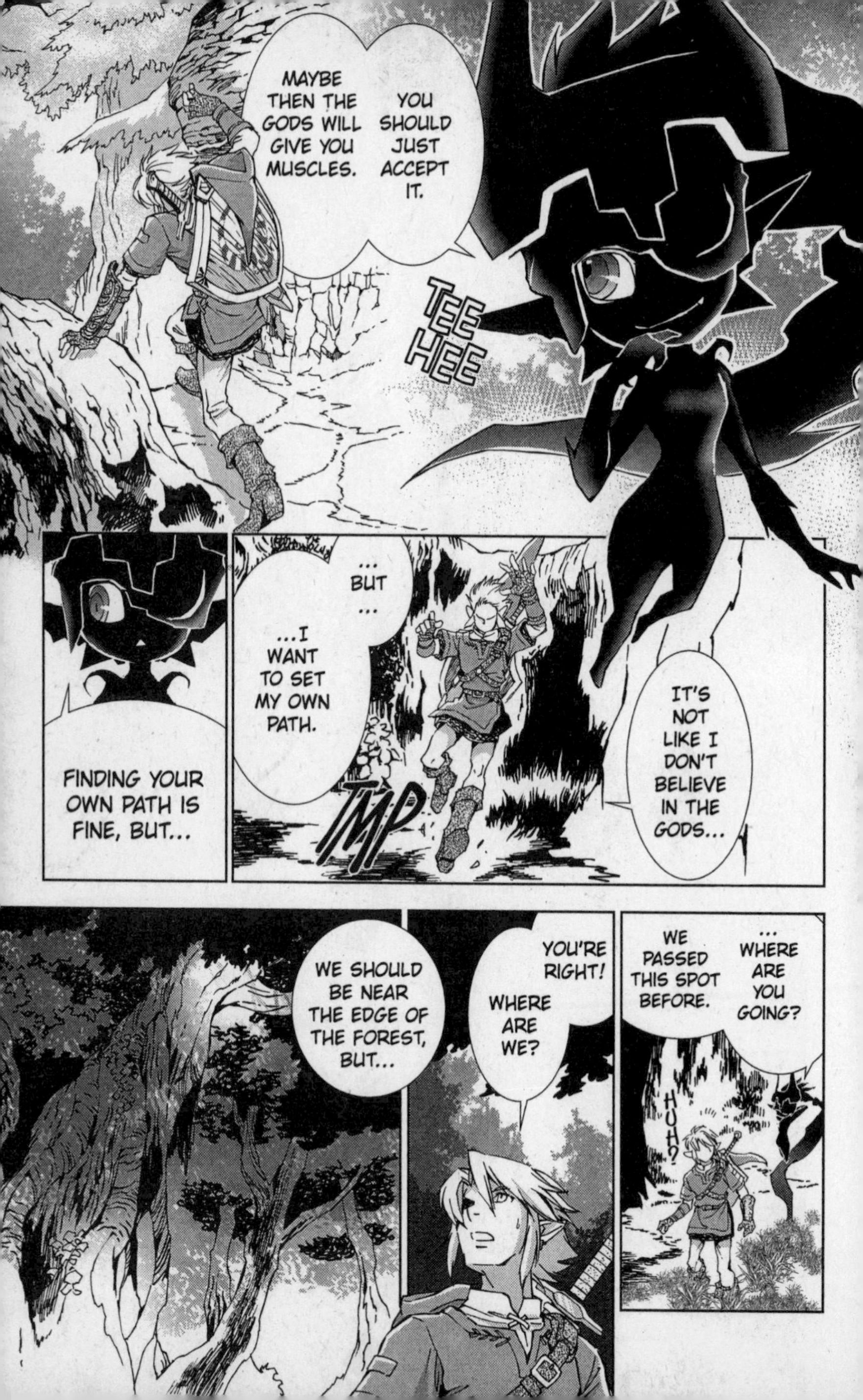
YOU SHOULD JUST ACCEPT IT.
MAYBE THEN THE GODS WILL GIVE YOU MUSCLES.
TEE HEE
IT'S NOT LIKE I DON'T BELIEVE IN THE GODS...
...BUT...
...I WANT TO SET MY OWN PATH.
TMP
FINDING YOUR OWN PATH IS FINE, BUT...
...WHERE ARE YOU GOING?
WE PASSED THIS SPOT BEFORE.
HUH?
YOU'RE RIGHT!
WHERE ARE WE?
WE SHOULD BE NEAR THE EDGE OF THE FOREST, BUT...

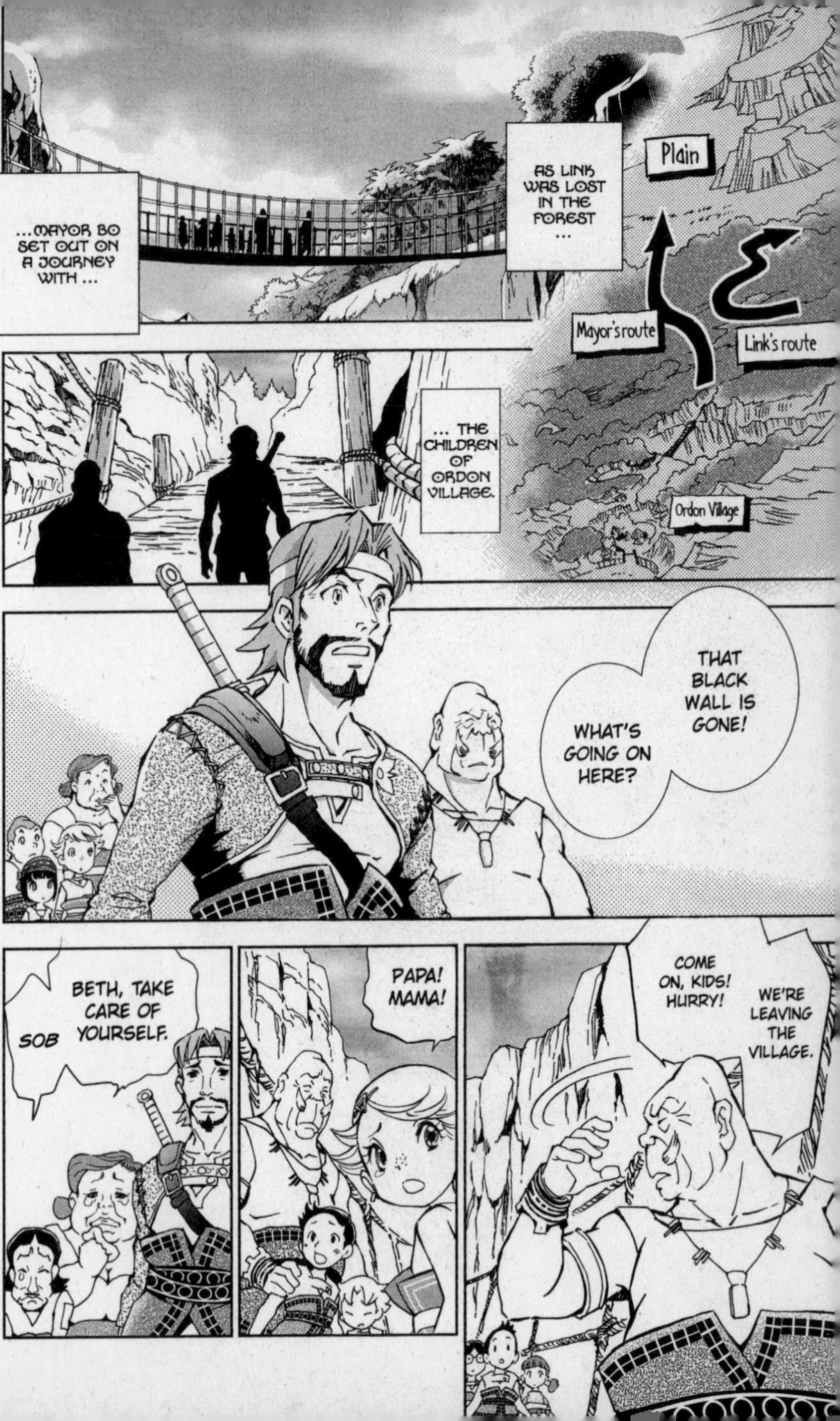
AS LINK WAS LOST IN THE FOREST ...
Plain
Mayor's route
Link's route
Ordon Village
...MAYOR BO SET OUT ON A JOURNEY WITH ...
... THE CHILDREN OF ORDON VILLAGE.
THAT BLACK WALL IS GONE!
WHAT'S GOING ON HERE?
COME ON, KIDS! HURRY!
WE'RE LEAVING THE VILLAGE.
PAPA! MAMA!
BETH, TAKE CARE OF YOURSELF.
SOB

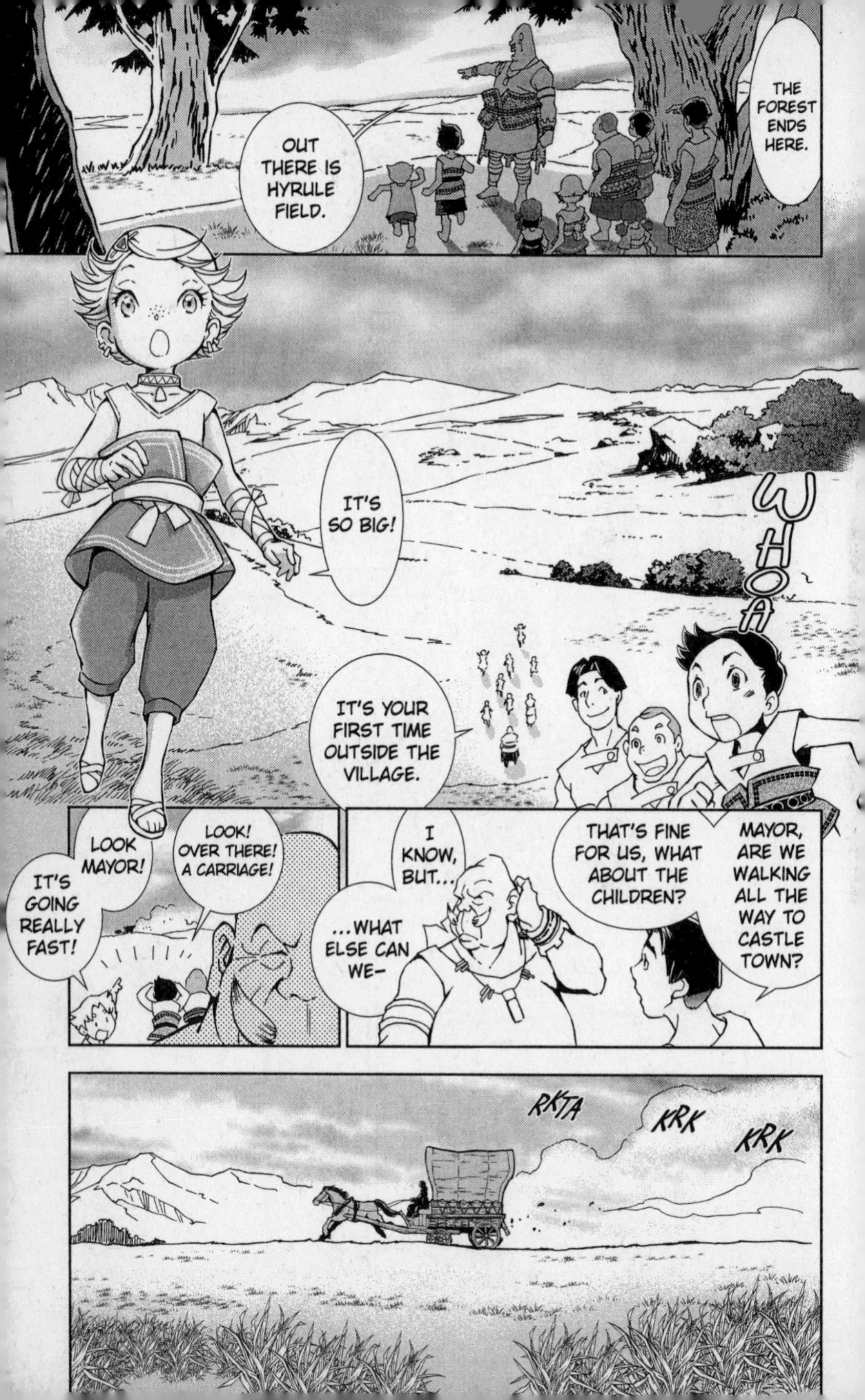
THE FOREST ENDS HERE.
OUT THERE IS HYRULE FIELD.
WHOA
IT'S SO BIG!
IT'S YOUR FIRST TIME OUTSIDE THE VILLAGE.
MAYOR, ARE WE WALKING ALL THE WAY TO CASTLE TOWN?
THAT'S FINE FOR US, WHAT ABOUT THE CHILDREN?
I KNOW, BUT...
...WHAT ELSE CAN WE-
LOOK! OVER THERE! A CARRIAGE!
LOOK MAYOR!
IT'S GOING REALLY FAST!
RKTA
KRK
KRK

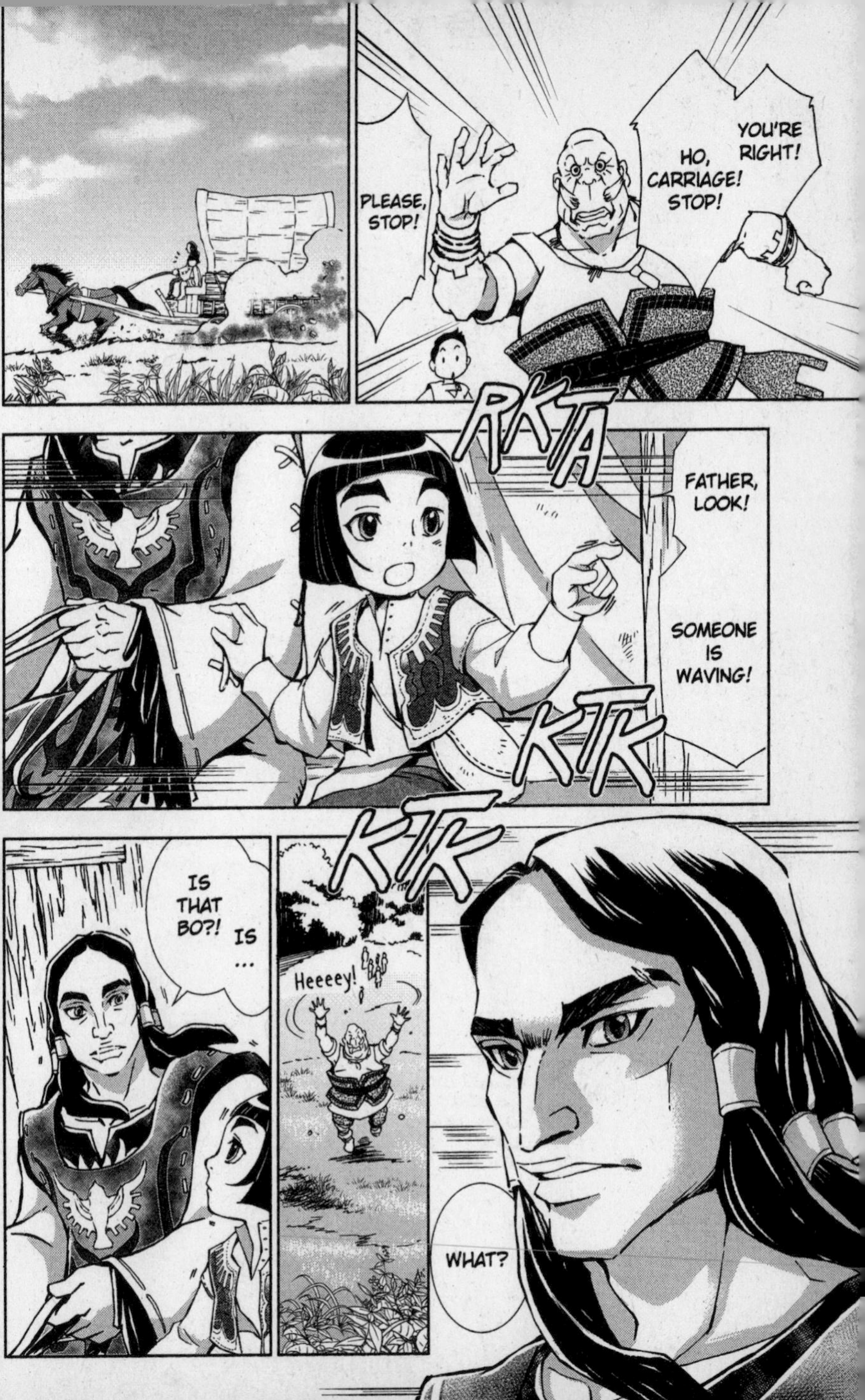
YOU'RE RIGHT!
HO, CARRIAGE! STOP!
PLEASE, STOP!
RKTA
FATHER, LOOK!
SOMEONE IS WAVING!
KTK
KTK
WHAT?
Heeeey!
IS THAT BO?!
IS ...

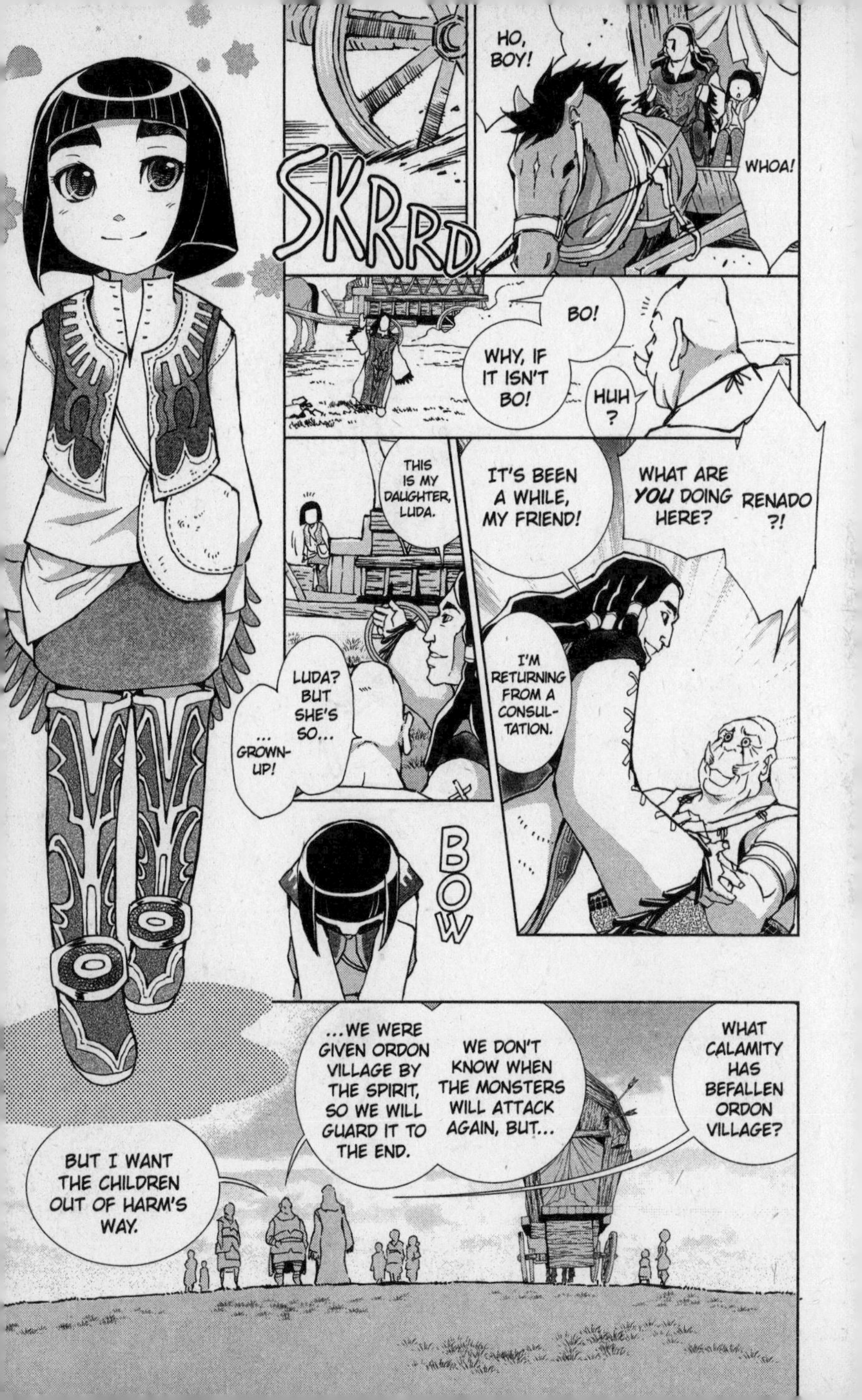
HO, BOY!
WHOA!
SKRRD
BO!
WHY, IF IT ISN'T BO!
HUH?
RENADO?!
WHAT ARE YOU DOING HERE?
IT'S BEEN A WHILE, MY FRIEND!
I'M RETURNING FROM A CONSULTATION.
THIS IS MY DAUGHTER, LUDA.
LUDA? BUT SHE'S SO...
...GROWN-UP!
BOW
WHAT CALAMITY HAS BEFALLEN ORDON VILLAGE?
WE DON'T KNOW WHEN THE MONSTERS WILL ATTACK AGAIN, BUT...
...WE WERE GIVEN ORDON VILLAGE BY THE SPIRIT, SO WE WILL GUARD IT TO THE END.
BUT I WANT THE CHILDREN OUT OF HARM'S WAY.

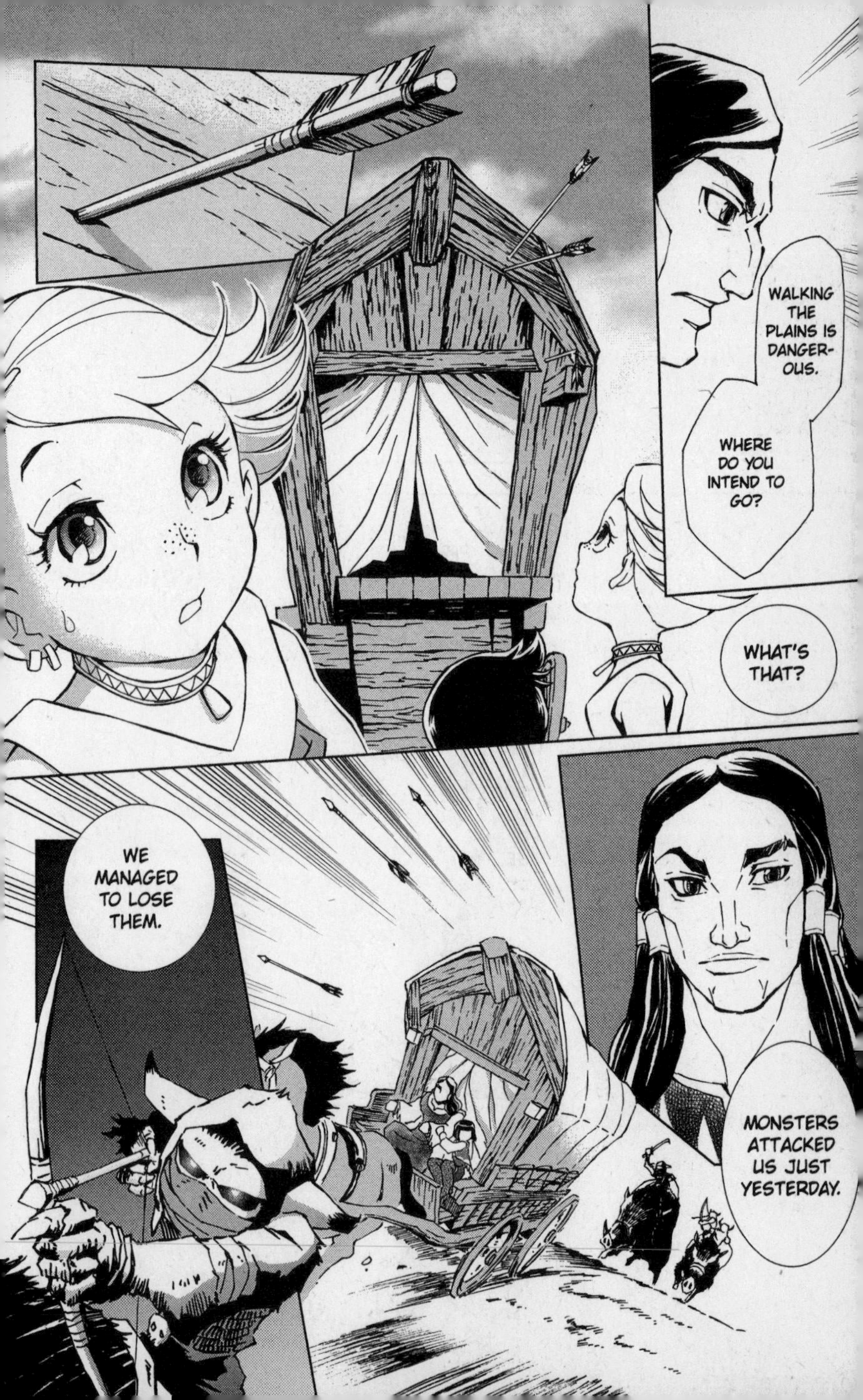
WALKING THE PLAINS IS DANGER-OUS.
WHERE DO YOU INTEND TO GO?
WHAT'S THAT?
MONSTERS ATTACKED US JUST YESTERDAY.
WE MANAGED TO LOSE THEM.

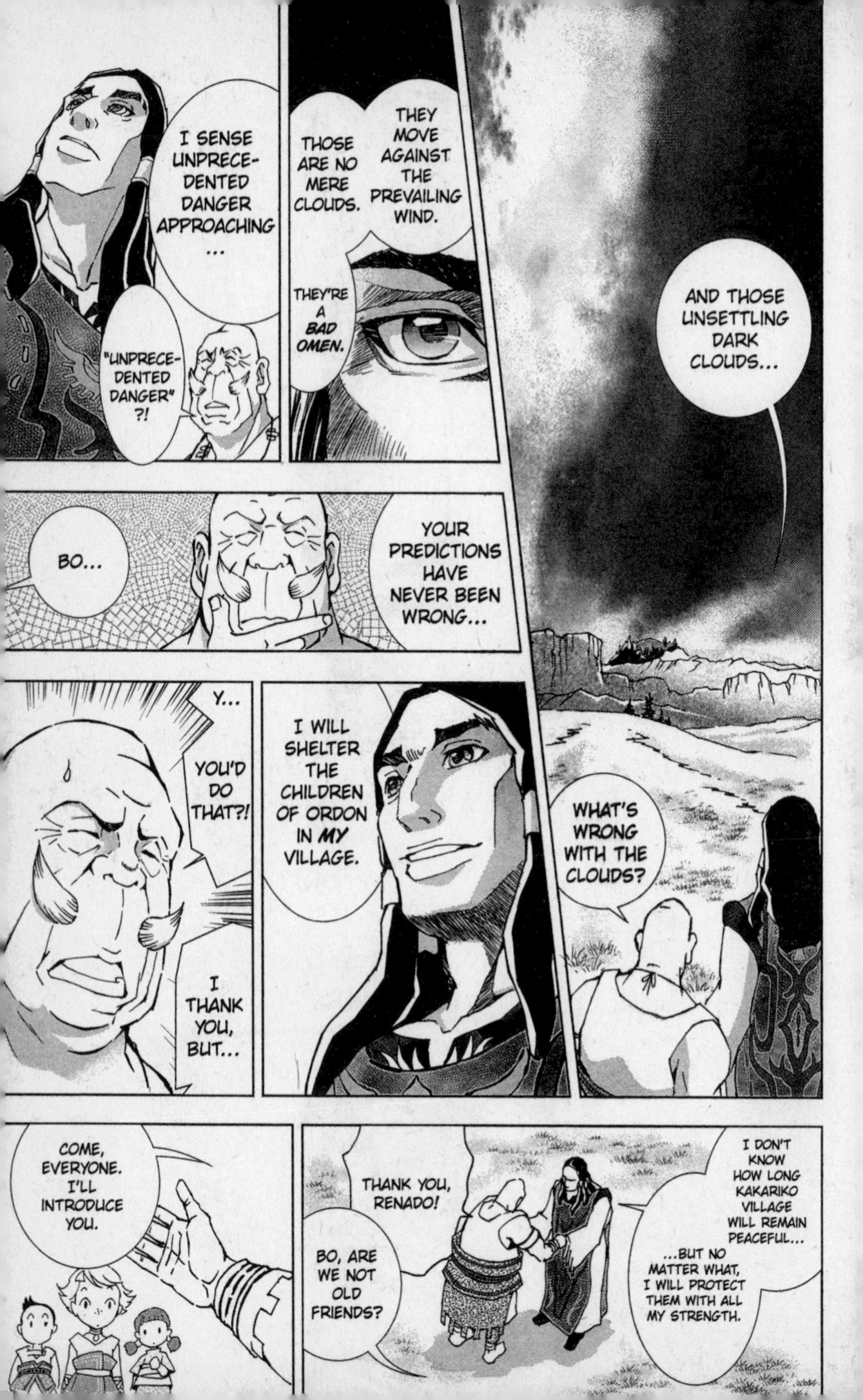
AND THOSE UNSETTLING DARK CLOUDS...
WHAT'S WRONG WITH THE CLOUDS?
THEY MOVE AGAINST THE PREVAILING WIND.
THOSE ARE NO MERE CLOUDS.
THEY'RE A *BAD OMEN.*
I SENSE UNPRECEDENTED DANGER APPROACHING ...
"UNPRECEDENTED DANGER" ?!
YOUR PREDICTIONS HAVE NEVER BEEN WRONG...
BO...
I WILL SHELTER THE CHILDREN OF ORDON IN *MY* VILLAGE.
Y...
YOU'D DO THAT?!
I THANK YOU, BUT...
I DON'T KNOW HOW LONG KAKARIKO VILLAGE WILL REMAIN PEACEFUL...
...BUT NO MATTER WHAT, I WILL PROTECT THEM WITH ALL MY STRENGTH.
THANK YOU, RENADO!
BO, ARE WE NOT OLD FRIENDS?
COME, EVERYONE. I'LL INTRODUCE YOU.

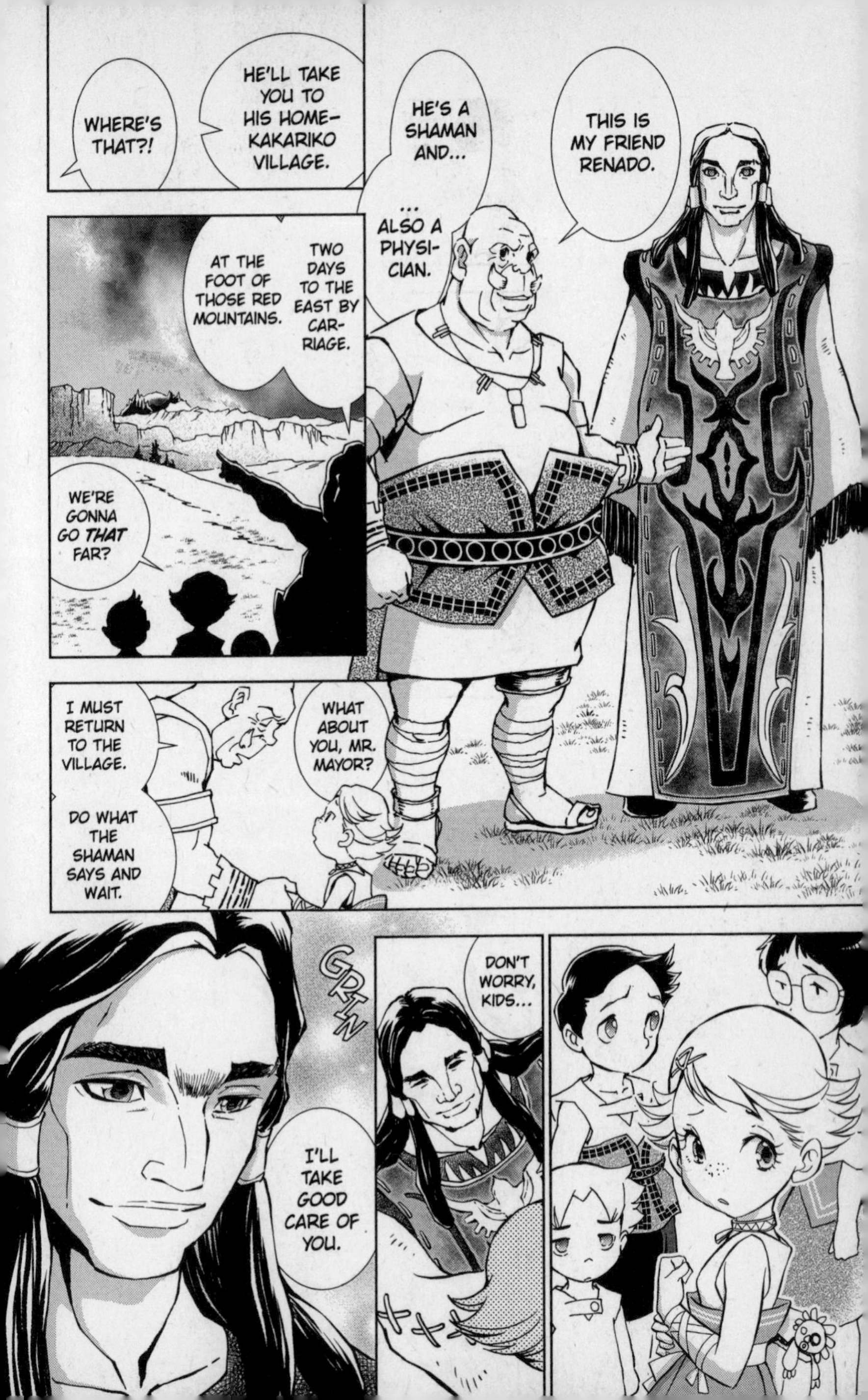
THIS IS MY FRIEND RENADO.
HE'S A SHAMAN AND...
... ALSO A PHYSICIAN.
HE'LL TAKE YOU TO HIS HOME-KAKARIKO VILLAGE.
WHERE'S THAT?!
TWO DAYS TO THE EAST BY CARRIAGE.
AT THE FOOT OF THOSE RED MOUNTAINS.
WE'RE GONNA GO *THAT* FAR?
WHAT ABOUT YOU, MR. MAYOR?
I MUST RETURN TO THE VILLAGE.
DO WHAT THE SHAMAN SAYS AND WAIT.
DON'T WORRY, KIDS...
GRIN
I'LL TAKE GOOD CARE OF YOU.

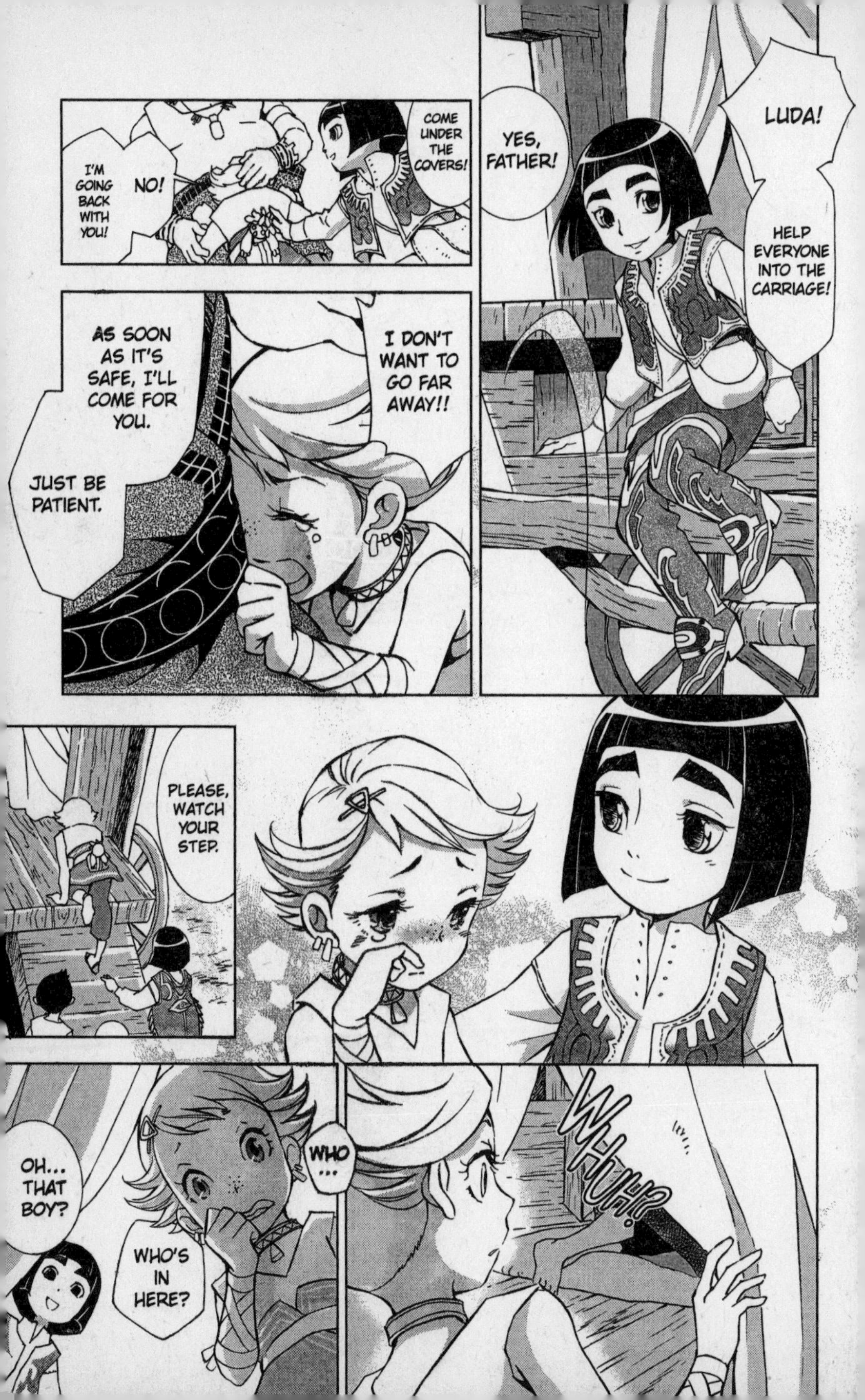
LUDA!
HELP EVERYONE INTO THE CARRIAGE!
YES, FATHER!
COME UNDER THE COVERS!
NO!
I'M GOING BACK WITH YOU!
I DON'T WANT TO GO FAR AWAY!!
AS SOON AS IT'S SAFE, I'LL COME FOR YOU.
JUST BE PATIENT.
PLEASE, WATCH YOUR STEP.
WHUH!?
WHO...
WHO'S IN HERE?
OH... THAT BOY?

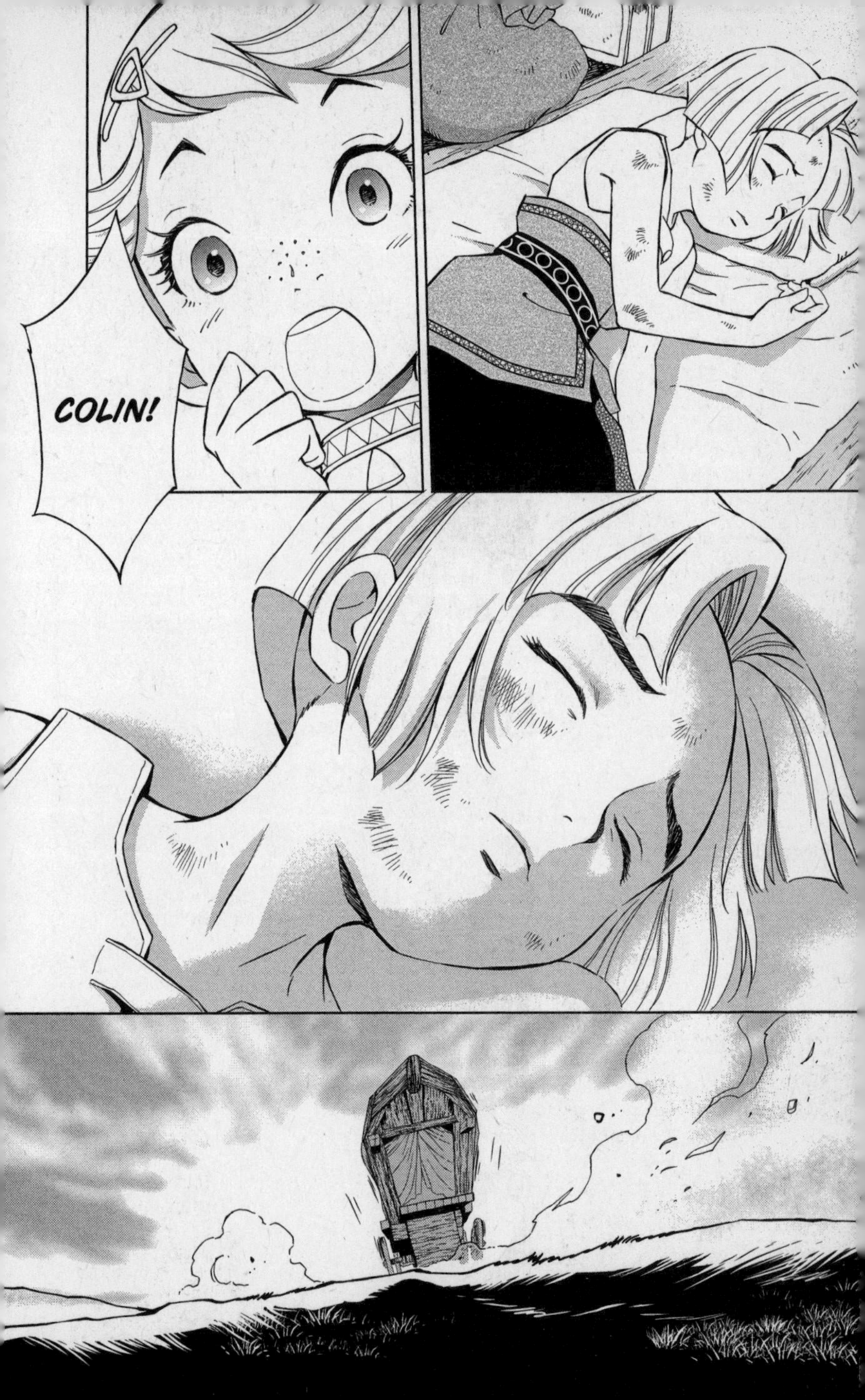
COLIN!

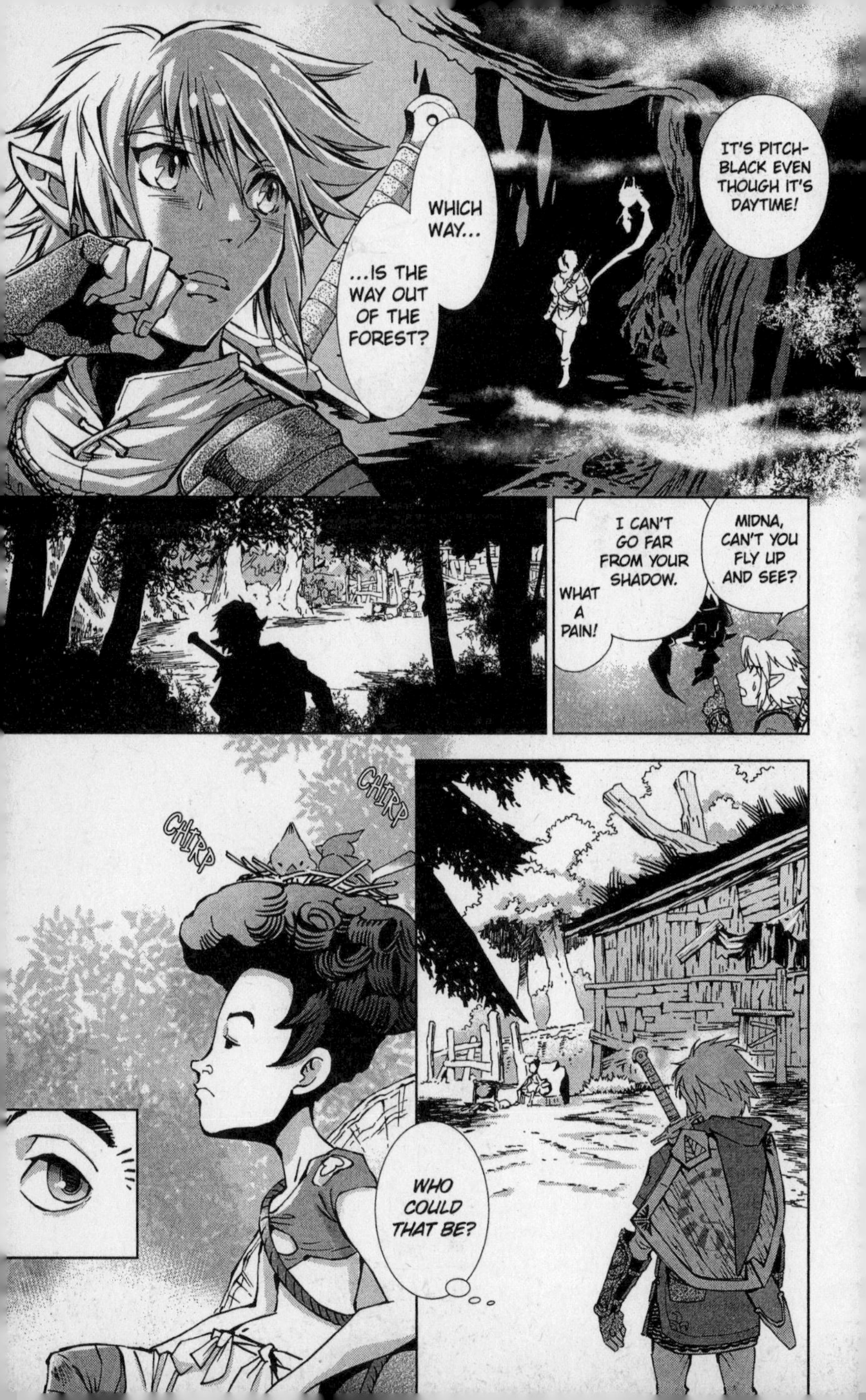
IT'S PITCH-BLACK EVEN THOUGH IT'S DAYTIME!
WHICH WAY...
...IS THE WAY OUT OF THE FOREST?
MIDNA, CAN'T YOU FLY UP AND SEE?
I CAN'T GO FAR FROM YOUR SHADOW.
WHAT A PAIN!
CHIRP
CHIRP
WHO COULD THAT BE?

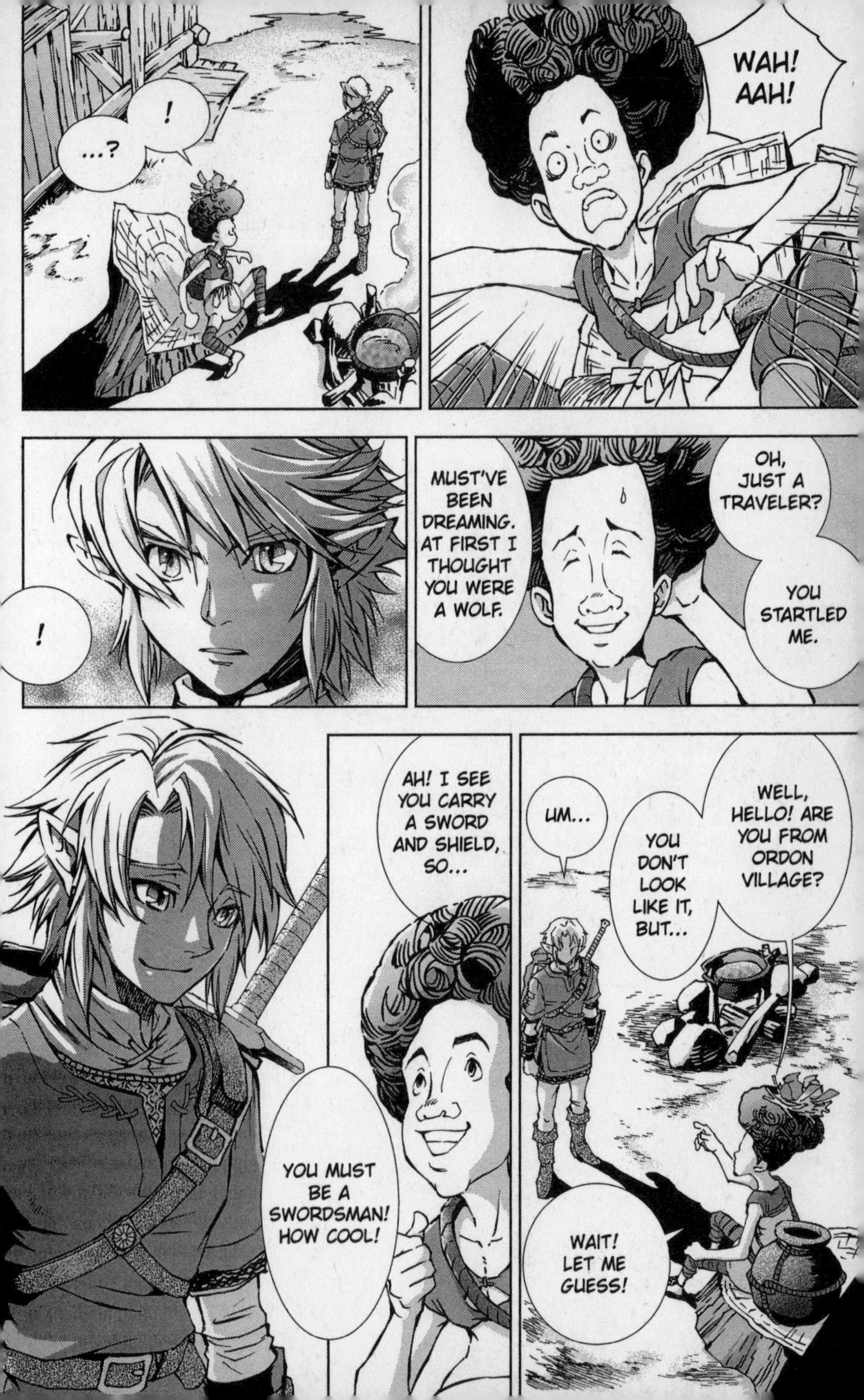
WAH! AAH!
!
...?
OH, JUST A TRAVELER?
YOU STARTLED ME.
MUST'VE BEEN DREAMING. AT FIRST I THOUGHT YOU WERE A WOLF.
!
WELL, HELLO! ARE YOU FROM ORDON VILLAGE?
YOU DON'T LOOK LIKE IT, BUT...
UM...
WAIT! LET ME GUESS!
AH! I SEE YOU CARRY A SWORD AND SHIELD, SO...
YOU MUST BE A SWORDSMAN! HOW COOL!

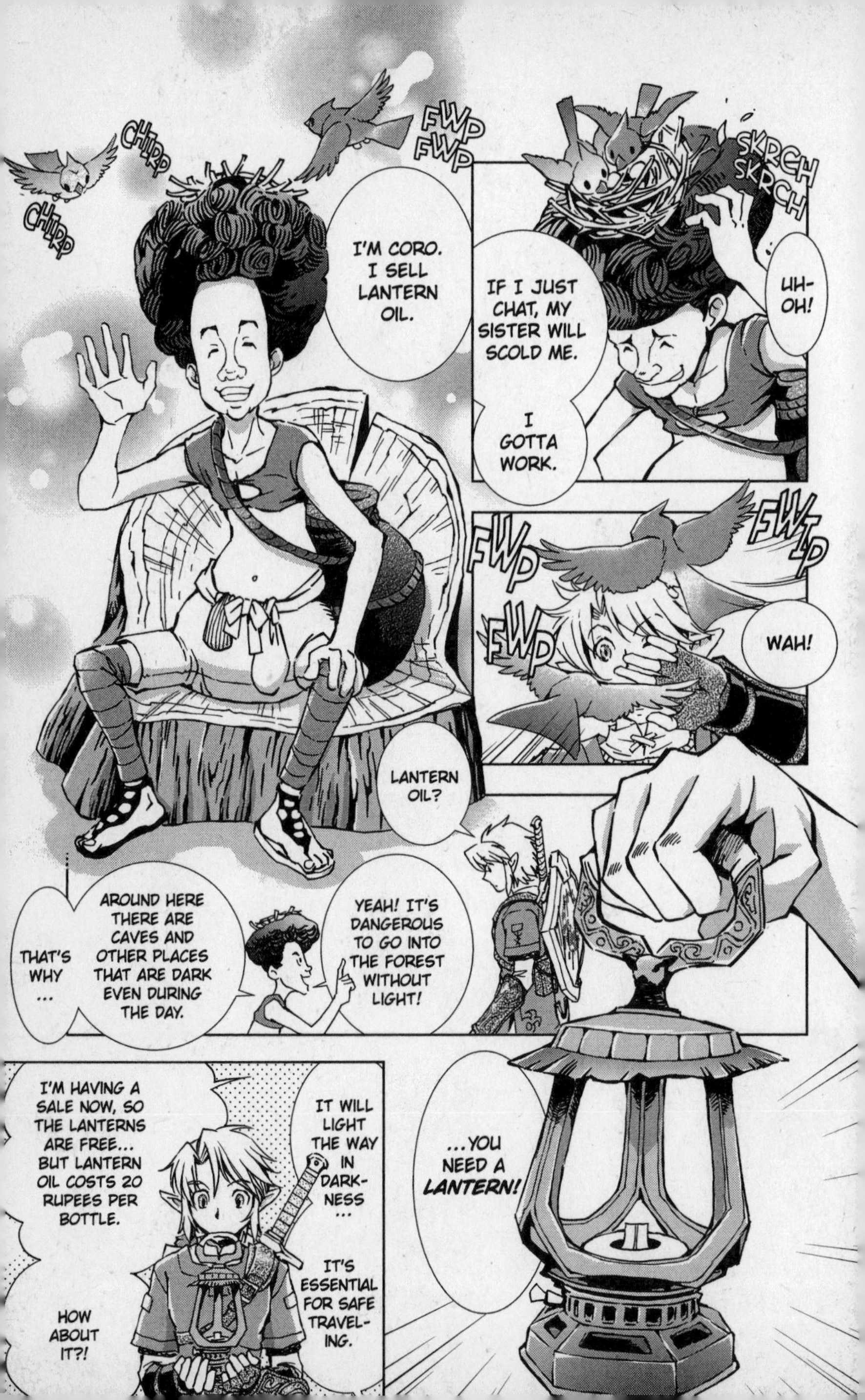
CHIRP
CHIRP
FWP FWP
I'M CORO. I SELL LANTERN OIL.
SKRCH SKRCH
IF I JUST CHAT, MY SISTER WILL SCOLD ME.
I GOTTA WORK.
UH-OH!
FWIP
FWP
FWP
WAH!
LANTERN OIL?
YEAH! IT'S DANGEROUS TO GO INTO THE FOREST WITHOUT LIGHT!
AROUND HERE THERE ARE CAVES AND OTHER PLACES THAT ARE DARK EVEN DURING THE DAY.
THAT'S WHY ...
...YOU NEED A *LANTERN!*
IT WILL LIGHT THE WAY IN DARKNESS ...
IT'S ESSENTIAL FOR SAFE TRAVELING.
I'M HAVING A SALE NOW, SO THE LANTERNS ARE FREE... BUT LANTERN OIL COSTS 20 RUPEES PER BOTTLE.
HOW ABOUT IT?!

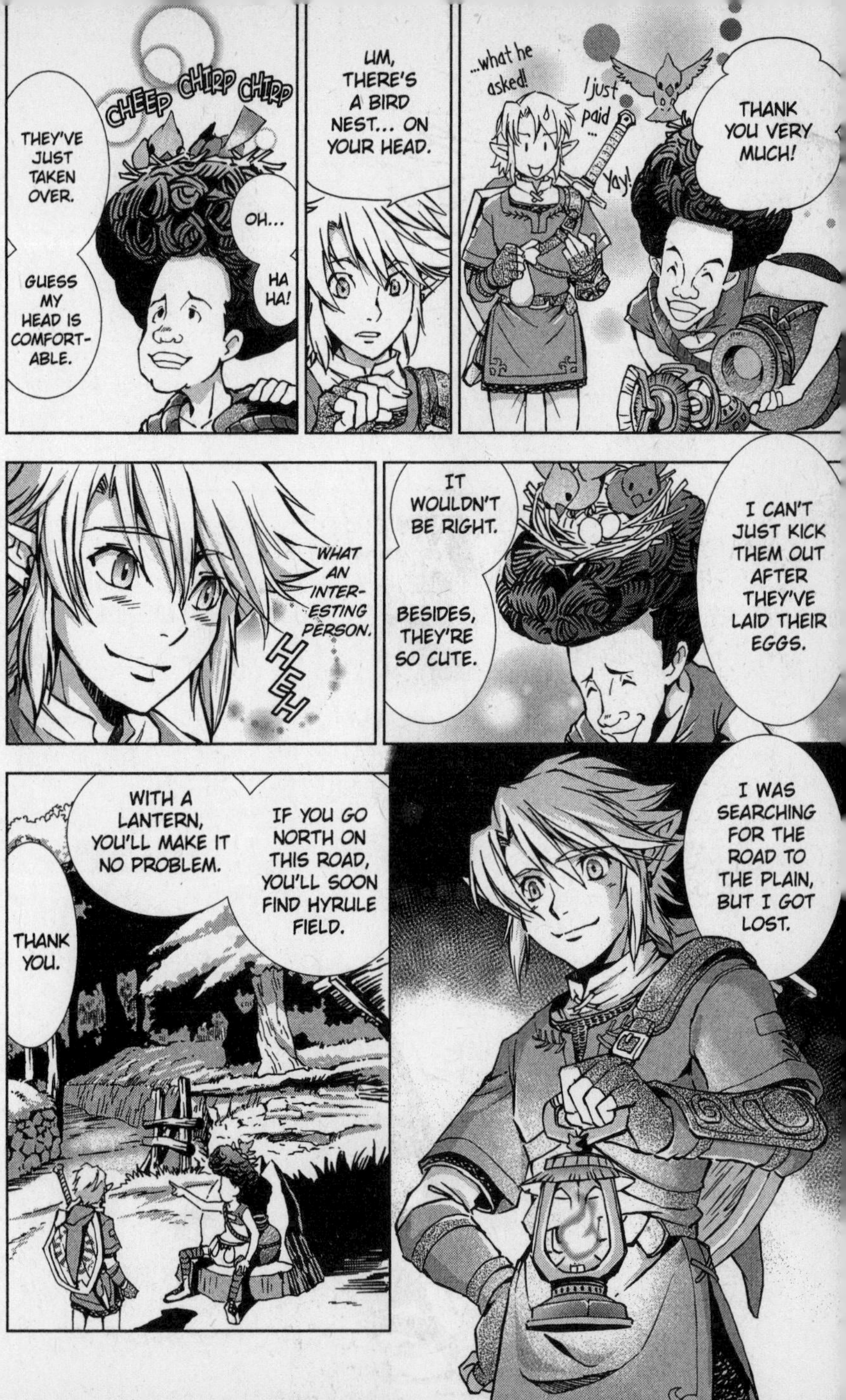
THANK YOU VERY MUCH!
I just paid ...
...what he asked!
Yay!
UM, THERE'S A BIRD NEST... ON YOUR HEAD.
OH...
HA HA!
CHEEP CHIRP CHIRP
THEY'VE JUST TAKEN OVER.
GUESS MY HEAD IS COMFORTABLE.
I CAN'T JUST KICK THEM OUT AFTER THEY'VE LAID THEIR EGGS.
IT WOULDN'T BE RIGHT.
BESIDES, THEY'RE SO CUTE.
WHAT AN INTERESTING PERSON.
HEH
I WAS SEARCHING FOR THE ROAD TO THE PLAIN, BUT I GOT LOST.
IF YOU GO NORTH ON THIS ROAD, YOU'LL SOON FIND HYRULE FIELD.
WITH A LANTERN, YOU'LL MAKE IT NO PROBLEM.
THANK YOU.

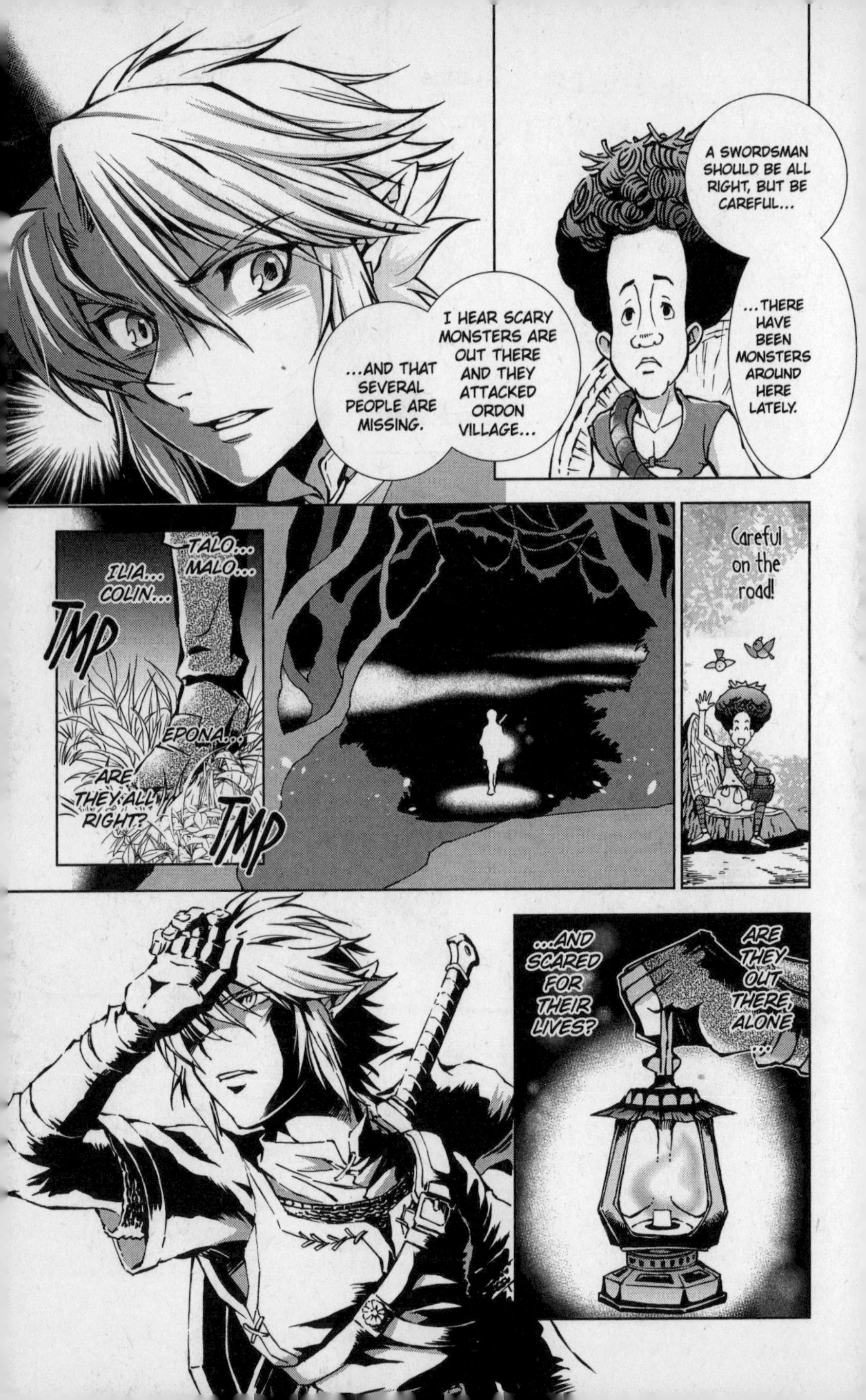
A SWORDSMAN SHOULD BE ALL RIGHT, BUT BE CAREFUL...
...THERE HAVE BEEN MONSTERS AROUND HERE LATELY.
I HEAR SCARY MONSTERS ARE OUT THERE AND THEY ATTACKED ORDON VILLAGE...
...AND THAT SEVERAL PEOPLE ARE MISSING.
Careful on the road!
TALO... MALO...
ILIA... COLIN...
TMP
EPONA...
ARE THEY ALL RIGHT?
TMP
ARE THEY OUT THERE, ALONE...
...AND SCARED FOR THEIR LIVES?

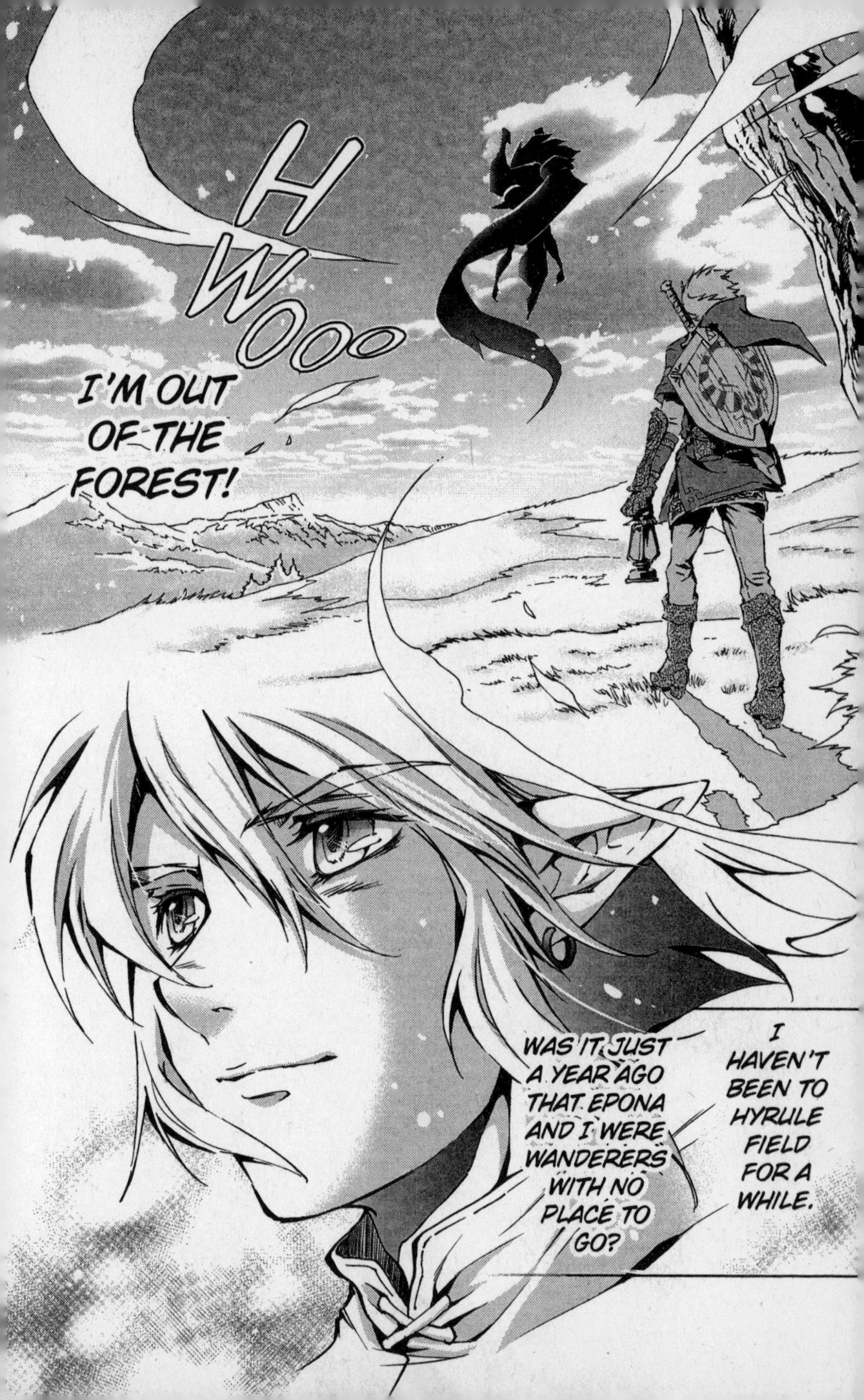
HWOOO
I'M OUT OF THE FOREST!
I HAVEN'T BEEN TO HYRULE FIELD FOR A WHILE.
WAS IT JUST A YEAR AGO THAT EPONA AND I WERE WANDERERS WITH NO PLACE TO GO?

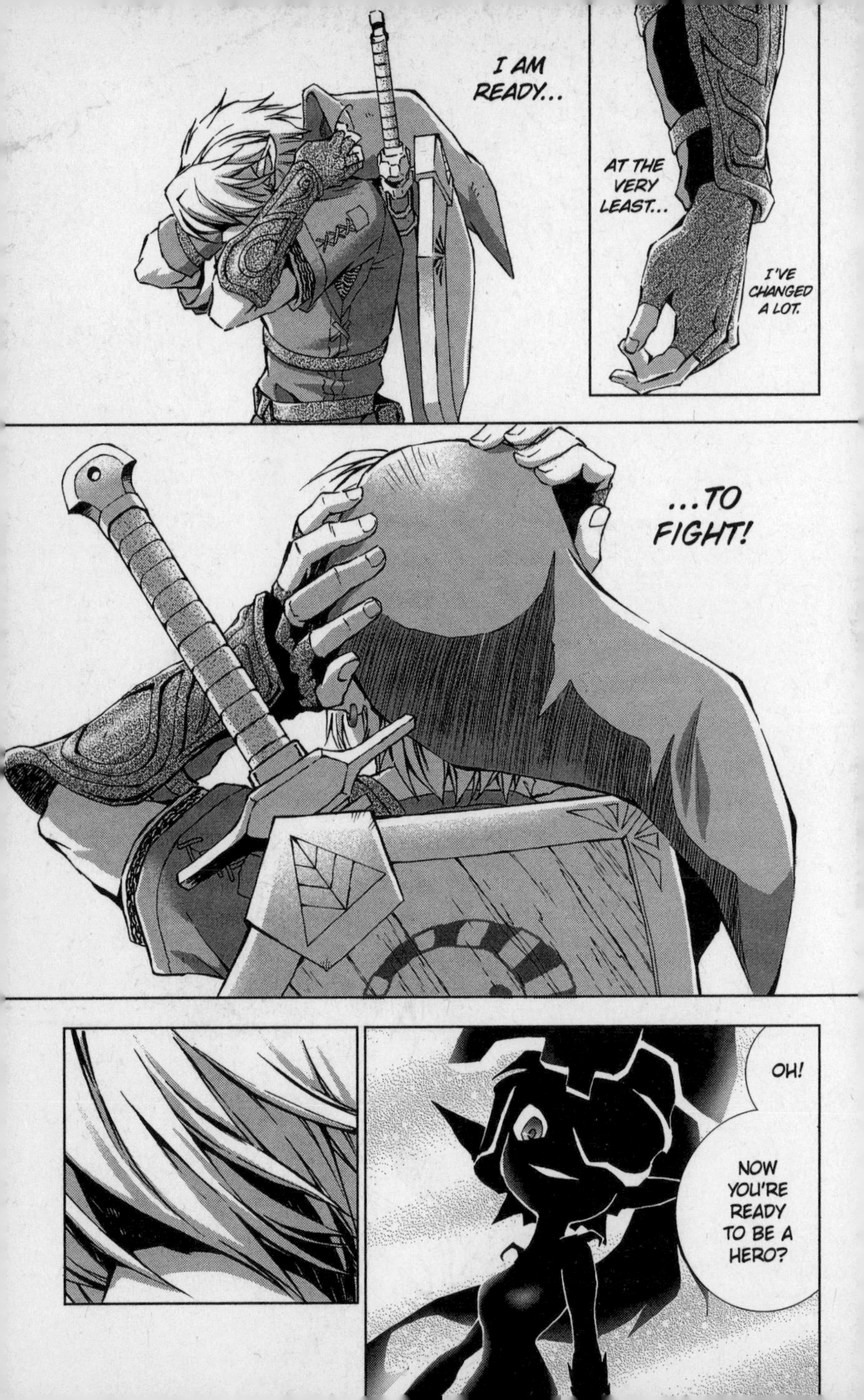
AT THE VERY LEAST...
I'VE CHANGED A LOT.
I AM READY...
...TO FIGHT!
OH!
NOW YOU'RE READY TO BE A HERO?

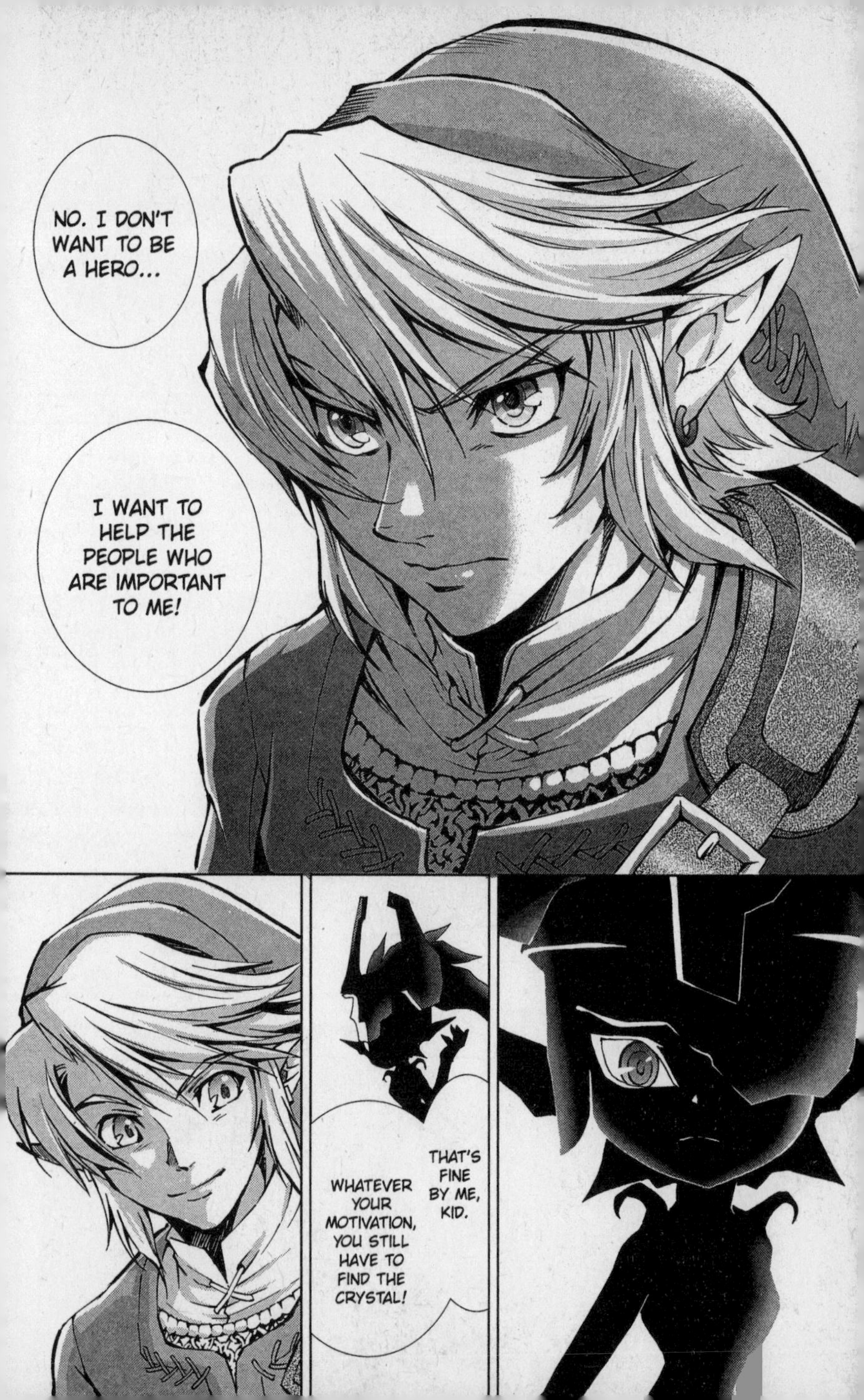
NO. I DON'T WANT TO BE A HERO...
I WANT TO HELP THE PEOPLE WHO ARE IMPORTANT TO ME!
THAT'S FINE BY ME, KID.
WHATEVER YOUR MOTIVATION, YOU STILL HAVE TO FIND THE CRYSTAL!

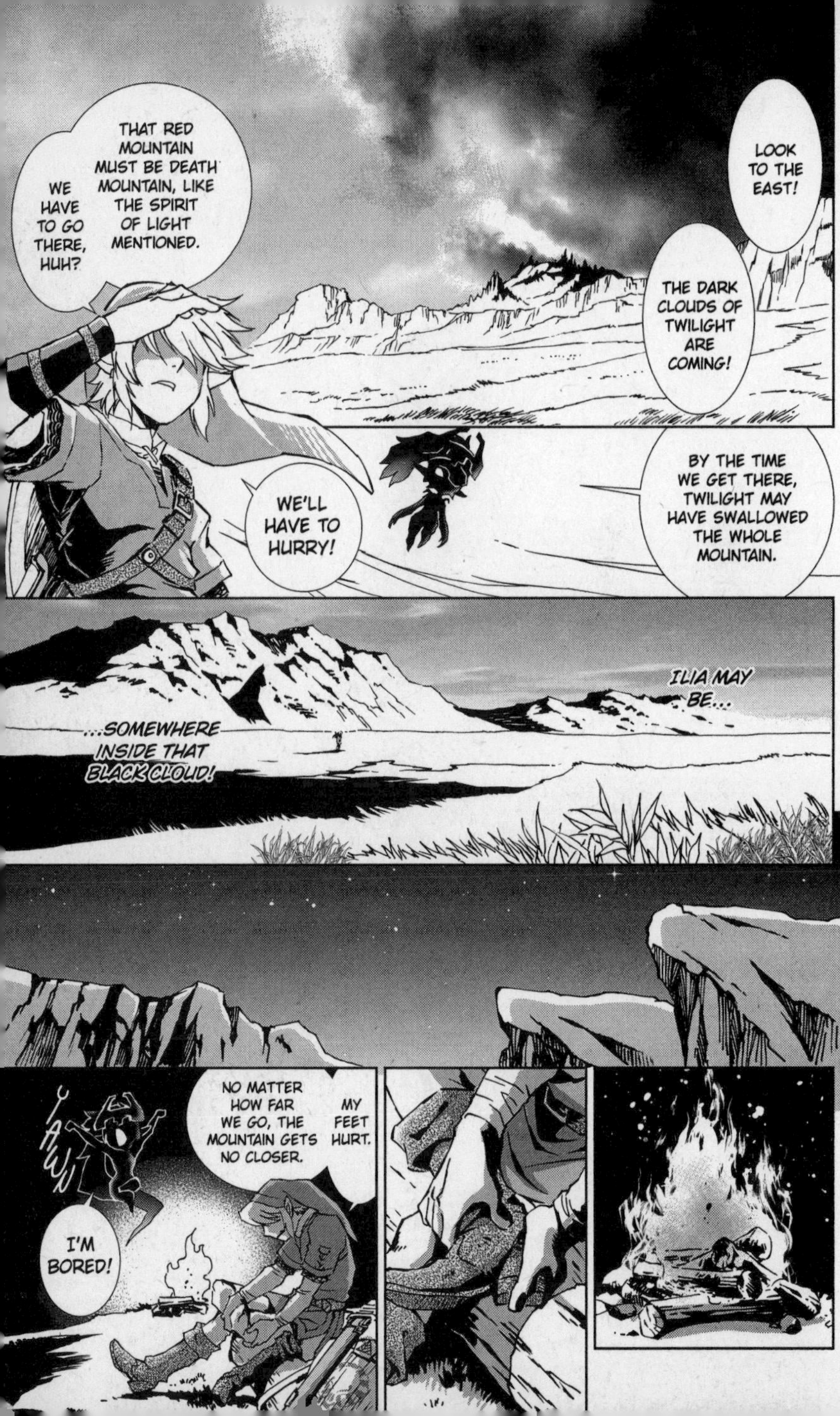
LOOK TO THE EAST!
THE DARK CLOUDS OF TWILIGHT ARE COMING!
THAT RED MOUNTAIN MUST BE DEATH MOUNTAIN, LIKE THE SPIRIT OF LIGHT MENTIONED.
WE HAVE TO GO THERE, HUH?
BY THE TIME WE GET THERE, TWILIGHT MAY HAVE SWALLOWED THE WHOLE MOUNTAIN.
WE'LL HAVE TO HURRY!
ILIA MAY BE...
...SOMEWHERE INSIDE THAT BLACK CLOUD!
MY FEET HURT.
NO MATTER HOW FAR WE GO, THE MOUNTAIN GETS NO CLOSER.
YAWN
I'M BORED!

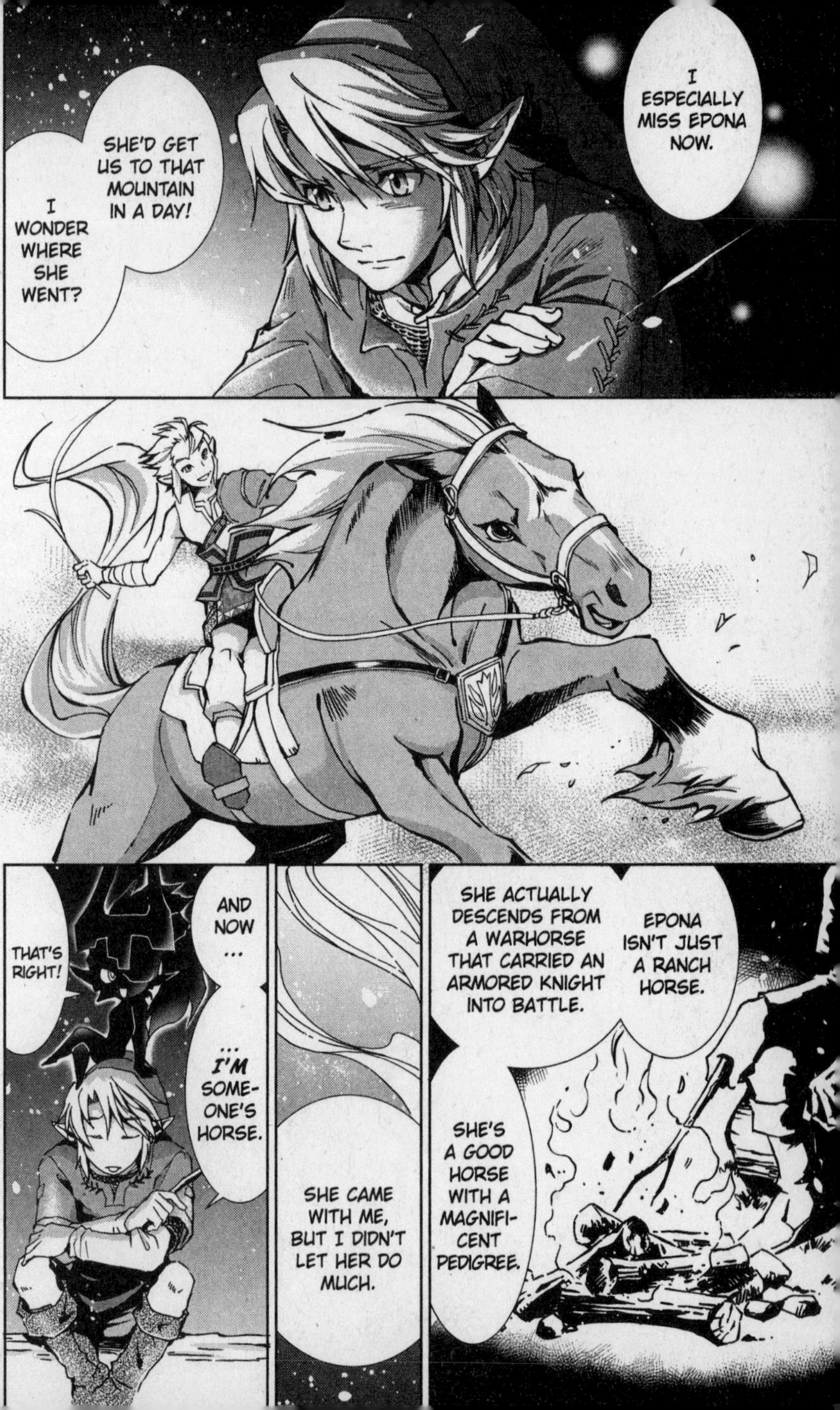
I ESPECIALLY MISS EPONA NOW.
SHE'D GET US TO THAT MOUNTAIN IN A DAY!
I WONDER WHERE SHE WENT?
EPONA ISN'T JUST A RANCH HORSE.
SHE ACTUALLY DESCENDS FROM A WARHORSE THAT CARRIED AN ARMORED KNIGHT INTO BATTLE.
SHE'S A GOOD HORSE WITH A MAGNIFICENT PEDIGREE.
SHE CAME WITH ME, BUT I DIDN'T LET HER DO MUCH.
AND NOW ...
... I'M SOMEONE'S HORSE.
THAT'S RIGHT!

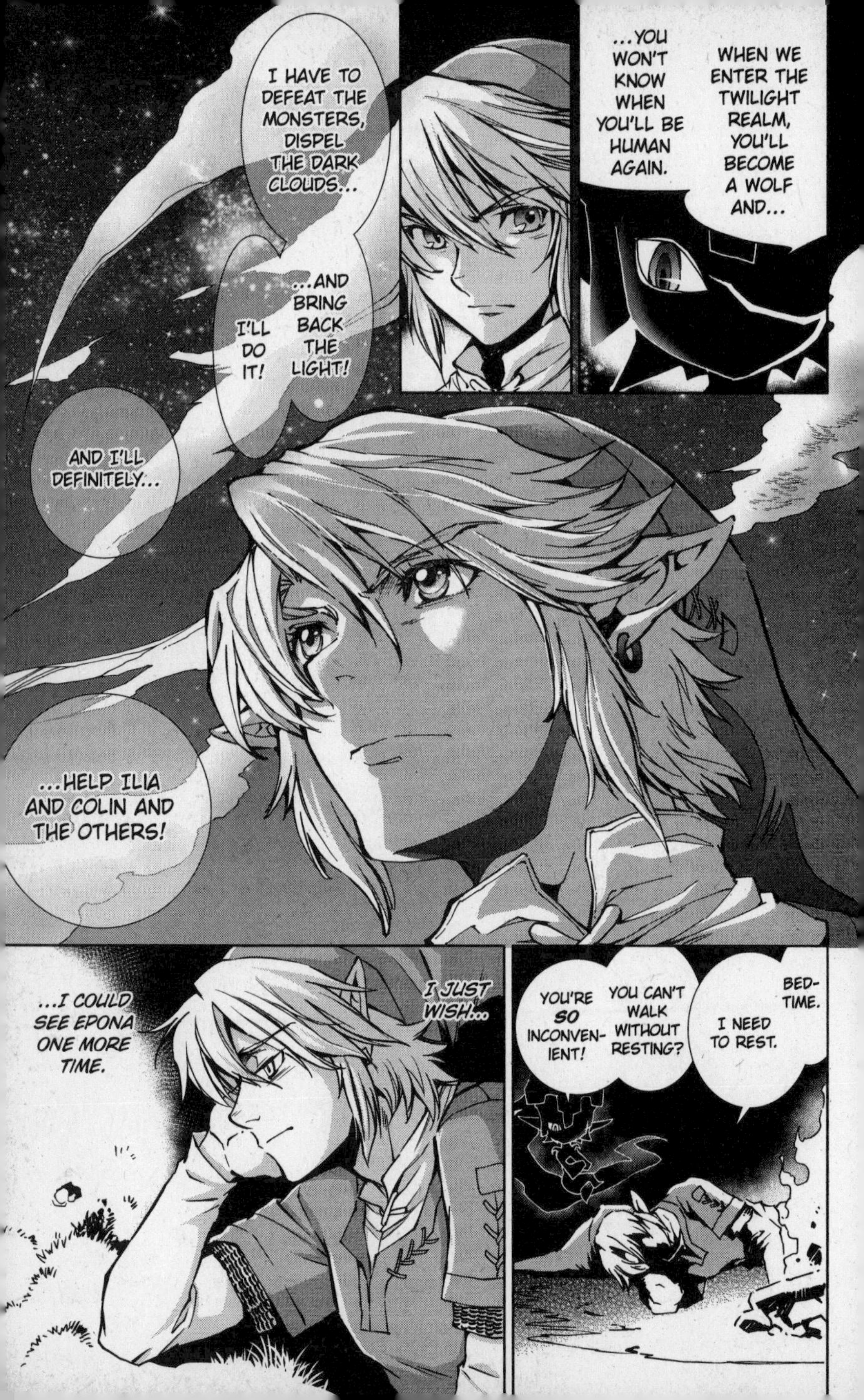
WHEN WE ENTER THE TWILIGHT REALM, YOU'LL BECOME A WOLF AND...
...YOU WON'T KNOW WHEN YOU'LL BE HUMAN AGAIN.
I HAVE TO DEFEAT THE MONSTERS, DISPEL THE DARK CLOUDS...
...AND BRING BACK THE LIGHT!
I'LL DO IT!
AND I'LL DEFINITELY...
...HELP ILIA AND COLIN AND THE OTHERS!
BED-TIME.
I NEED TO REST.
YOU CAN'T WALK WITHOUT RESTING?
YOU'RE *SO* INCONVEN-IENT!
I JUST WISH...
...I COULD SEE EPONA ONE MORE TIME.

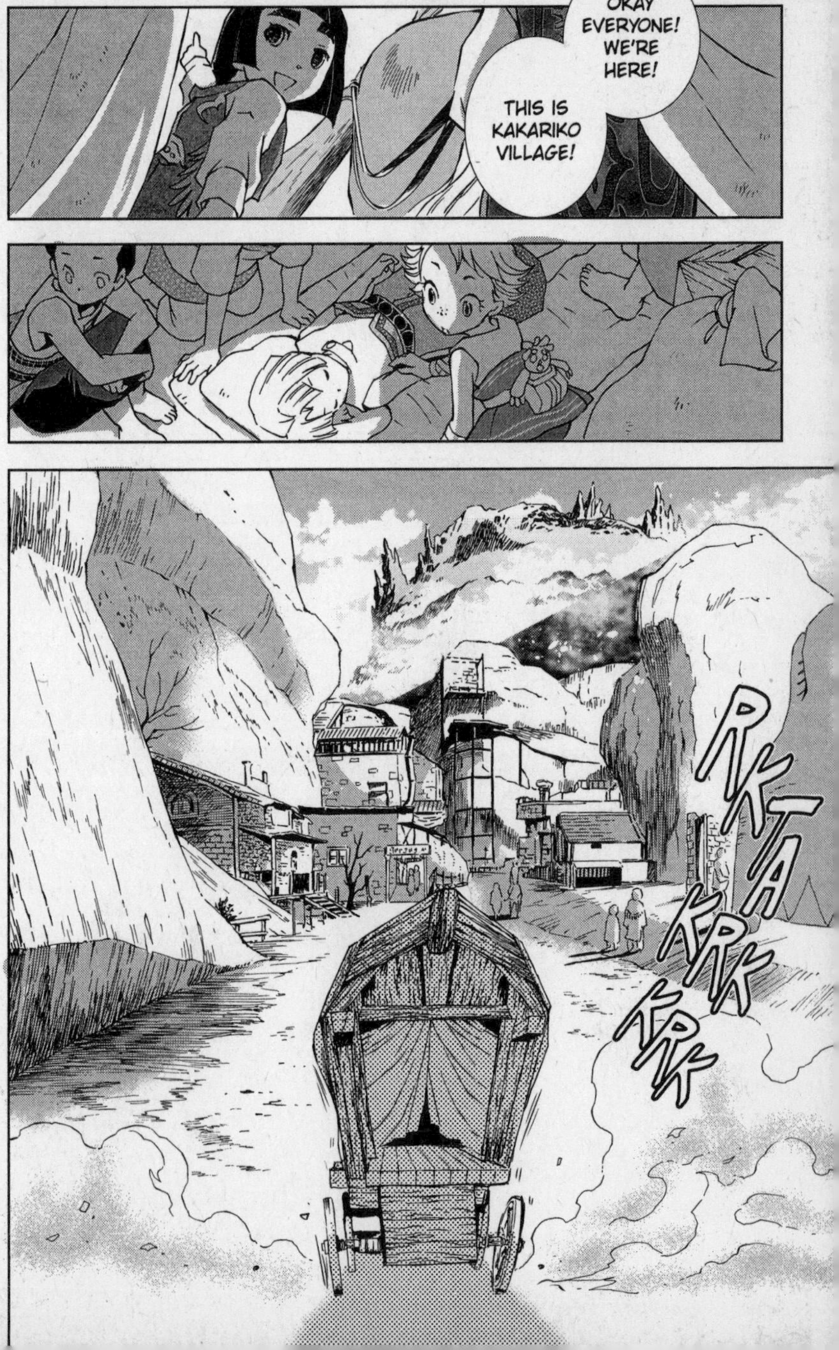
OKAY EVERYONE! WE'RE HERE!
THIS IS KAKARIKO VILLAGE!
RKTA KRK KRK

#19. KAKARIKO VILLAGE

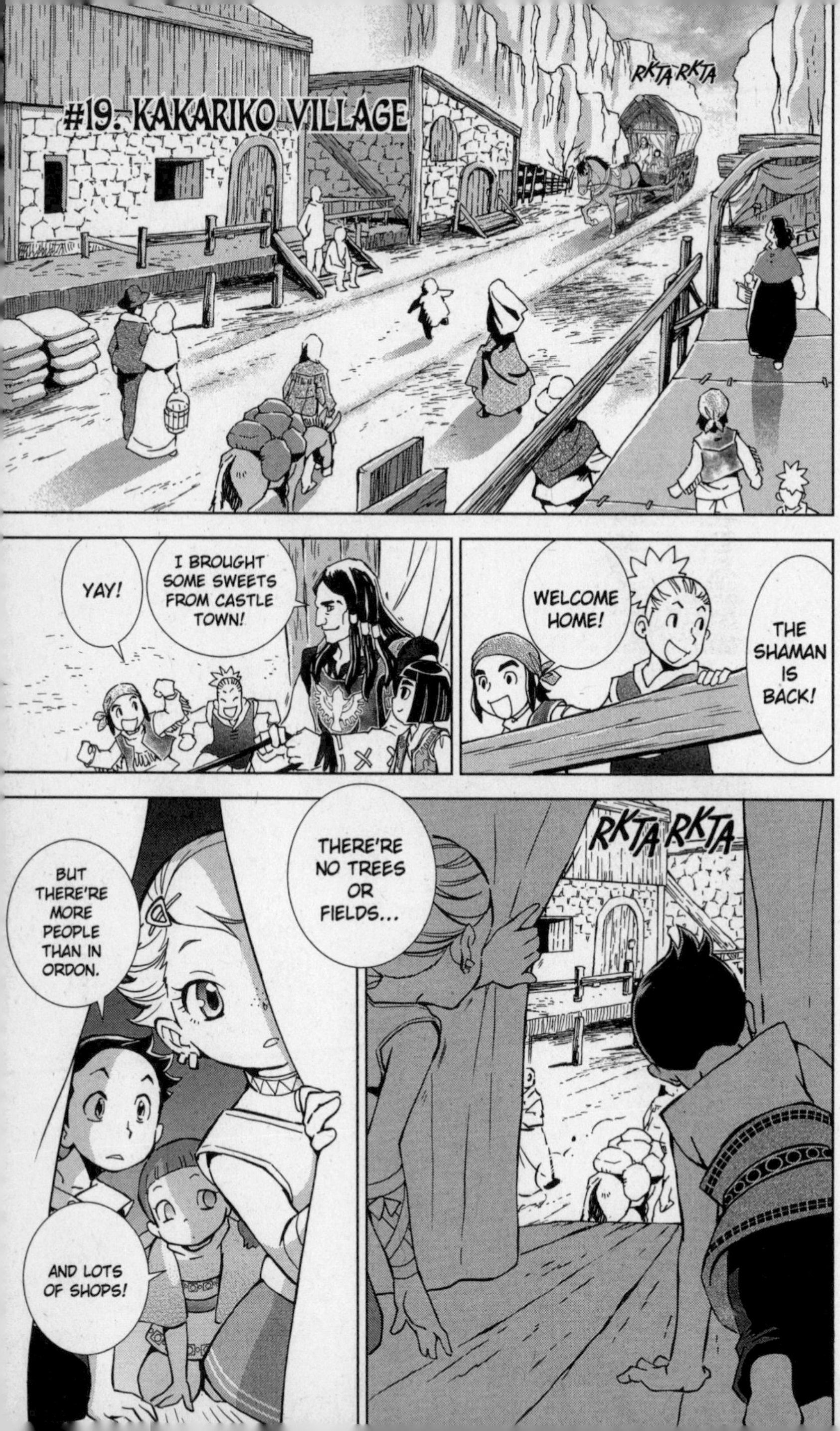
RKTA RKTA
THE SHAMAN IS BACK!
WELCOME HOME!
I BROUGHT SOME SWEETS FROM CASTLE TOWN!
YAY!
RKTA RKTA
THERE'RE NO TREES OR FIELDS...
BUT THERE'RE MORE PEOPLE THAN IN ORDON.
AND LOTS OF SHOPS!

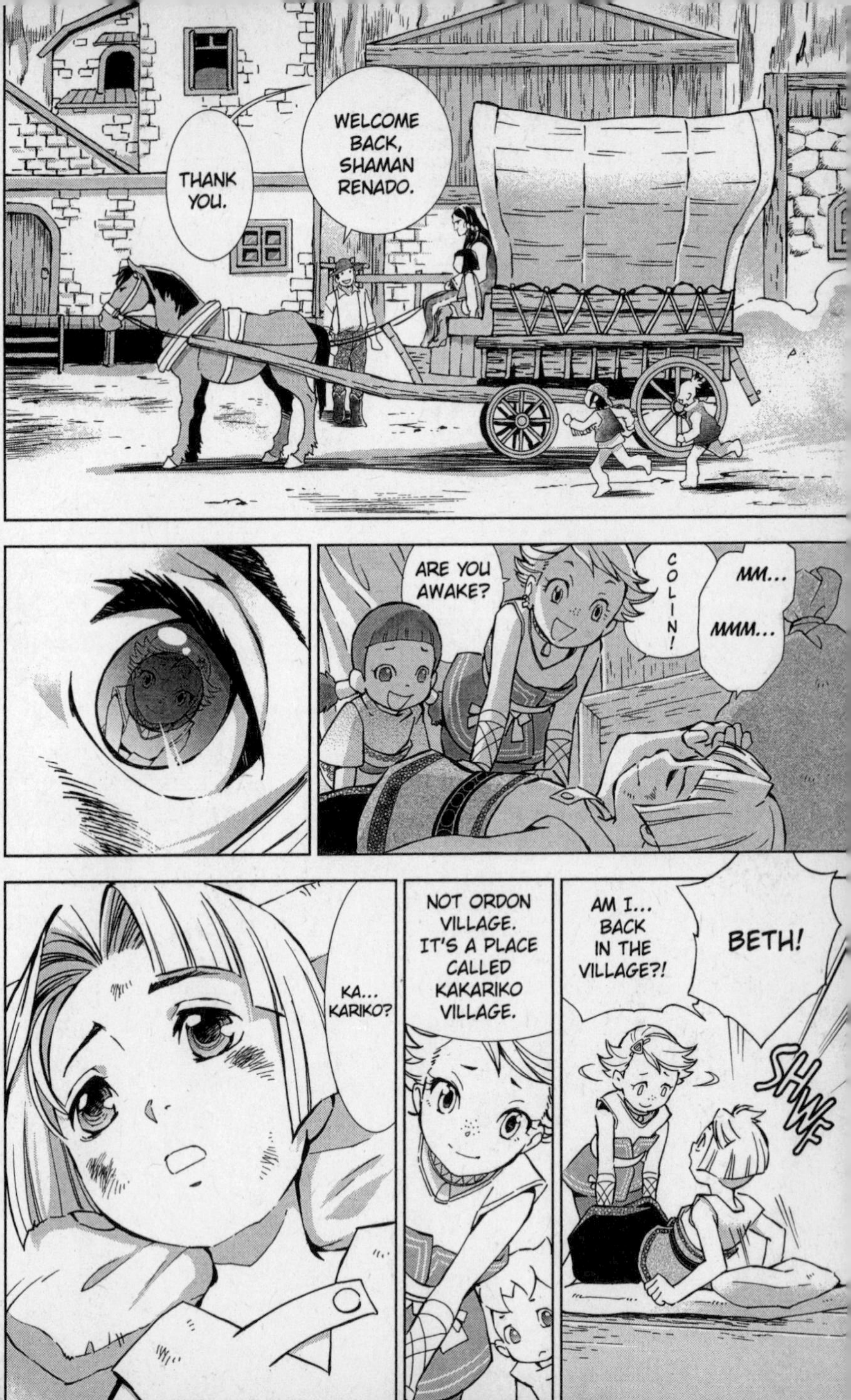
WELCOME BACK, SHAMAN RENADO.
THANK YOU.
MM...
MMM...
COLIN!
ARE YOU AWAKE?
BETH!
AM I... BACK IN THE VILLAGE?!
SHWF
NOT ORDON VILLAGE. IT'S A PLACE CALLED KAKARIKO VILLAGE.
KA... KARIKO?

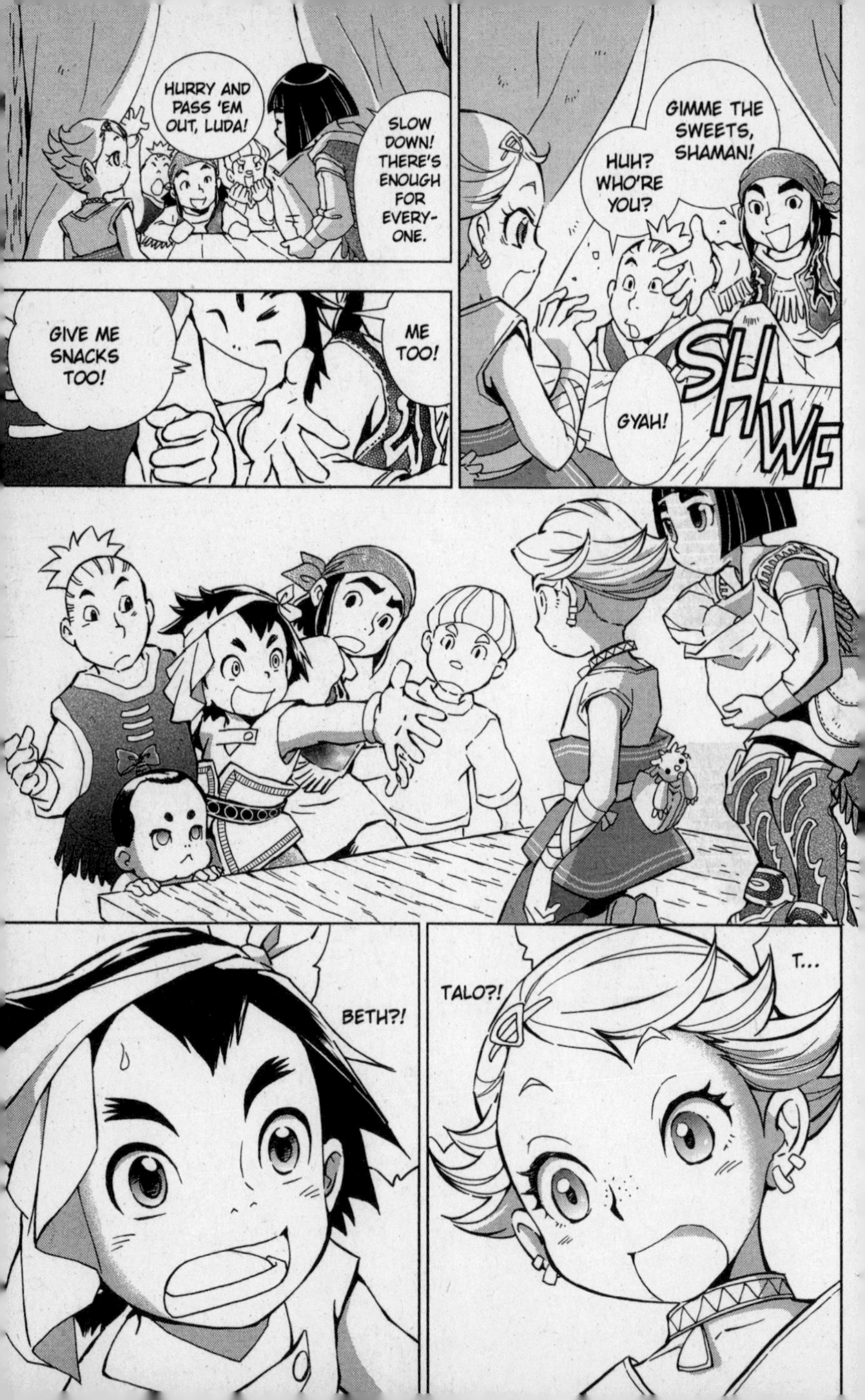
GIMME THE SWEETS, SHAMAN!
HUH? WHO'RE YOU?
SHWF
GYAH!
HURRY AND PASS 'EM OUT, LUDA!
SLOW DOWN! THERE'S ENOUGH FOR EVERY-ONE.
ME TOO!
GIVE ME SNACKS TOO!
T...
TALO?!
BETH?!

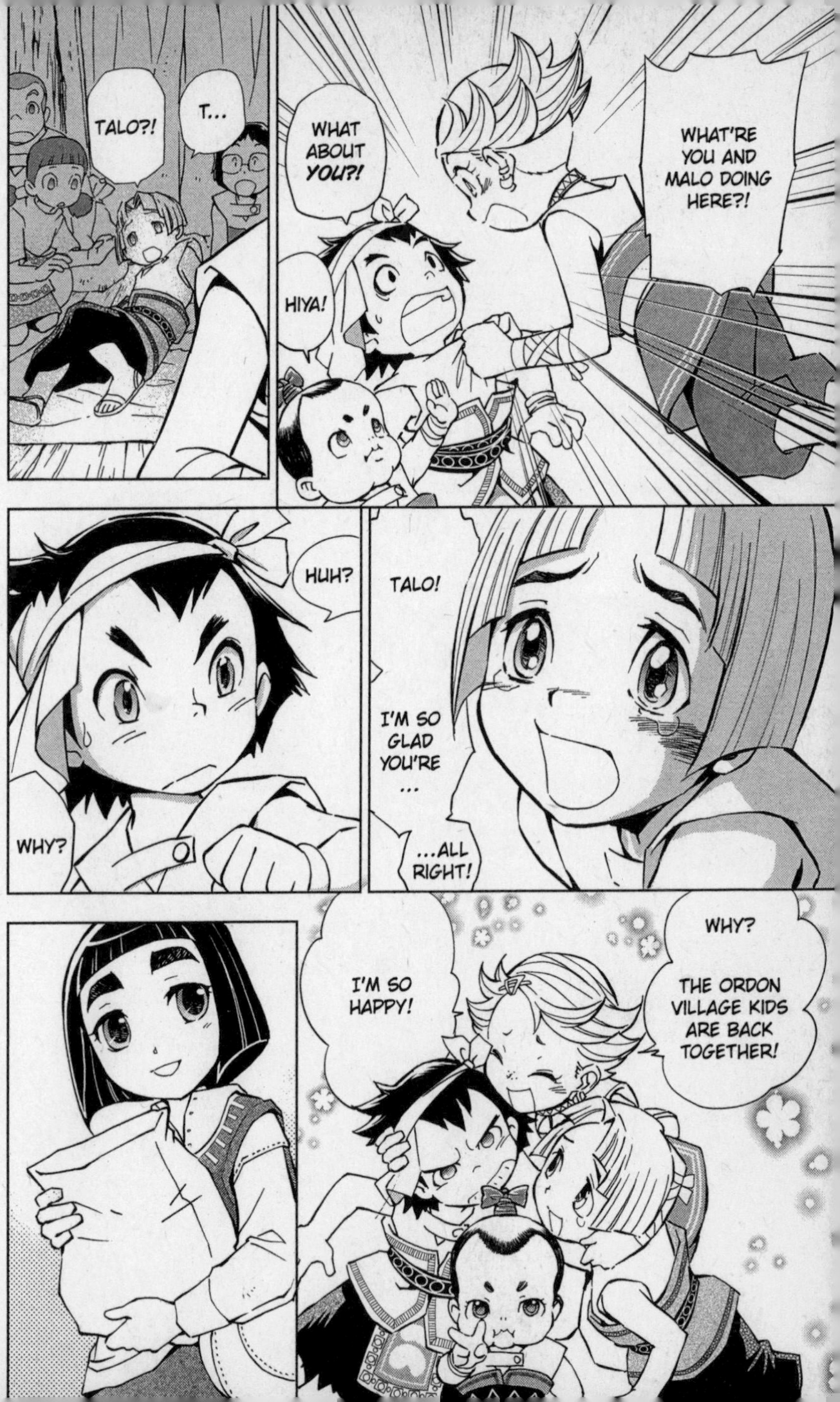
WHAT'RE YOU AND MALO DOING HERE?!
WHAT ABOUT *YOU?!*
HIYA!
T...
TALO?!
TALO!
I'M SO GLAD YOU'RE ...
...ALL RIGHT!
HUH?
WHY?
WHY?
THE ORDON VILLAGE KIDS ARE BACK TOGETHER!
I'M SO HAPPY!

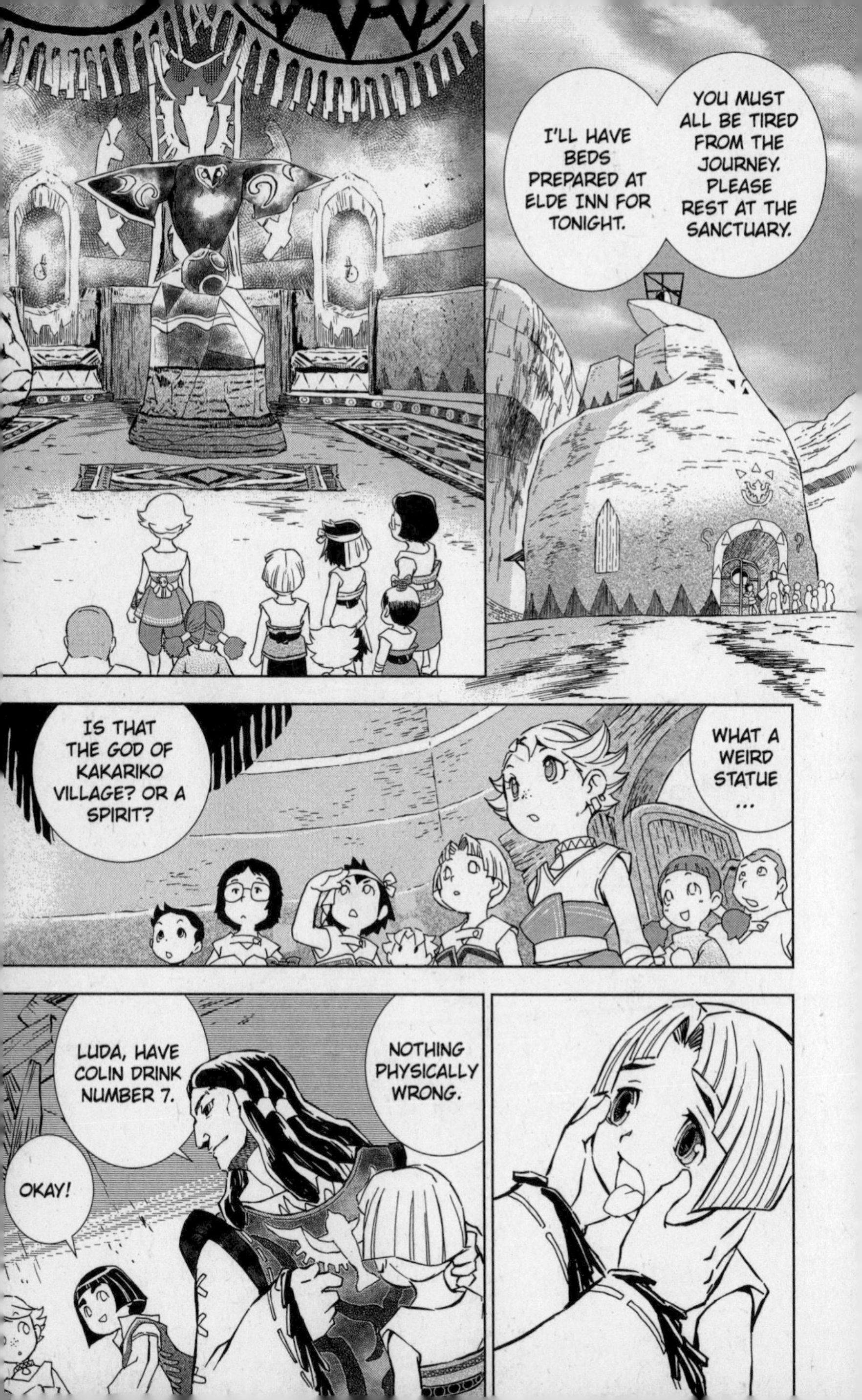
YOU MUST ALL BE TIRED FROM THE JOURNEY. PLEASE REST AT THE SANCTUARY.
I'LL HAVE BEDS PREPARED AT ELDE INN FOR TONIGHT.
WHAT A WEIRD STATUE ...
IS THAT THE GOD OF KAKARIKO VILLAGE? OR A SPIRIT?
NOTHING PHYSICALLY WRONG.
LUDA, HAVE COLIN DRINK NUMBER 7.
OKAY!

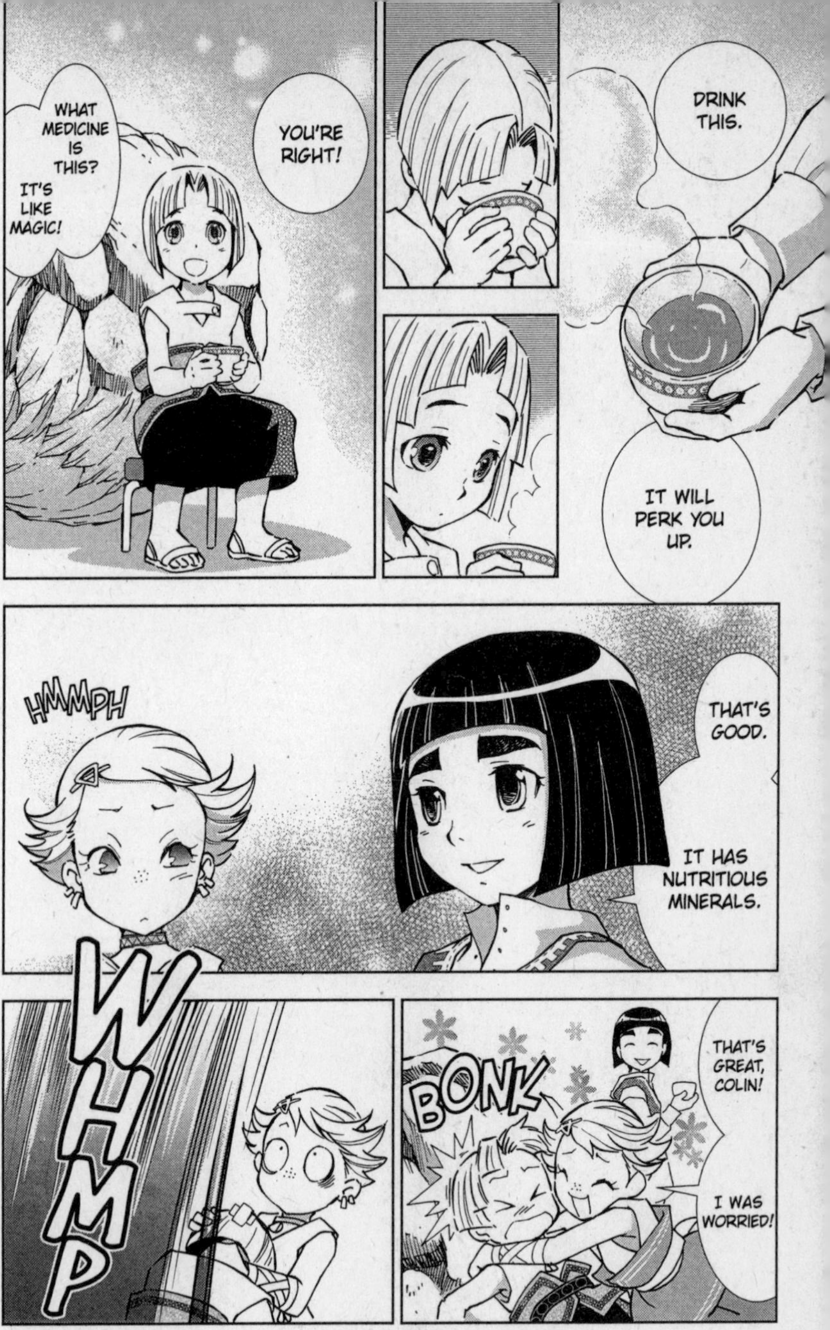
DRINK THIS.
IT WILL PERK YOU UP.
YOU'RE RIGHT!
WHAT MEDICINE IS THIS? IT'S LIKE MAGIC!
THAT'S GOOD.
IT HAS NUTRITIOUS MINERALS.
HMMMPH
BONK
THAT'S GREAT, COLIN!
I WAS WORRIED!
WHMMP

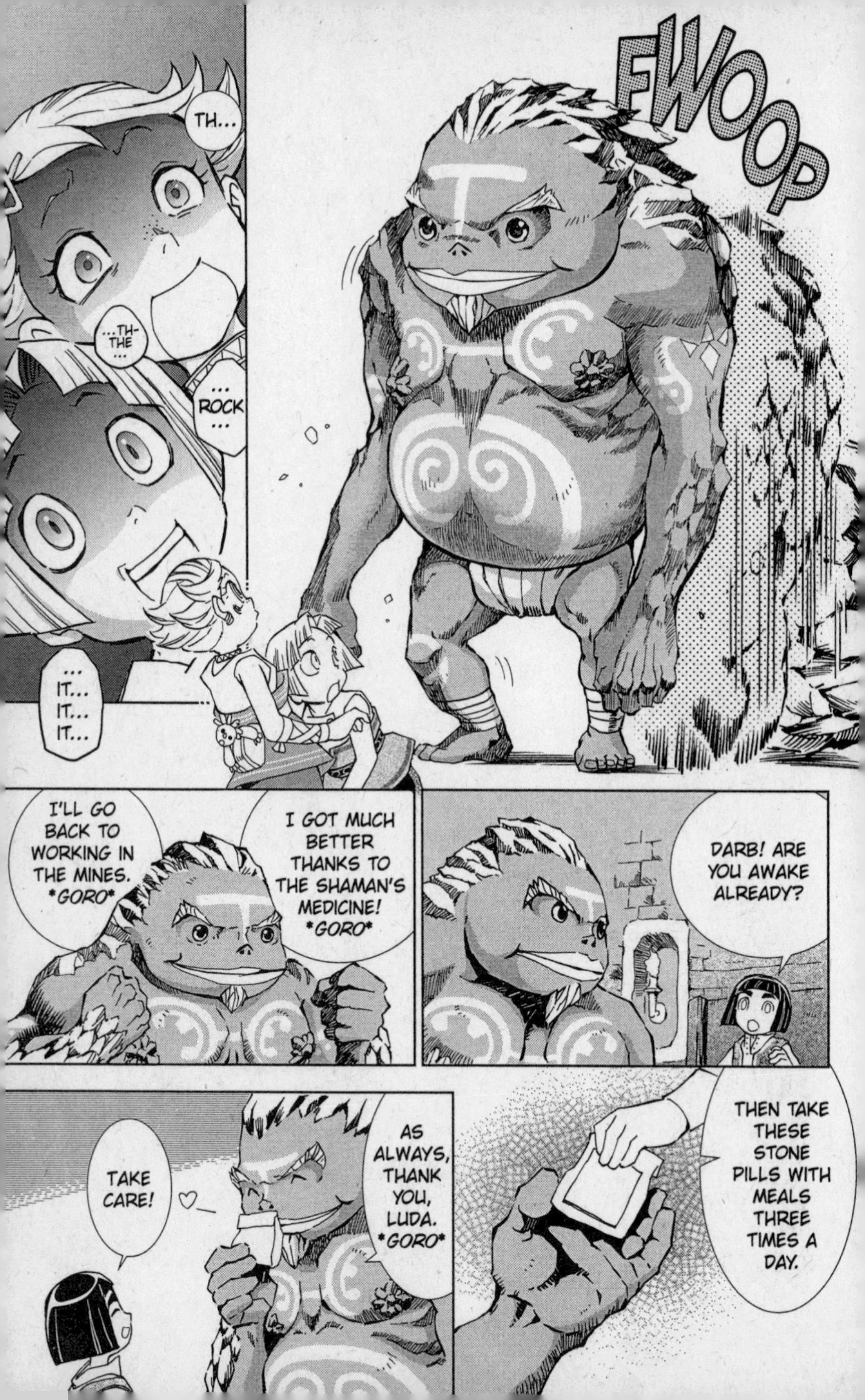
FWOOP
TH...
...TH-THE...
...ROCK...
...IT... IT... IT...
DARB! ARE YOU AWAKE ALREADY?
I GOT MUCH BETTER THANKS TO THE SHAMAN'S MEDICINE! *GORO*
I'LL GO BACK TO WORKING IN THE MINES. *GORO*
THEN TAKE THESE STONE PILLS WITH MEALS THREE TIMES A DAY.
AS ALWAYS, THANK YOU, LUDA. *GORO*
TAKE CARE!

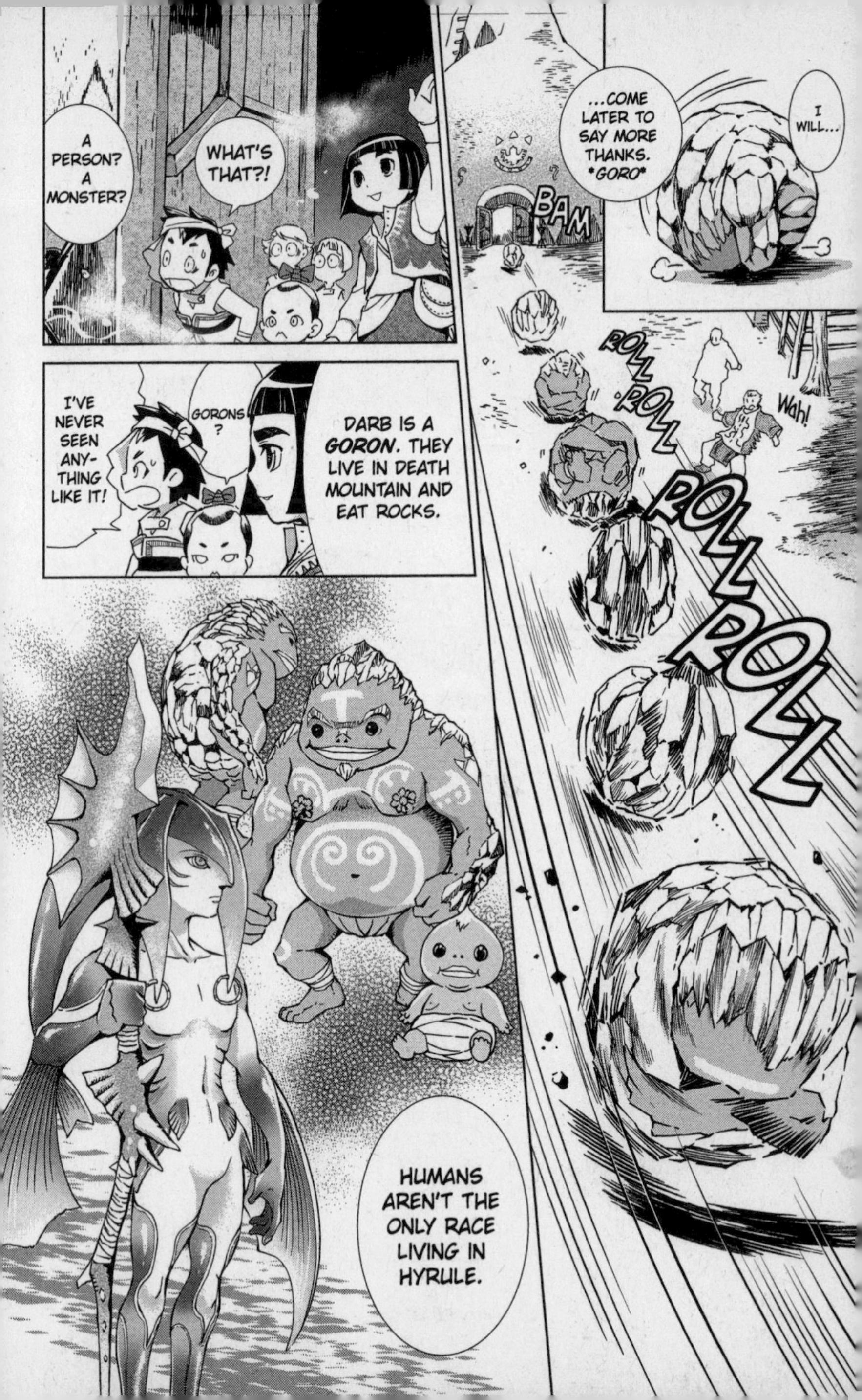
I WILL...
...COME LATER TO SAY MORE THANKS. *GORO*
BAM
ROLL ROLL
Wah!
ROLL ROLL
WHAT'S THAT?!
A PERSON? A MONSTER?
DARB IS A GORON. THEY LIVE IN DEATH MOUNTAIN AND EAT ROCKS.
GORONS?
I'VE NEVER SEEN ANYTHING LIKE IT!
HUMANS AREN'T THE ONLY RACE LIVING IN HYRULE.

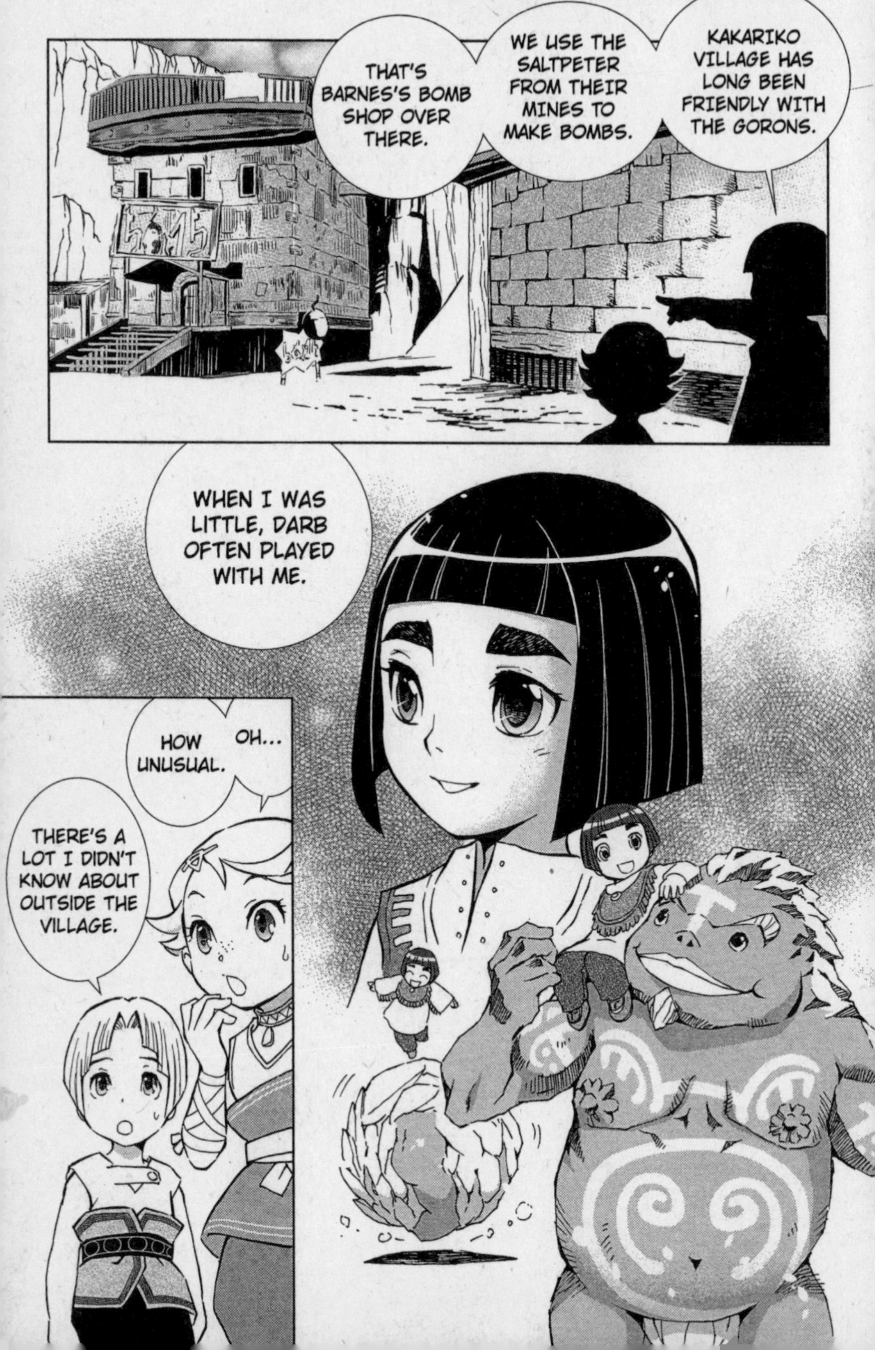
KAKARIKO VILLAGE HAS LONG BEEN FRIENDLY WITH THE GORONS.
WE USE THE SALTPETER FROM THEIR MINES TO MAKE BOMBS.
THAT'S BARNES'S BOMB SHOP OVER THERE.
WHEN I WAS LITTLE, DARB OFTEN PLAYED WITH ME.
OH...
HOW UNUSUAL.
THERE'S A LOT I DIDN'T KNOW ABOUT OUTSIDE THE VILLAGE.

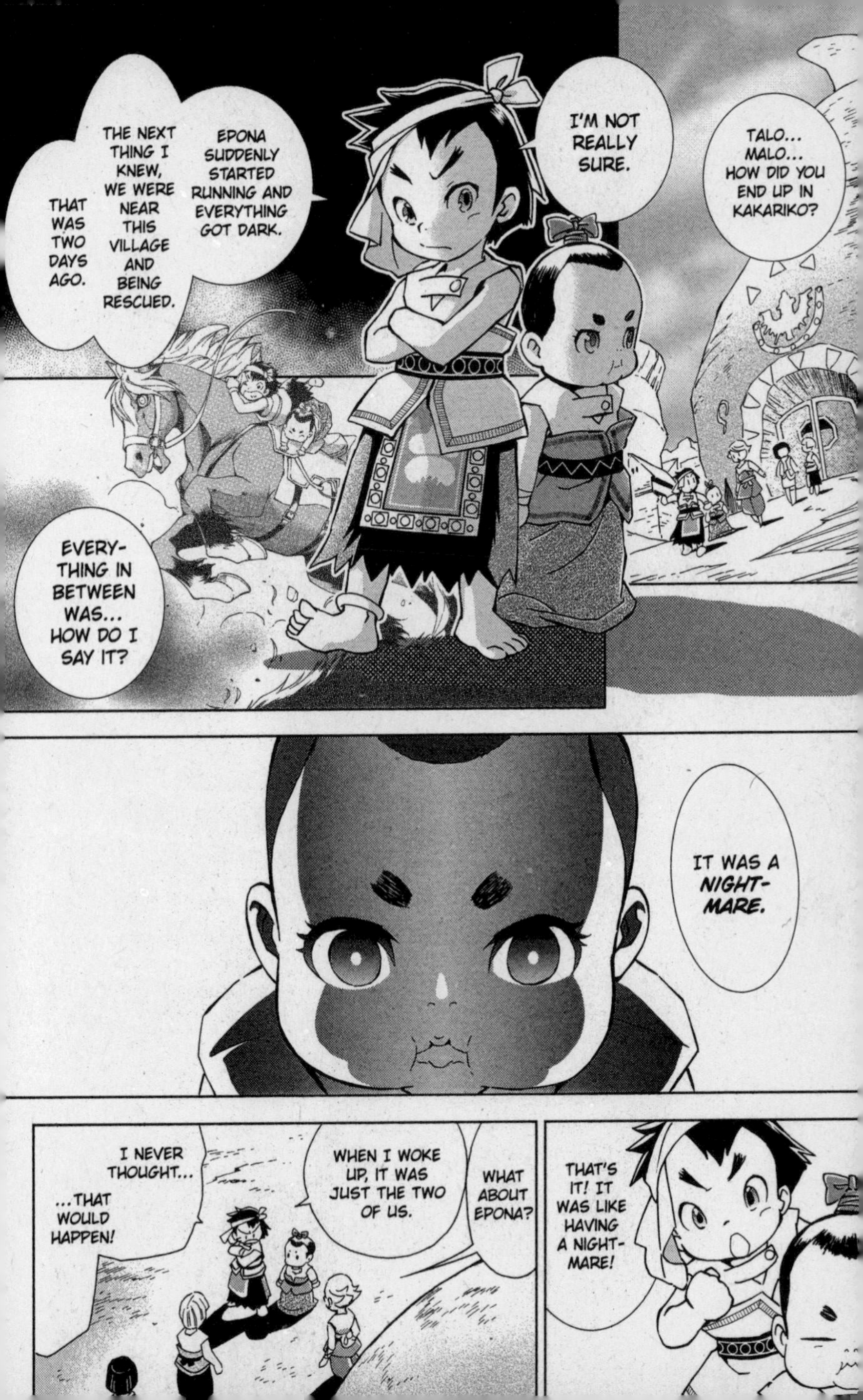
TALO... MALO... HOW DID YOU END UP IN KAKARIKO?
I'M NOT REALLY SURE.
EPONA SUDDENLY STARTED RUNNING AND EVERYTHING GOT DARK.
THE NEXT THING I KNEW, WE WERE NEAR THIS VILLAGE AND BEING RESCUED.
THAT WAS TWO DAYS AGO.
EVERY-THING IN BETWEEN WAS... HOW DO I SAY IT?
IT WAS A *NIGHT-MARE.*
THAT'S IT! IT WAS LIKE HAVING A NIGHT-MARE!
WHAT ABOUT EPONA?
WHEN I WOKE UP, IT WAS JUST THE TWO OF US.
I NEVER THOUGHT...
...THAT WOULD HAPPEN!

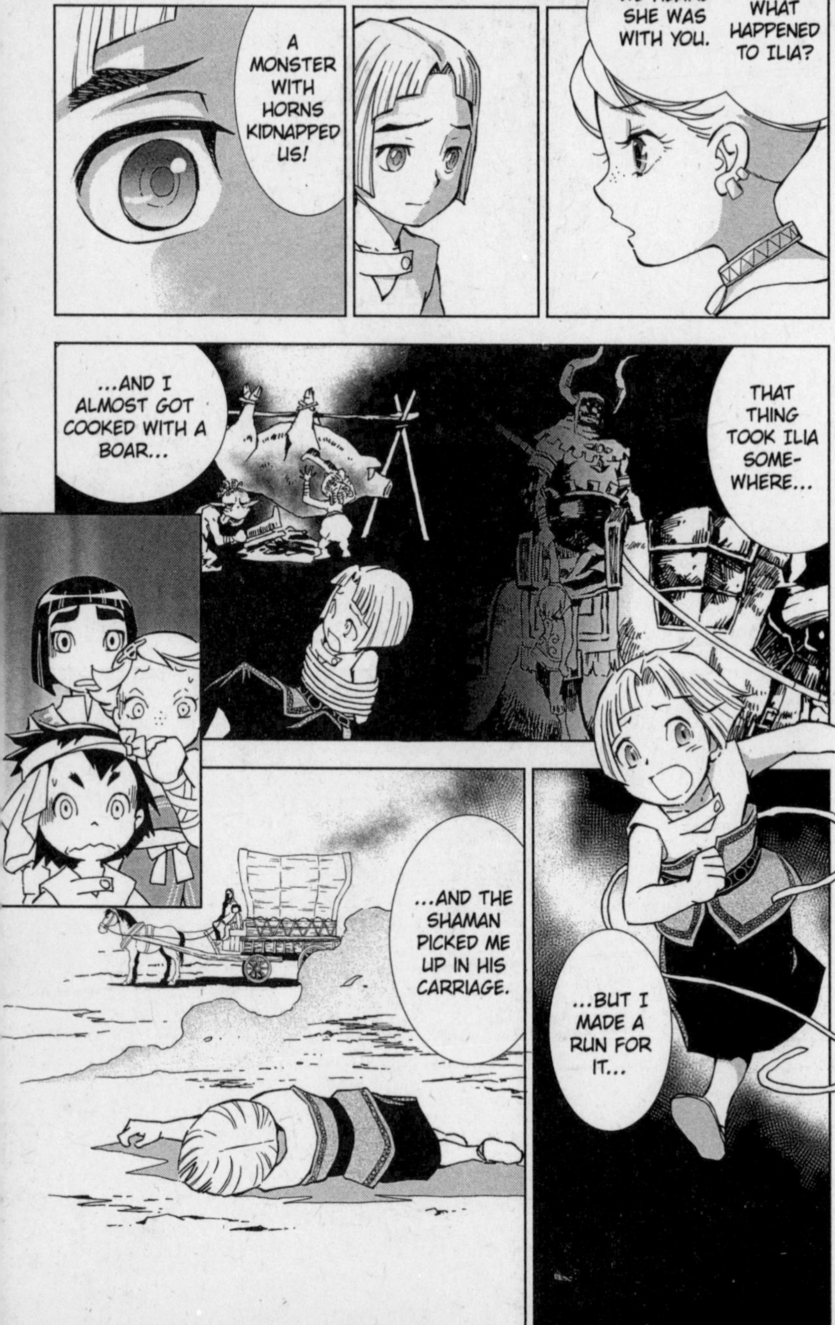
COLIN, WHAT HAPPENED TO ILIA?
WE HEARD SHE WAS WITH YOU.
A MONSTER WITH HORNS KIDNAPPED US!
THAT THING TOOK ILIA SOME-WHERE...
...AND I ALMOST GOT COOKED WITH A BOAR...
...BUT I MADE A RUN FOR IT...
...AND THE SHAMAN PICKED ME UP IN HIS CARRIAGE.

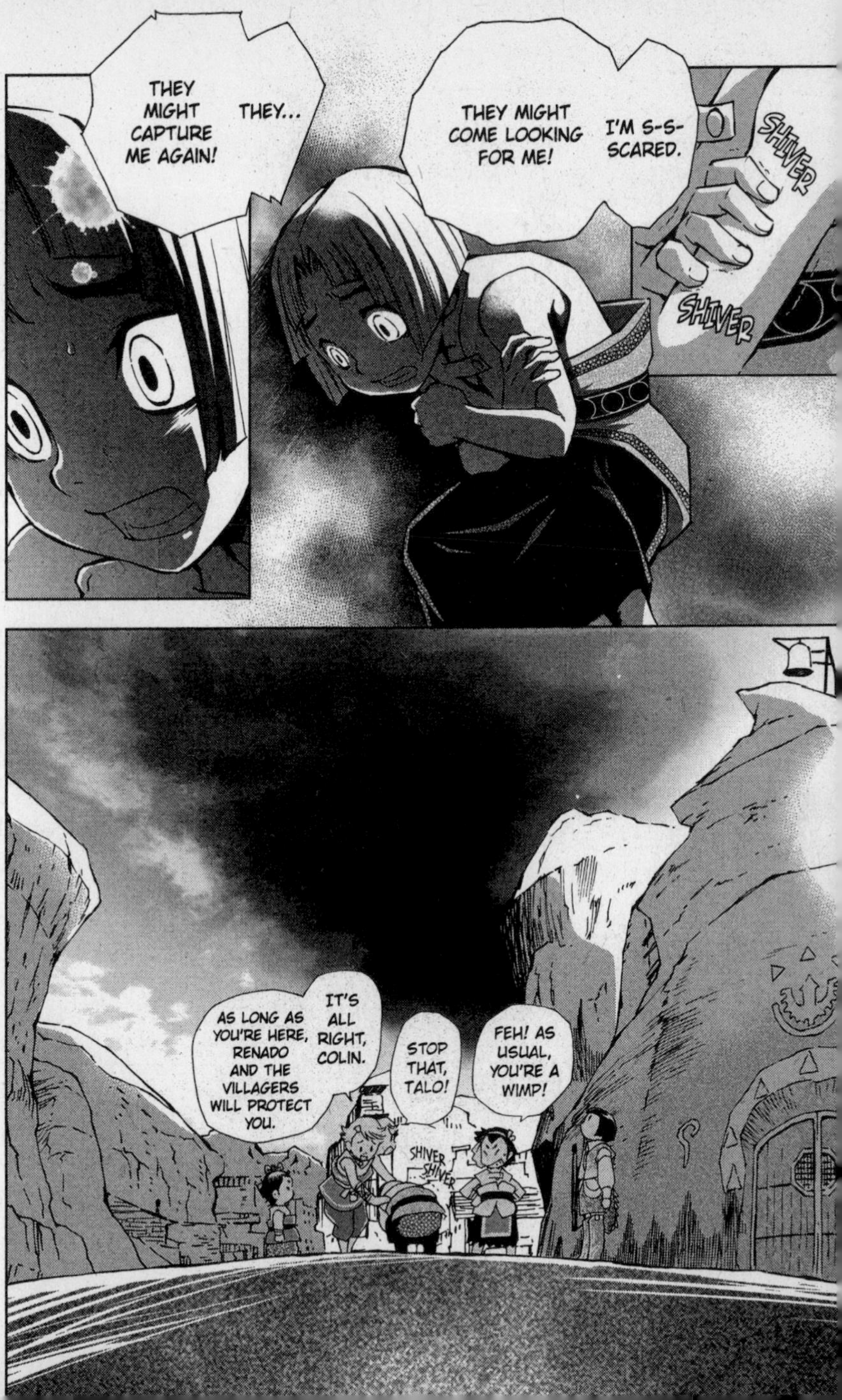
I'M S-S-SCARED.
THEY MIGHT COME LOOKING FOR ME!
SHIVER
SHIVER
THEY...
THEY MIGHT CAPTURE ME AGAIN!
FEH! AS USUAL, YOU'RE A WIMP!
STOP THAT, TALO!
IT'S ALL RIGHT, COLIN.
AS LONG AS YOU'RE HERE, RENADO AND THE VILLAGERS WILL PROTECT YOU.
SHIVER SHIVER

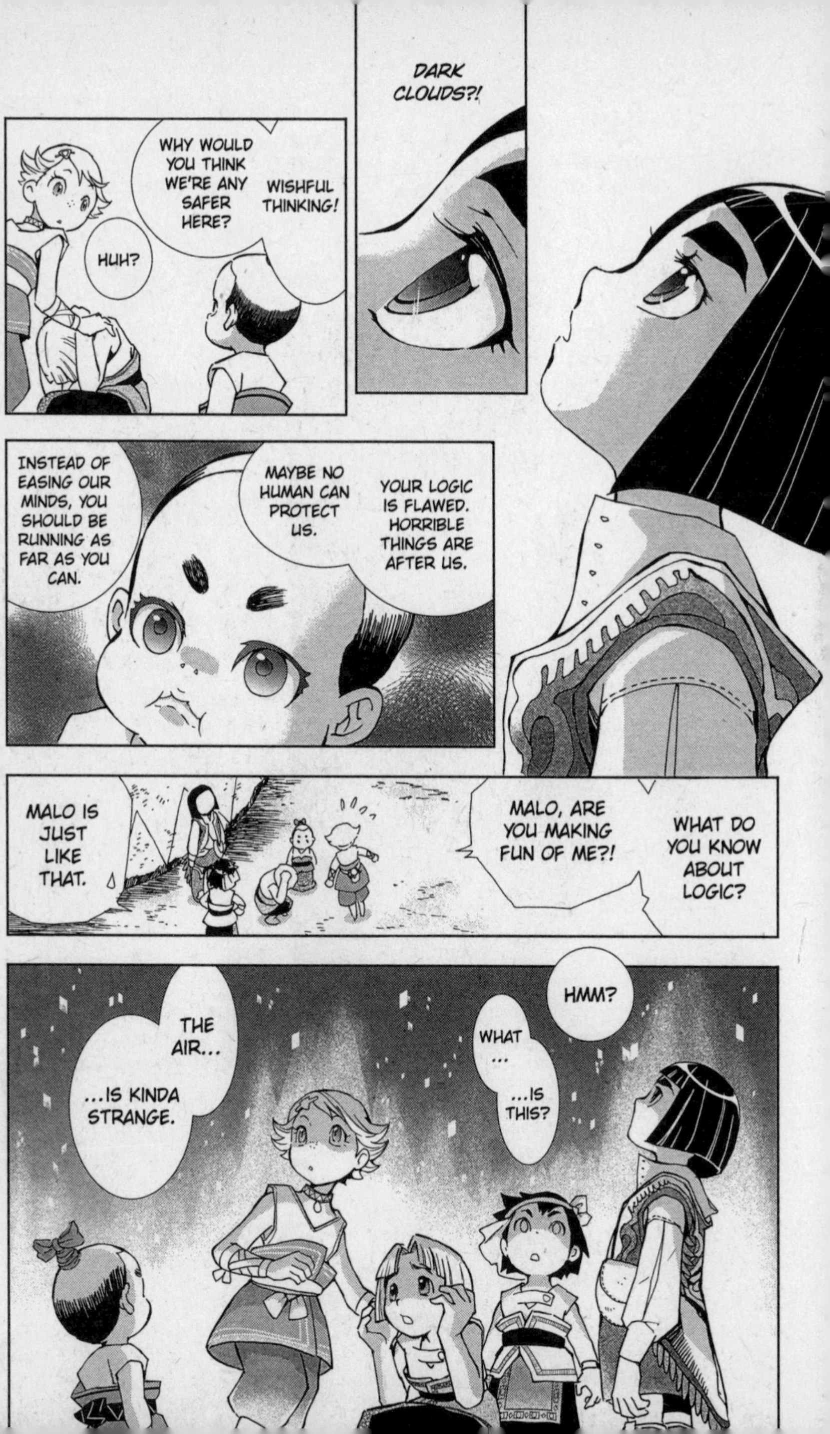
DARK CLOUDS?!
WHY WOULD YOU THINK WE'RE ANY SAFER HERE?
WISHFUL THINKING!
HUH?
YOUR LOGIC IS FLAWED. HORRIBLE THINGS ARE AFTER US.
MAYBE NO HUMAN CAN PROTECT US.
INSTEAD OF EASING OUR MINDS, YOU SHOULD BE RUNNING AS FAR AS YOU CAN.
WHAT DO YOU KNOW ABOUT LOGIC?
MALO, ARE YOU MAKING FUN OF ME?!
MALO IS JUST LIKE THAT.
HMM?
WHAT...
...IS THIS?
THE AIR...
...IS KINDA STRANGE.

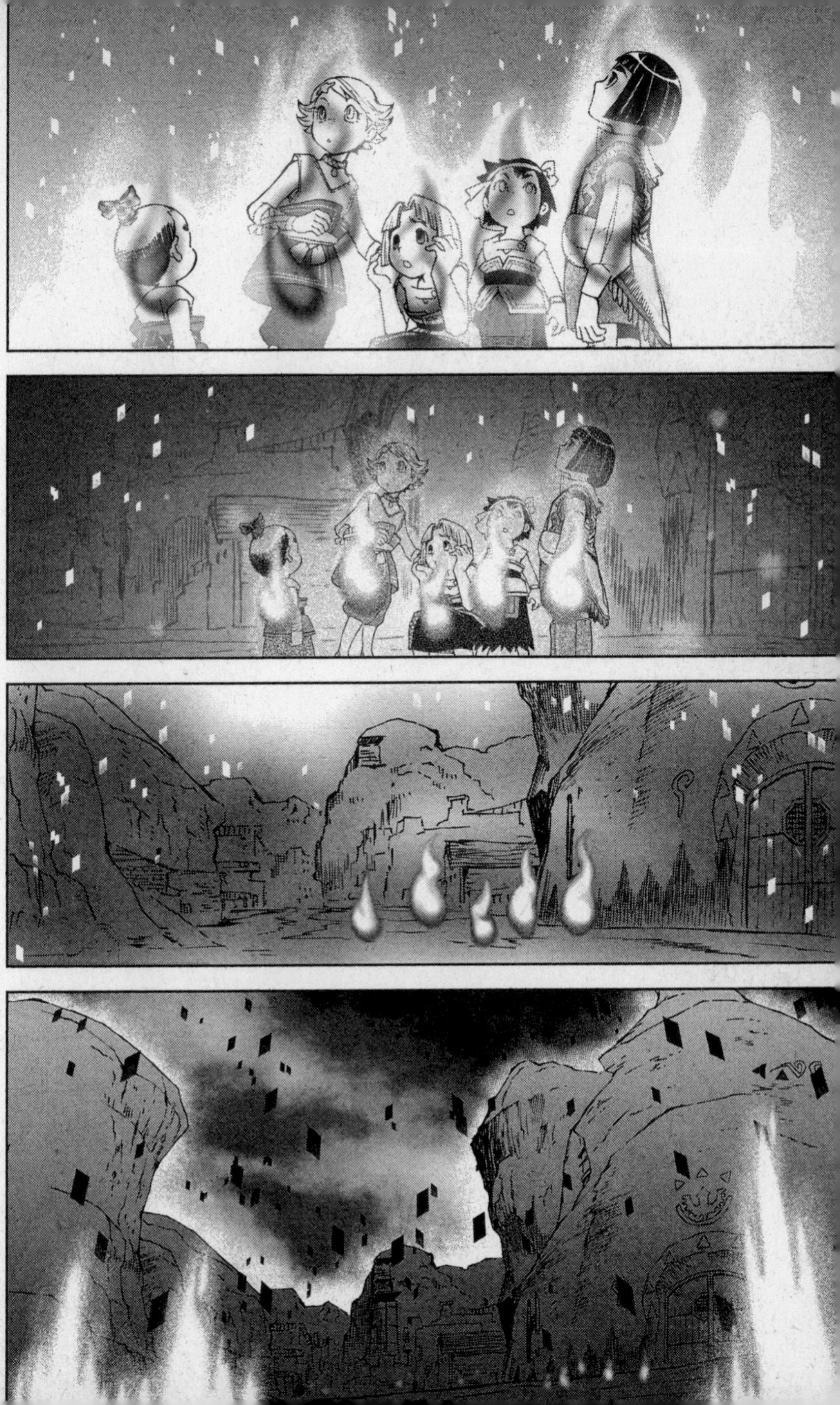

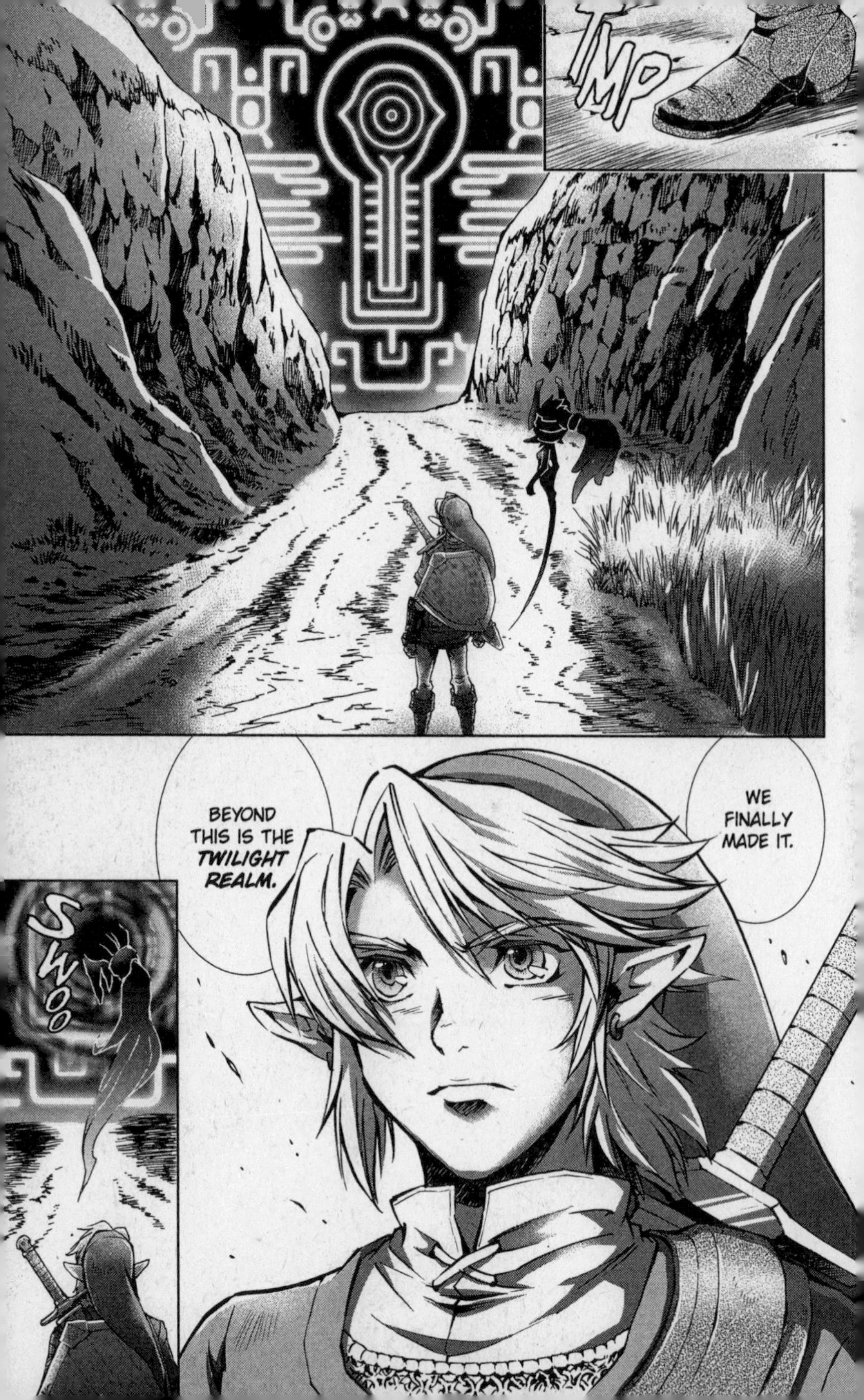
TMP
WE FINALLY MADE IT.
BEYOND THIS IS THE *TWILIGHT REALM.*
SWOO

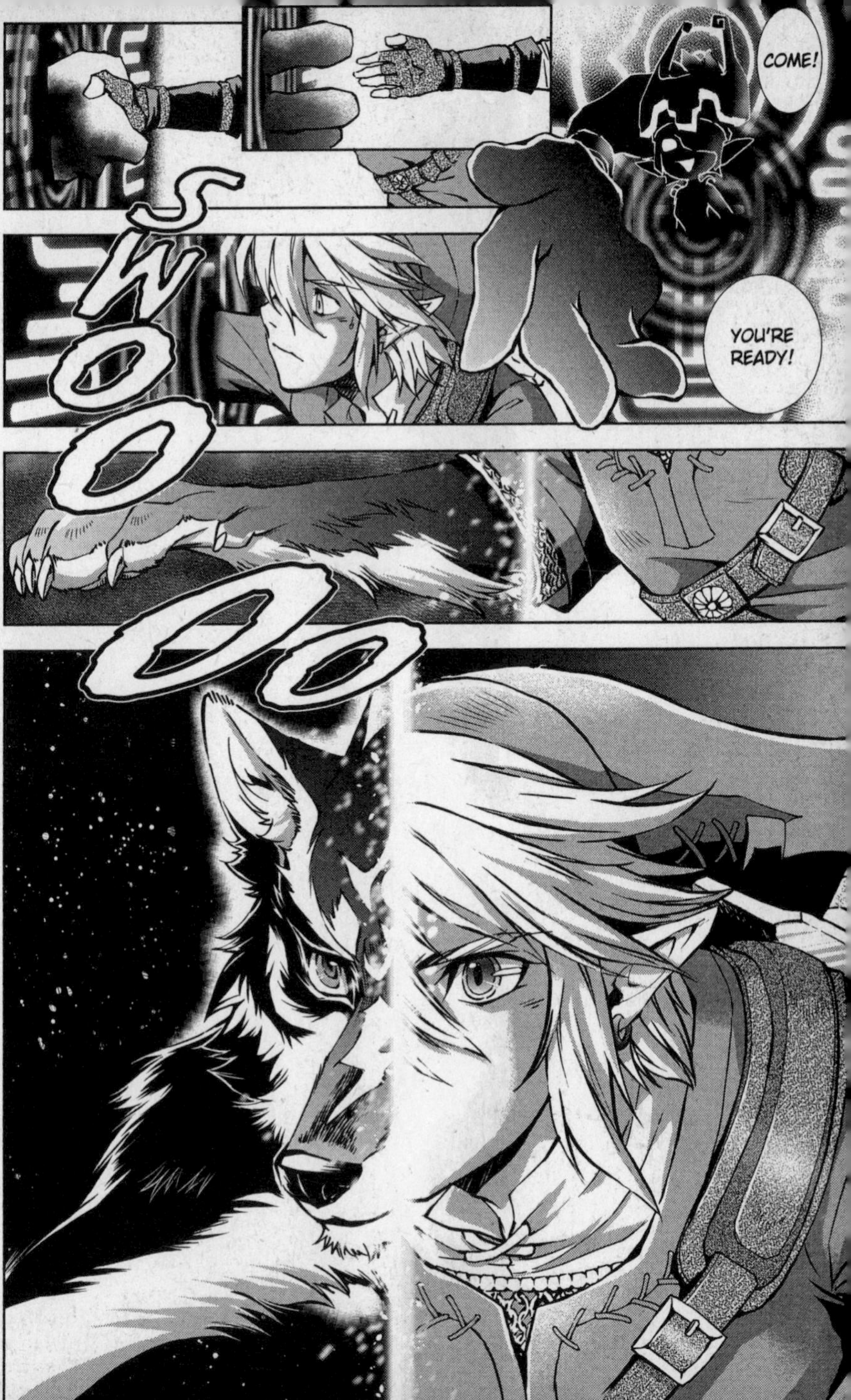
COME!
YOU'RE READY!
SWOOOOOO

#20. INTO TWILIGHT ONCE MORE

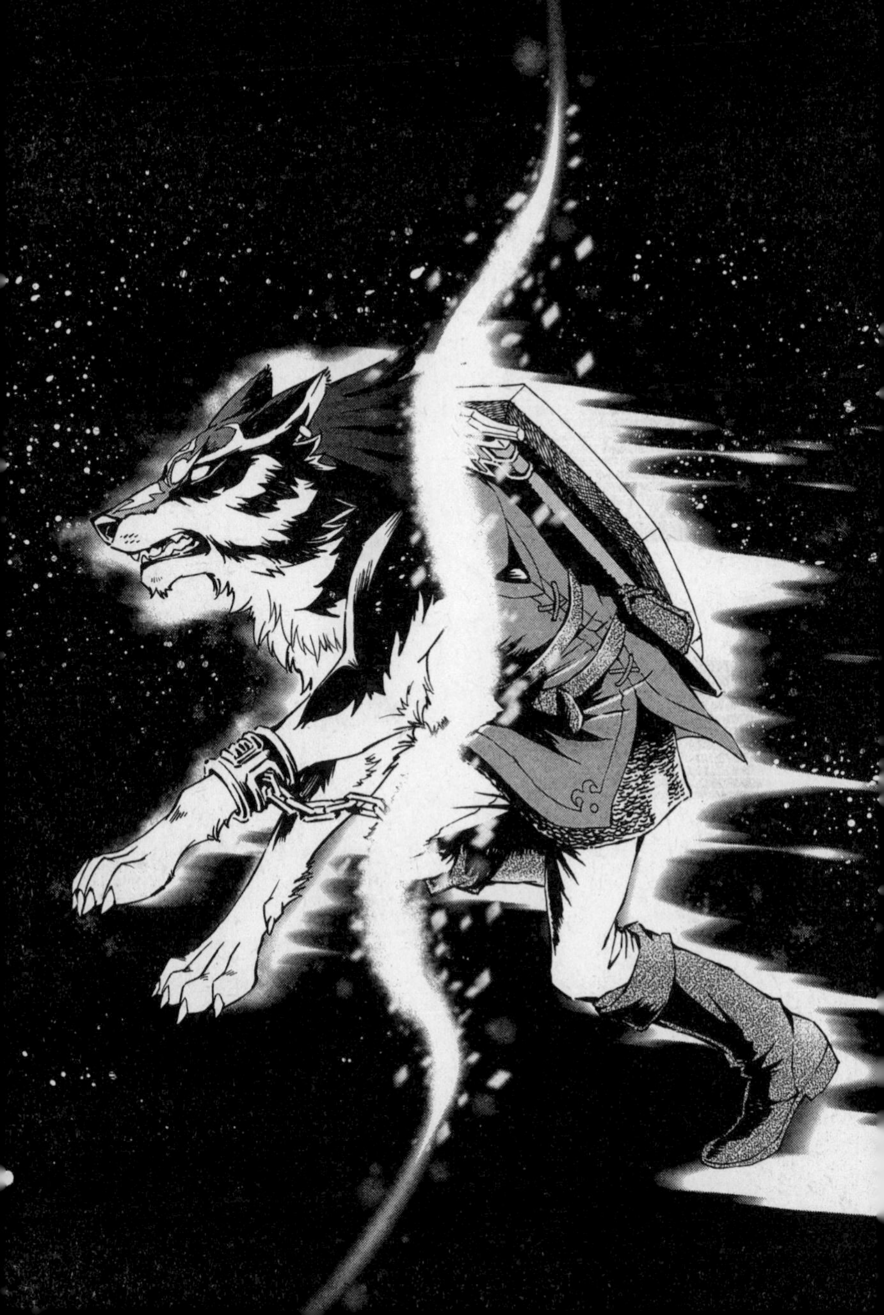

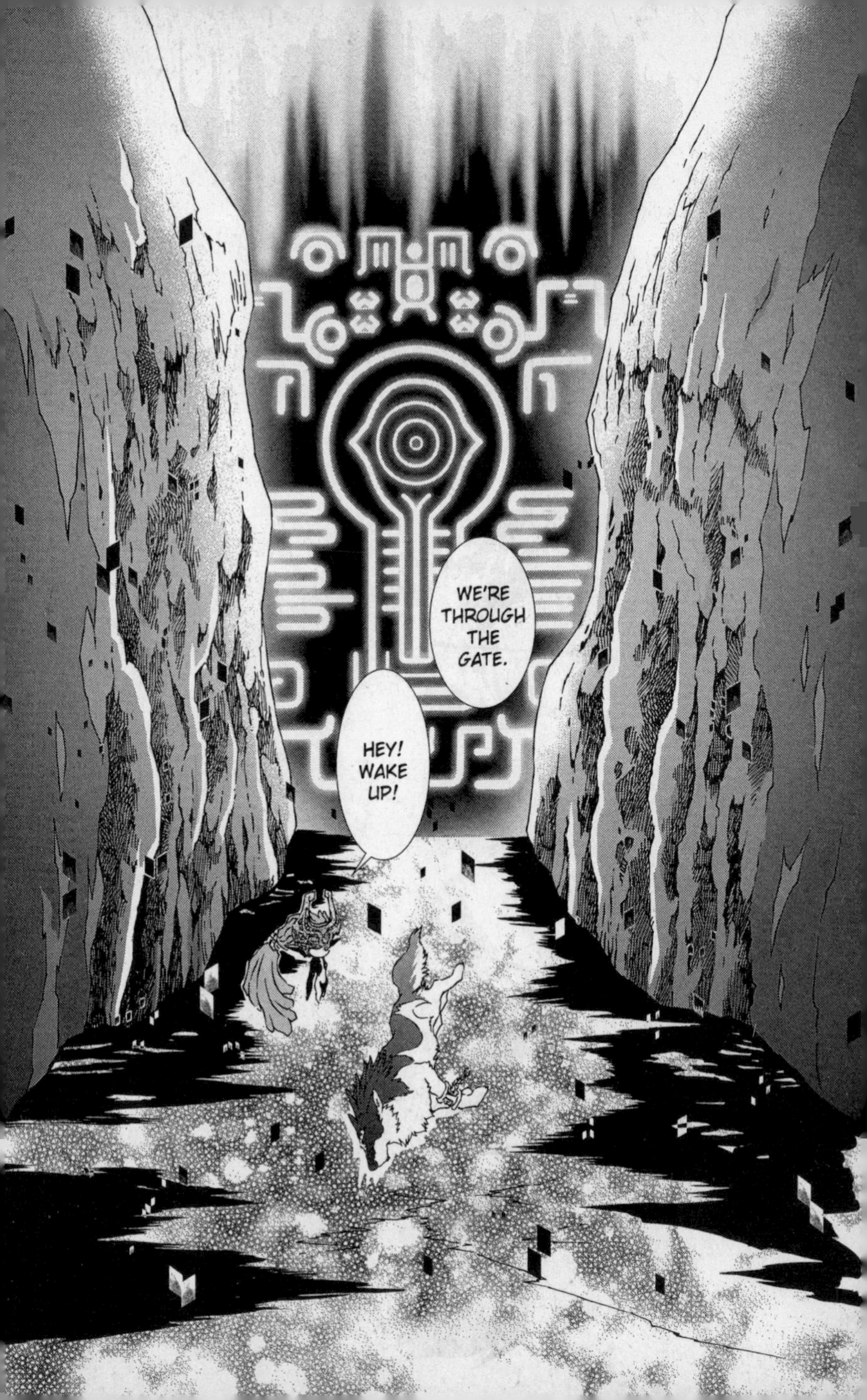
WE'RE THROUGH THE GATE.
HEY! WAKE UP!

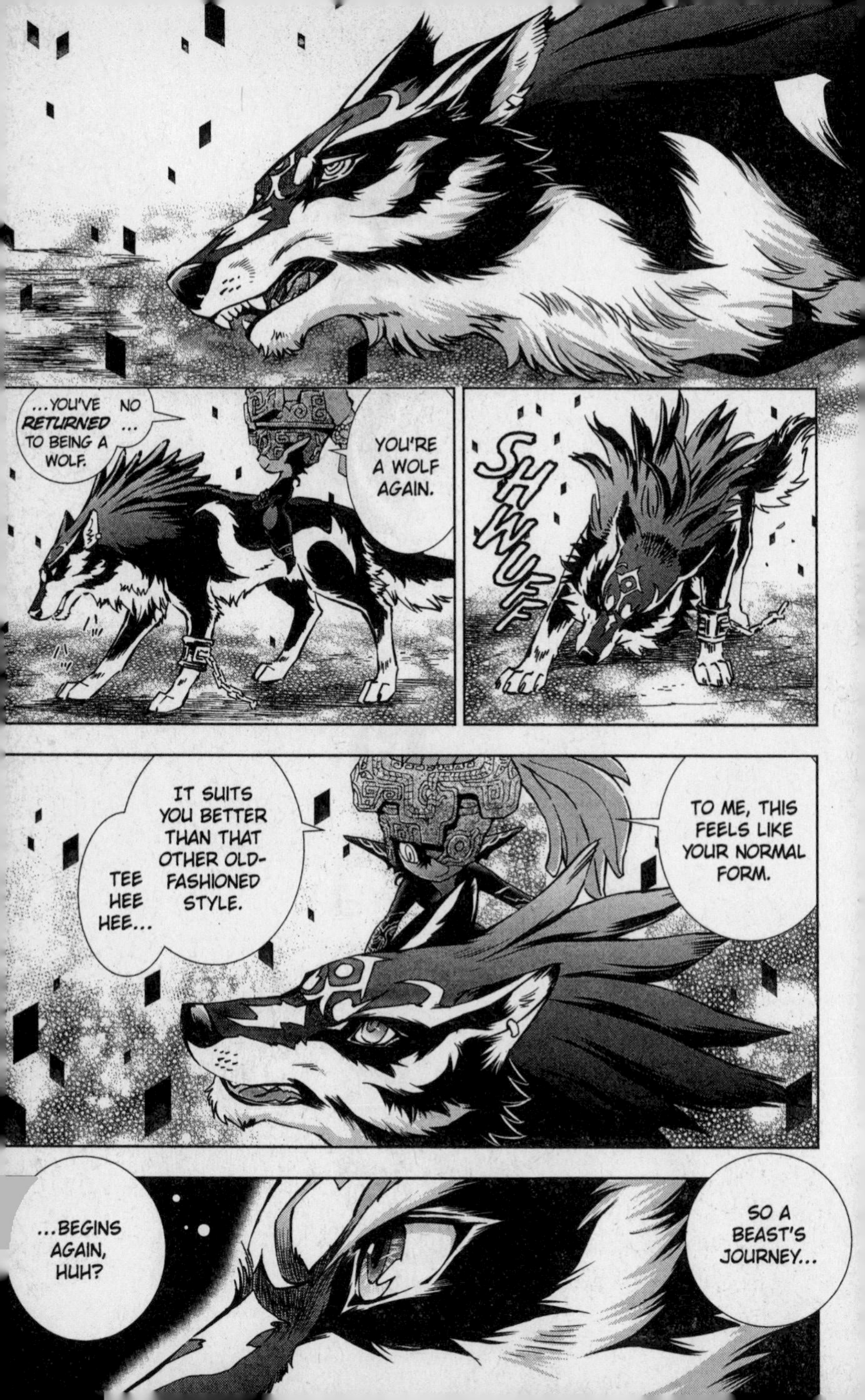
SHWUFF
YOU'RE A WOLF AGAIN.
NO... ...YOU'VE ***RETURNED*** TO BEING A WOLF.
TO ME, THIS FEELS LIKE YOUR NORMAL FORM.
IT SUITS YOU BETTER THAN THAT OTHER OLD-FASHIONED STYLE.
TEE HEE HEE...
SO A BEAST'S JOURNEY...
...BEGINS AGAIN, HUH?

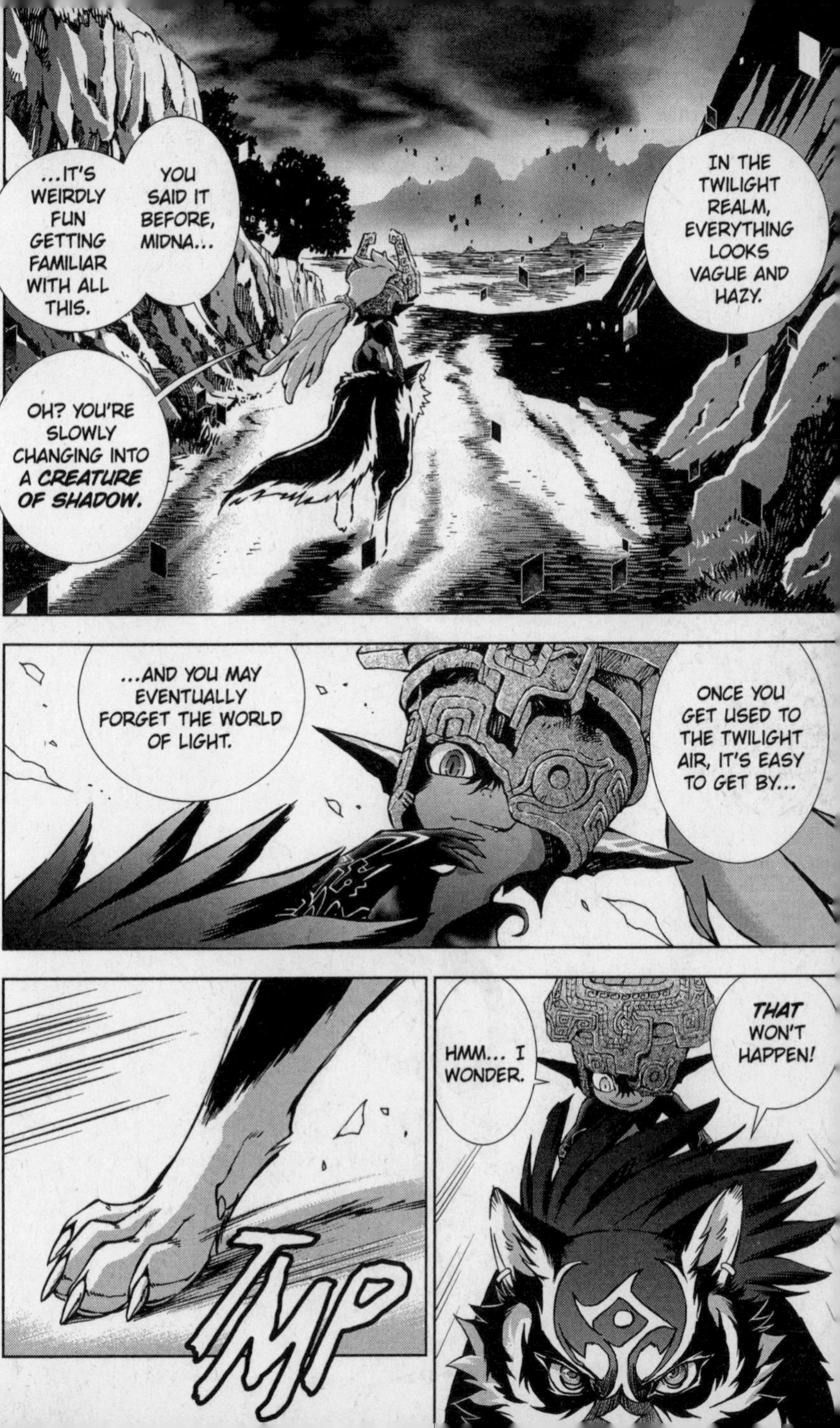
IN THE TWILIGHT REALM, EVERYTHING LOOKS VAGUE AND HAZY.
YOU SAID IT BEFORE, MIDNA...
...IT'S WEIRDLY FUN GETTING FAMILIAR WITH ALL THIS.
OH? YOU'RE SLOWLY CHANGING INTO A *CREATURE OF SHADOW.*
ONCE YOU GET USED TO THE TWILIGHT AIR, IT'S EASY TO GET BY...
...AND YOU MAY EVENTUALLY FORGET THE WORLD OF LIGHT.
THAT WON'T HAPPEN!
HMM... I WONDER.
TMP

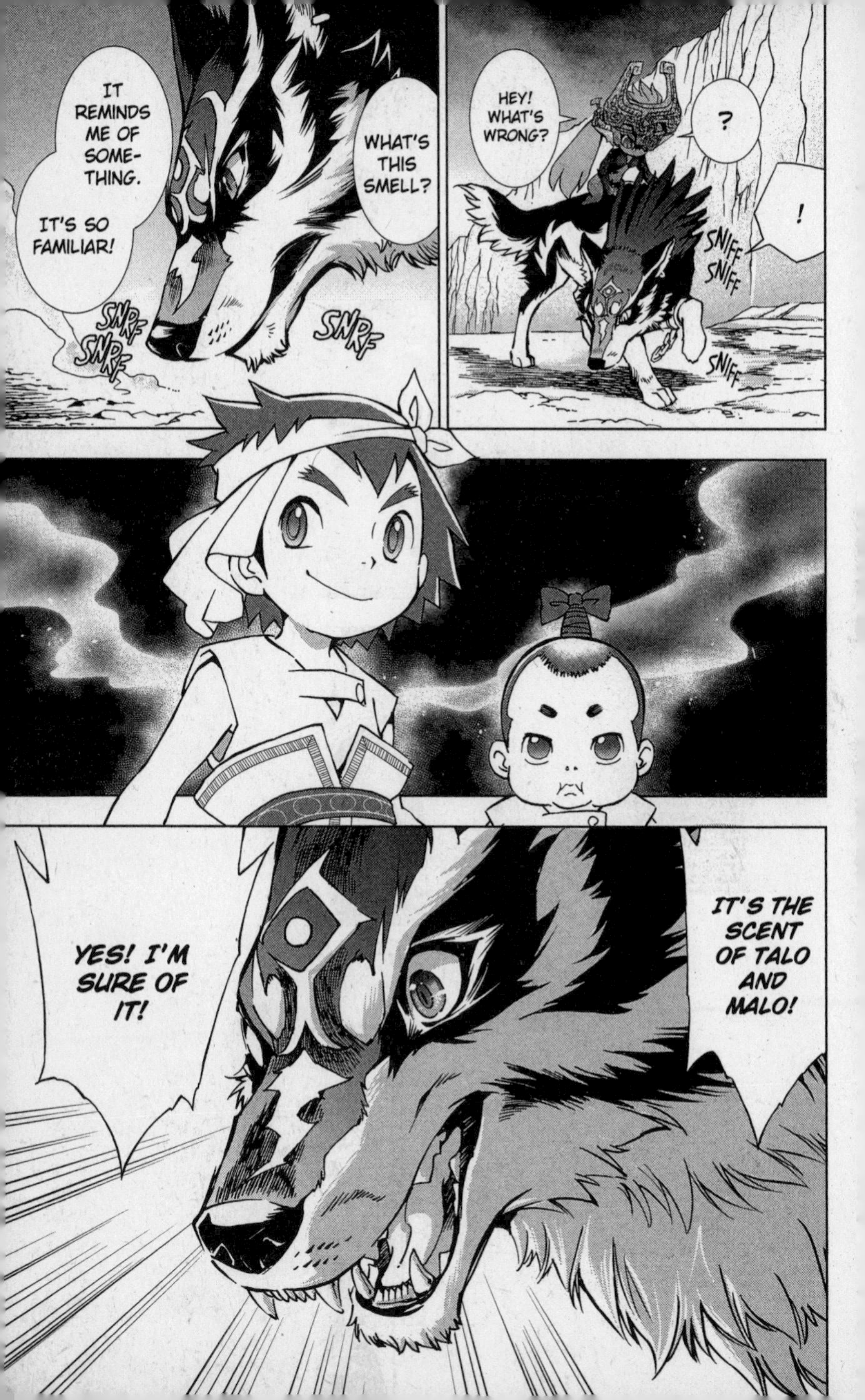
?
HEY! WHAT'S WRONG?
!
SNIFF SNIFF
SNIFF
WHAT'S THIS SMELL?
IT REMINDS ME OF SOME-THING.
IT'S SO FAMILIAR!
SNRF
SNRF SNRF
IT'S THE SCENT OF TALO AND MALO!
YES! I'M SURE OF IT!

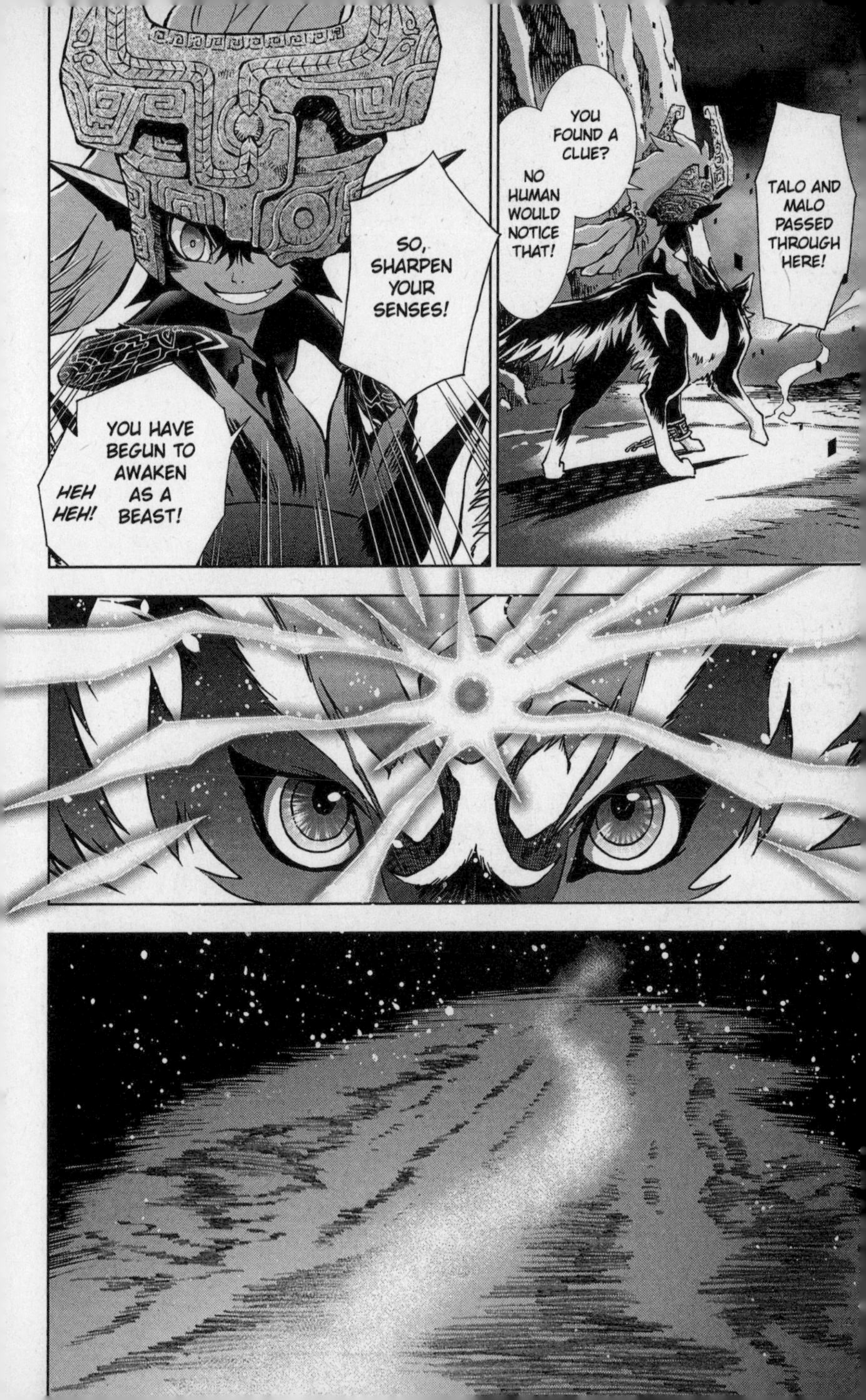
TALO AND MALO PASSED THROUGH HERE!
YOU FOUND A CLUE?
NO HUMAN WOULD NOTICE THAT!
SO, SHARPEN YOUR SENSES!
YOU HAVE BEGUN TO AWAKEN AS A BEAST!
HEH HEH!

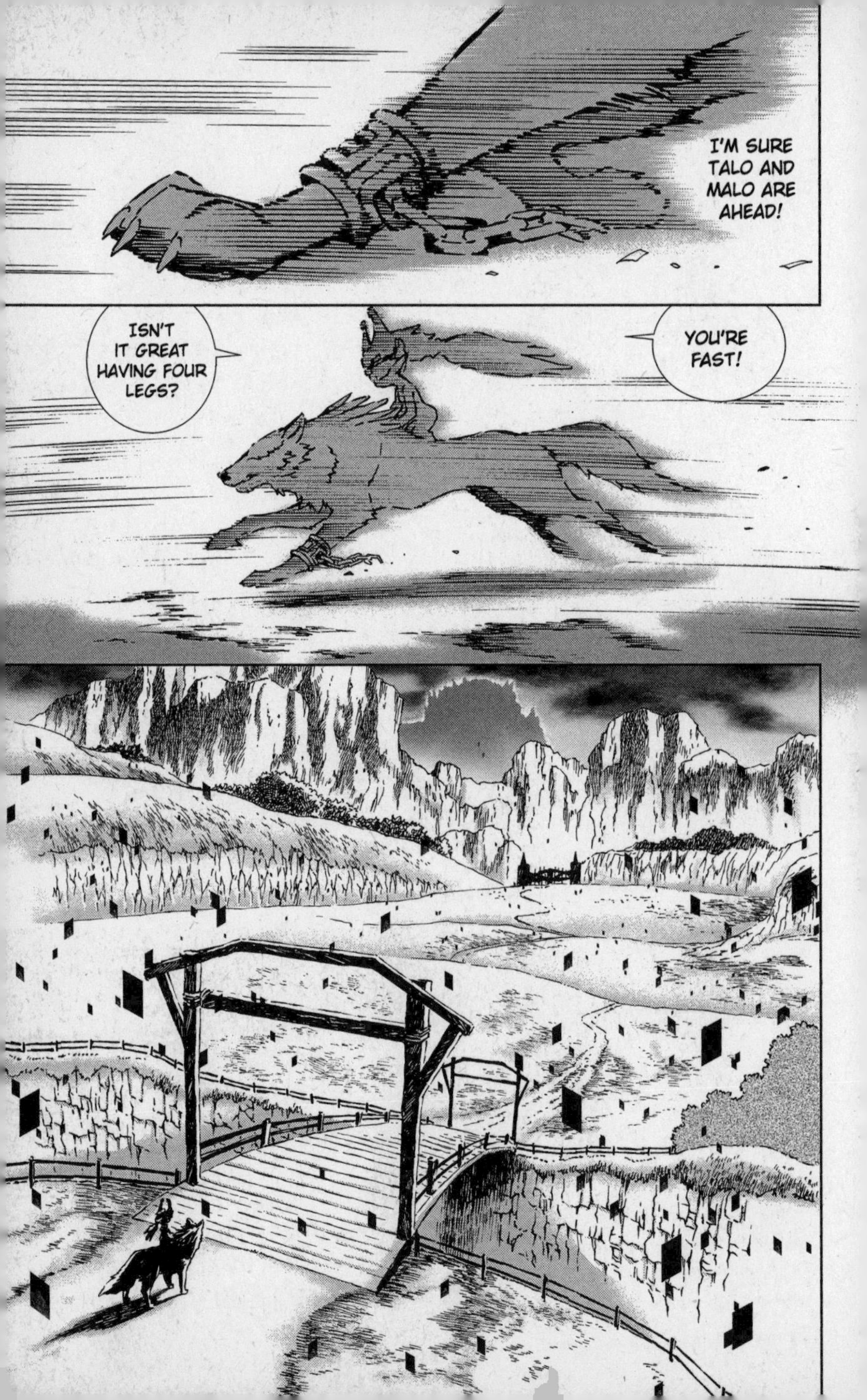
I'M SURE TALO AND MALO ARE AHEAD!
YOU'RE FAST!
ISN'T IT GREAT HAVING FOUR LEGS?

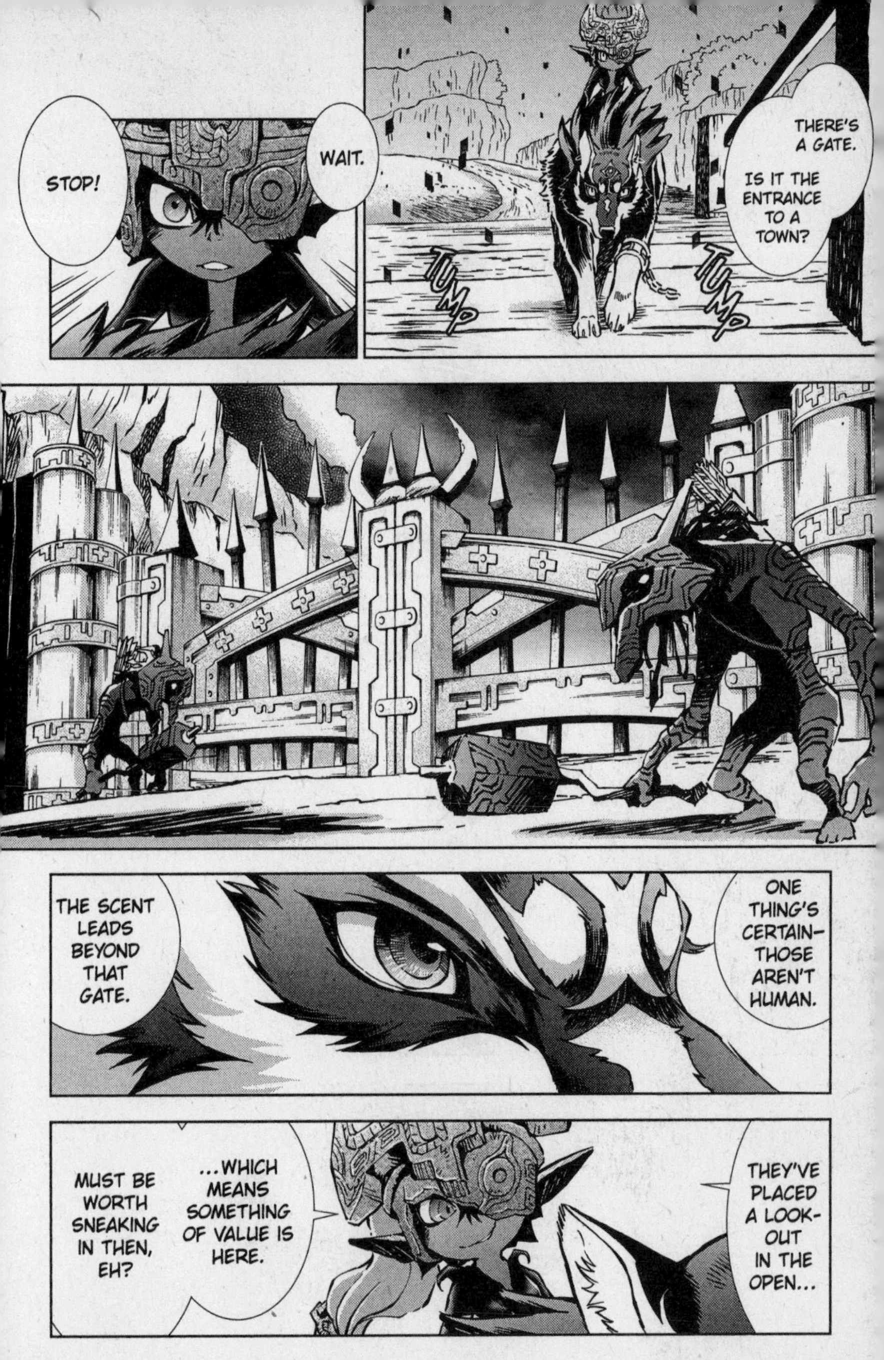
THERE'S A GATE.
IS IT THE ENTRANCE TO A TOWN?
TUMP
TUMP
WAIT.
STOP!
ONE THING'S CERTAIN— THOSE AREN'T HUMAN.
THE SCENT LEADS BEYOND THAT GATE.
THEY'VE PLACED A LOOK-OUT IN THE OPEN...
...WHICH MEANS SOMETHING OF VALUE IS HERE.
MUST BE WORTH SNEAKING IN THEN, EH?

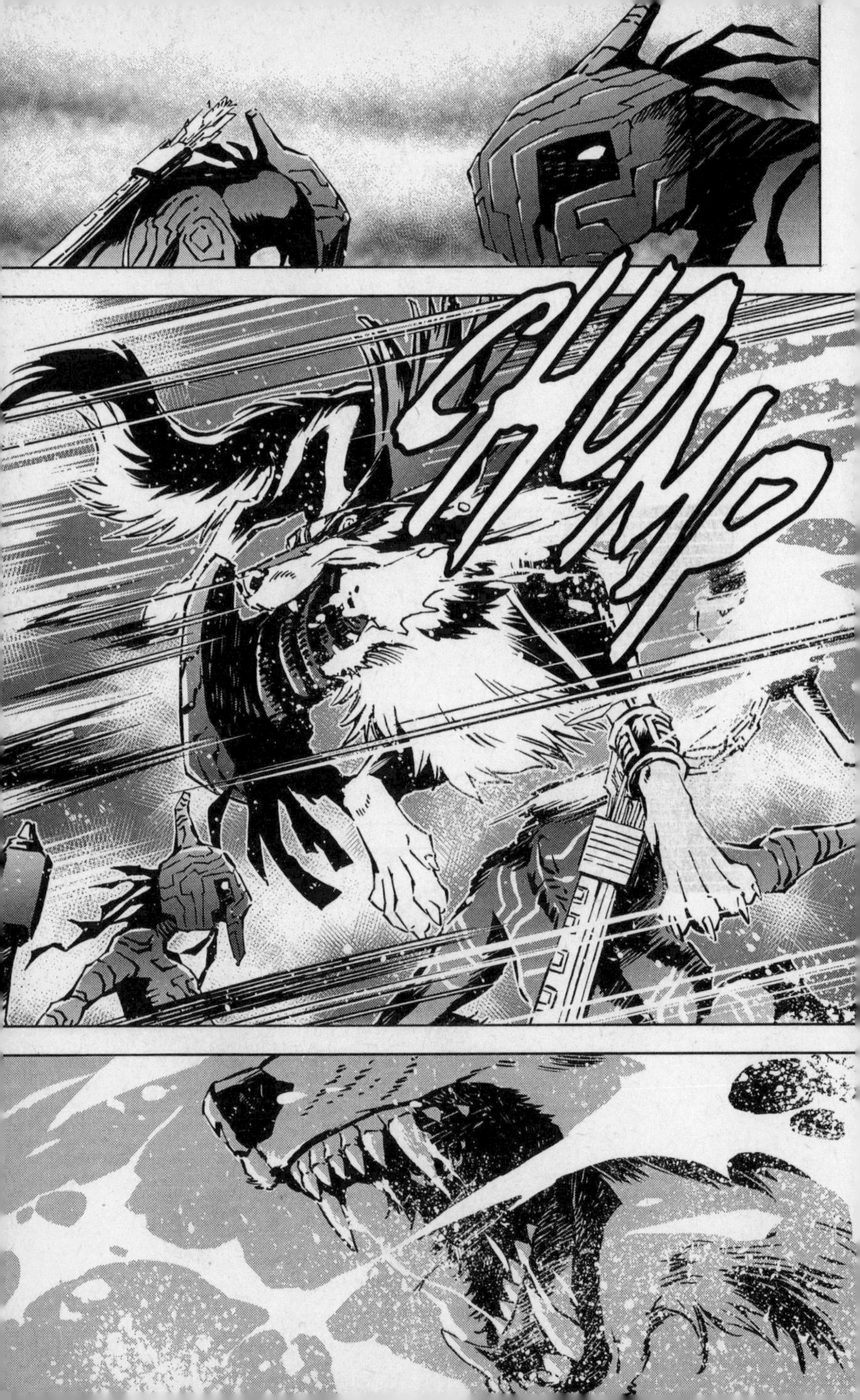
CHOMP

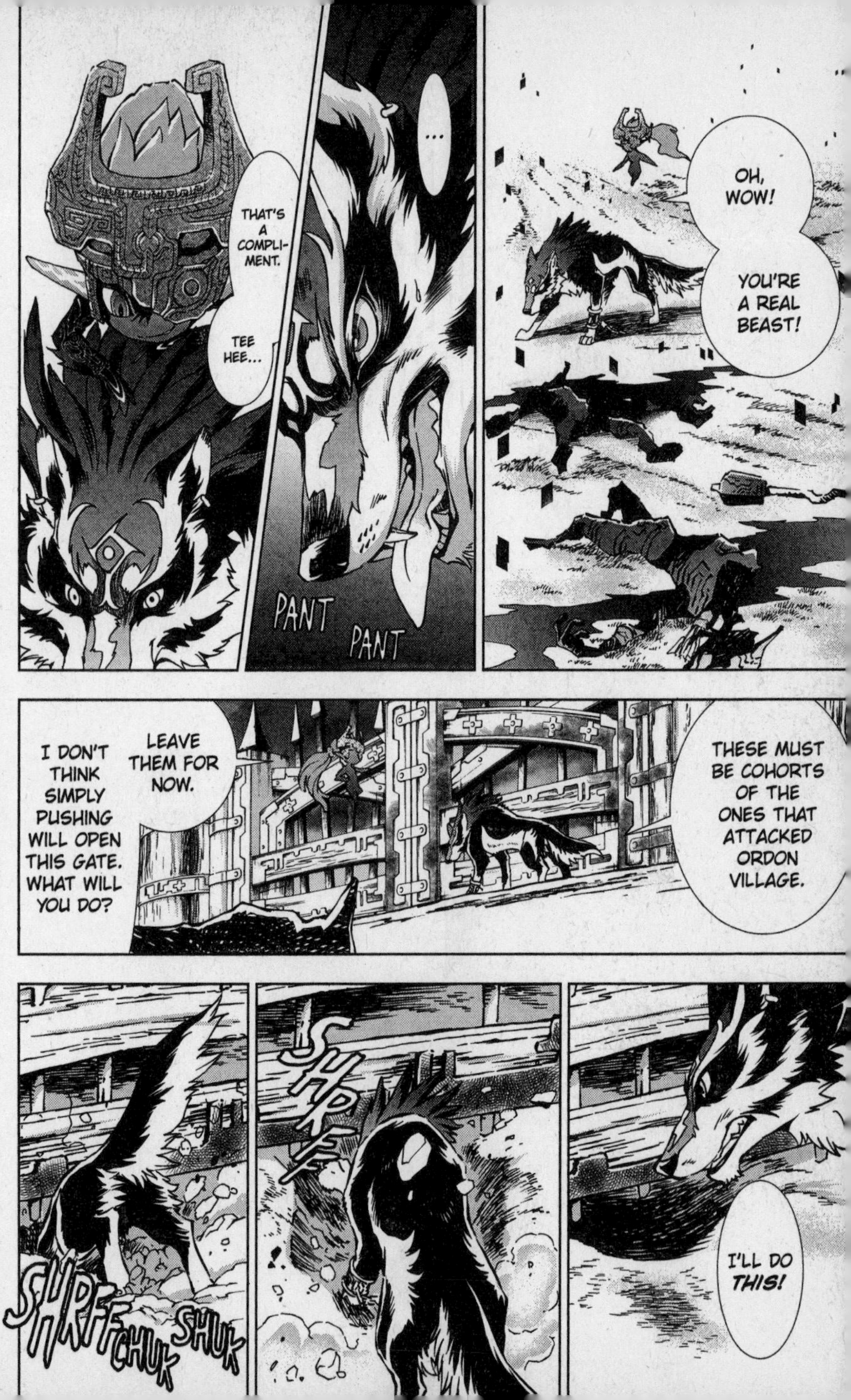
OH, WOW!
YOU'RE A REAL BEAST!
...
PANT PANT
THAT'S A COMPLI- MENT.
TEE HEE...
THESE MUST BE COHORTS OF THE ONES THAT ATTACKED ORDON VILLAGE.
LEAVE THEM FOR NOW.
I DON'T THINK SIMPLY PUSHING WILL OPEN THIS GATE. WHAT WILL YOU DO?
I'LL DO *THIS!*
SHRFF CHUK SHUK

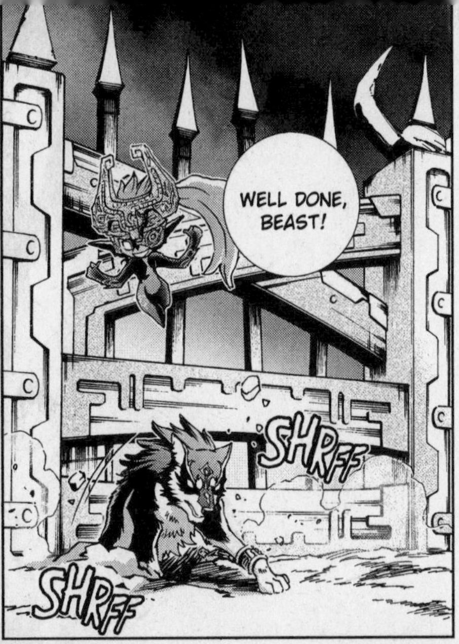
WELL DONE, BEAST!
SHRFF
SHRFF

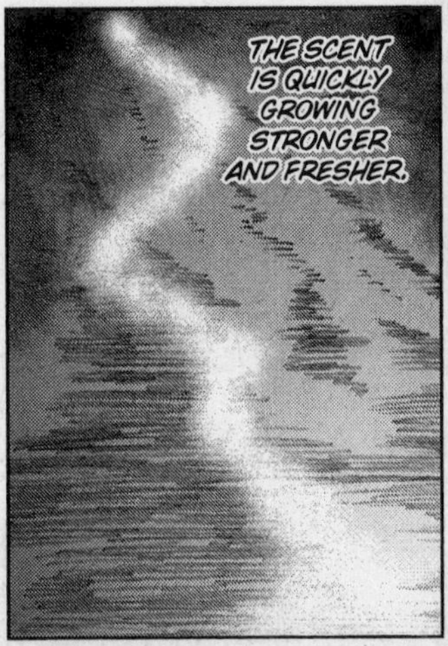
THE SCENT IS QUICKLY GROWING STRONGER AND FRESHER.

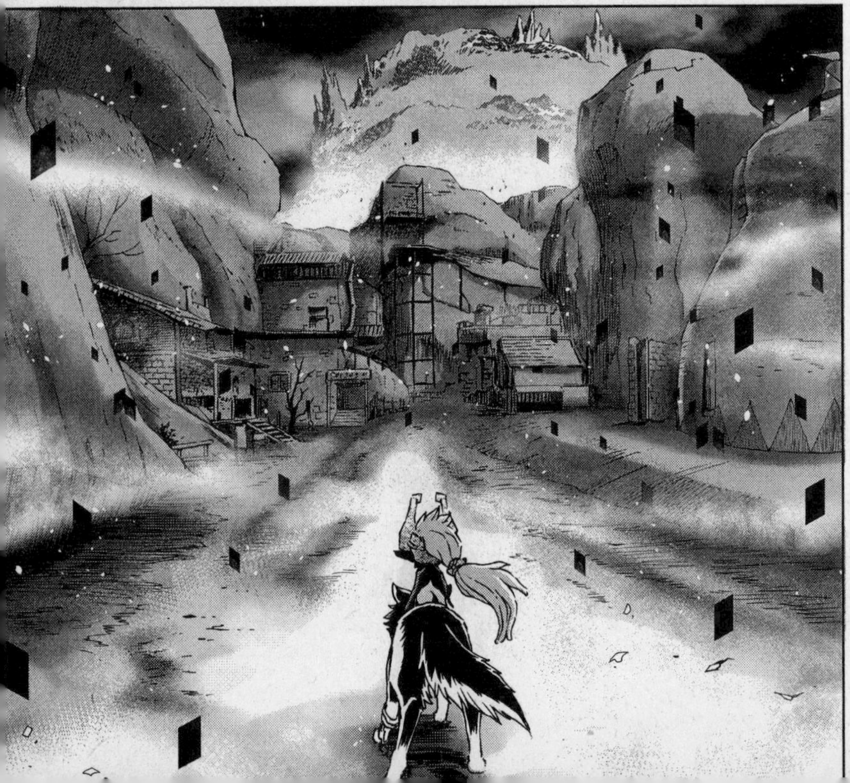

IT'S A GHOST TOWN THAT THE TWILIGHT SWALLOWED UP.

A SETTLE-MENT?

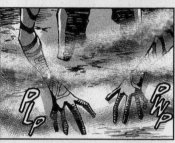

PLp

PWp

GO UP.

TROT

SHADOW BEASTS!

KRAK

SNIFF

?

IF THEY FIND YOU, IT'LL BE TROUBLE.

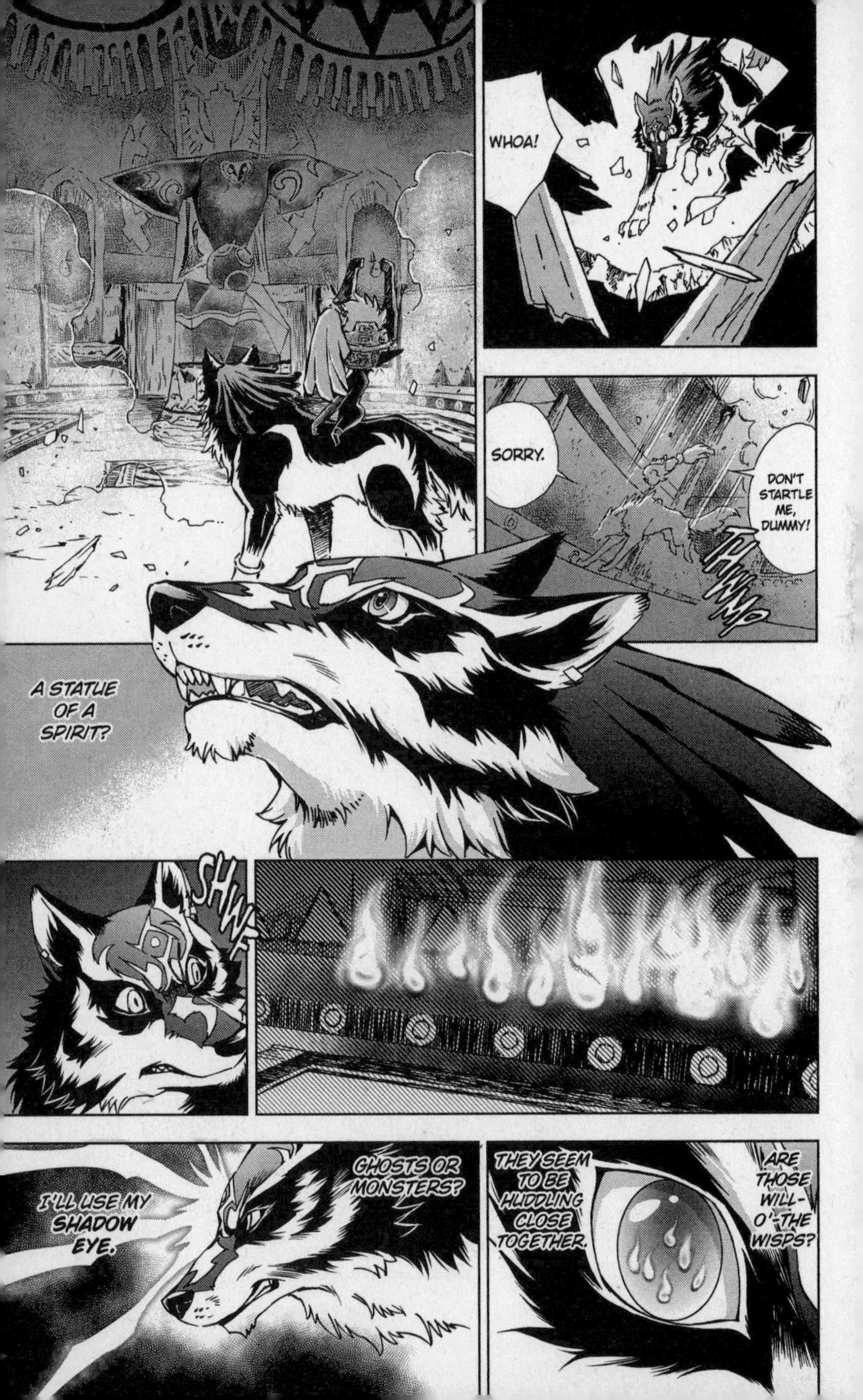
WHOA!
DON'T STARTLE ME, DUMMY!
THUMP
SORRY.
A STATUE OF A SPIRIT?
SHWF
ARE THOSE WILL-O'-THE WISPS?
THEY SEEM TO BE HUDDLING CLOSE TOGETHER.
GHOSTS OR MONSTERS?
I'LL USE MY SHADOW EYE.

#22. LIFE AND DEATH

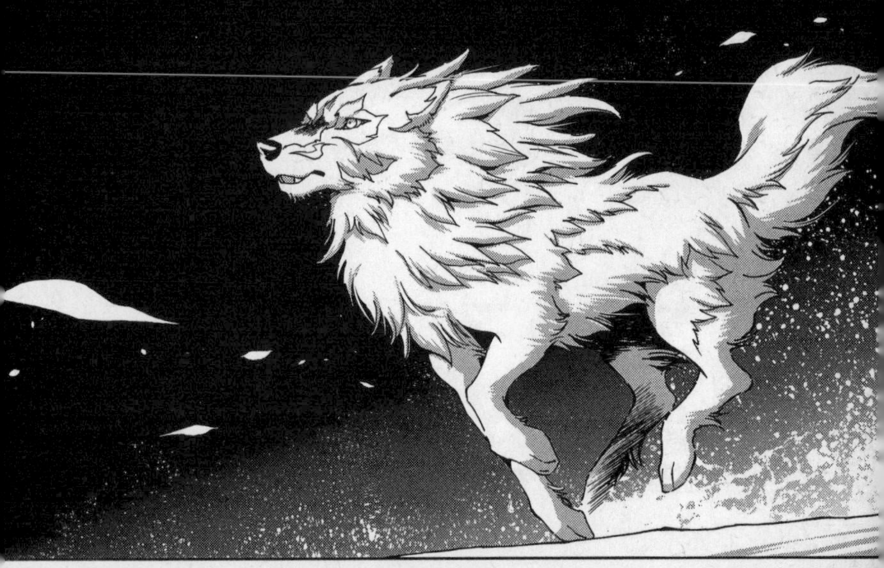

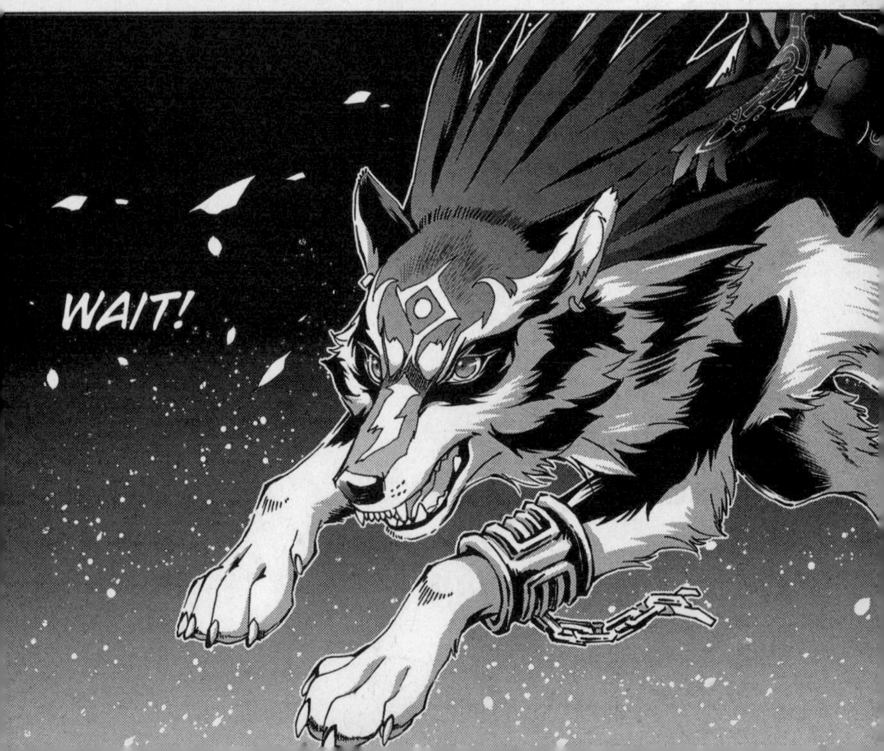
WAIT!

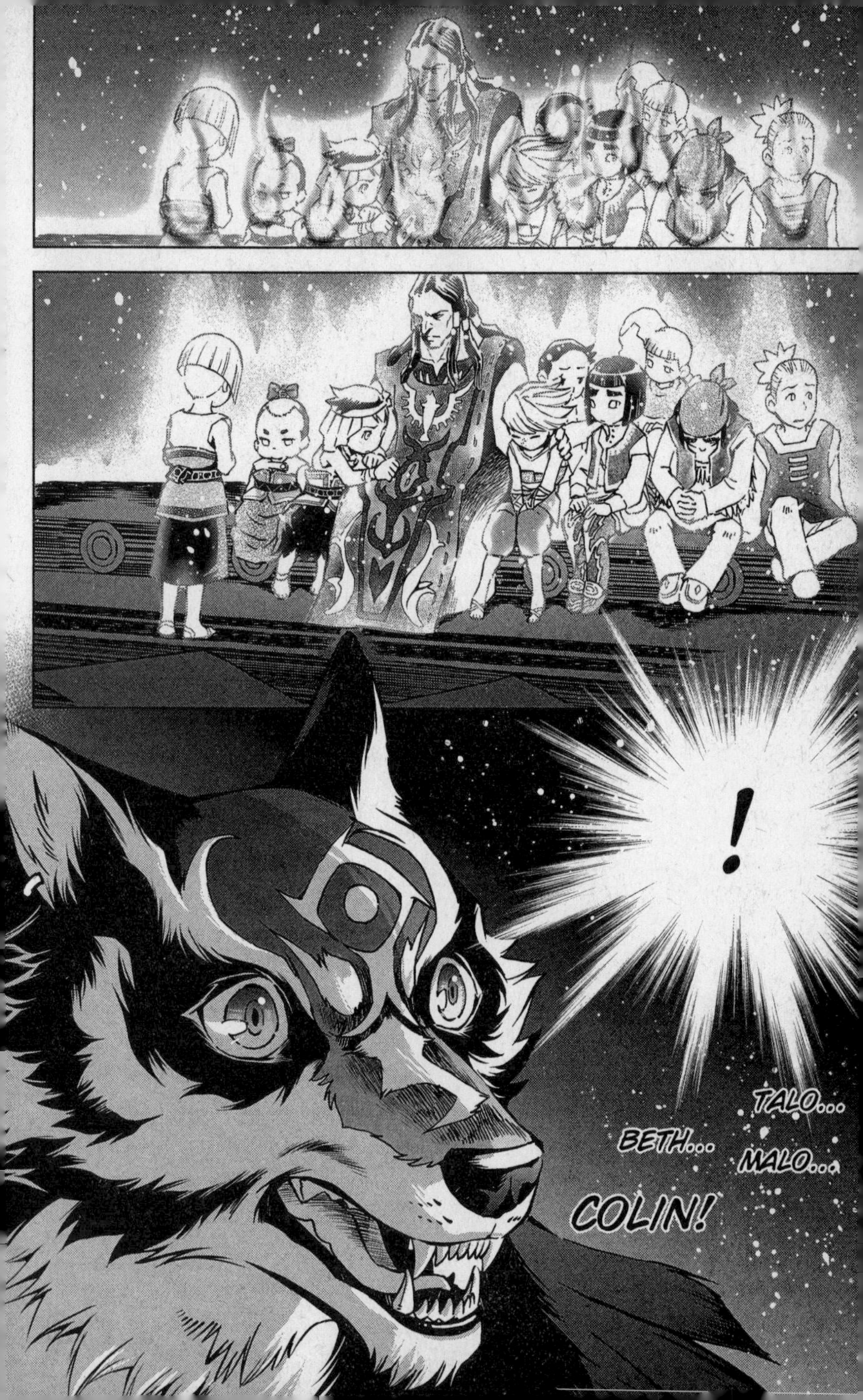
!
TALO...
MALO...
BETH...
COLIN!

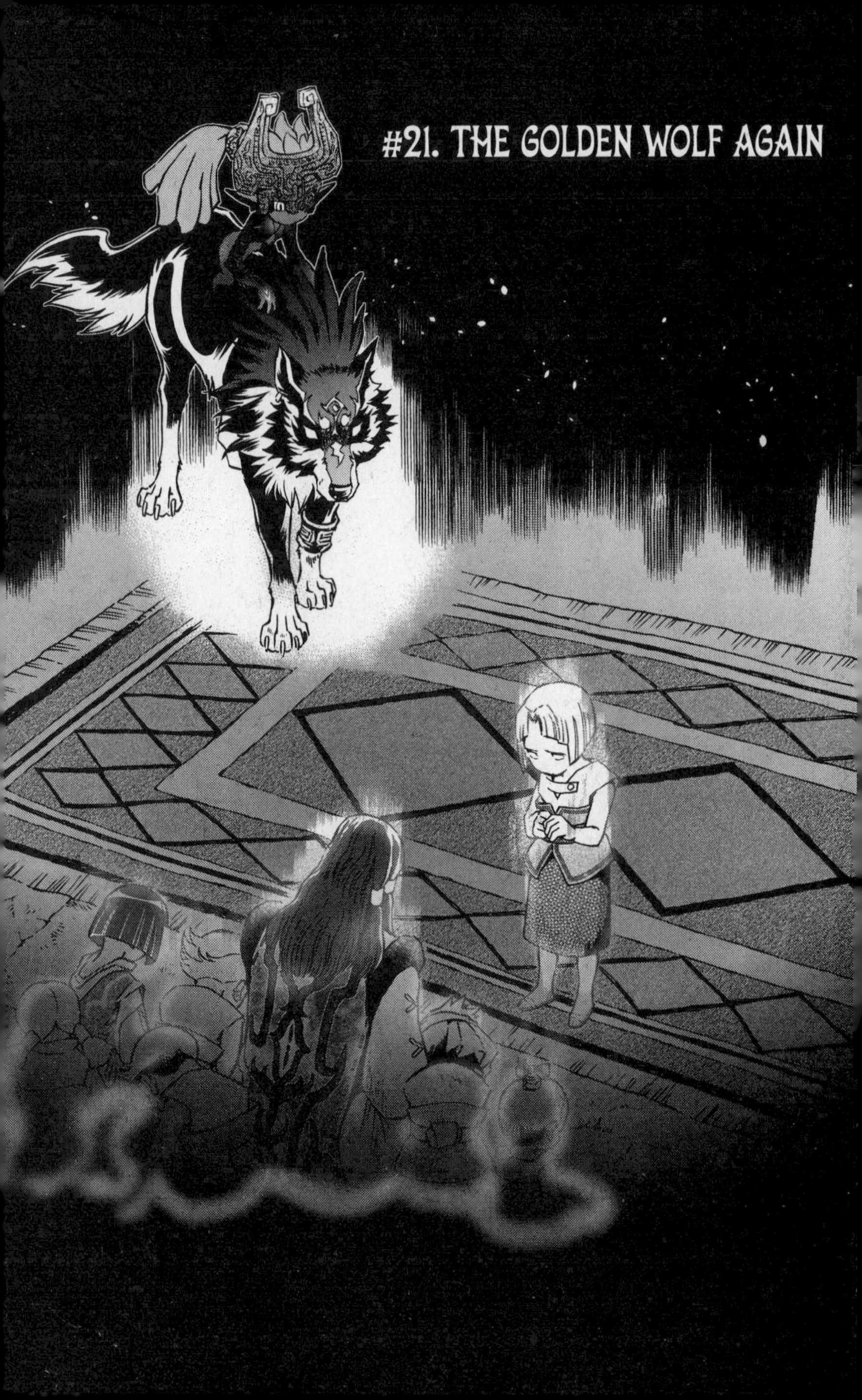
#21. THE GOLDEN WOLF AGAIN

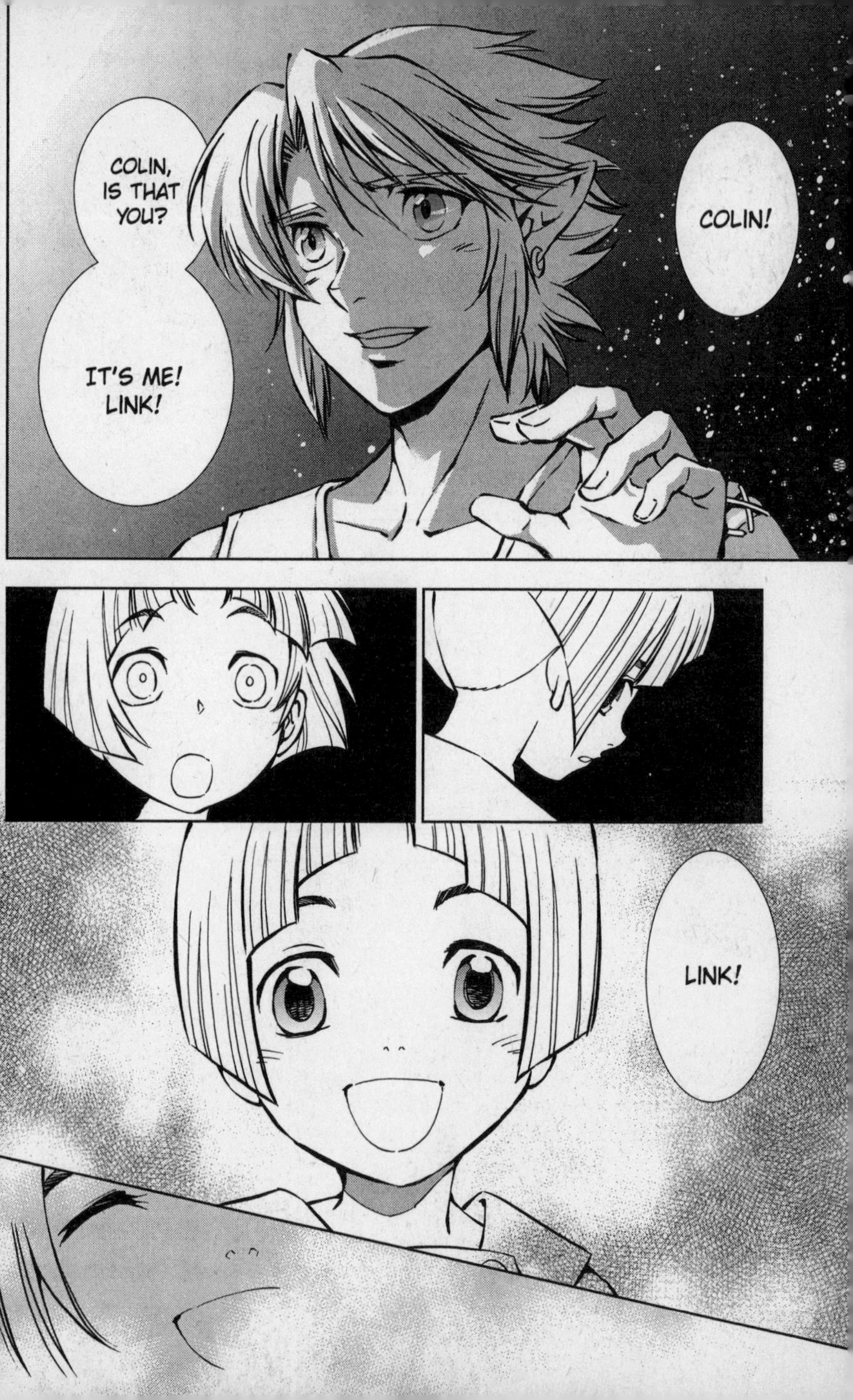
COLIN!
COLIN, IS THAT YOU?
IT'S ME! LINK!
LINK!

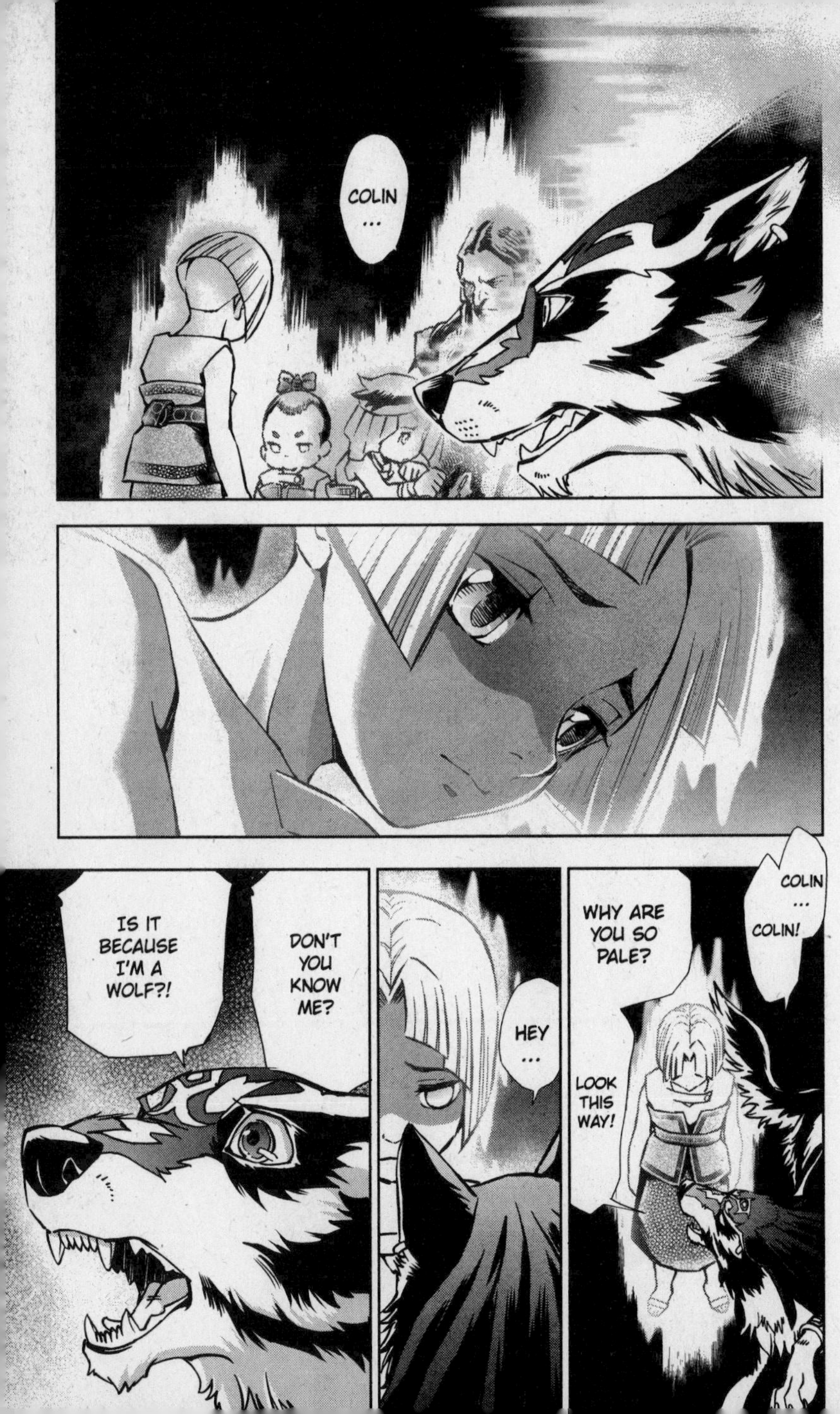
COLIN ...
COLIN ... COLIN!
WHY ARE YOU SO PALE?
LOOK THIS WAY!
HEY ...
DON'T YOU KNOW ME?
IS IT BECAUSE I'M A WOLF?!

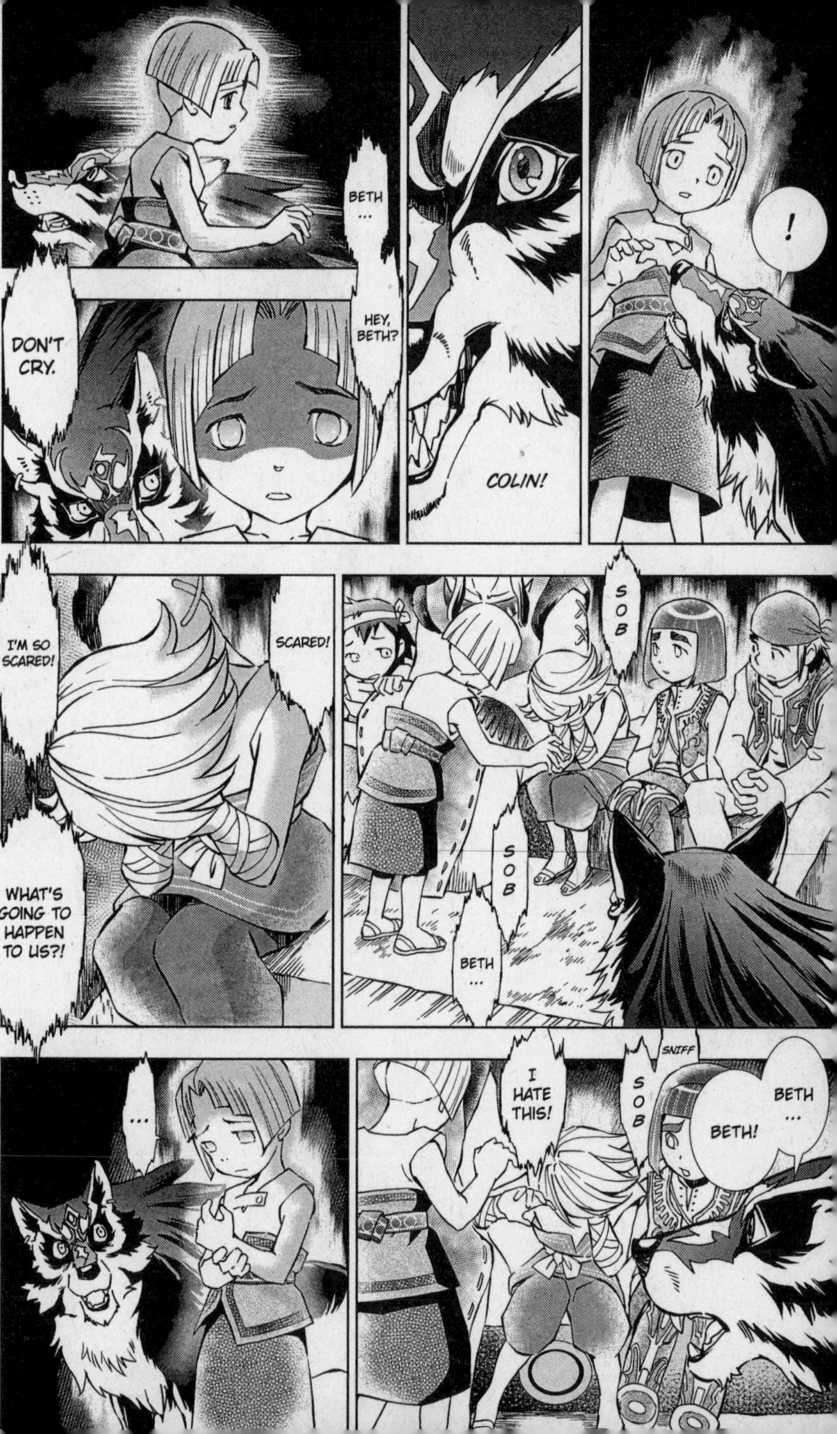
!
BETH ...
HEY, BETH?
COLIN!
DON'T CRY.
SOB
SOB
BETH ...
I'M SO SCARED!
SCARED!
WHAT'S GOING TO HAPPEN TO US?!
BETH ...
BETH!
SNIFF
SOB
I HATE THIS!
...

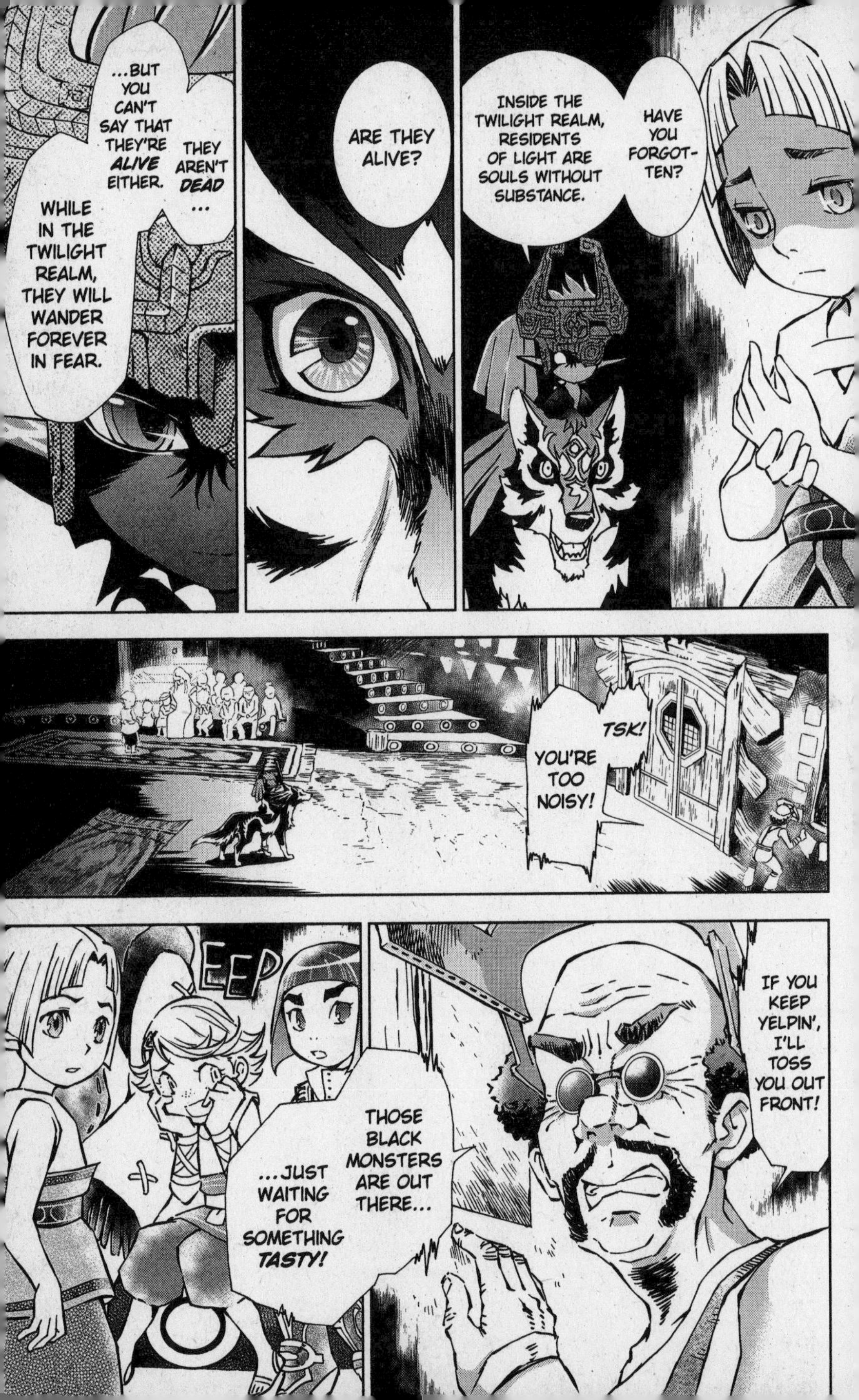
HAVE YOU FORGOTTEN?
INSIDE THE TWILIGHT REALM, RESIDENTS OF LIGHT ARE SOULS WITHOUT SUBSTANCE.
ARE THEY ALIVE?
THEY AREN'T *DEAD*...
...BUT YOU CAN'T SAY THAT THEY'RE *ALIVE* EITHER.
WHILE IN THE TWILIGHT REALM, THEY WILL WANDER FOREVER IN FEAR.
TSK!
YOU'RE TOO NOISY!
IF YOU KEEP YELPIN', I'LL TOSS YOU OUT FRONT!
EEEP
THOSE BLACK MONSTERS ARE OUT THERE...
...JUST WAITING FOR SOMETHING *TASTY!*

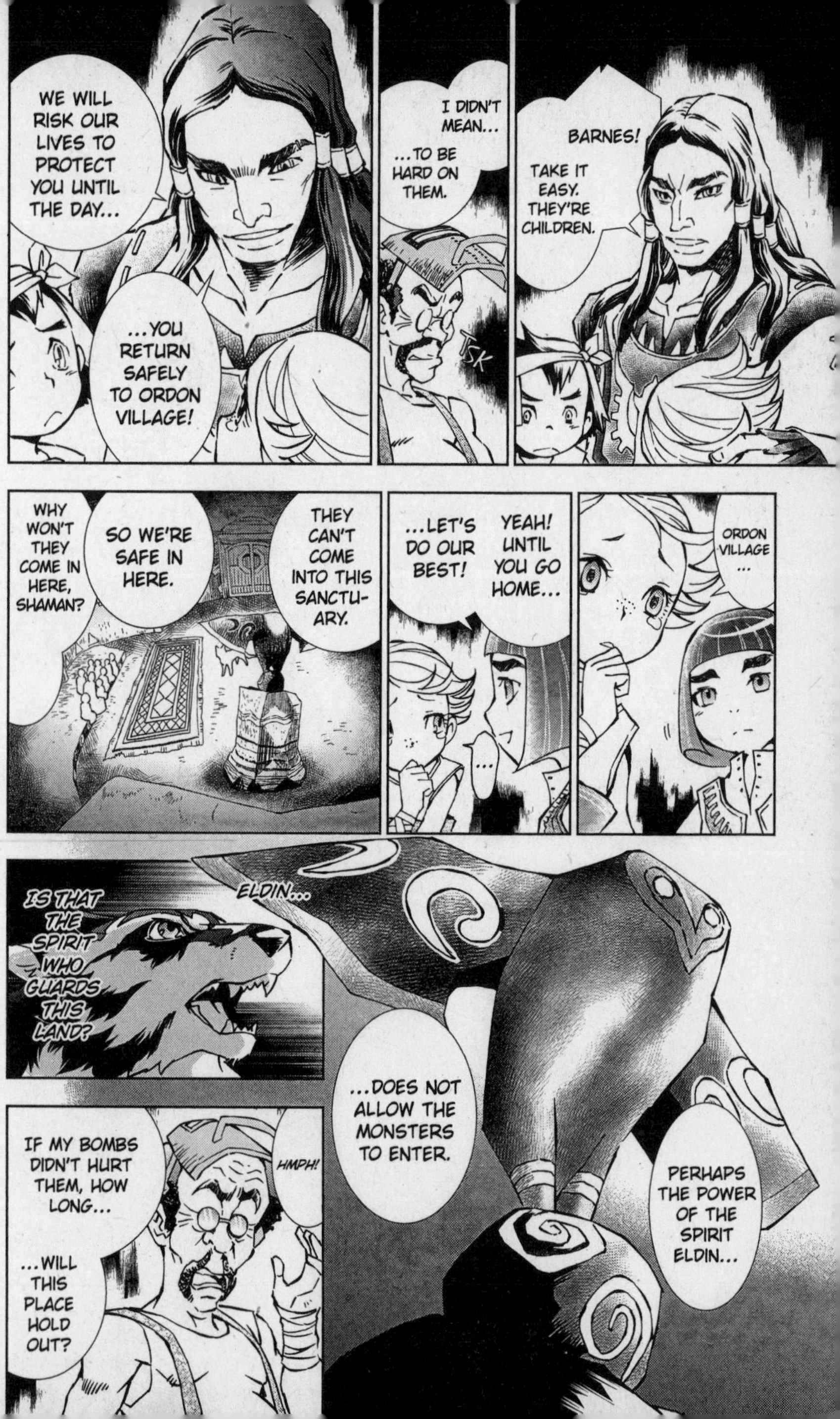
BARNES!
TAKE IT EASY. THEY'RE CHILDREN.
I DIDN'T MEAN...
...TO BE HARD ON THEM.
TSK
WE WILL RISK OUR LIVES TO PROTECT YOU UNTIL THE DAY...
...YOU RETURN SAFELY TO ORDON VILLAGE!
ORDON VILLAGE...
YEAH! UNTIL YOU GO HOME...
...LET'S DO OUR BEST!
...
THEY CAN'T COME INTO THIS SANCTUARY.
SO WE'RE SAFE IN HERE.
WHY WON'T THEY COME IN HERE, SHAMAN?
PERHAPS THE POWER OF THE SPIRIT ELDIN...
...DOES NOT ALLOW THE MONSTERS TO ENTER.
ELDIN...
IS THAT THE SPIRIT WHO GUARDS THIS LAND?
HMPH!
IF MY BOMBS DIDN'T HURT THEM, HOW LONG...
...WILL THIS PLACE HOLD OUT?

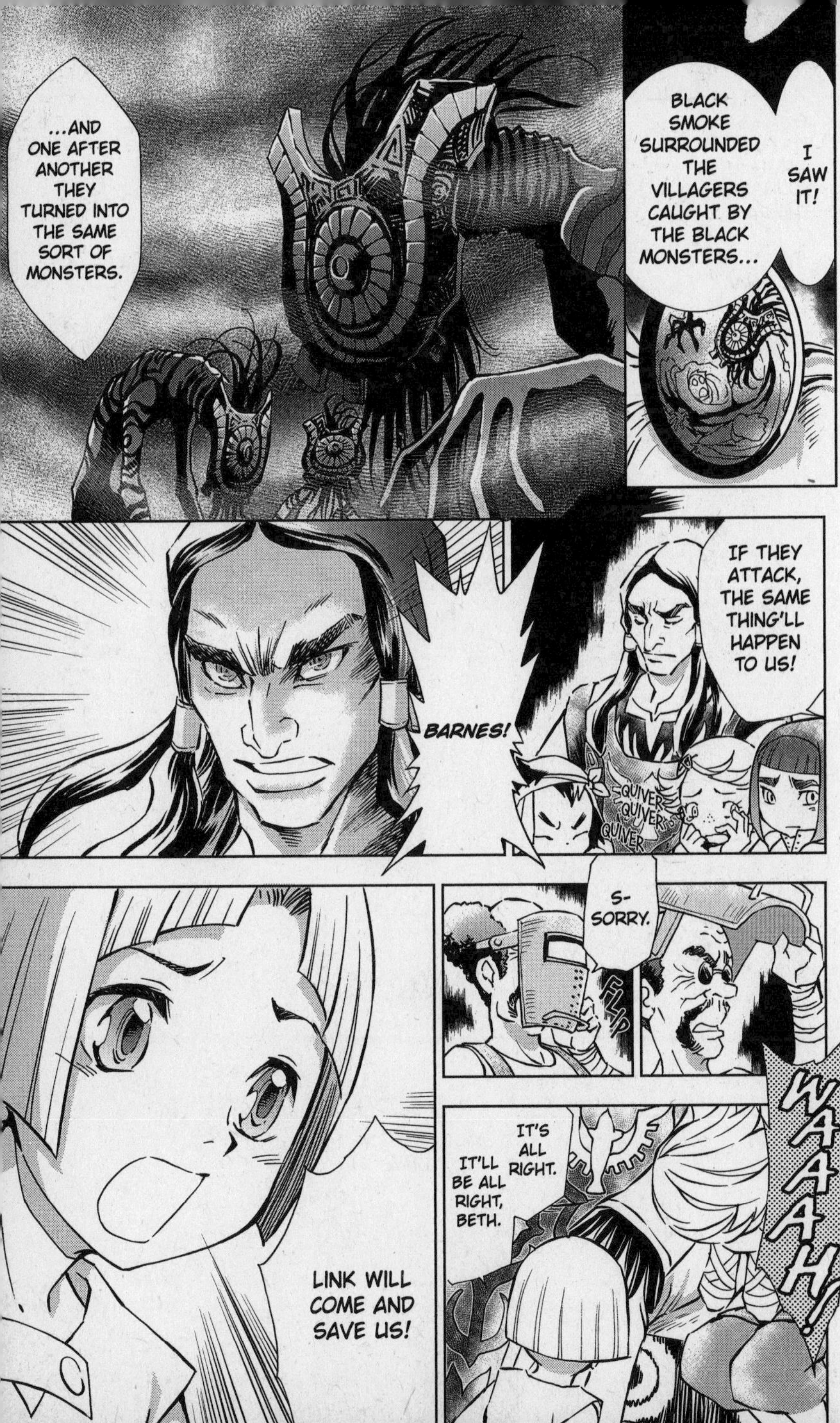
I SAW IT!
BLACK SMOKE SURROUNDED THE VILLAGERS CAUGHT BY THE BLACK MONSTERS...
...AND ONE AFTER ANOTHER THEY TURNED INTO THE SAME SORT OF MONSTERS.
IF THEY ATTACK, THE SAME THING'LL HAPPEN TO US!
QUIVER QUIVER QUIVER
BARNES!
S-SORRY.
FLIP
IT'S ALL RIGHT.
IT'LL BE ALL RIGHT, BETH.
WAAAH!
LINK WILL COME AND SAVE US!

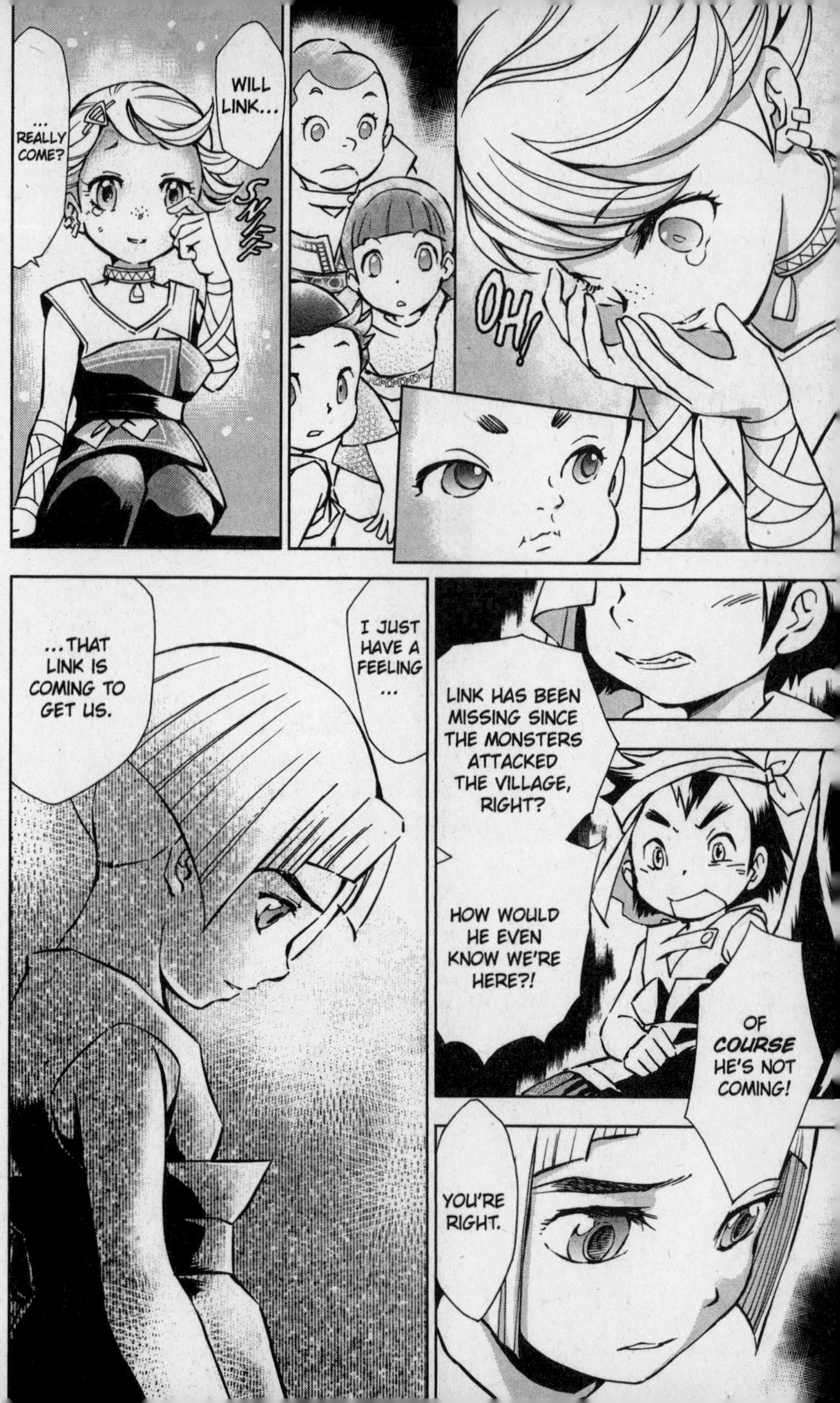
OH!
WILL LINK...
...REALLY COME?
SNIFF
LINK HAS BEEN MISSING SINCE THE MONSTERS ATTACKED THE VILLAGE, RIGHT?
HOW WOULD HE EVEN KNOW WE'RE HERE?!
OF COURSE HE'S NOT COMING!
YOU'RE RIGHT.
I JUST HAVE A FEELING...
...THAT LINK IS COMING TO GET US.

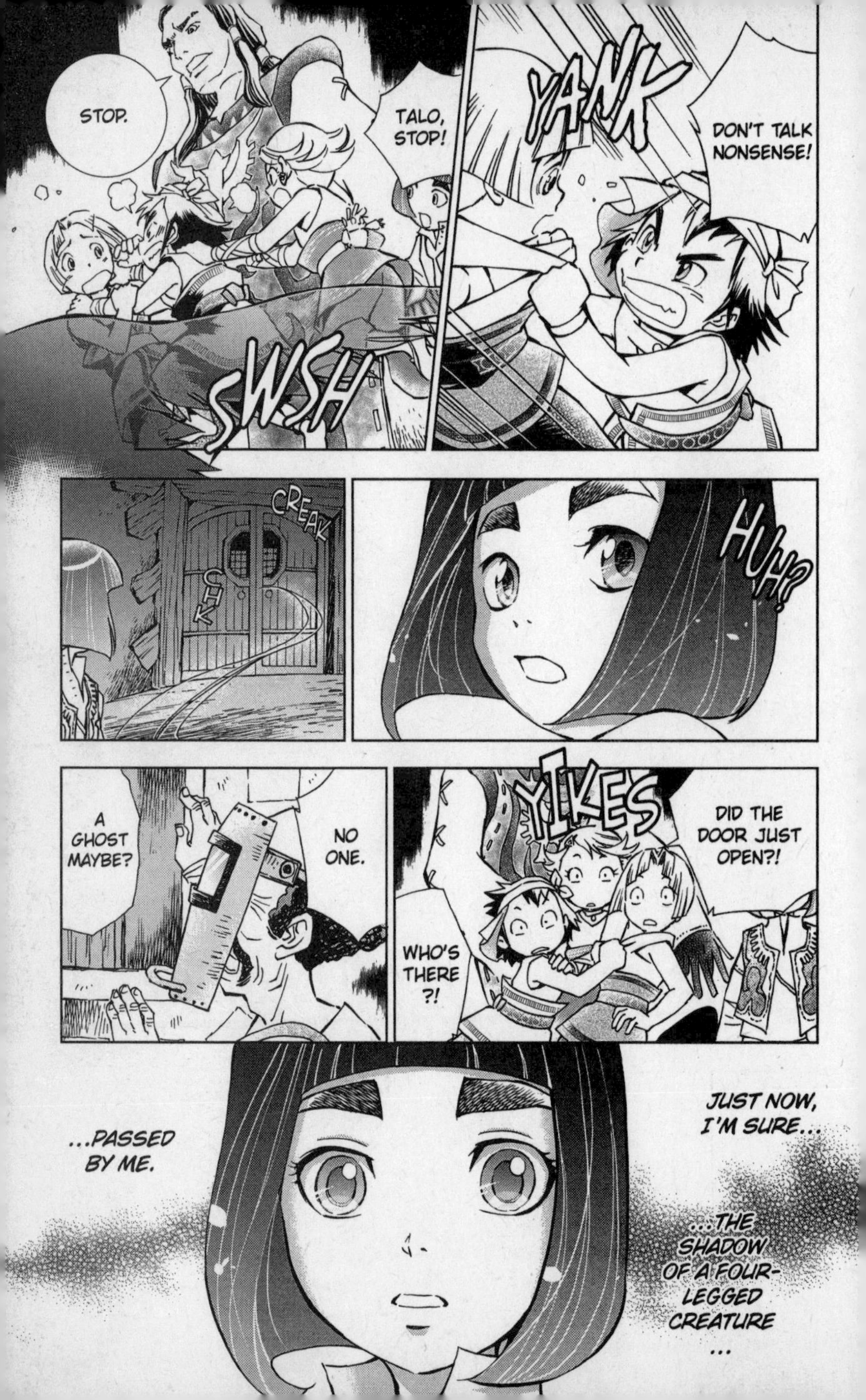
YANK
DON'T TALK NONSENSE!
TALO, STOP!
STOP.
SWSH
HUH?!
CREAK
CHK
YIKES
DID THE DOOR JUST OPEN?!
WHO'S THERE ?!
NO ONE.
A GHOST MAYBE?
JUST NOW, I'M SURE...
...THE SHADOW OF A FOUR-LEGGED CREATURE ...
...PASSED BY ME.

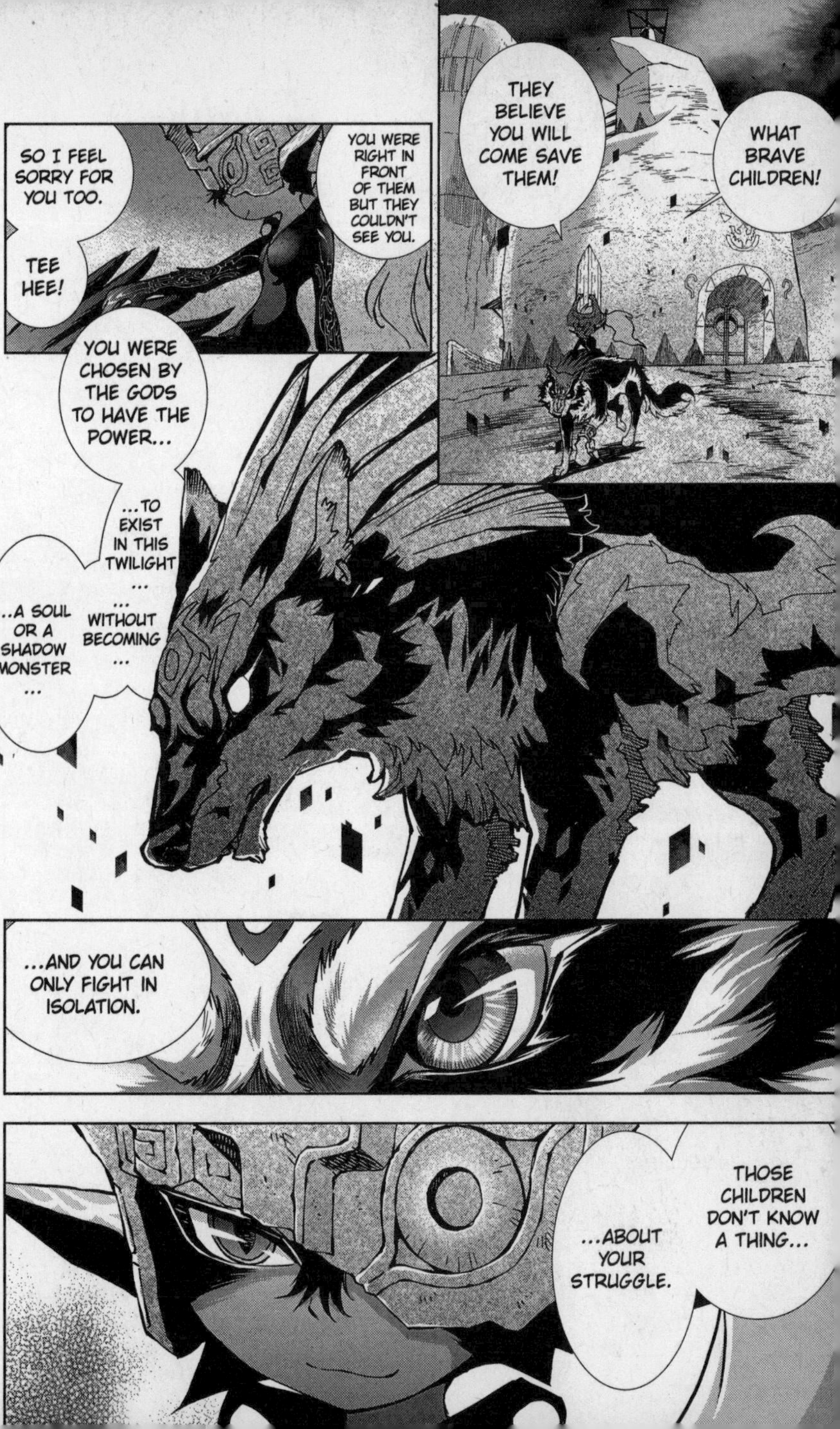
WHAT BRAVE CHILDREN!
THEY BELIEVE YOU WILL COME SAVE THEM!
YOU WERE RIGHT IN FRONT OF THEM BUT THEY COULDN'T SEE YOU.
SO I FEEL SORRY FOR YOU TOO.
TEE HEE!
YOU WERE CHOSEN BY THE GODS TO HAVE THE POWER...
...TO EXIST IN THIS TWILIGHT...
...WITHOUT BECOMING...
...A SOUL OR A SHADOW MONSTER...
...AND YOU CAN ONLY FIGHT IN ISOLATION.
THOSE CHILDREN DON'T KNOW A THING...
...ABOUT YOUR STRUGGLE.

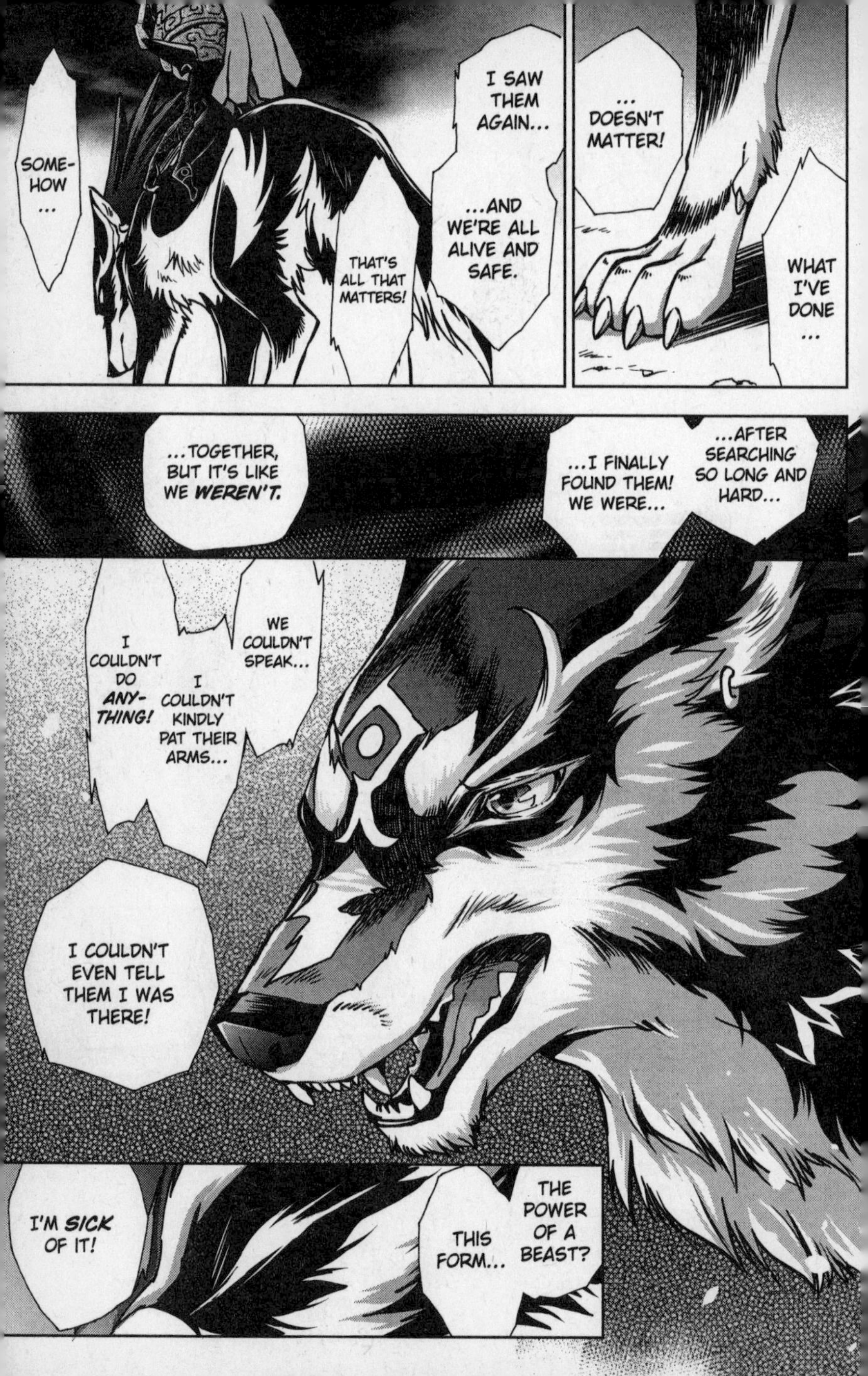
WHAT I'VE DONE ...
... DOESN'T MATTER!
I SAW THEM AGAIN...
...AND WE'RE ALL ALIVE AND SAFE.
THAT'S ALL THAT MATTERS!
SOME-HOW ...
...AFTER SEARCHING SO LONG AND HARD...
...I FINALLY FOUND THEM! WE WERE...
...TOGETHER, BUT IT'S LIKE WE WEREN'T.
WE COULDN'T SPEAK...
I COULDN'T KINDLY PAT THEIR ARMS...
I COULDN'T DO ANY-THING!
I COULDN'T EVEN TELL THEM I WAS THERE!
THE POWER OF A BEAST?
THIS FORM...
I'M SICK OF IT!

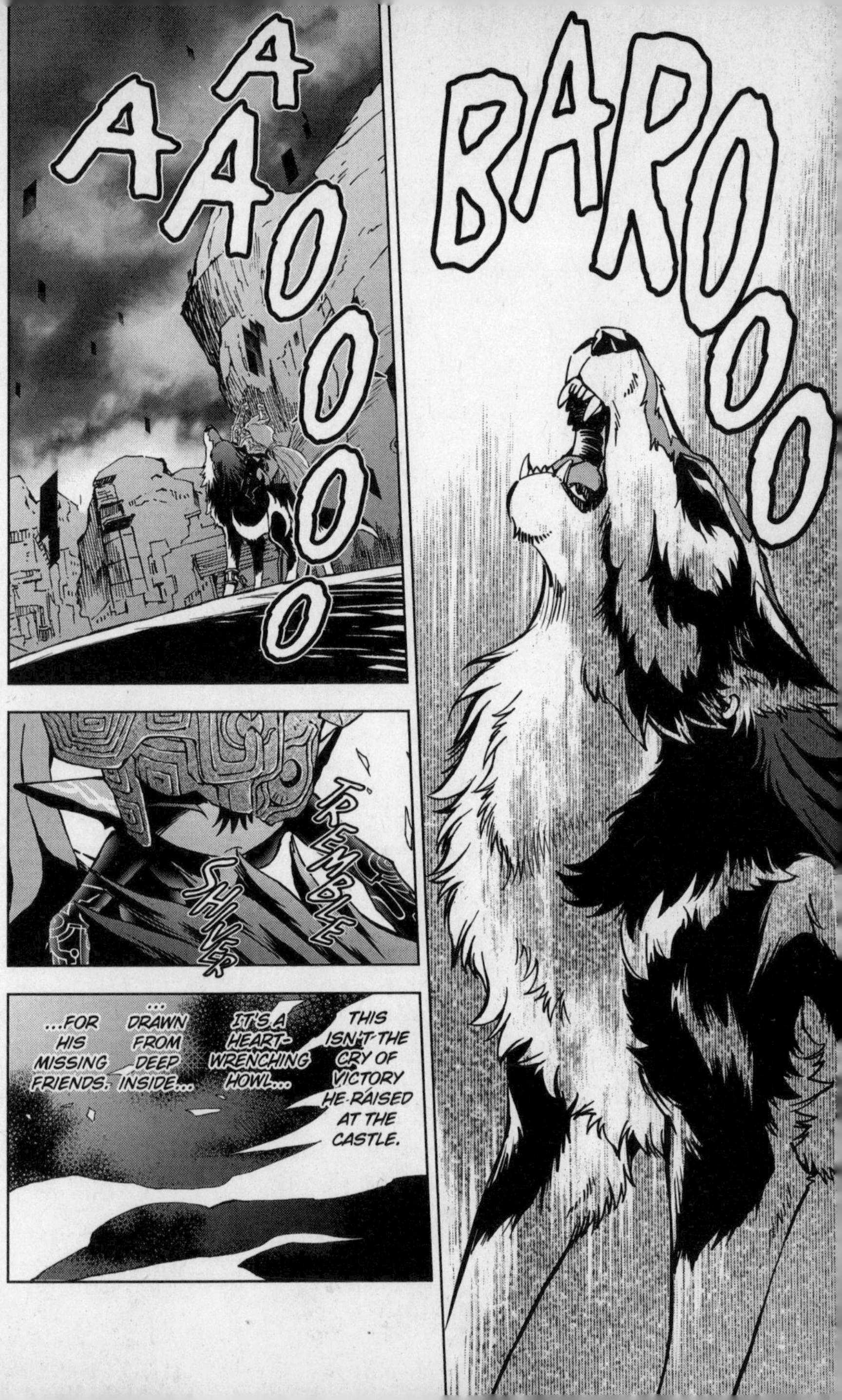

BAROOO
AAAOOOOO
TREMBLE
SHIVER
THIS ISN'T THE CRY OF VICTORY HE RAISED AT THE CASTLE.
IT'S A HEART-WRENCHING HOWL...
...DRAWN FROM DEEP INSIDE...
...FOR HIS MISSING FRIENDS.

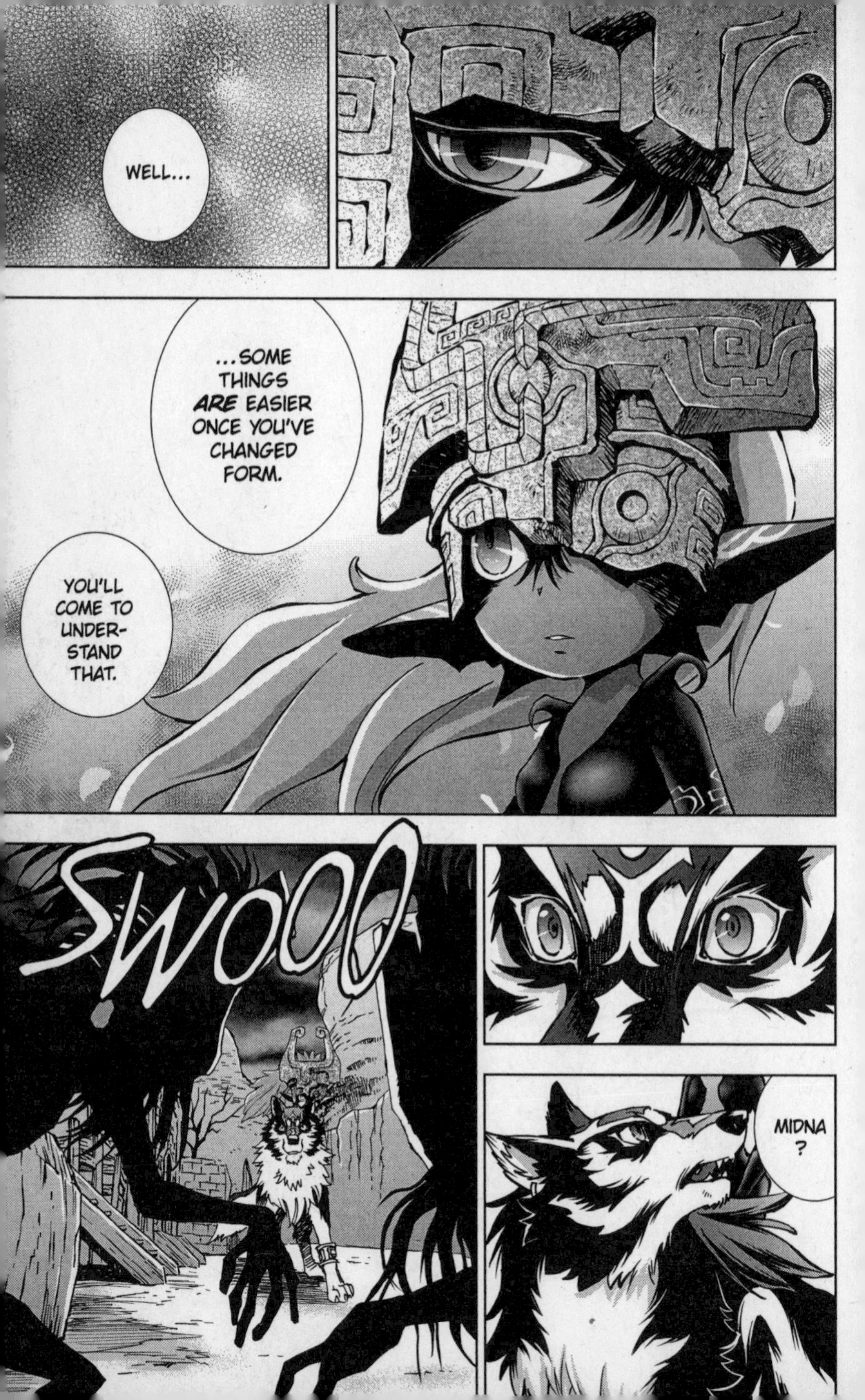
WELL...
...SOME THINGS ARE EASIER ONCE YOU'VE CHANGED FORM.
YOU'LL COME TO UNDER-STAND THAT.
MIDNA ?
SWOOO

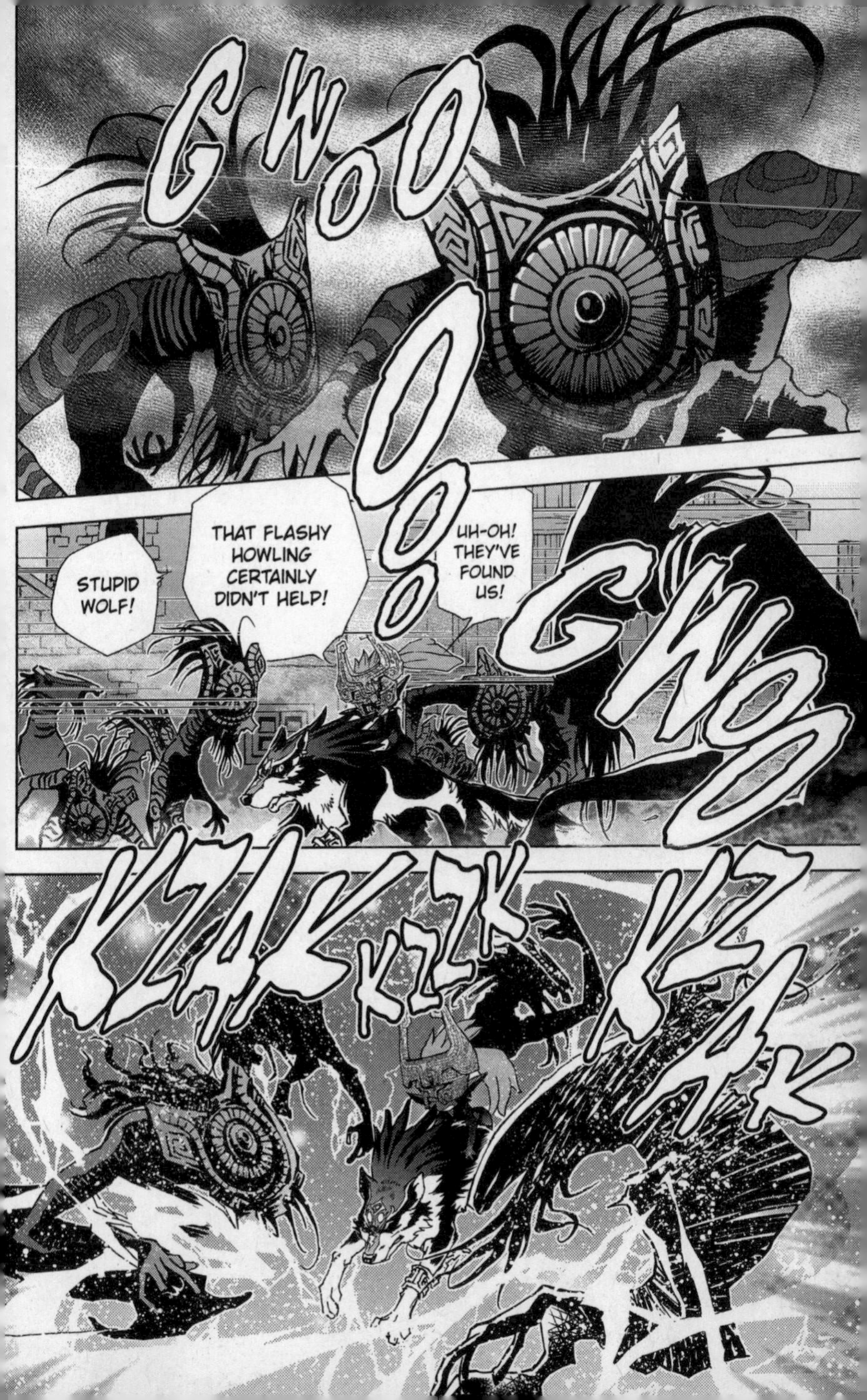
GWOO
UH-OH! THEY'VE FOUND US!
THAT FLASHY HOWLING CERTAINLY DIDN'T HELP!
STUPID WOLF!
KZAK
KZZK
KZAK

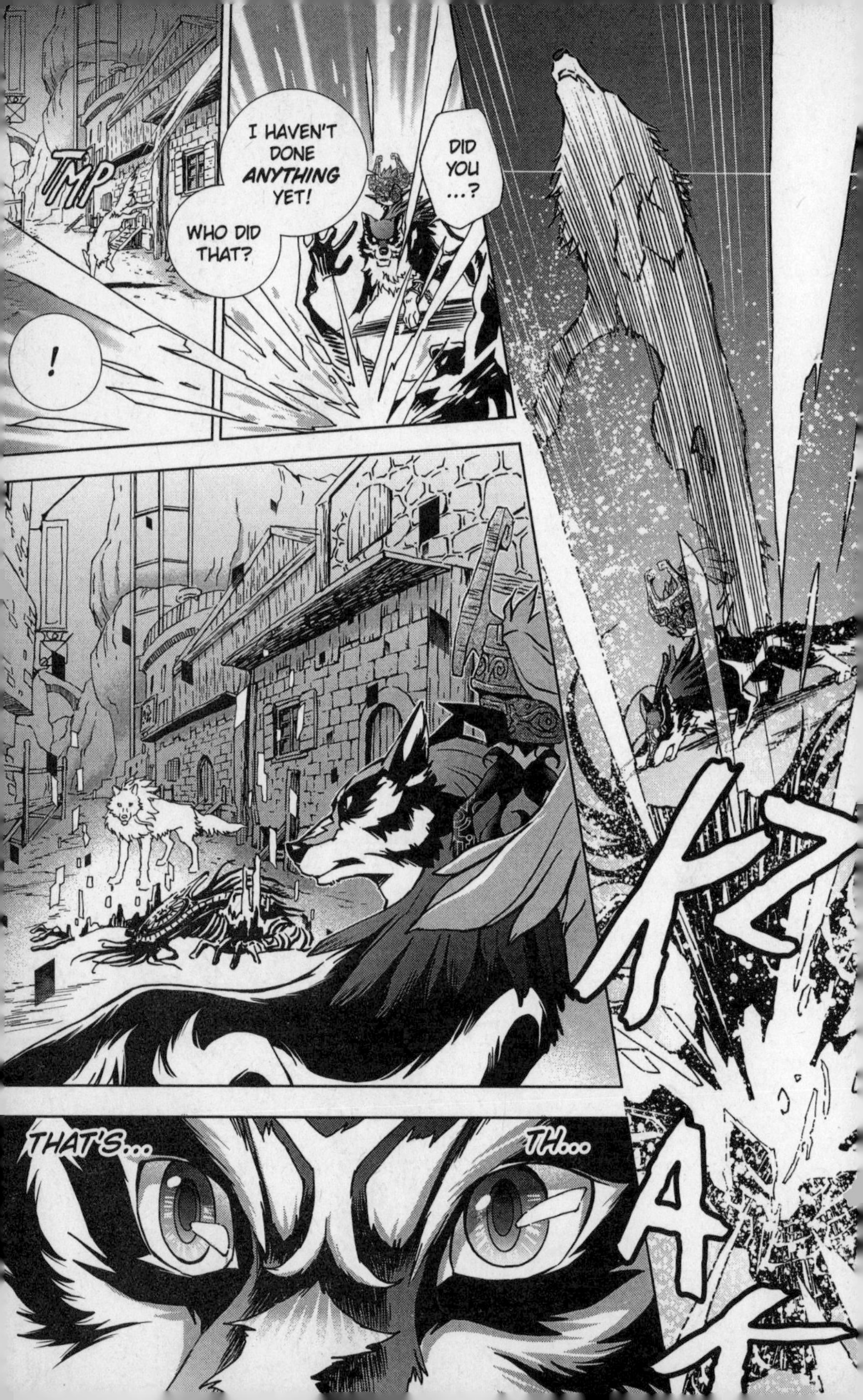
DID YOU ...?
I HAVEN'T DONE ANYTHING YET!
WHO DID THAT?
TMP
!
KRAK
THAT'S...
TH...

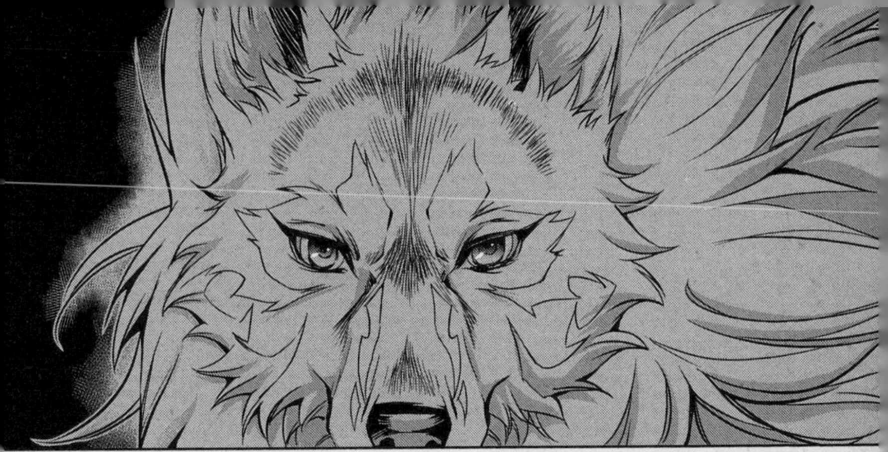
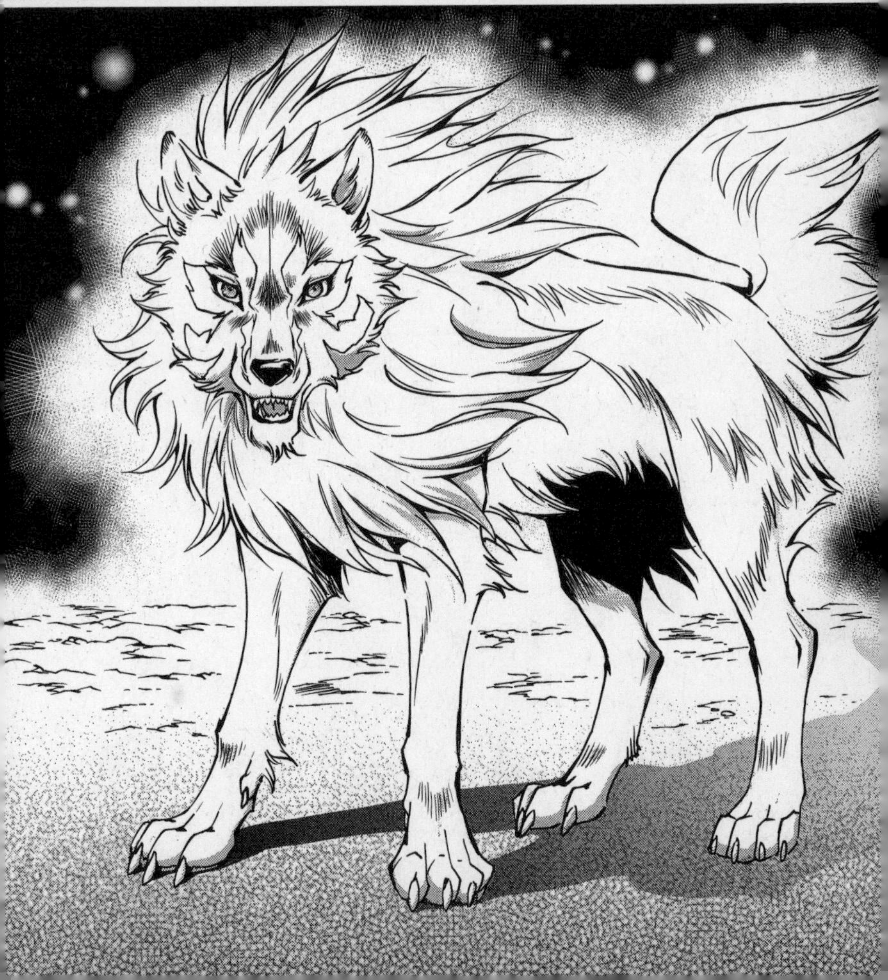

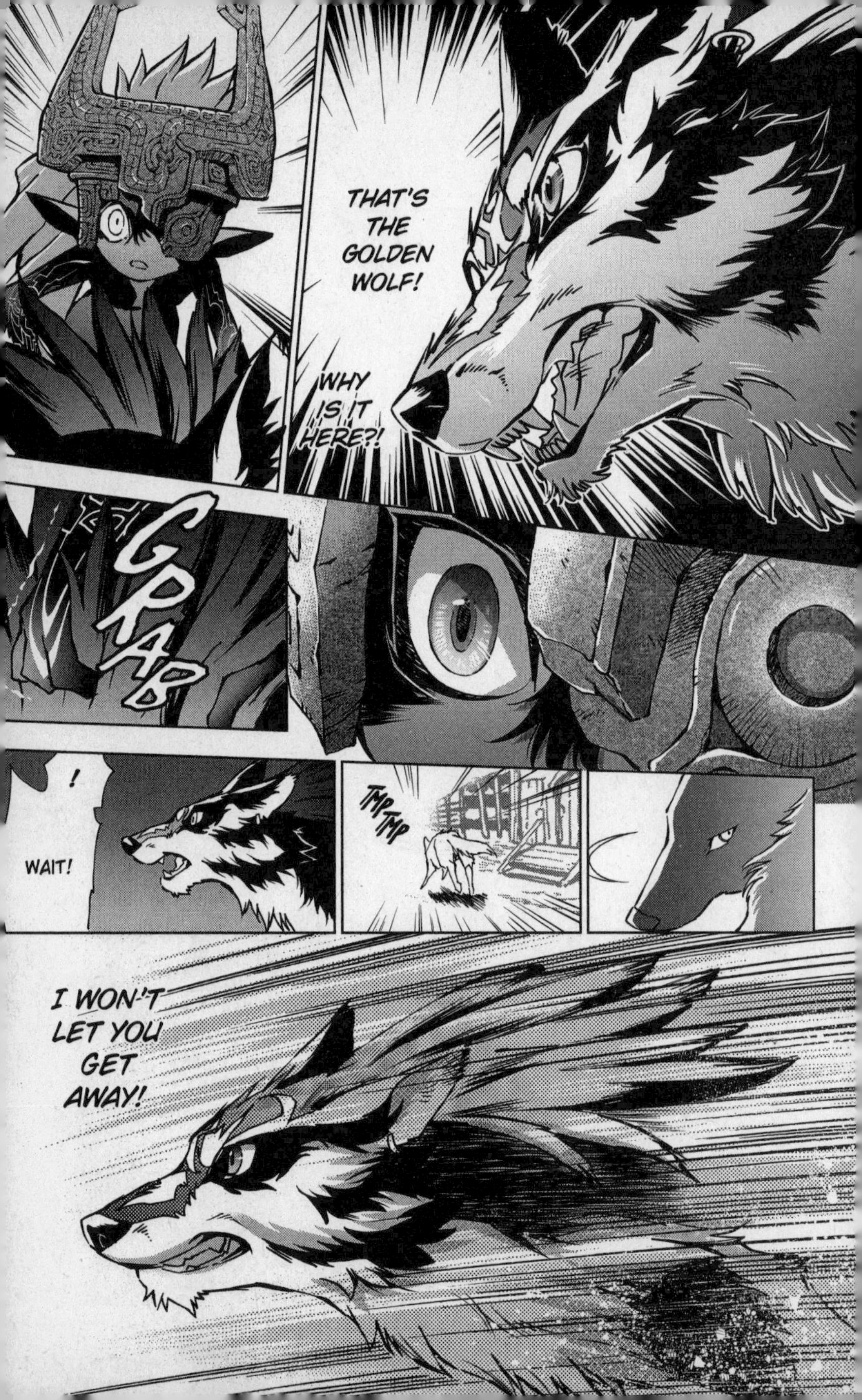
THAT'S THE GOLDEN WOLF!
WHY IS IT HERE?!
GRAB
TMP TMP
!
WAIT!
I WON'T LET YOU GET AWAY!

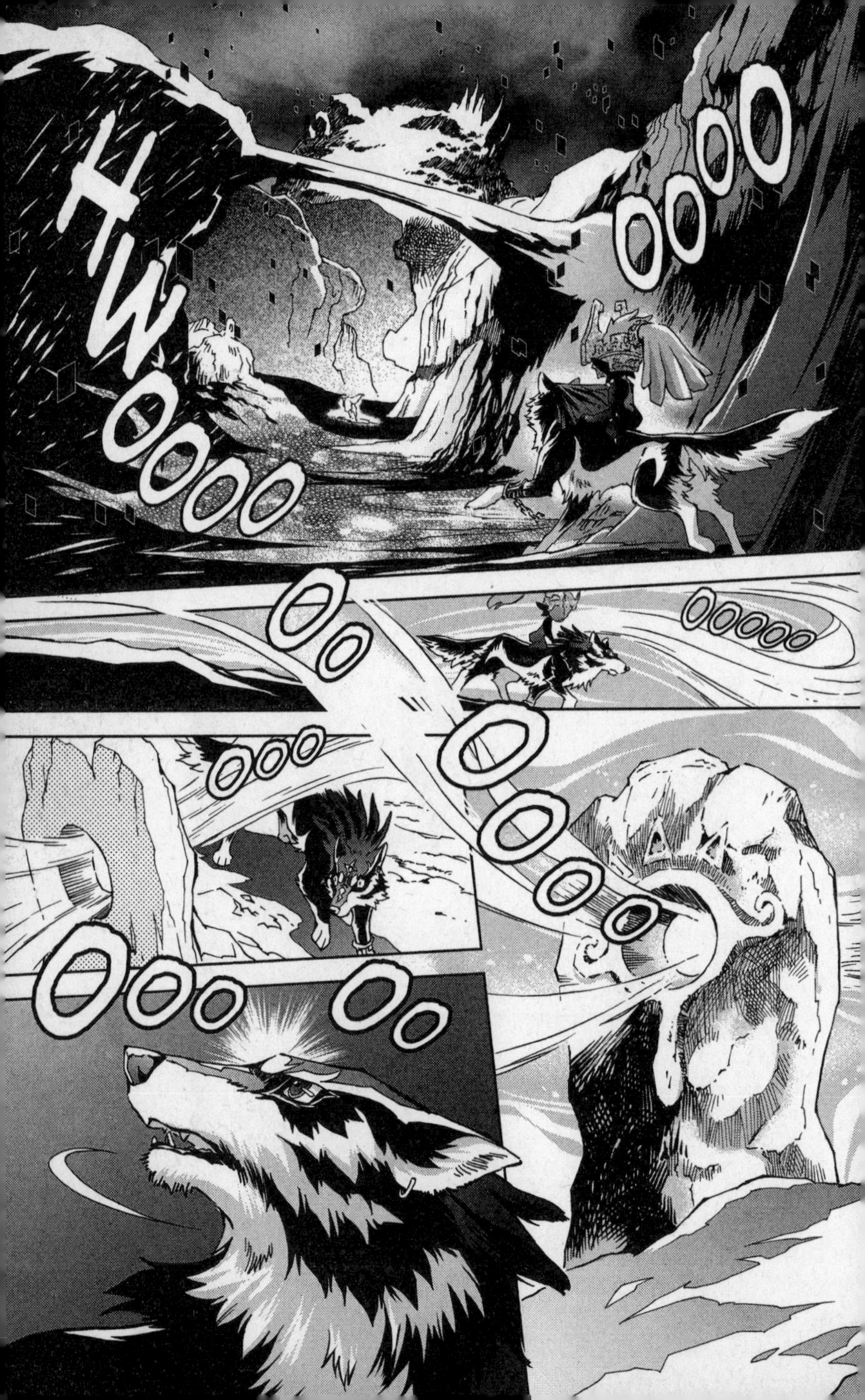
HWOOOOO
OOOOOO
OO
OOOOO
OOO
OOOOO
OOOO
OO

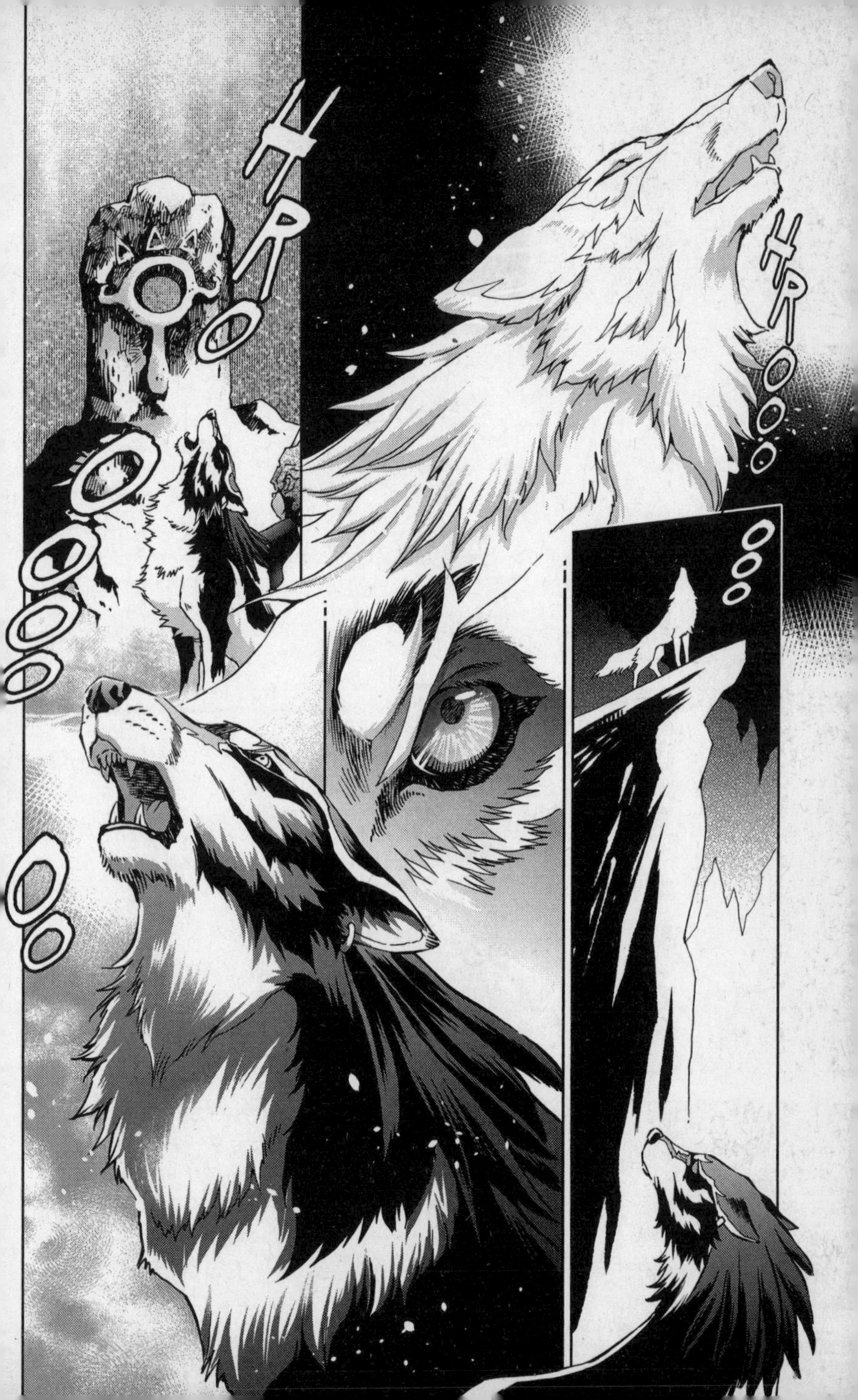
HROOOOO
OOO
HROOOOOO
OO

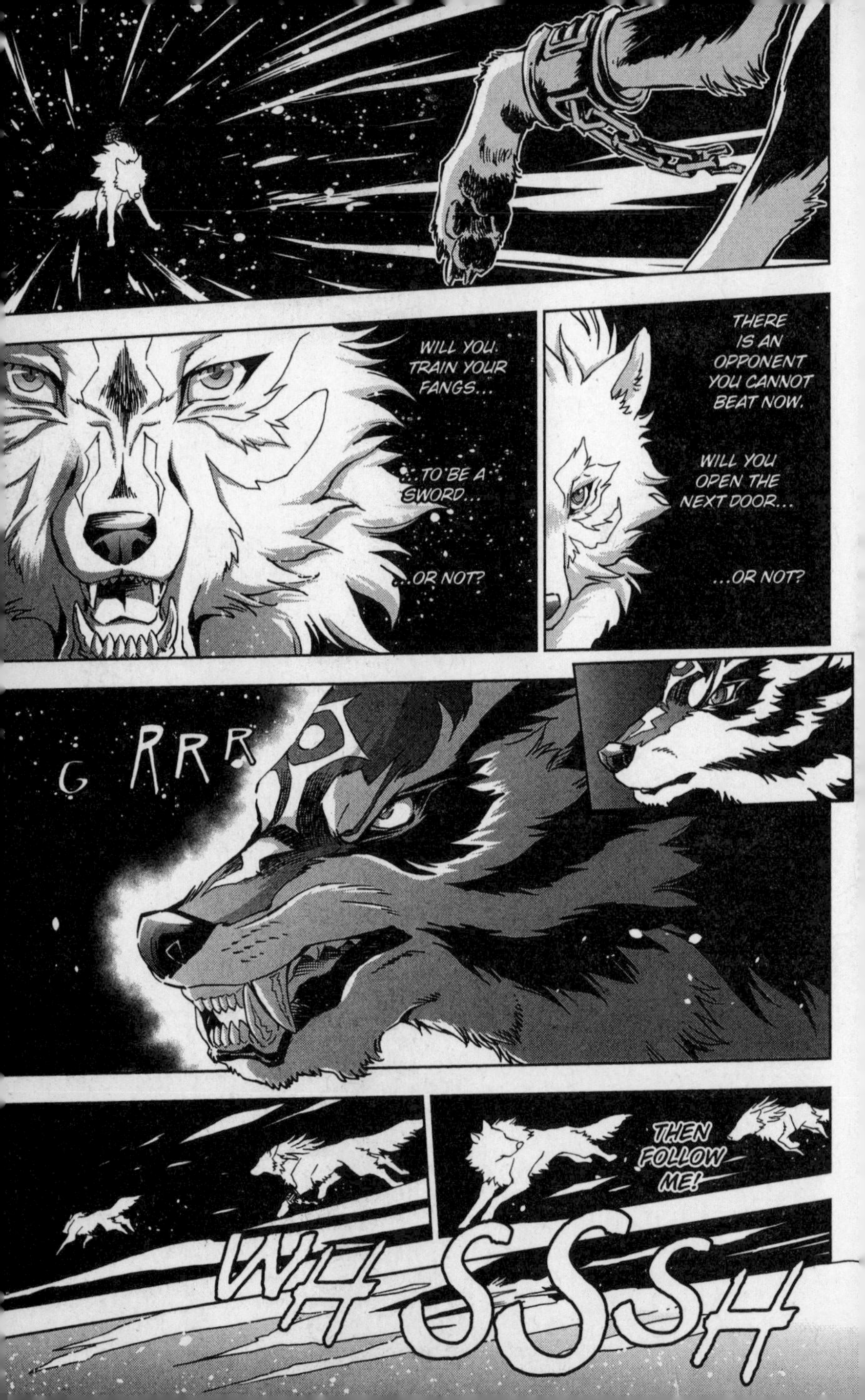
THERE IS AN OPPONENT YOU CANNOT BEAT NOW.
WILL YOU OPEN THE NEXT DOOR...
...OR NOT?
WILL YOU TRAIN YOUR FANGS...
...TO BE A SWORD...
...OR NOT?
GRRR
THEN FOLLOW ME!
WHSSSH

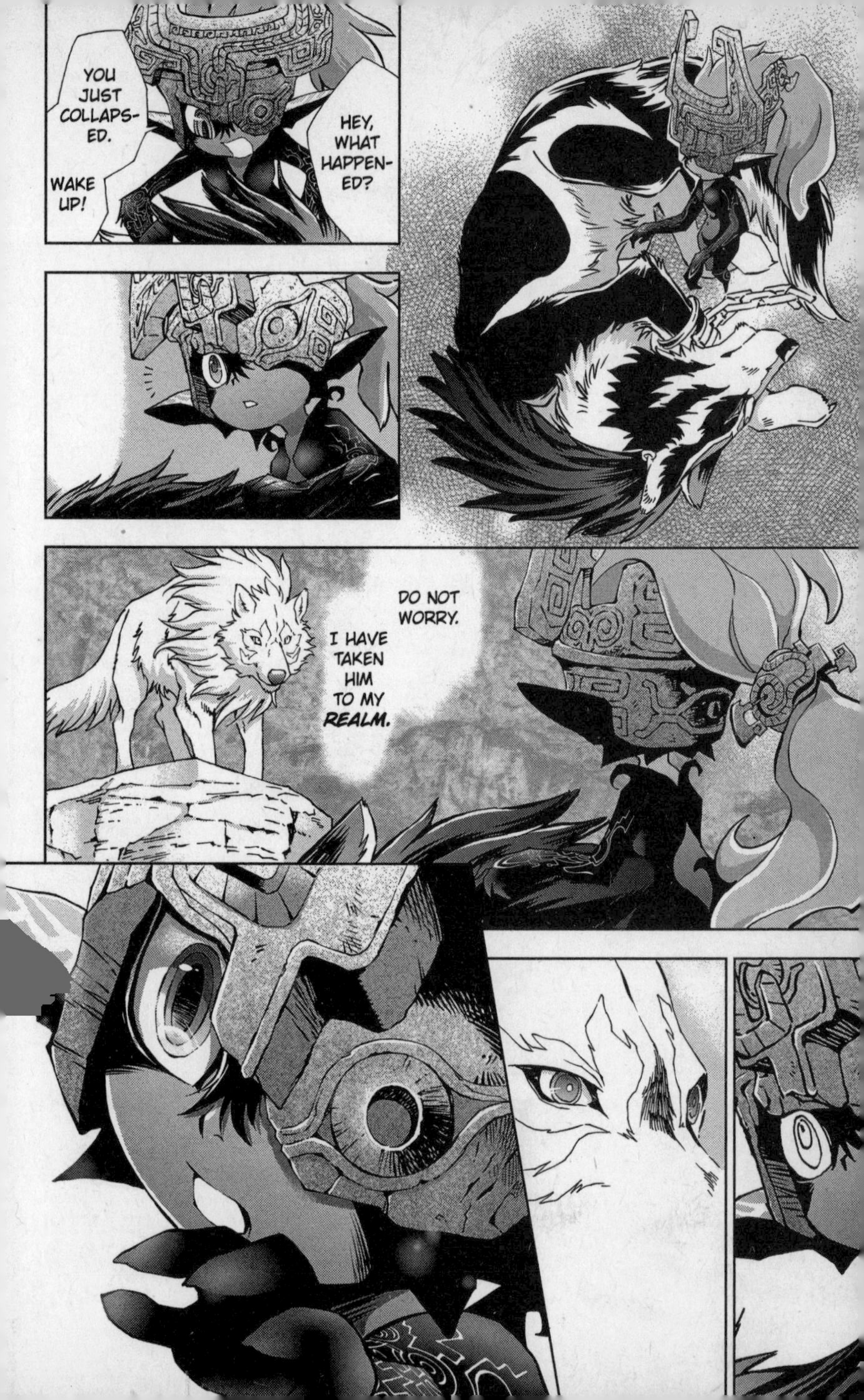
HEY, WHAT HAPPEN-ED?
YOU JUST COLLAPS-ED.
WAKE UP!
DO NOT WORRY.
I HAVE TAKEN HIM TO MY *REALM.*

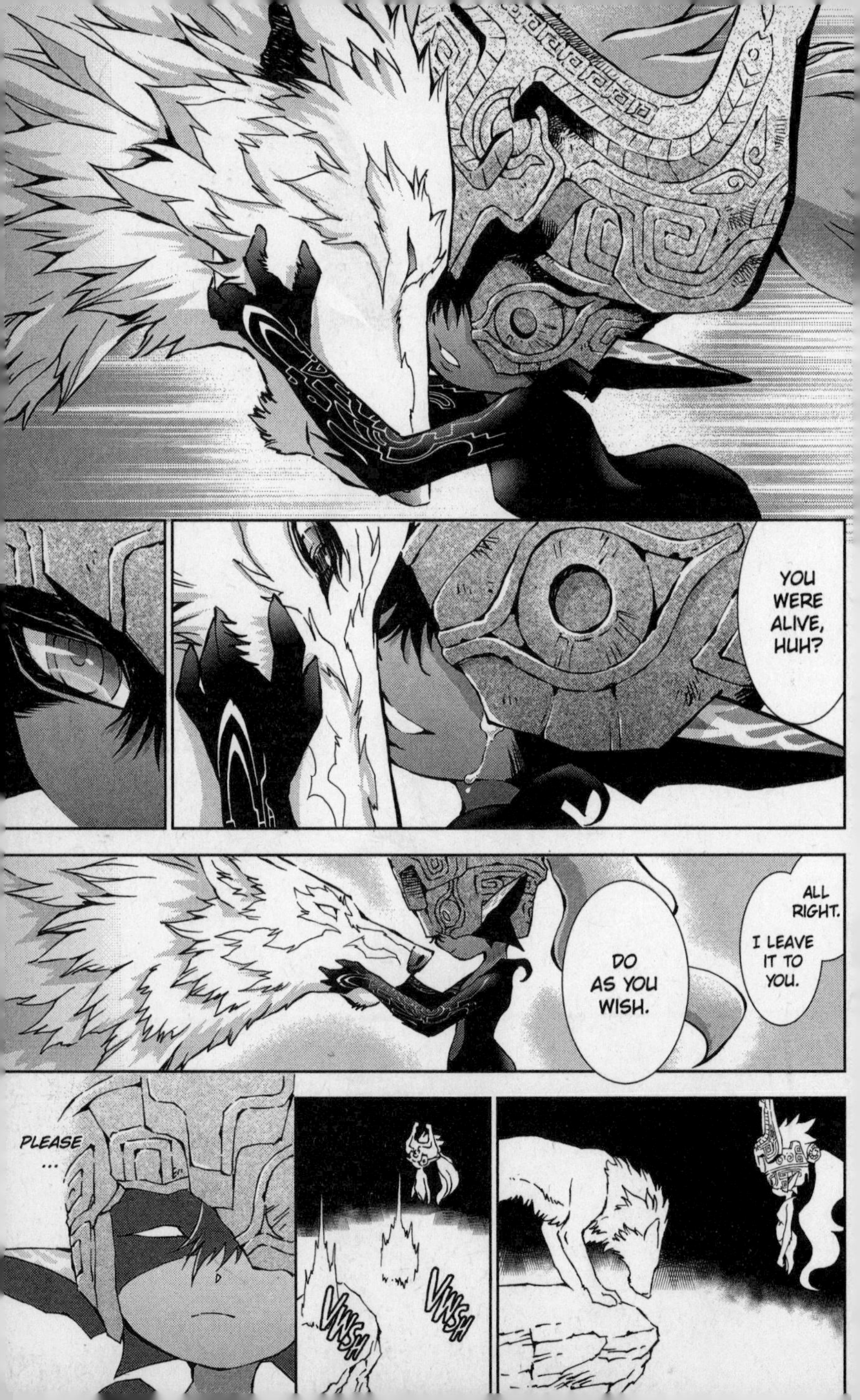
YOU WERE ALIVE, HUH?
ALL RIGHT.
I LEAVE IT TO YOU.
DO AS YOU WISH.
VWSH
VWSH
PLEASE ...

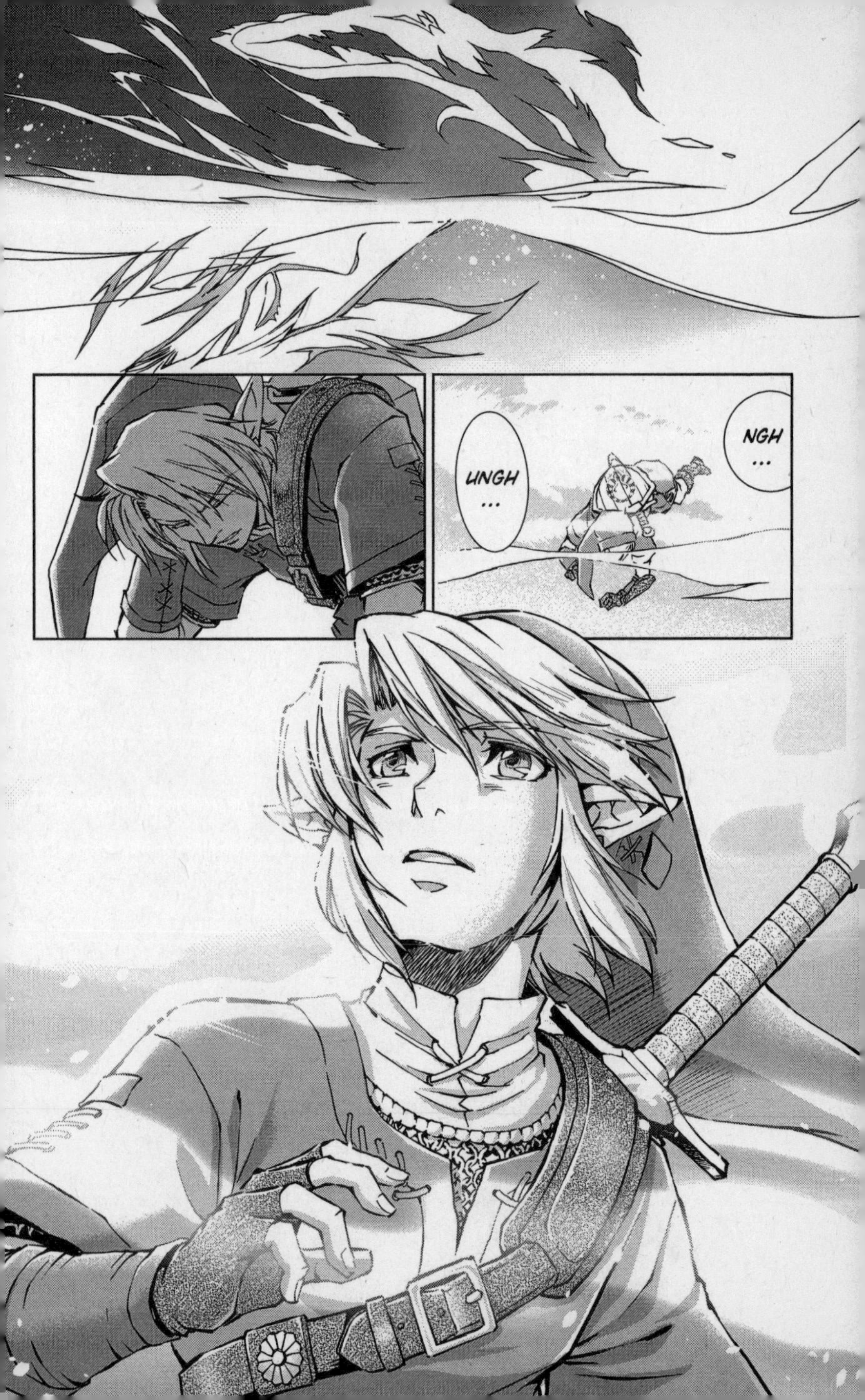
NGH ...
UNGH ...

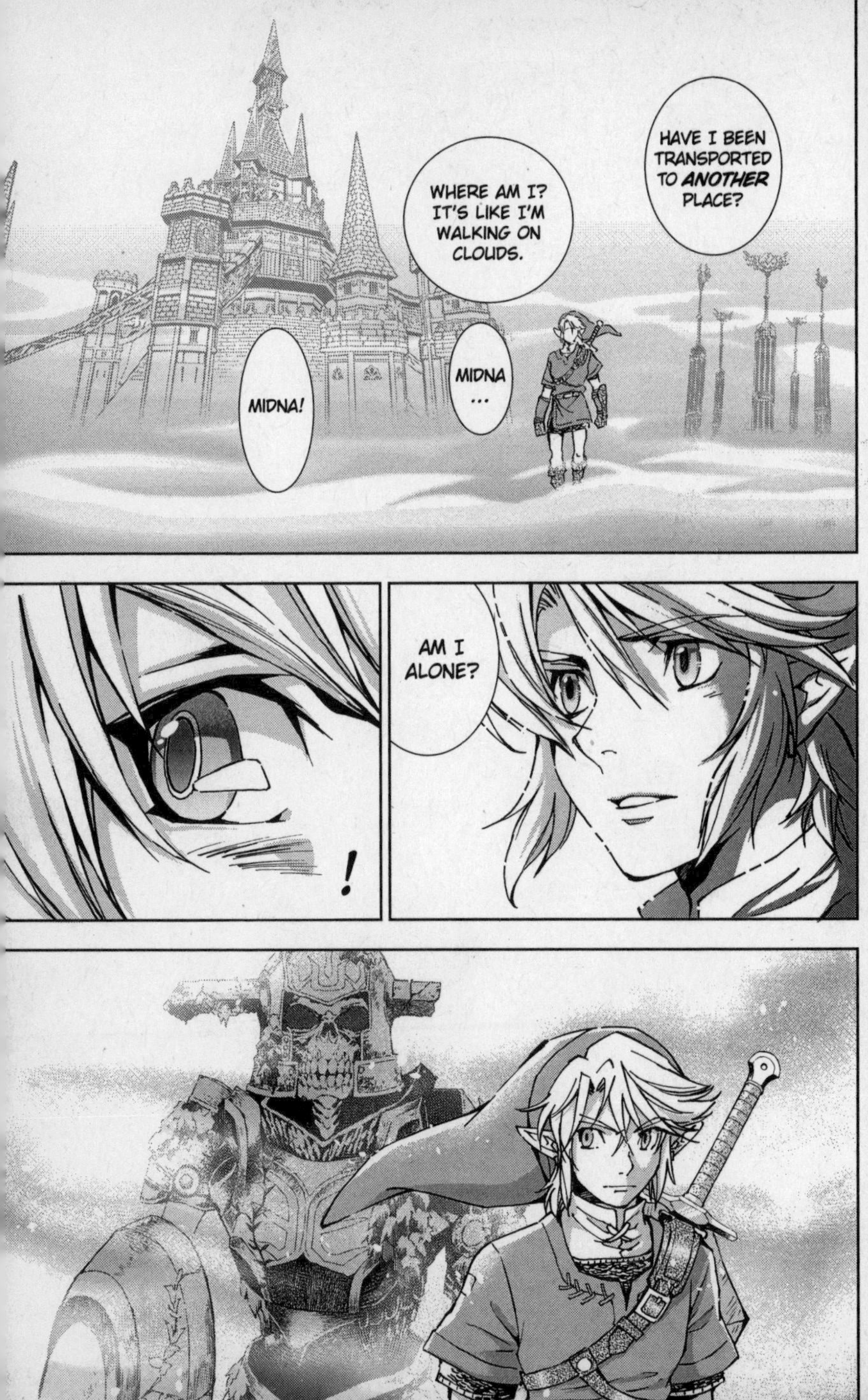
HAVE I BEEN TRANSPORTED TO ANOTHER PLACE?
WHERE AM I? IT'S LIKE I'M WALKING ON CLOUDS.
MIDNA ...
MIDNA!
AM I ALONE?
!

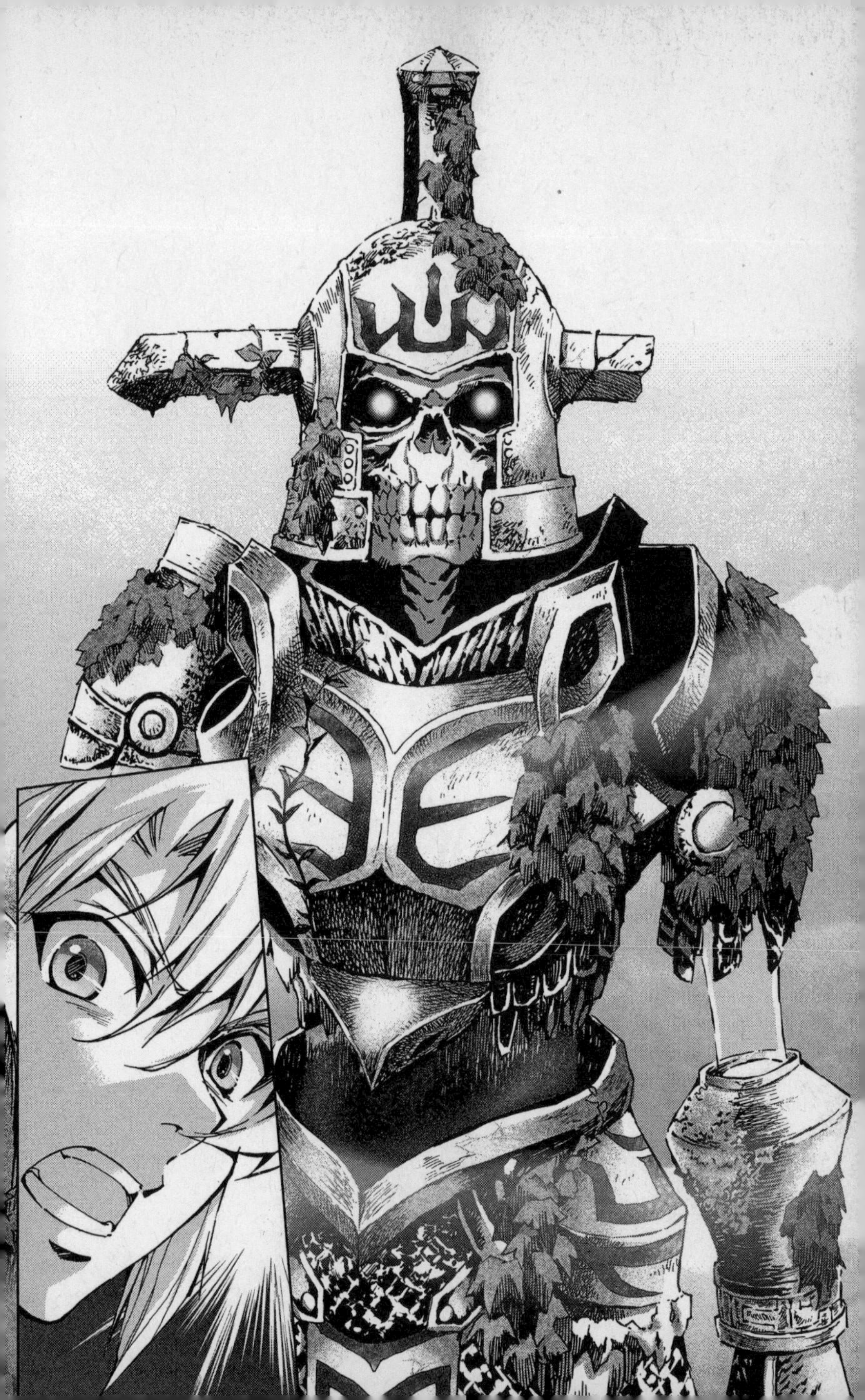

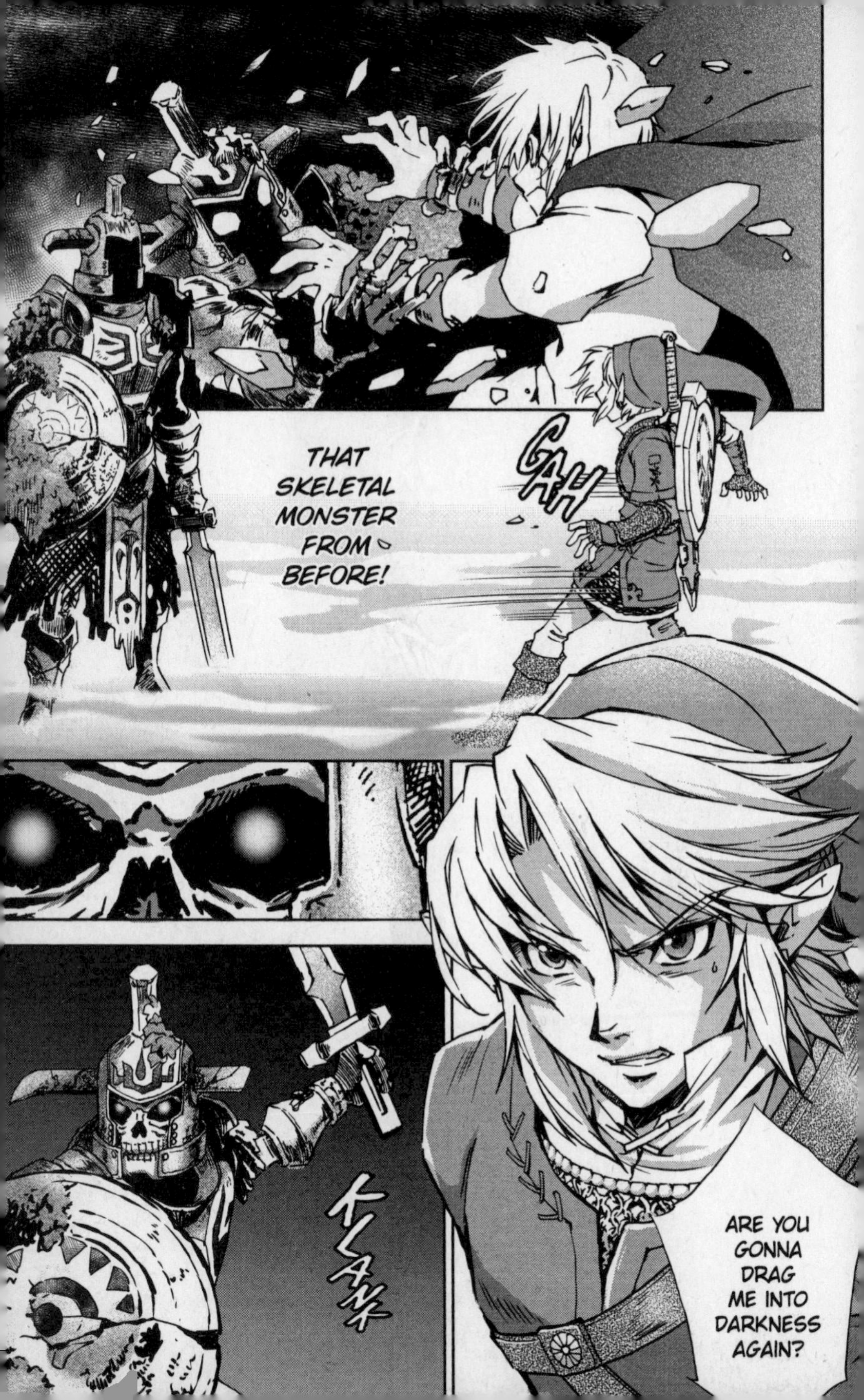
THAT SKELETAL MONSTER FROM BEFORE!
GAH
KLANK
ARE YOU GONNA DRAG ME INTO DARKNESS AGAIN?

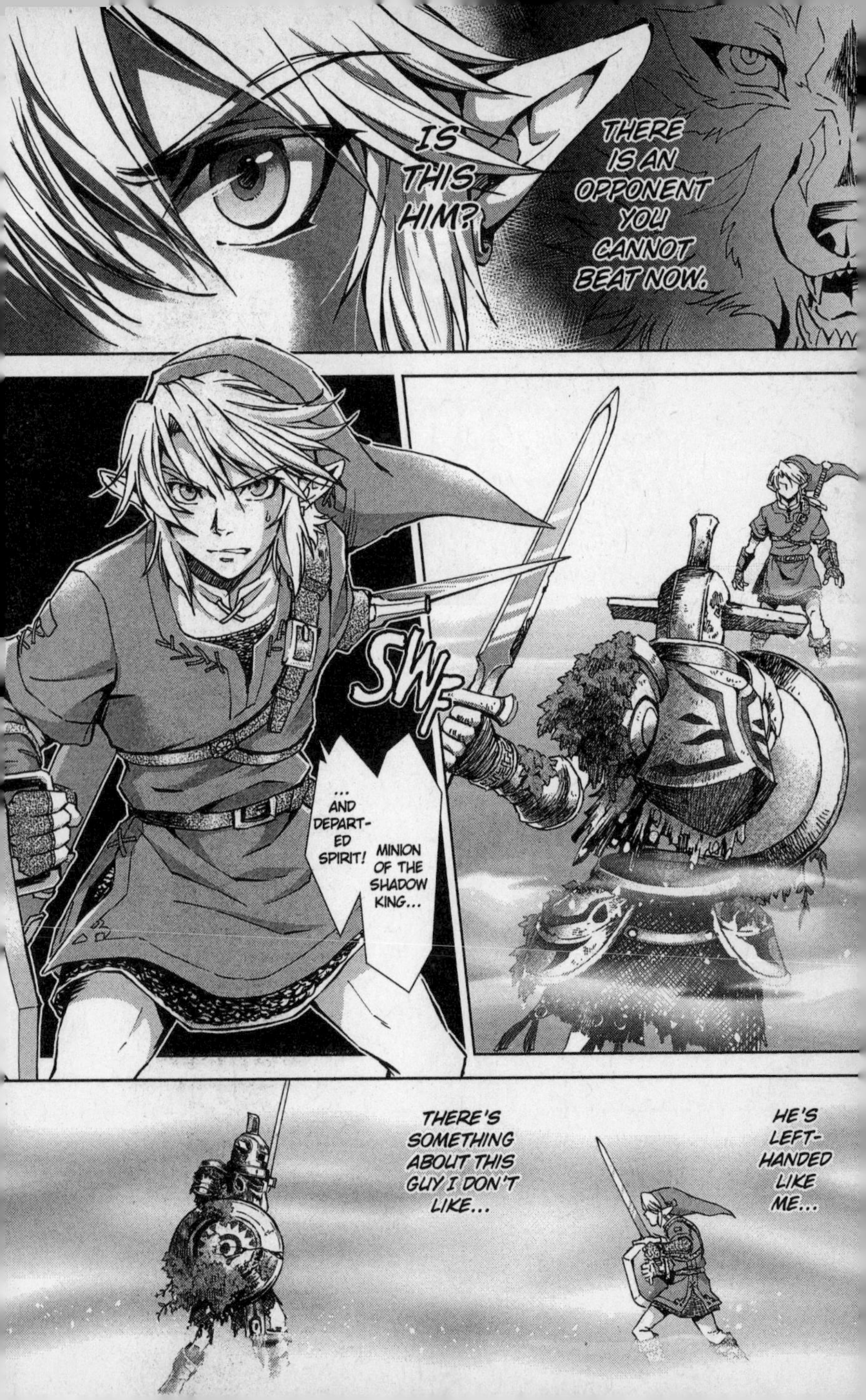
THERE IS AN OPPONENT YOU CANNOT BEAT NOW.
IS THIS HIM?
SWF
MINION OF THE SHADOW KING...
...AND DEPART-ED SPIRIT!
HE'S LEFT-HANDED LIKE ME...
THERE'S SOMETHING ABOUT THIS GUY I DON'T LIKE...

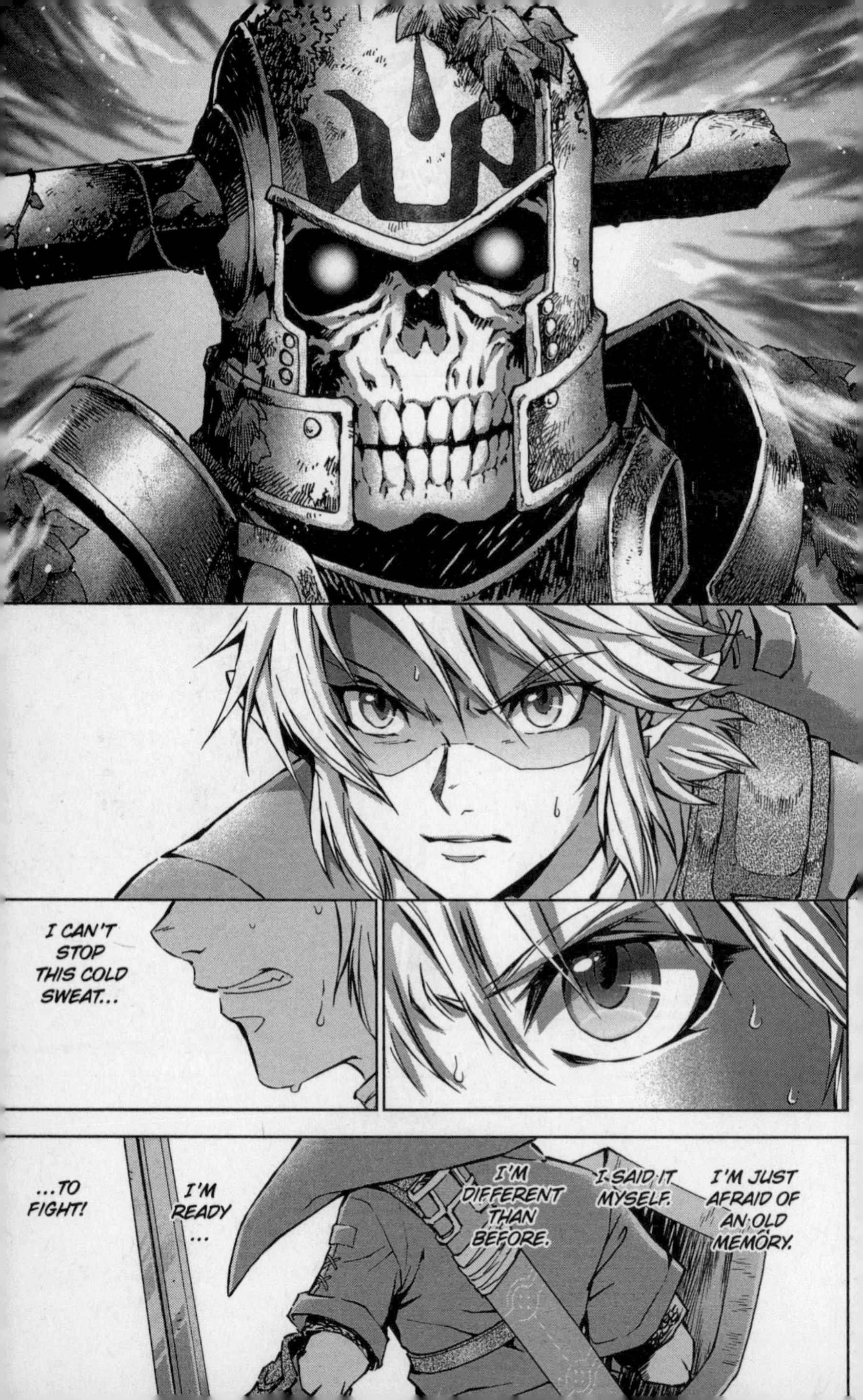
I CAN'T STOP THIS COLD SWEAT...
I'M JUST AFRAID OF AN OLD MEMORY.
I SAID IT MYSELF.
I'M DIFFERENT THAN BEFORE.
I'M READY ...
...TO FIGHT!

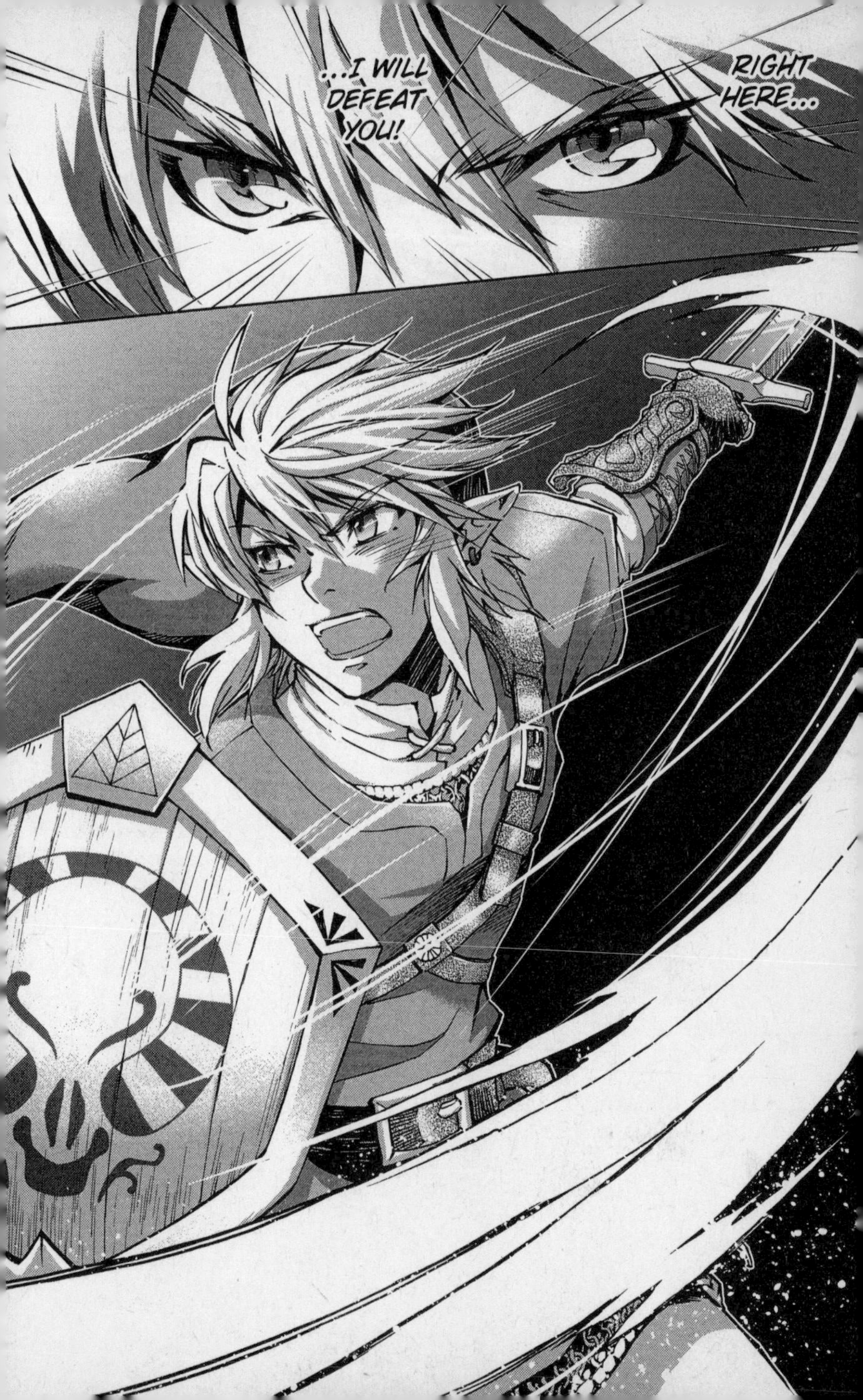
RIGHT HERE...
...I WILL DEFEAT YOU!

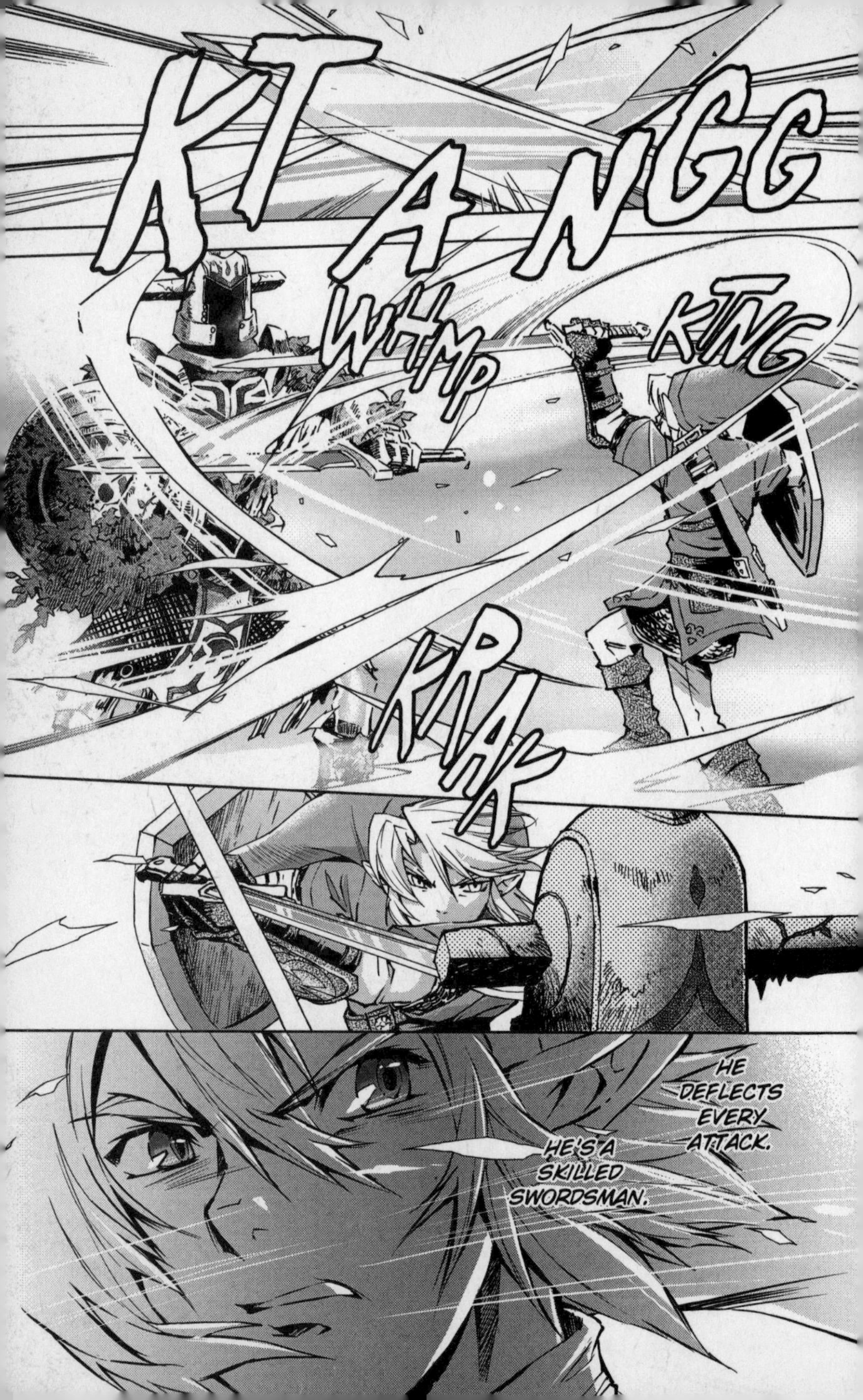
KTANGG
KTING
WHMP
KRAK
HE DEFLECTS EVERY ATTACK.
HE'S A SKILLED SWORDSMAN.

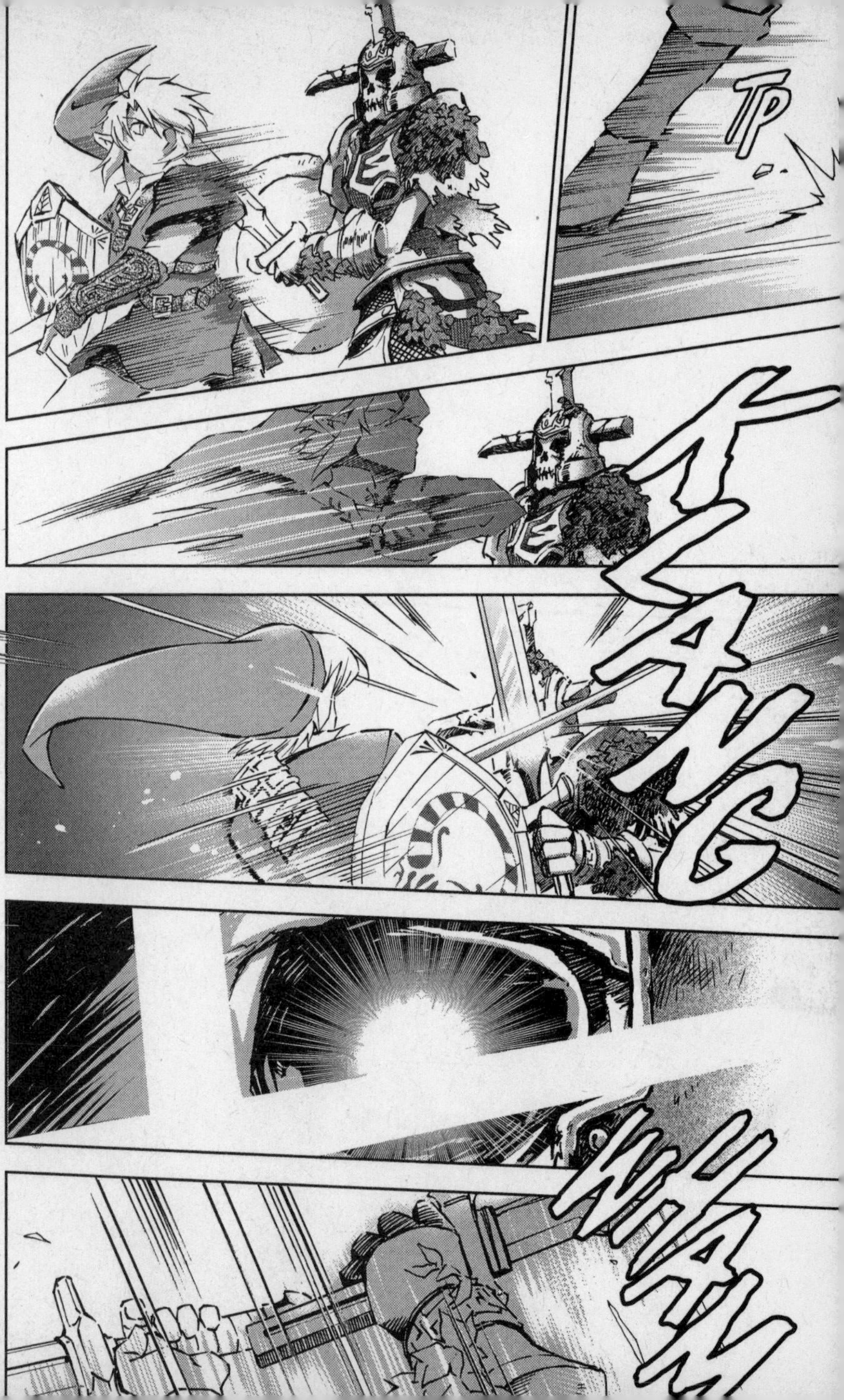
TP
KLANG
WHAM

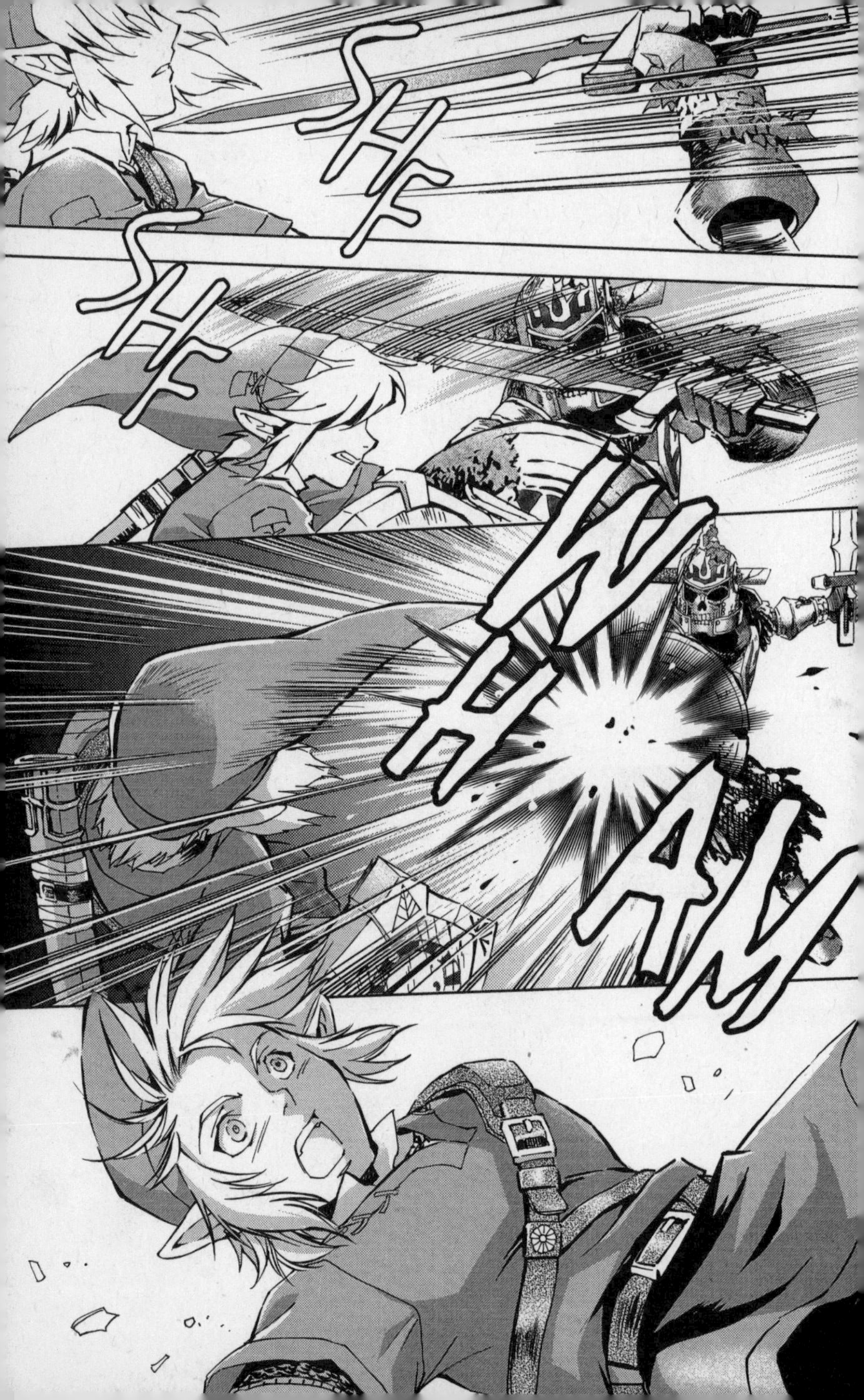
SHF
SHF
WHAM

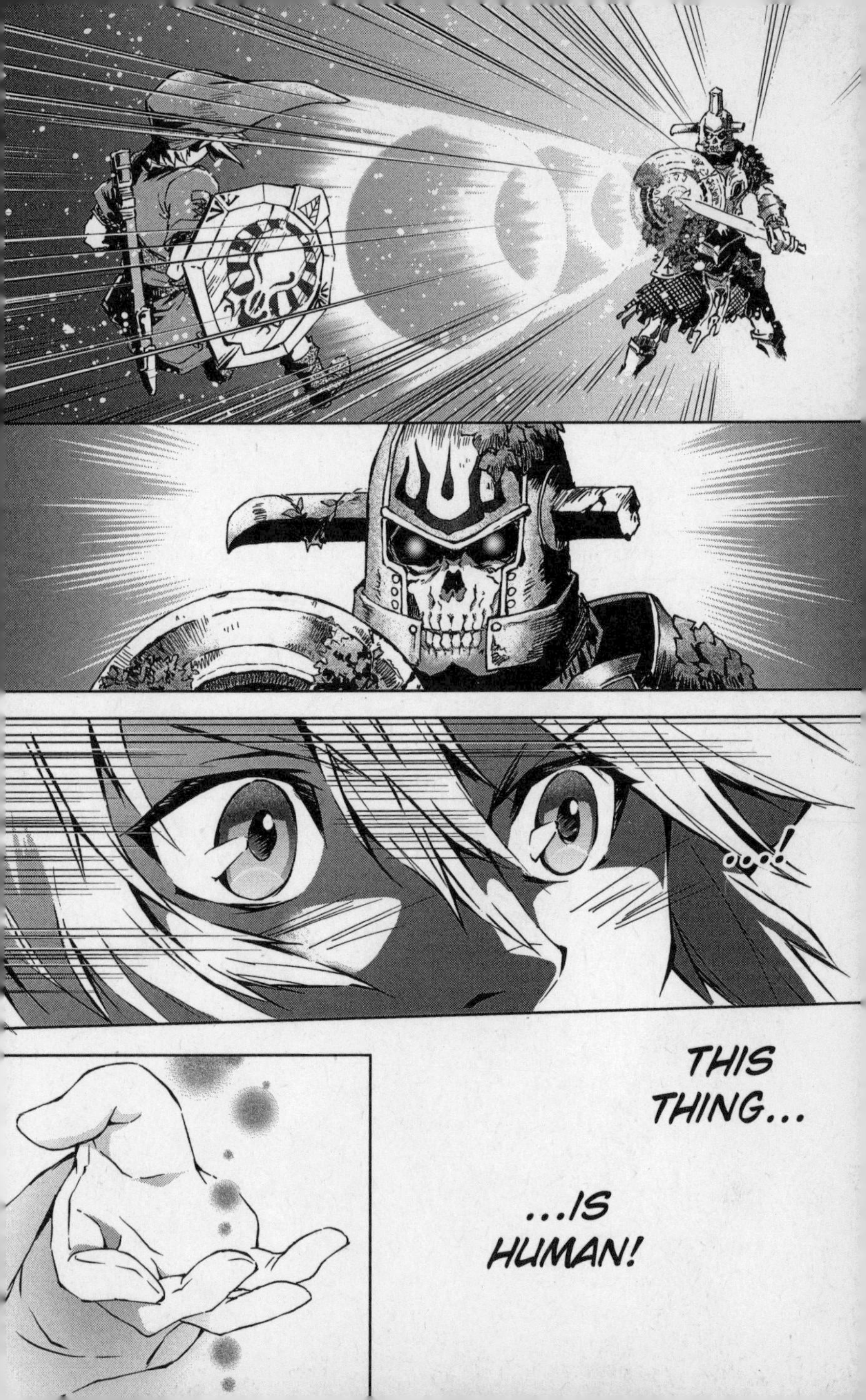
...!
THIS THING...
...IS HUMAN!

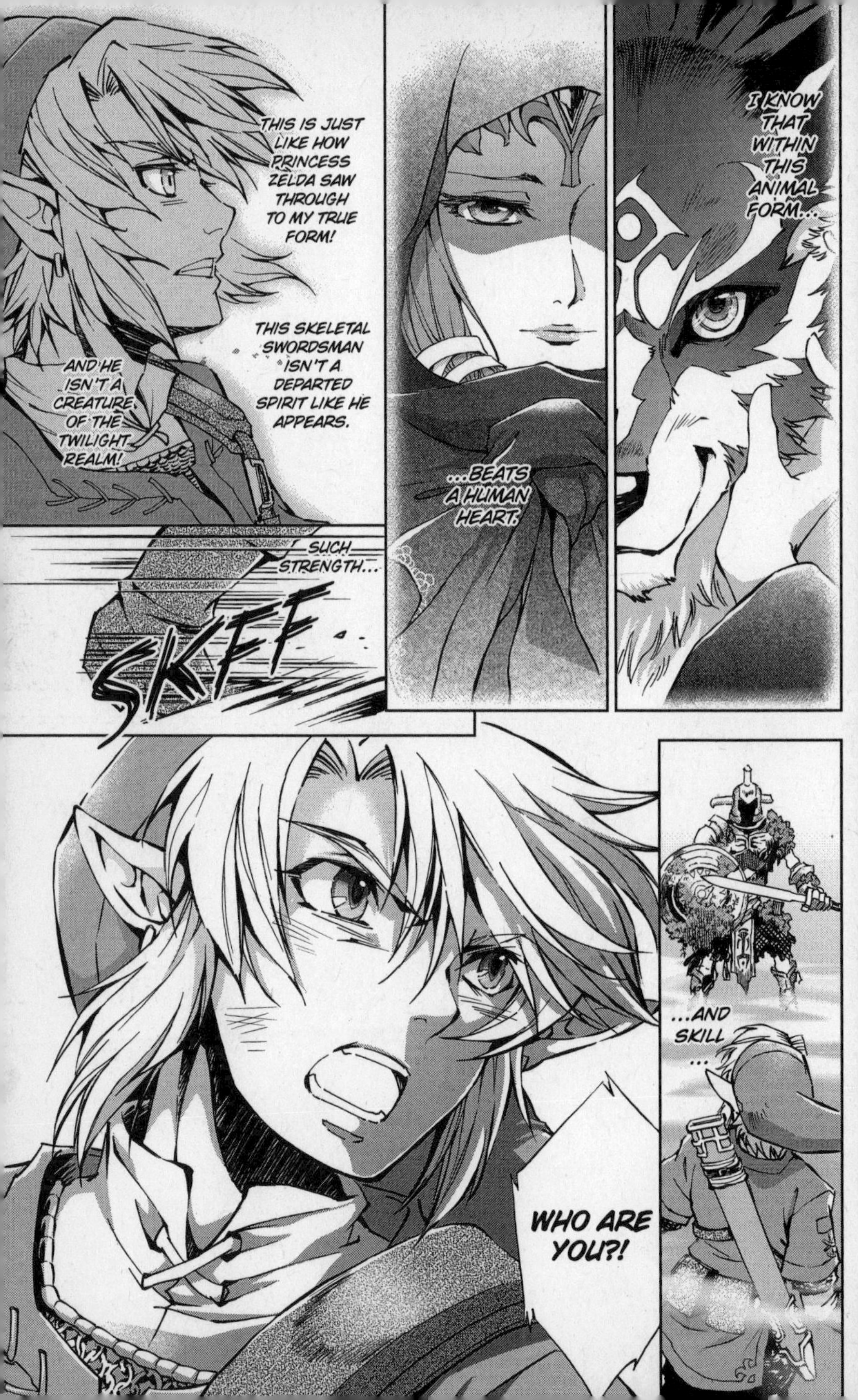
I KNOW THAT WITHIN THIS ANIMAL FORM...
...BEATS A HUMAN HEART.
THIS IS JUST LIKE HOW PRINCESS ZELDA SAW THROUGH TO MY TRUE FORM!
THIS SKELETAL SWORDSMAN ISN'T A DEPARTED SPIRIT LIKE HE APPEARS.
AND HE ISN'T A CREATURE OF THE TWILIGHT REALM!
SUCH STRENGTH...
SKFF
...AND SKILL...
WHO ARE YOU?!

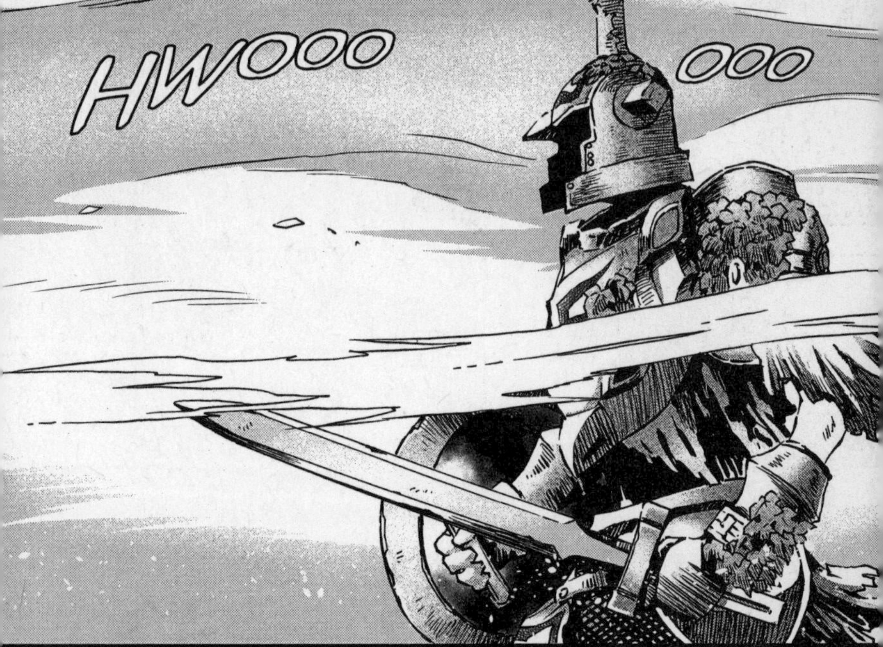
HWOOO
OOO
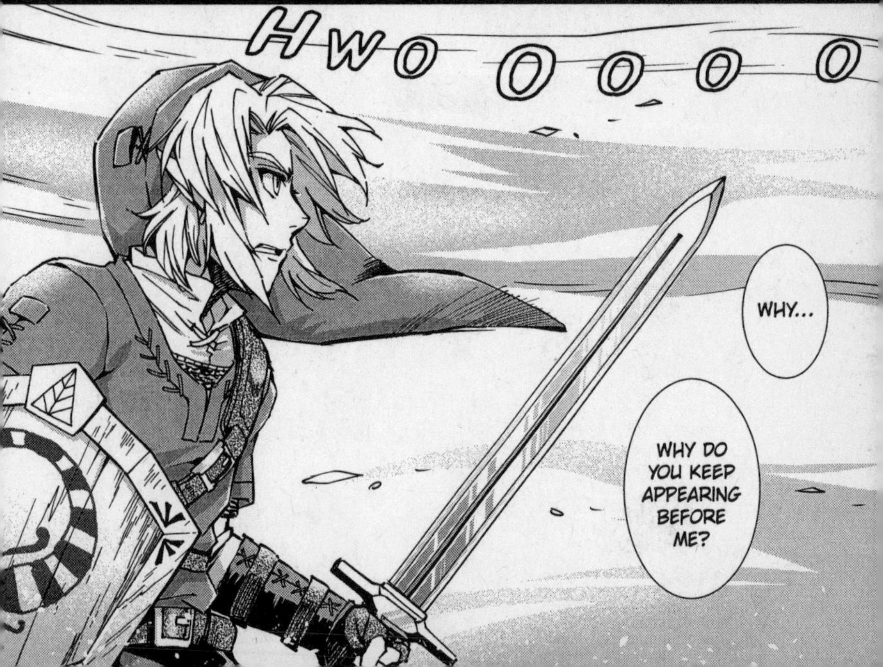
HWOOOOOO
WHY...
WHY DO YOU KEEP APPEARING BEFORE ME?

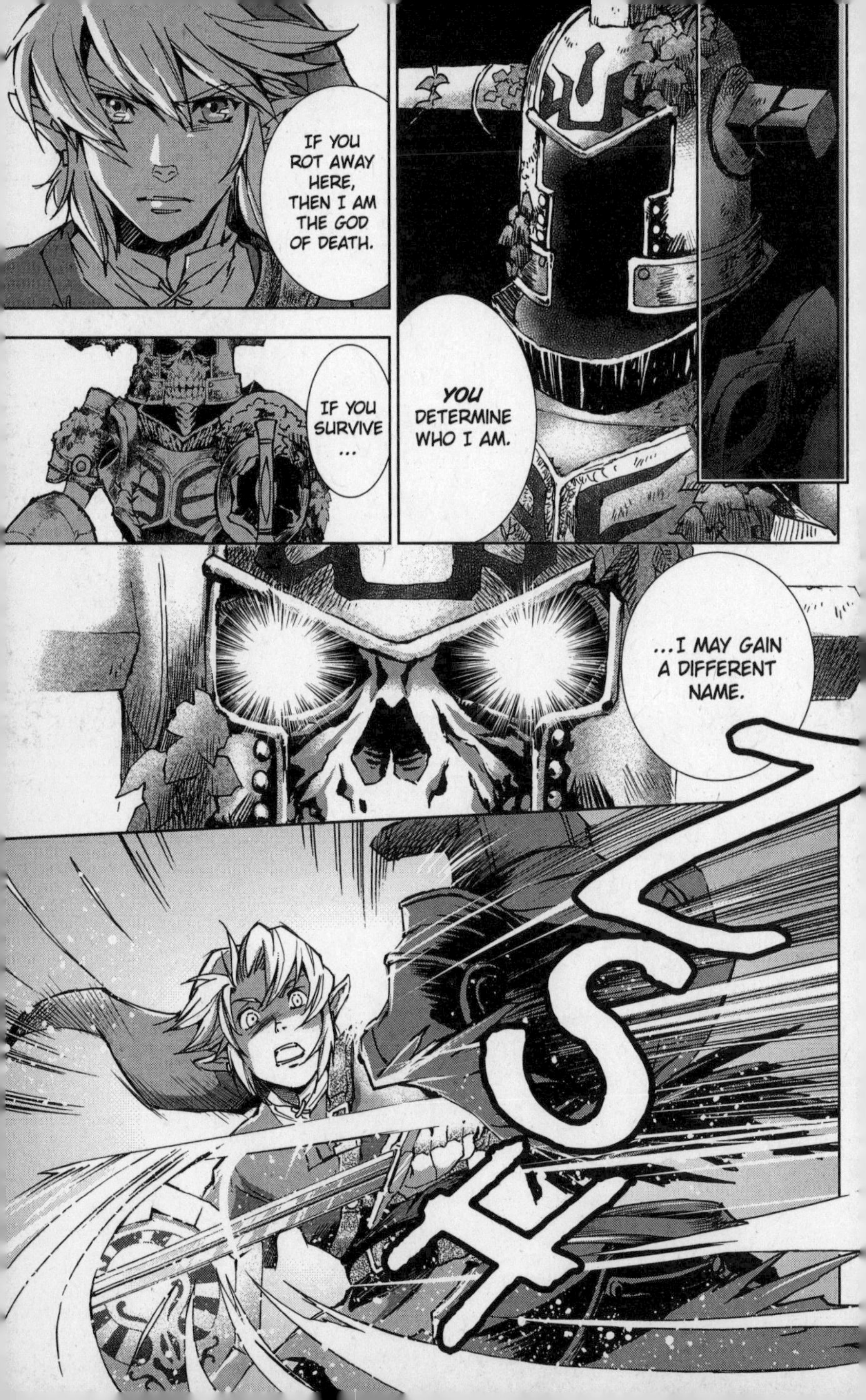
YOU DETERMINE WHO I AM.
IF YOU ROT AWAY HERE, THEN I AM THE GOD OF DEATH.
IF YOU SURVIVE ...
...I MAY GAIN A DIFFERENT NAME.

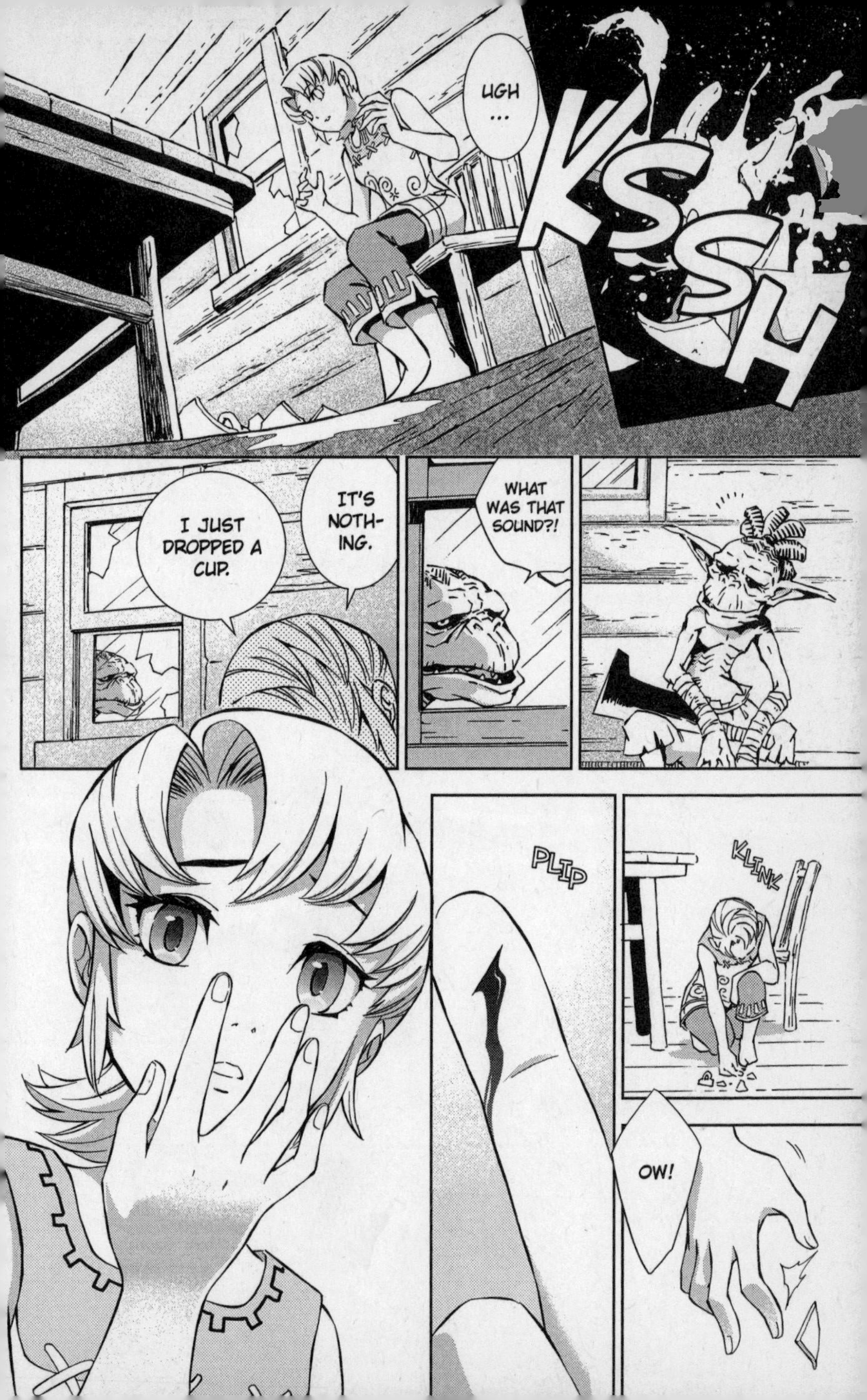
KSSH
UGH ...
WHAT WAS THAT SOUND?!
IT'S NOTH-ING.
I JUST DROPPED A CUP.
KLINK
OW!
PLIP

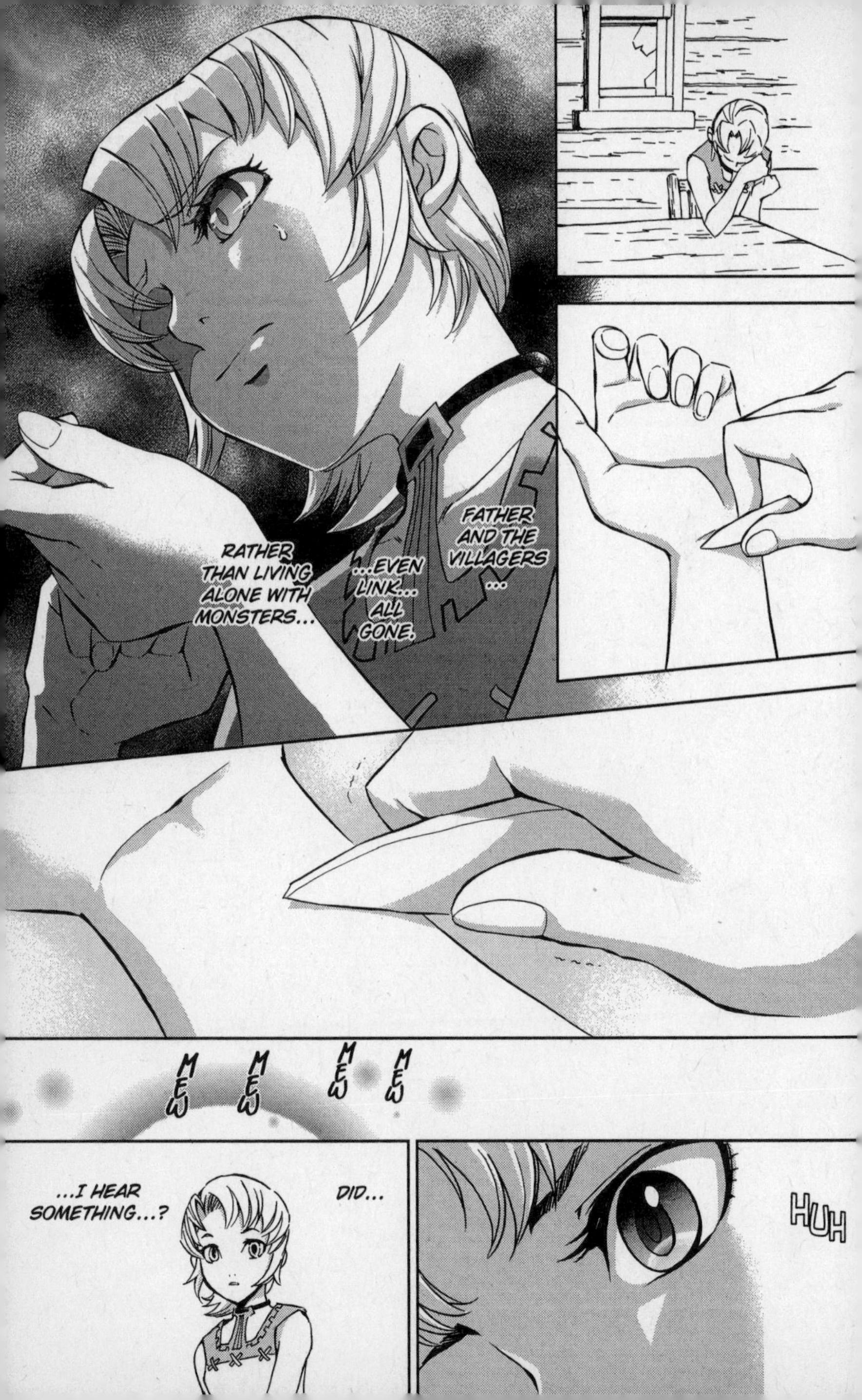
FATHER AND THE VILLAGERS...
...EVEN LINK... ALL GONE.
RATHER THAN LIVING ALONE WITH MONSTERS...
MEW
MEW
MEW
MEW
HUH
DID...
...I HEAR SOMETHING...?

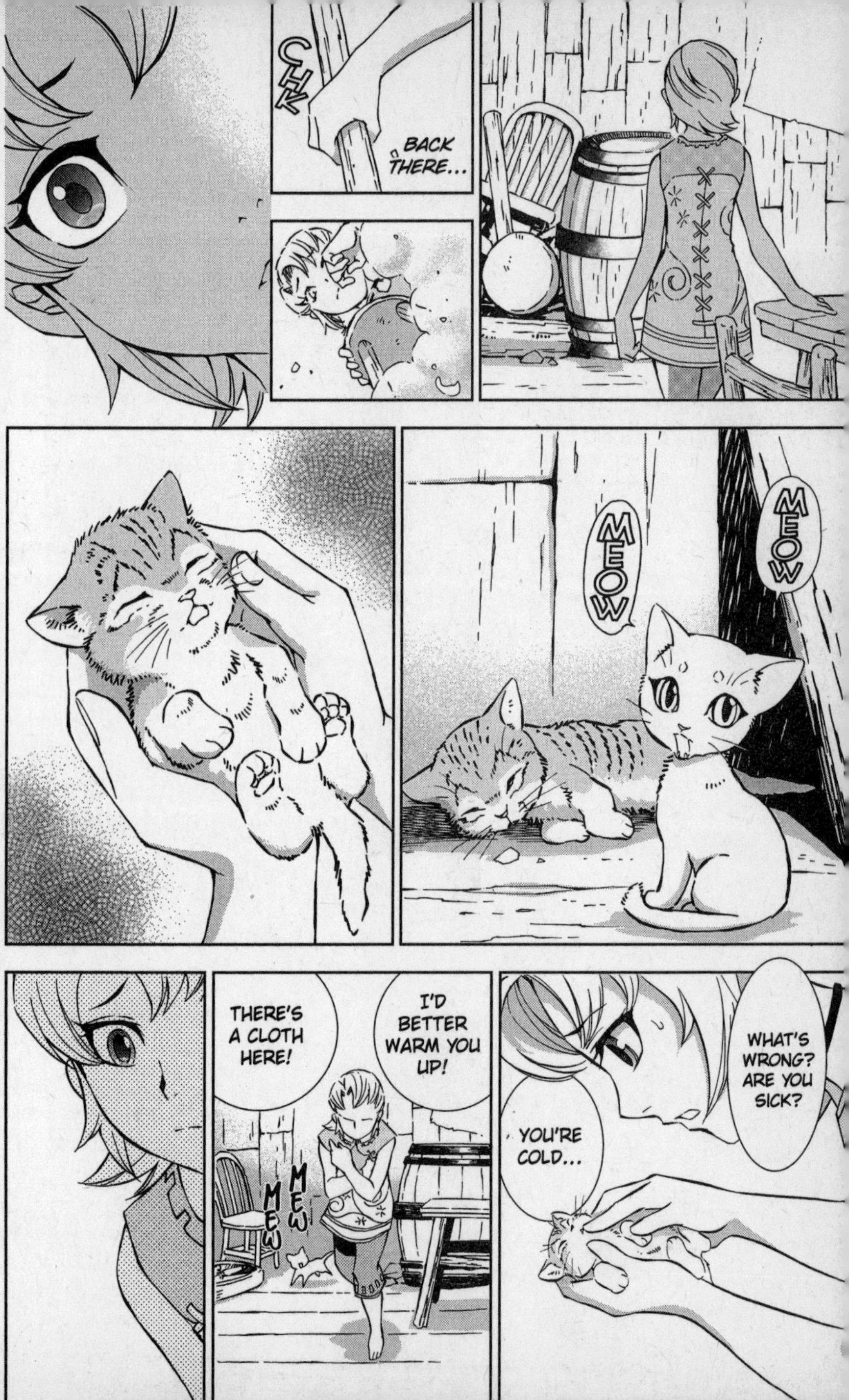
CHK
BACK THERE...
MEOW
MEOW
WHAT'S WRONG? ARE YOU SICK?
YOU'RE COLD...
I'D BETTER WARM YOU UP!
THERE'S A CLOTH HERE!
MEW
MEW

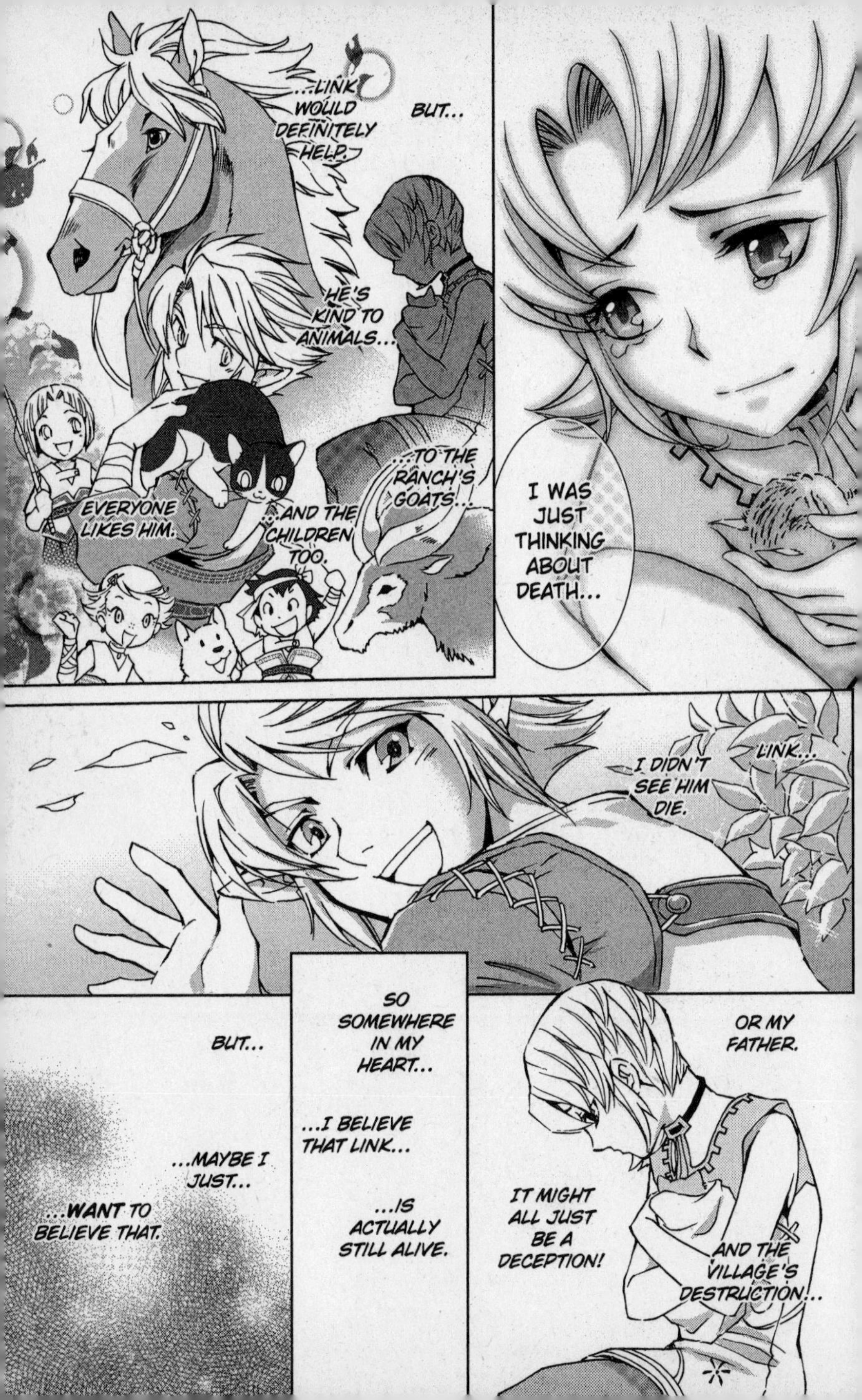
I WAS JUST THINKING ABOUT DEATH...
BUT...
...LINK WOULD DEFINITELY HELP.
HE'S KIND TO ANIMALS...
...TO THE RANCH'S GOATS...
...AND THE CHILDREN TOO.
EVERYONE LIKES HIM.
LINK...
I DIDN'T SEE HIM DIE.
OR MY FATHER.
AND THE VILLAGE'S DESTRUCTION...
IT MIGHT ALL JUST BE A DECEPTION!
SO SOMEWHERE IN MY HEART...
...I BELIEVE THAT LINK...
...IS ACTUALLY STILL ALIVE.
BUT...
...MAYBE I JUST...
...**WANT** TO BELIEVE THAT.

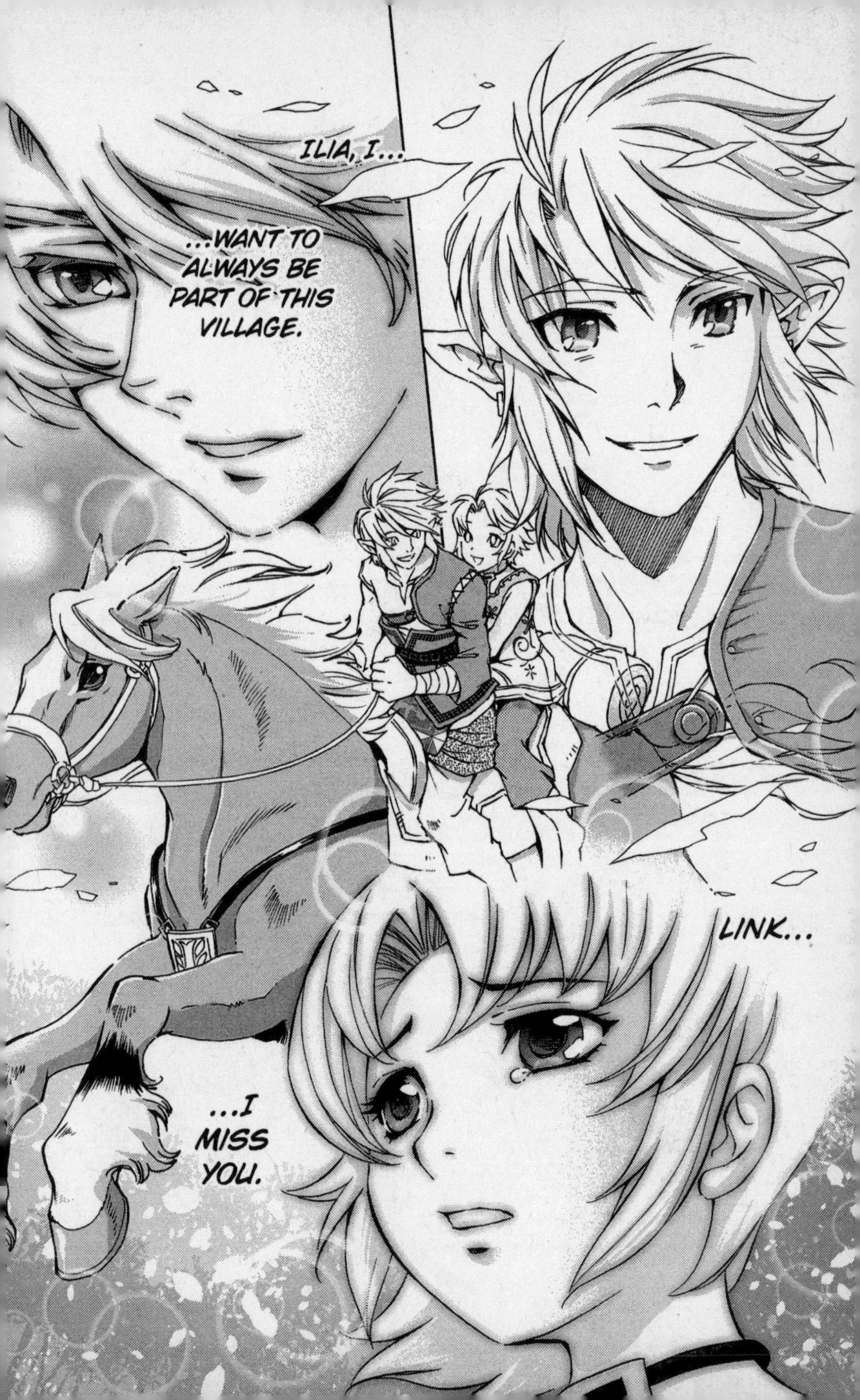
ILIA, I...
...WANT TO ALWAYS BE PART OF THIS VILLAGE.
LINK...
...I MISS YOU.

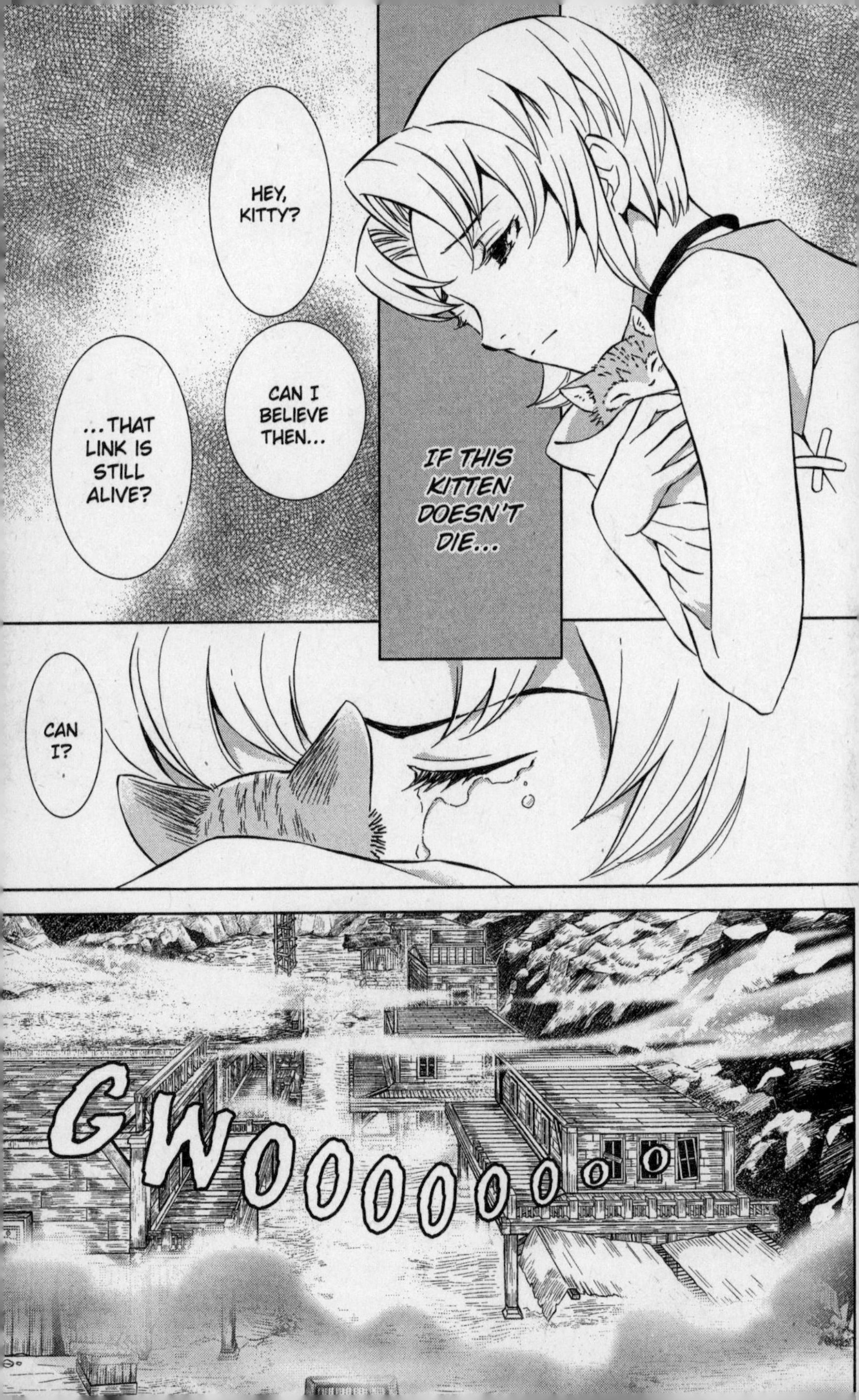
HEY, KITTY?
IF THIS KITTEN DOESN'T DIE...
CAN I BELIEVE THEN...
...THAT LINK IS STILL ALIVE?
CAN I?
GWOOOOOOOO

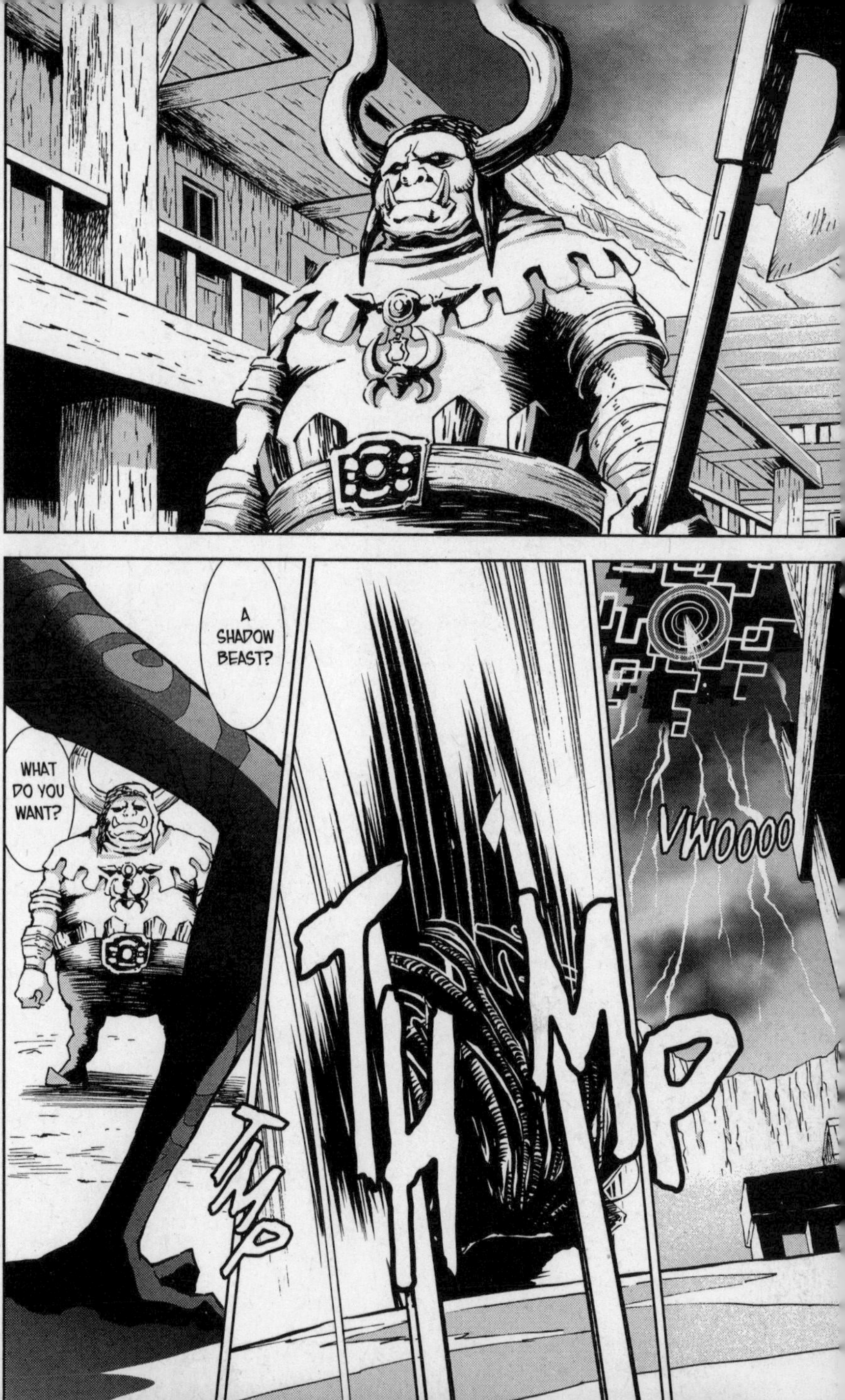
VWOOOO
THMP
THMP
A SHADOW BEAST?
WHAT DO YOU WANT?

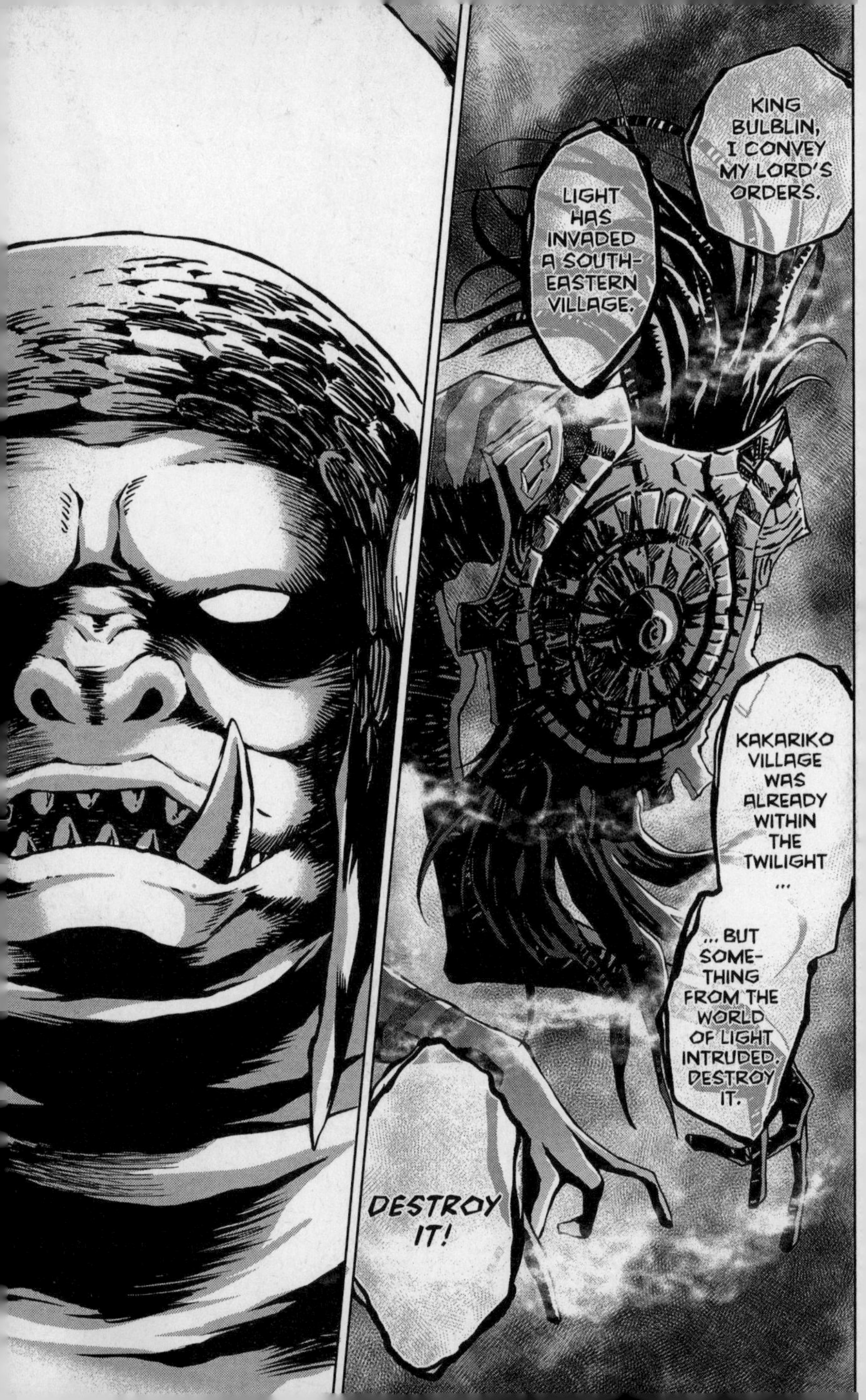
KING BULBLIN, I CONVEY MY LORD'S ORDERS.
LIGHT HAS INVADED A SOUTH-EASTERN VILLAGE.
KAKARIKO VILLAGE WAS ALREADY WITHIN THE TWILIGHT...
...BUT SOMETHING FROM THE WORLD OF LIGHT INTRUDED. DESTROY IT.
DESTROY IT!

#23. TRUE BRAVERY

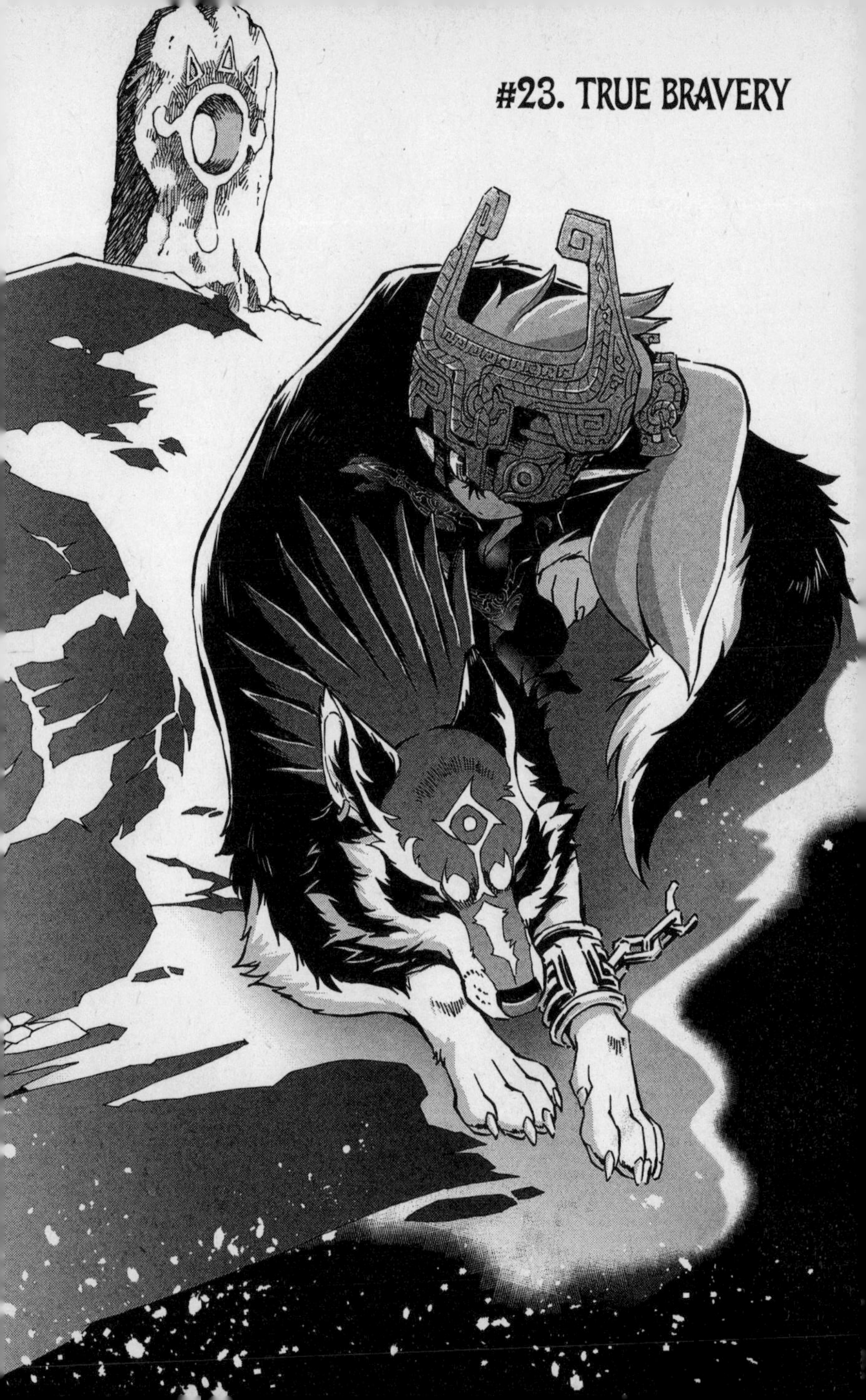

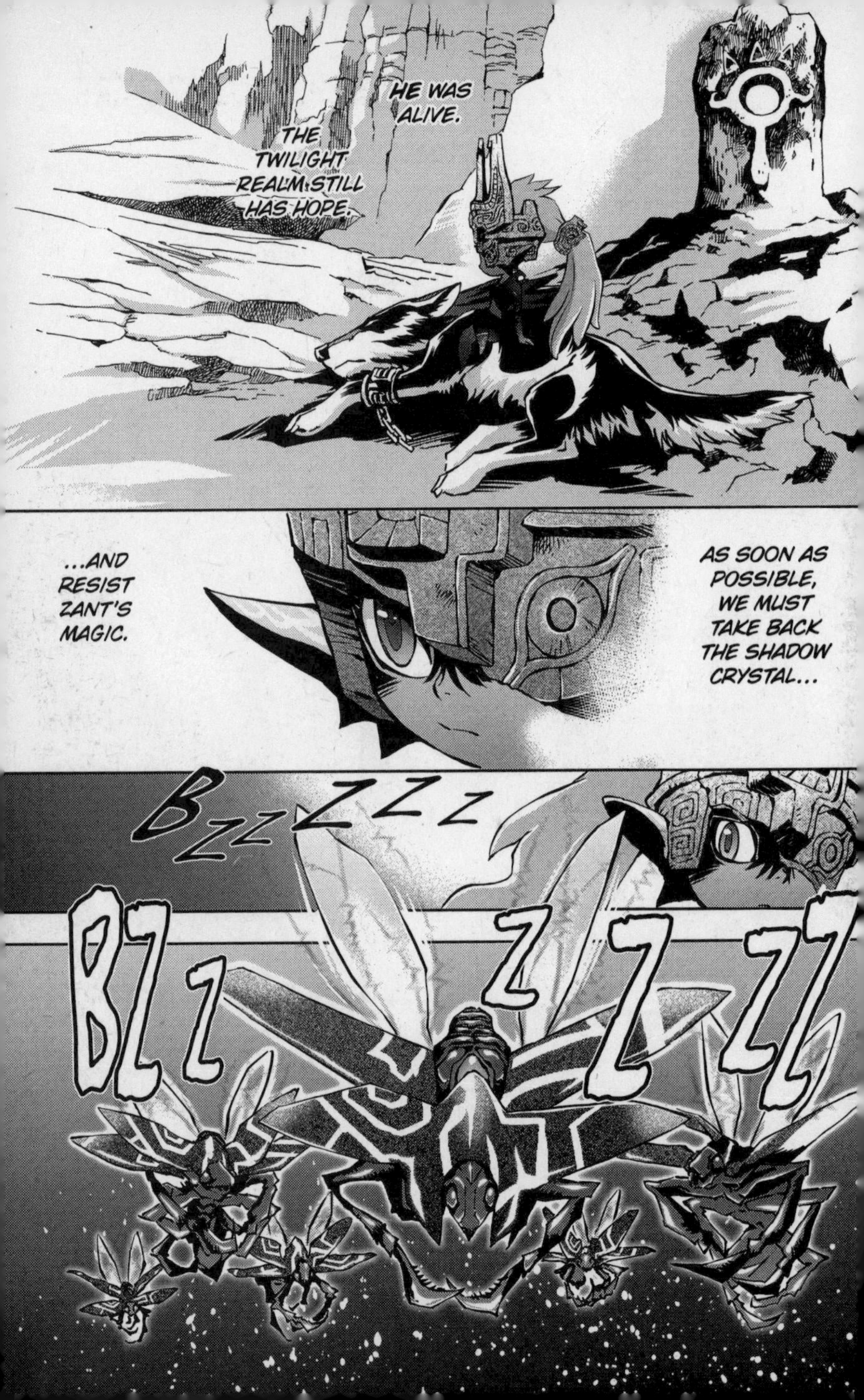
HE WAS ALIVE.
THE TWILIGHT REALM STILL HAS HOPE.
AS SOON AS POSSIBLE, WE MUST TAKE BACK THE SHADOW CRYSTAL...
...AND RESIST ZANT'S MAGIC.
BZZZZZZZ
BZZ ZZZZ

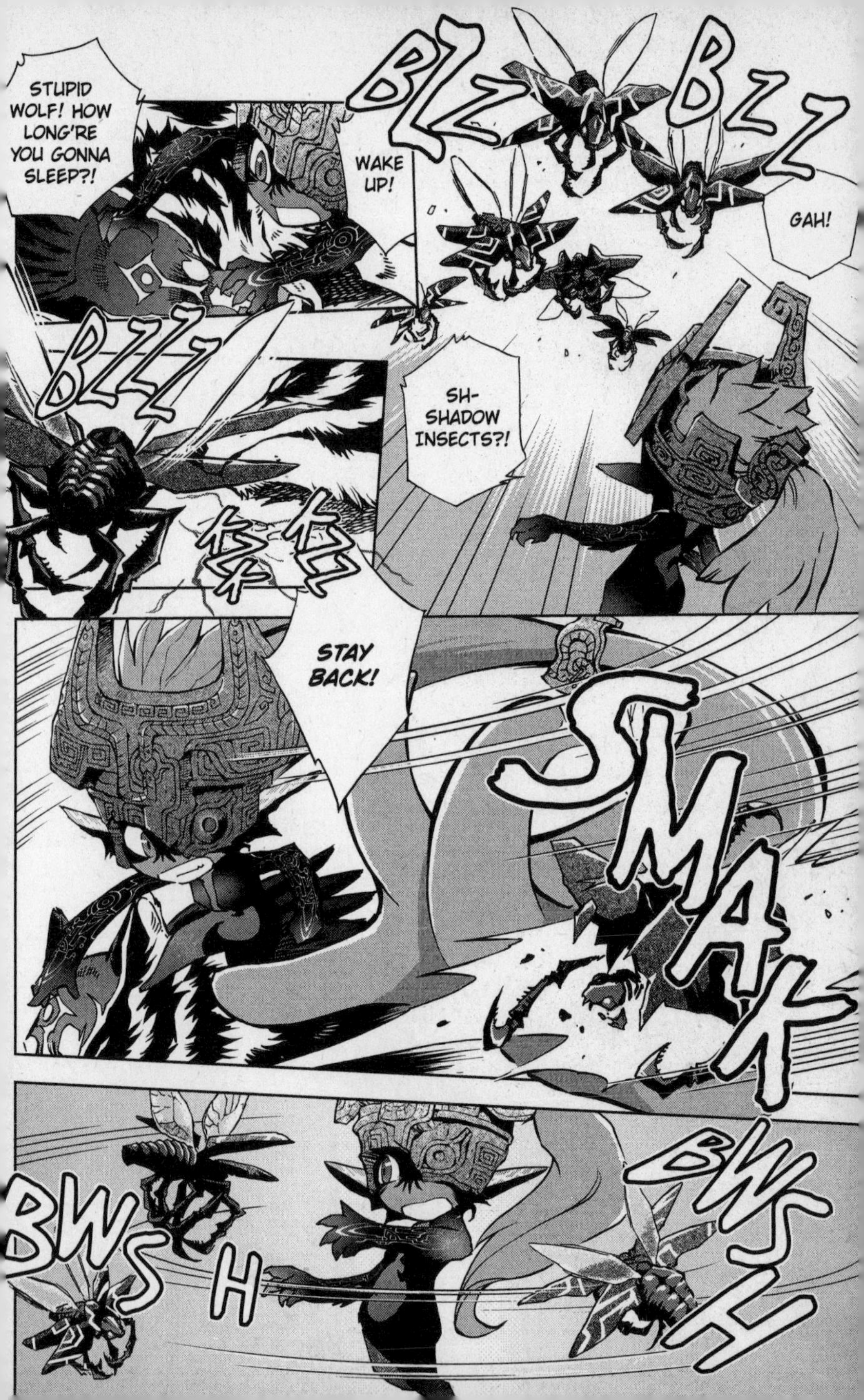
STUPID WOLF! HOW LONG'RE YOU GONNA SLEEP?!
WAKE UP!
BZZ BZZ
GAH!
SH-SHADOW INSECTS?!
BZZZ
KZZ KZZ
STAY BACK!
SMAK
BWSH BWSH

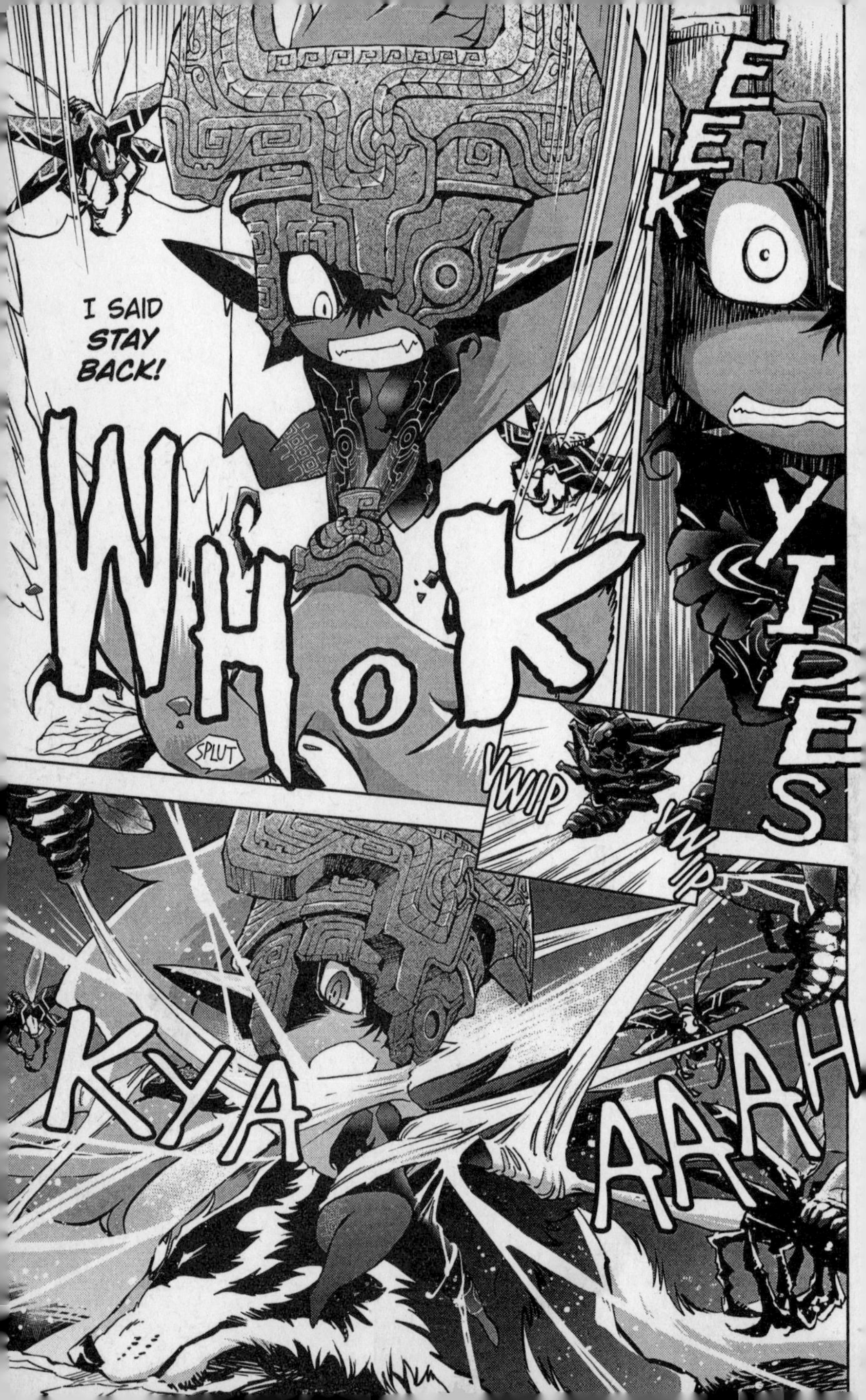
EEK
I SAID STAY BACK!
WHOK
SPLUT
YIPES
VWIP
VWIP
KYA
AAAH

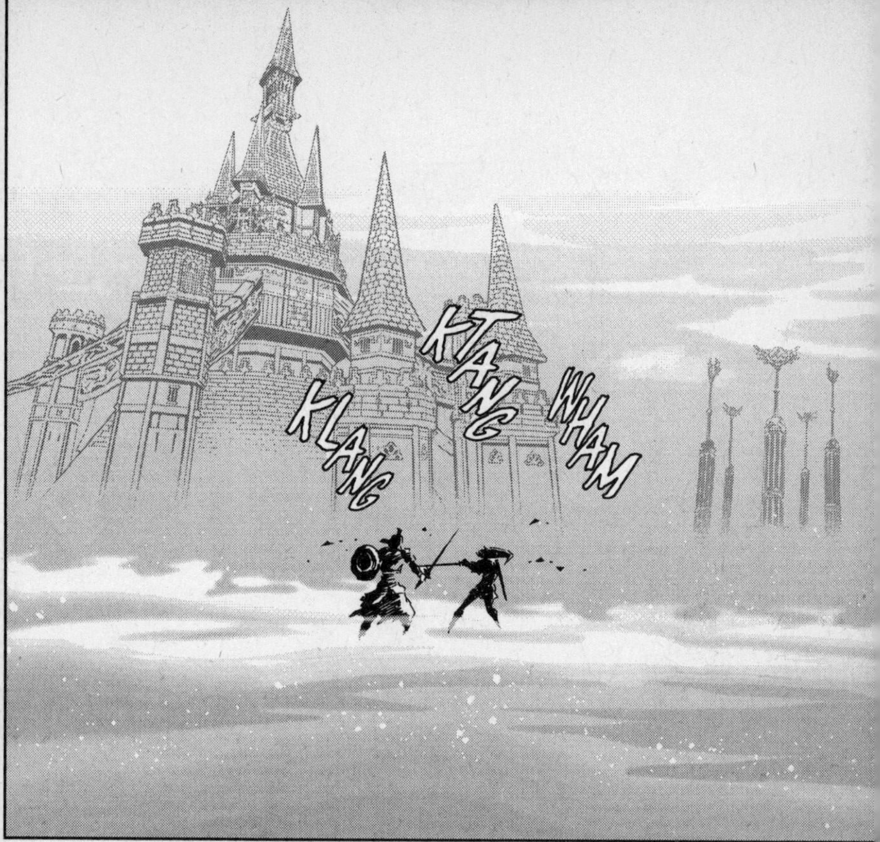
KTANG
WHAM
KLANG
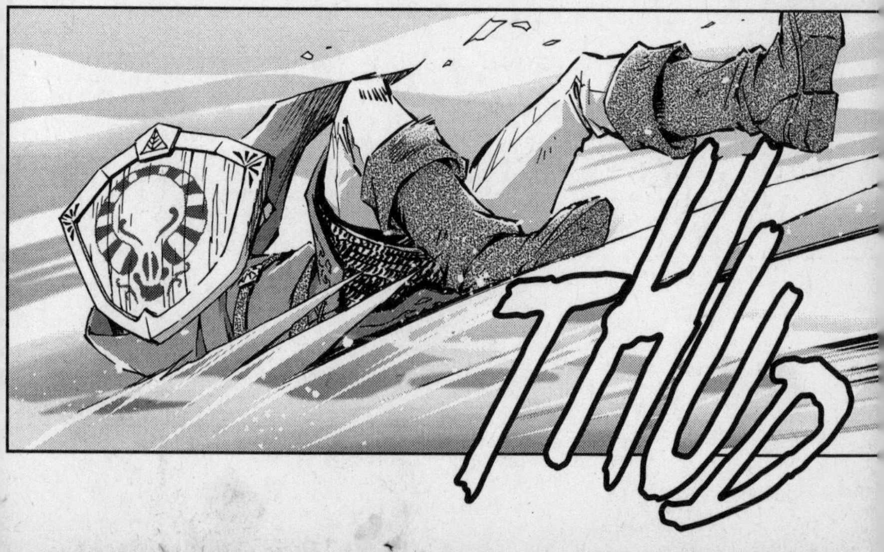
THUD

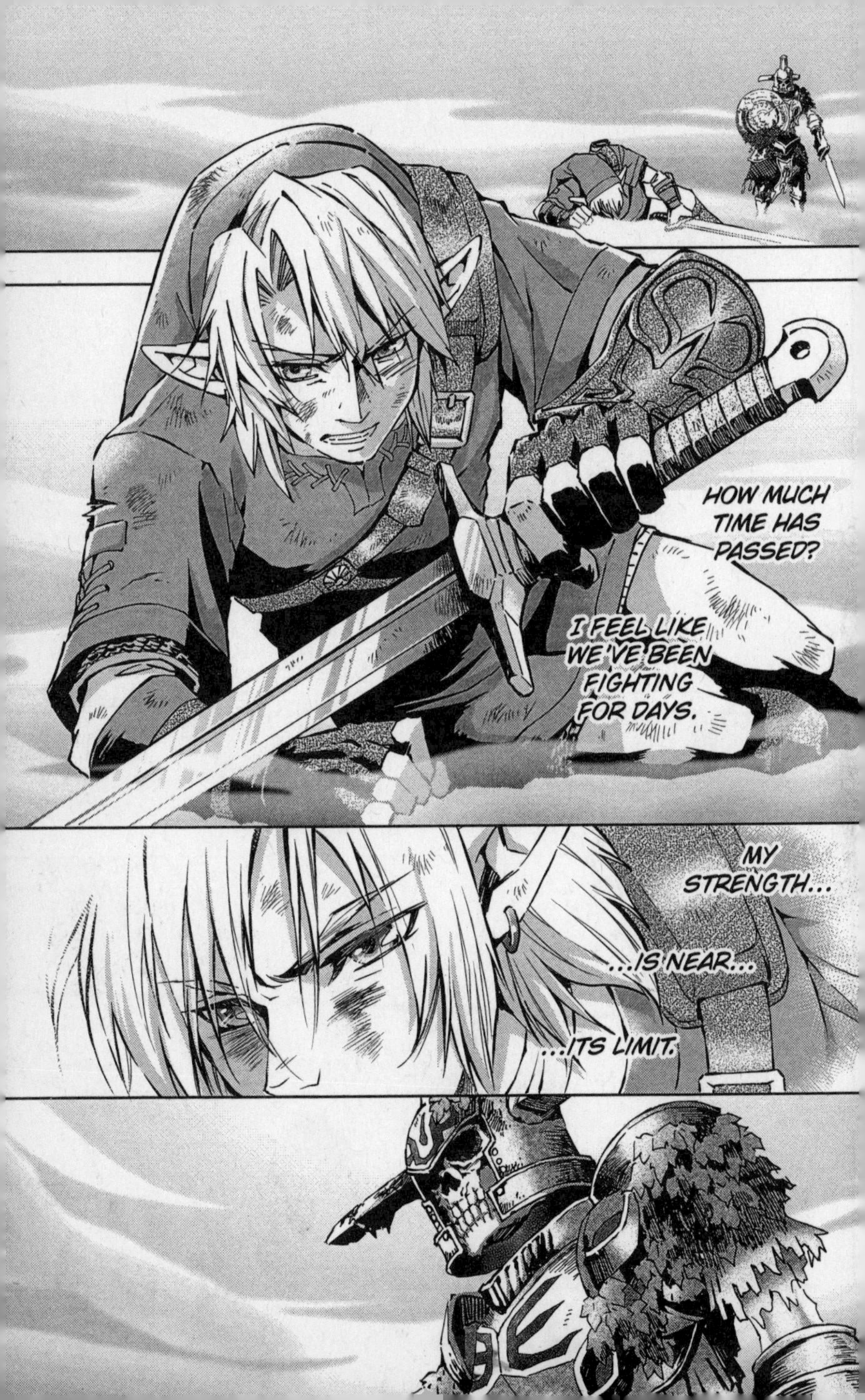
HOW MUCH TIME HAS PASSED?
I FEEL LIKE WE'VE BEEN FIGHTING FOR DAYS.
MY STRENGTH...
...IS NEAR...
...ITS LIMIT.

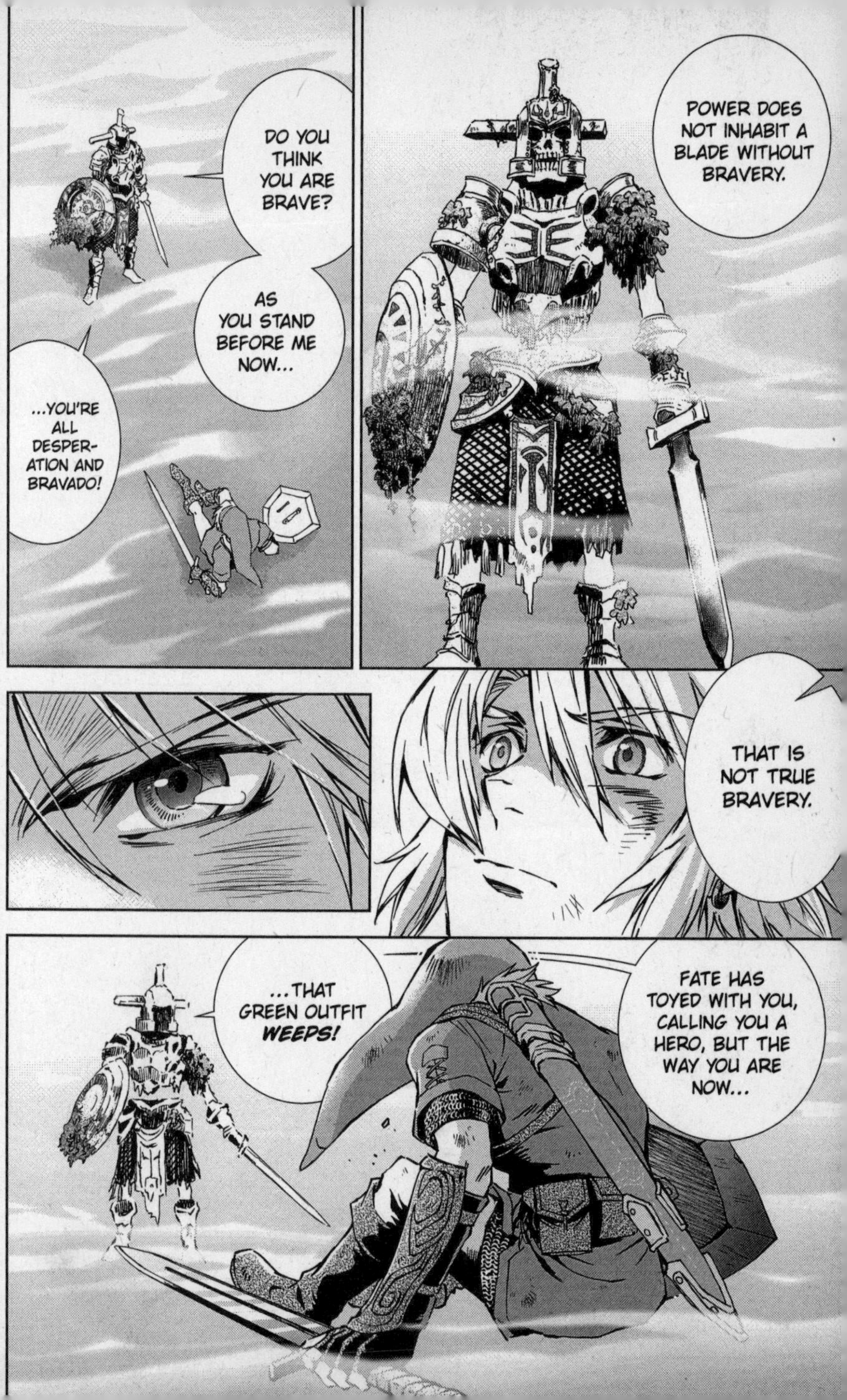
POWER DOES NOT INHABIT A BLADE WITHOUT BRAVERY.
DO YOU THINK YOU ARE BRAVE?
AS YOU STAND BEFORE ME NOW...
...YOU'RE ALL DESPER-ATION AND BRAVADO!
THAT IS NOT TRUE BRAVERY.
FATE HAS TOYED WITH YOU, CALLING YOU A HERO, BUT THE WAY YOU ARE NOW...
...THAT GREEN OUTFIT *WEEPS!*

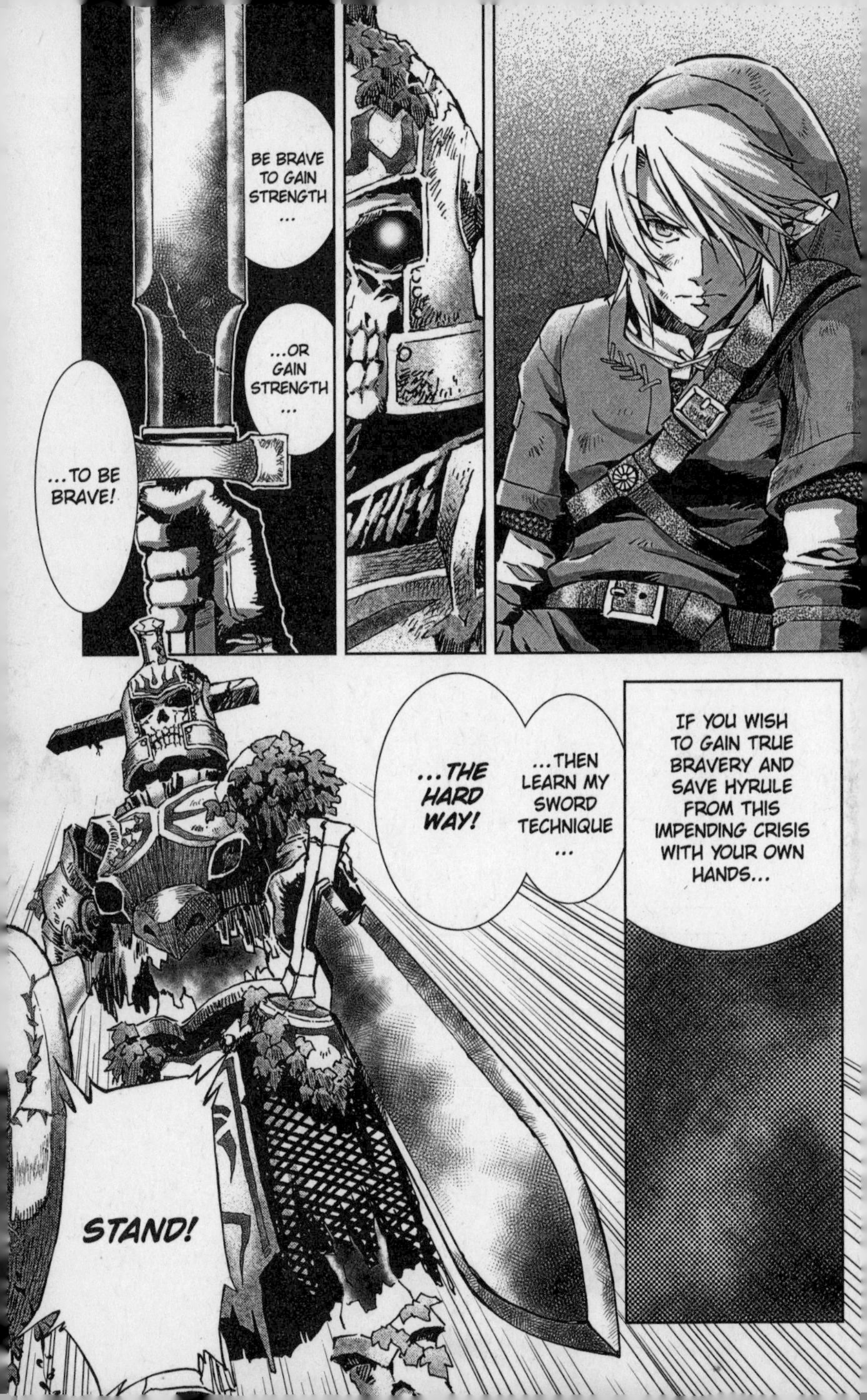
BE BRAVE TO GAIN STRENGTH ...
...OR GAIN STRENGTH ...
...TO BE BRAVE!
IF YOU WISH TO GAIN TRUE BRAVERY AND SAVE HYRULE FROM THIS IMPENDING CRISIS WITH YOUR OWN HANDS...
...THEN LEARN MY SWORD TECHNIQUE ...
...THE HARD WAY!
STAND!

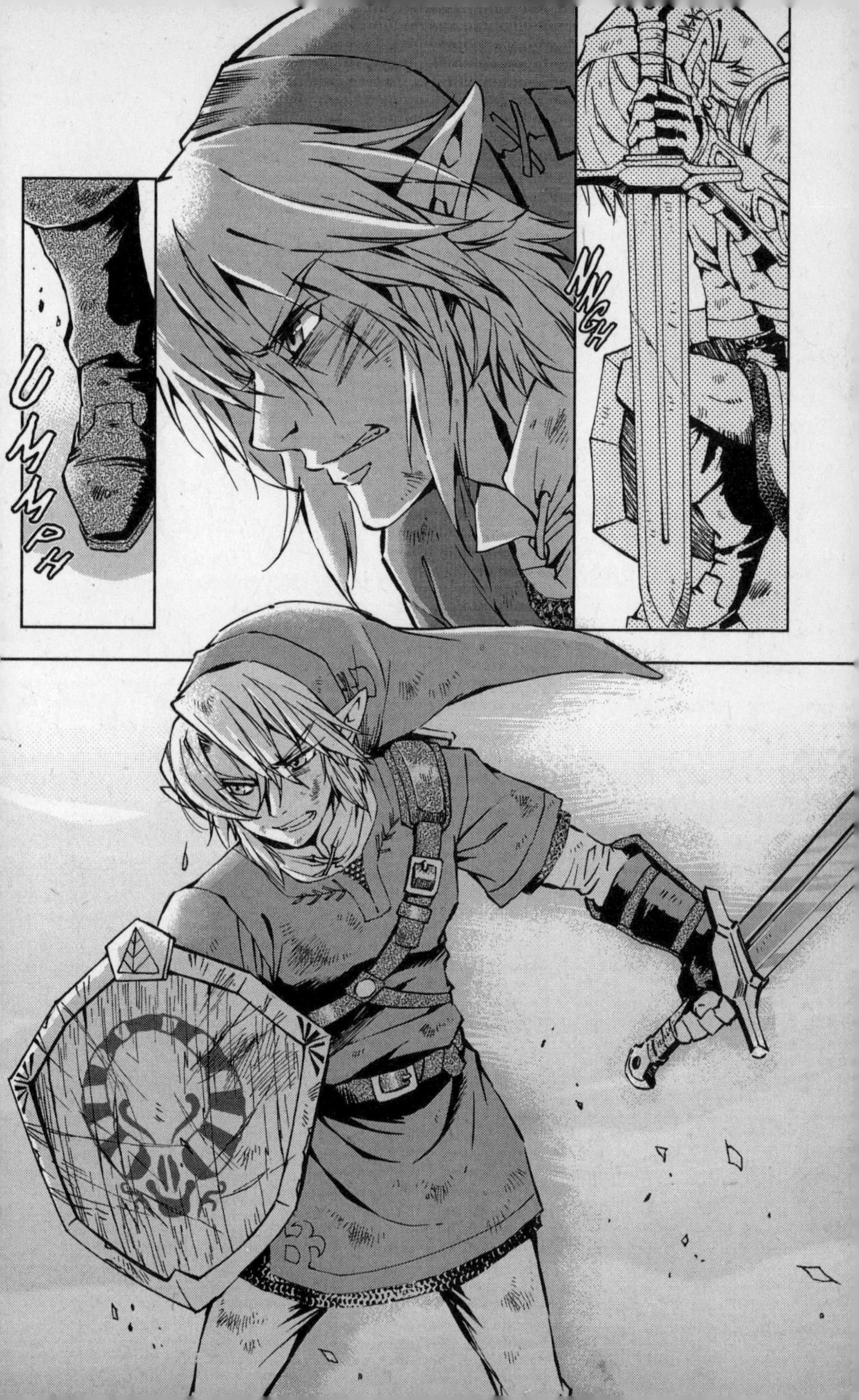
NNGH
UMMPH

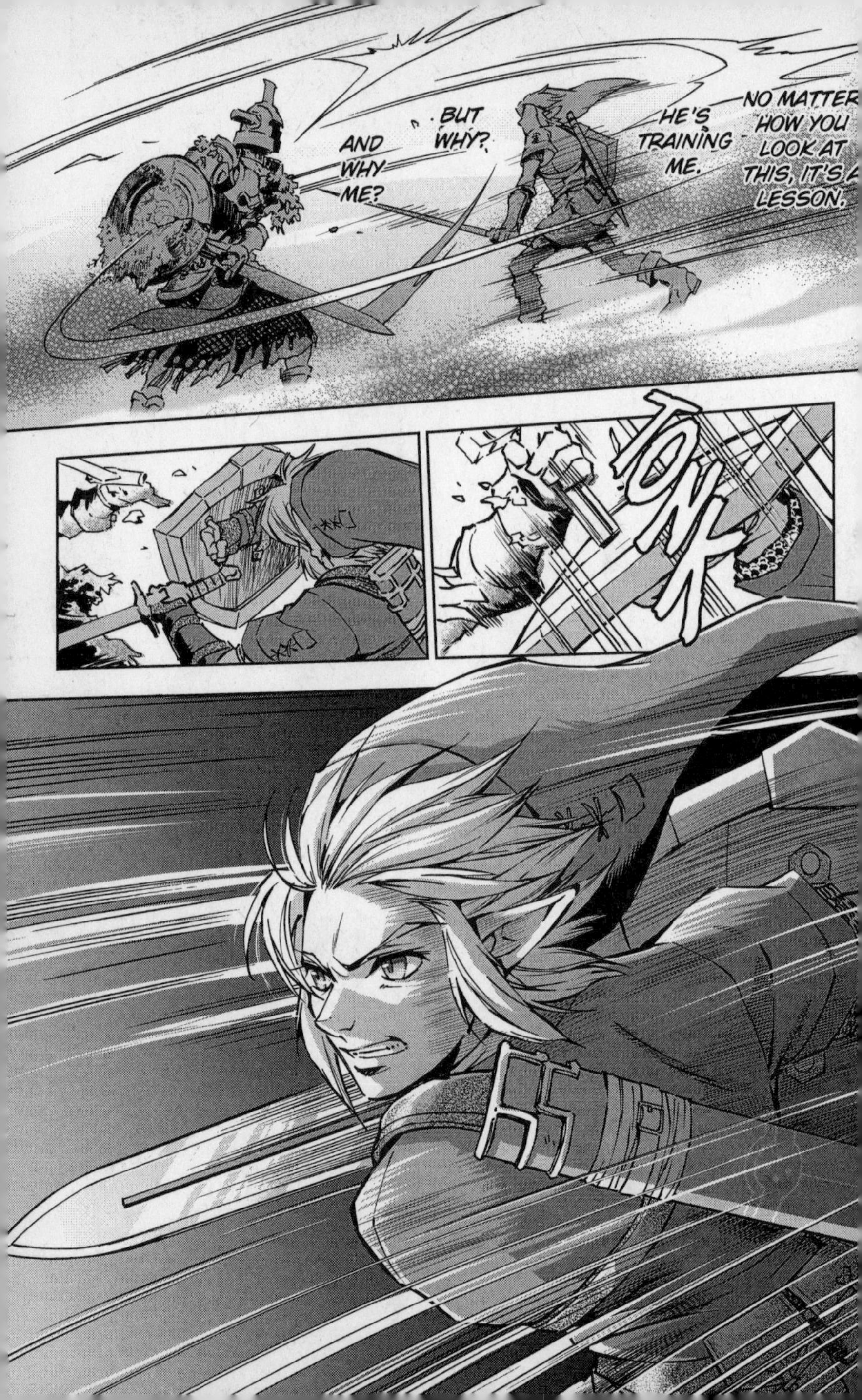
NO MATTER HOW YOU LOOK AT THIS, IT'S A LESSON.
HE'S TRAINING ME.
BUT WHY?
AND WHY ME?
TONK

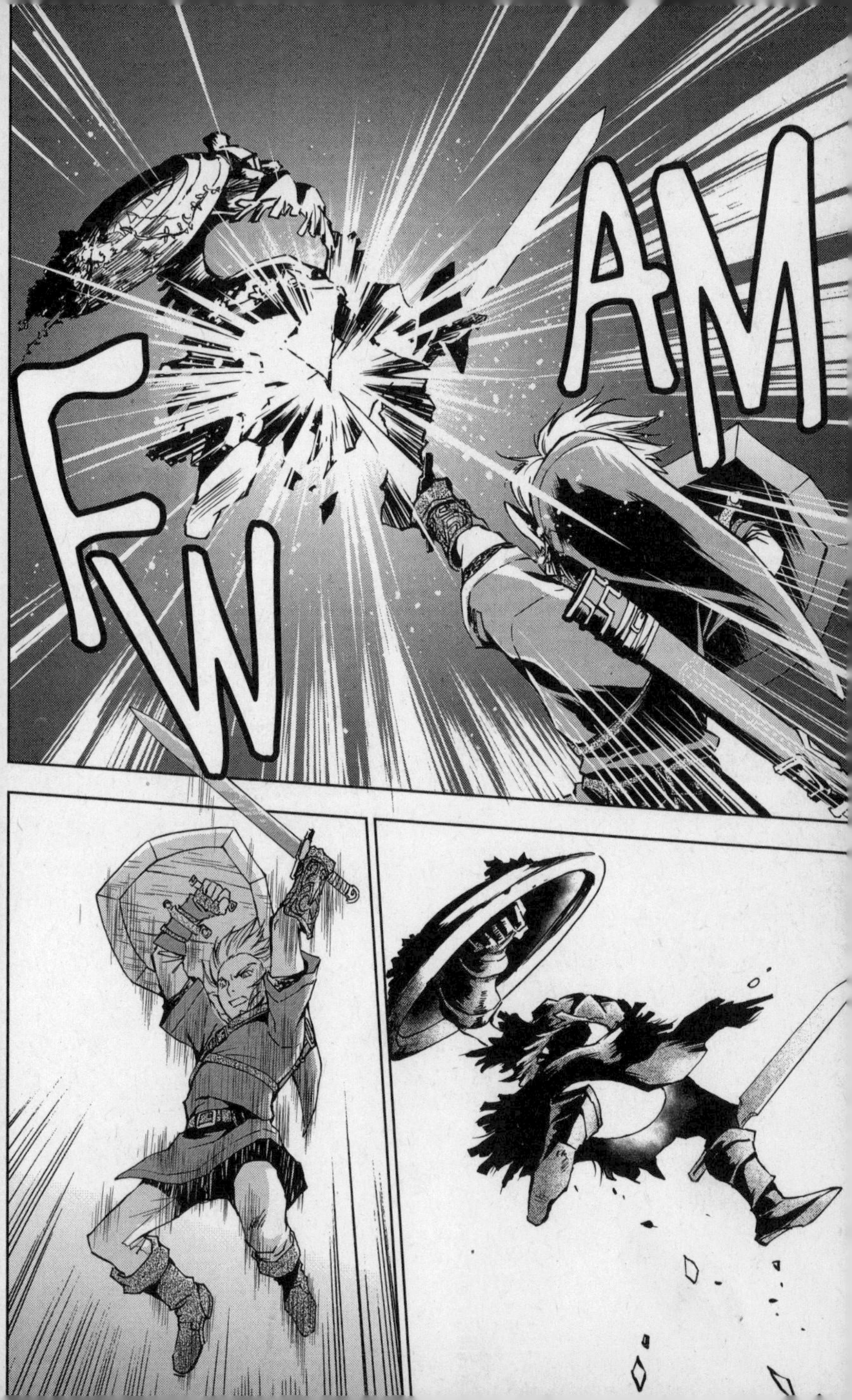
FWAM

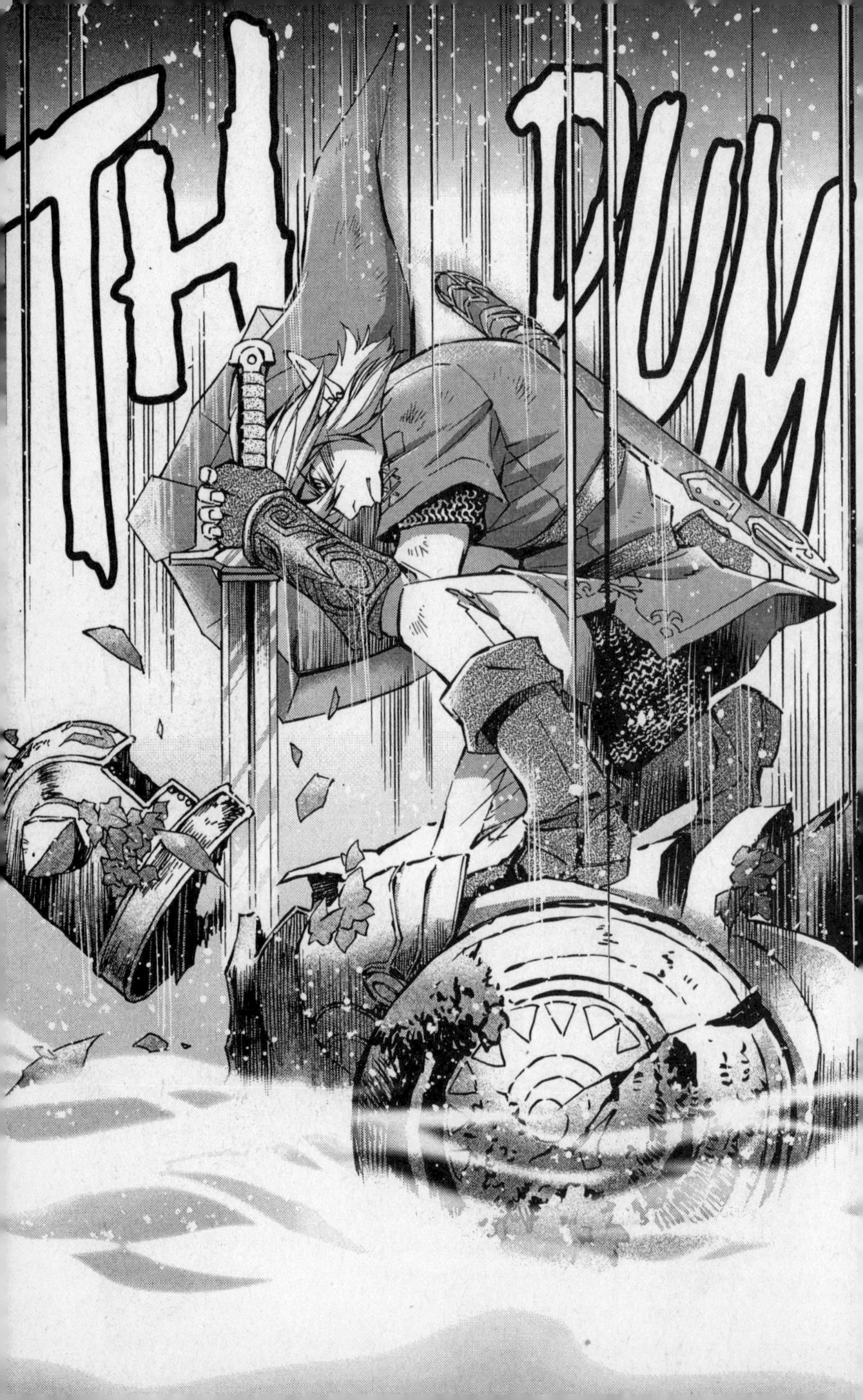
THUMP

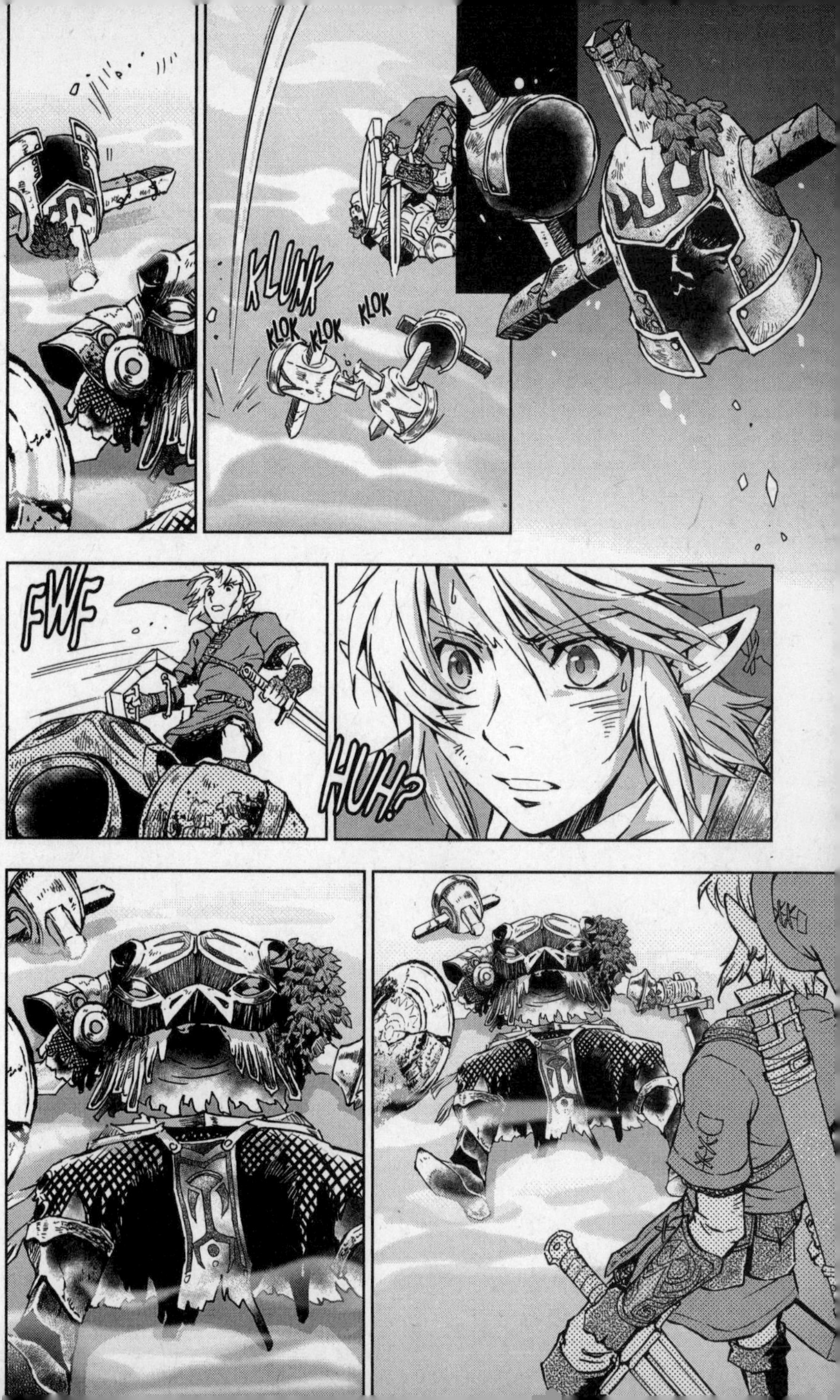
KLUNK
KLOK
KLOK
KLOK
HUH?
FWF

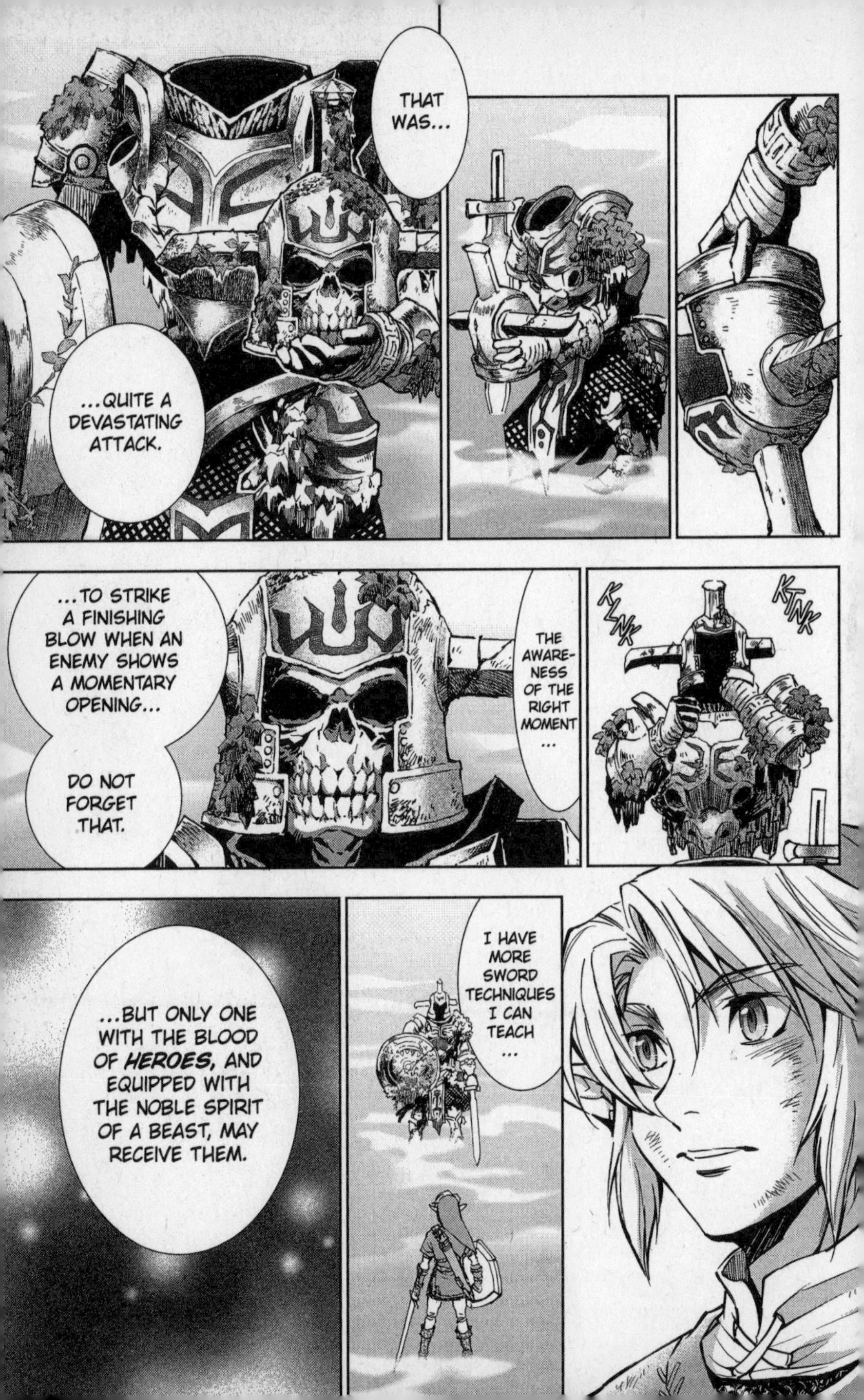
THAT WAS...
...QUITE A DEVASTATING ATTACK.
KTNK
KLNK
THE AWARENESS OF THE RIGHT MOMENT...
...TO STRIKE A FINISHING BLOW WHEN AN ENEMY SHOWS A MOMENTARY OPENING...
DO NOT FORGET THAT.
I HAVE MORE SWORD TECHNIQUES I CAN TEACH...
...BUT ONLY ONE WITH THE BLOOD OF *HEROES*, AND EQUIPPED WITH THE NOBLE SPIRIT OF A BEAST, MAY RECEIVE THEM.

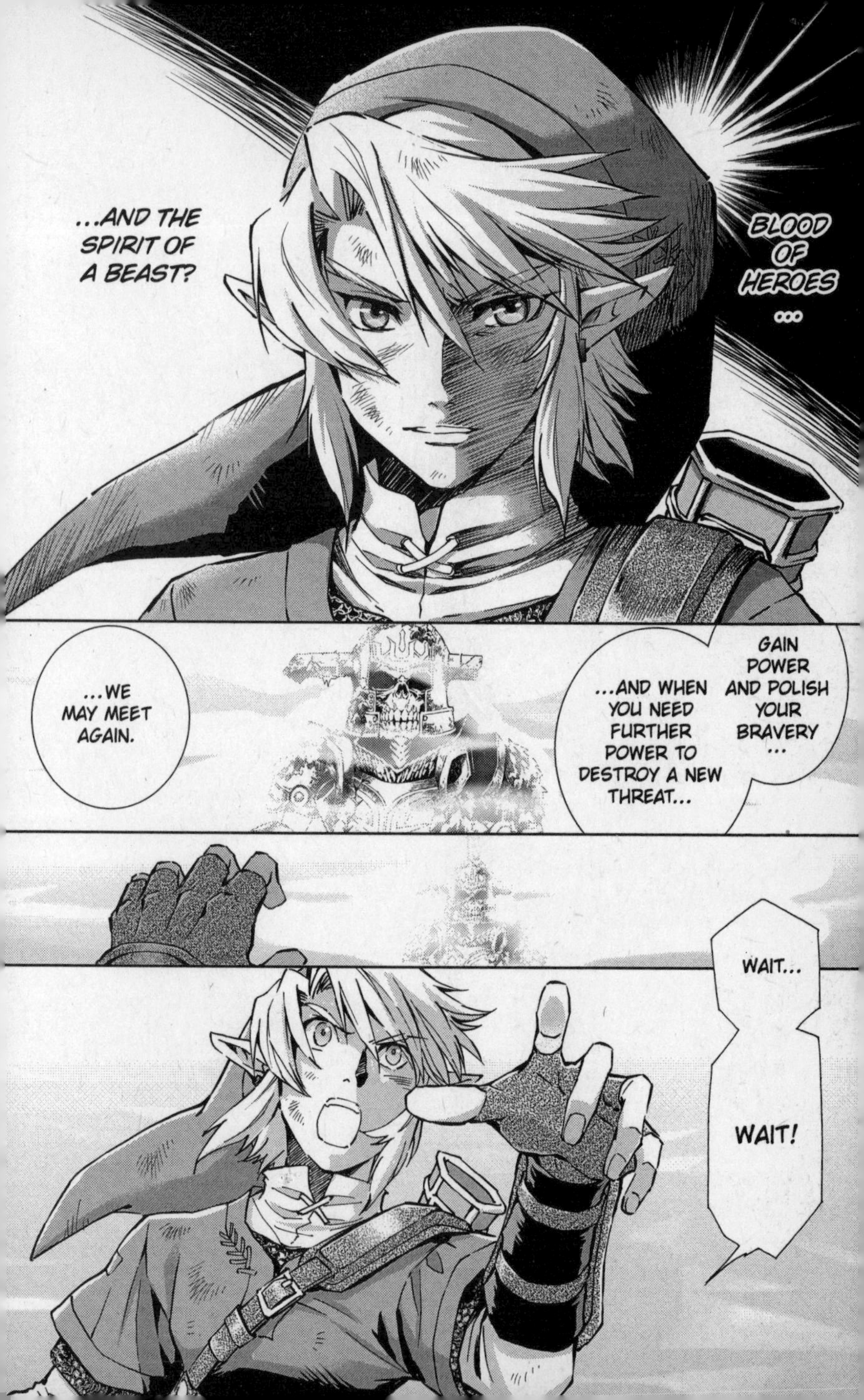
BLOOD OF HEROES...
...AND THE SPIRIT OF A BEAST?
GAIN POWER AND POLISH YOUR BRAVERY...
...AND WHEN YOU NEED FURTHER POWER TO DESTROY A NEW THREAT...
...WE MAY MEET AGAIN.
WAIT...
WAIT!

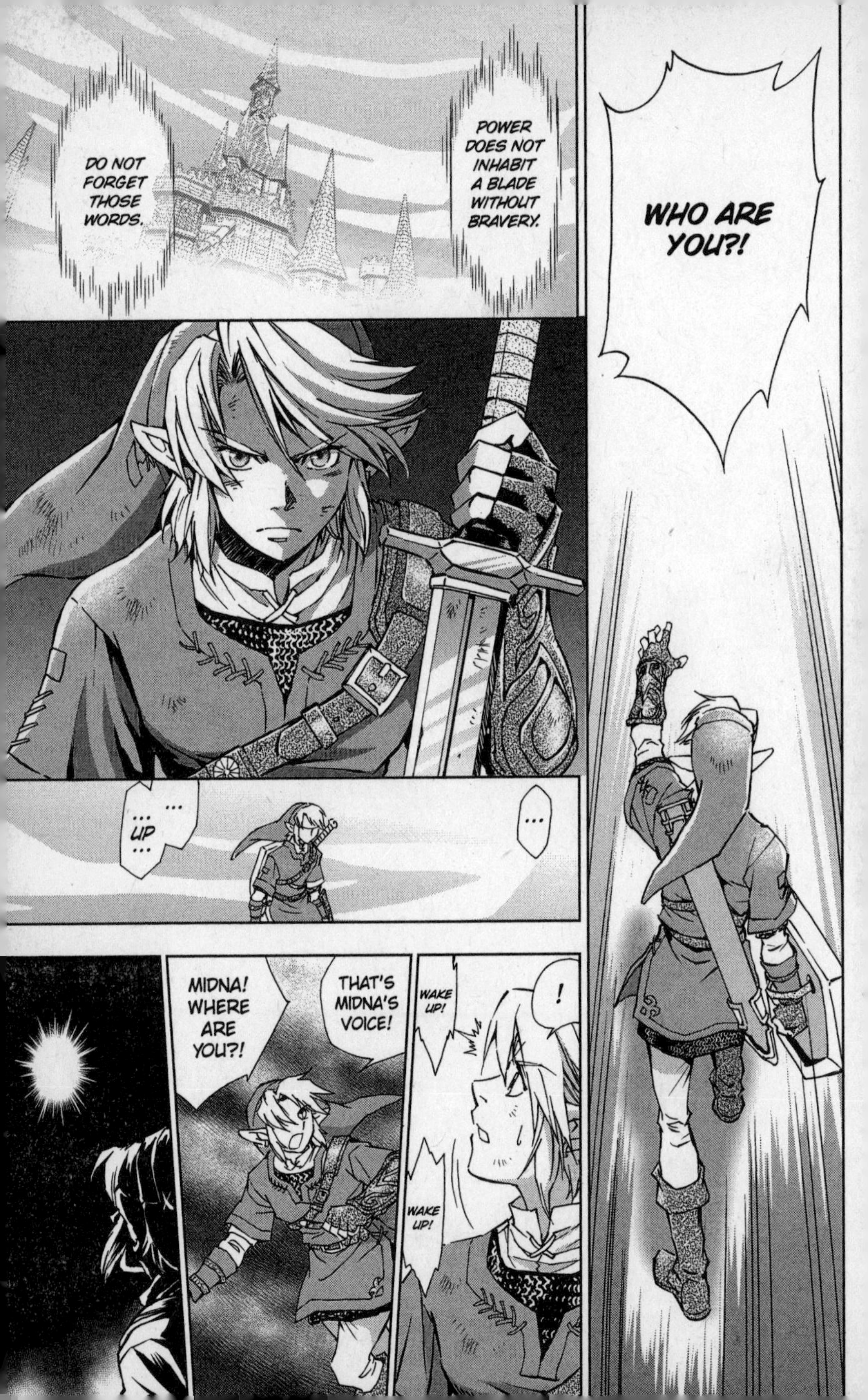
WHO ARE YOU?!
POWER DOES NOT INHABIT A BLADE WITHOUT BRAVERY.
DO NOT FORGET THOSE WORDS.
...
... ... UP ...
!
WAKE UP!
WAKE UP!
THAT'S MIDNA'S VOICE!
MIDNA! WHERE ARE YOU?!

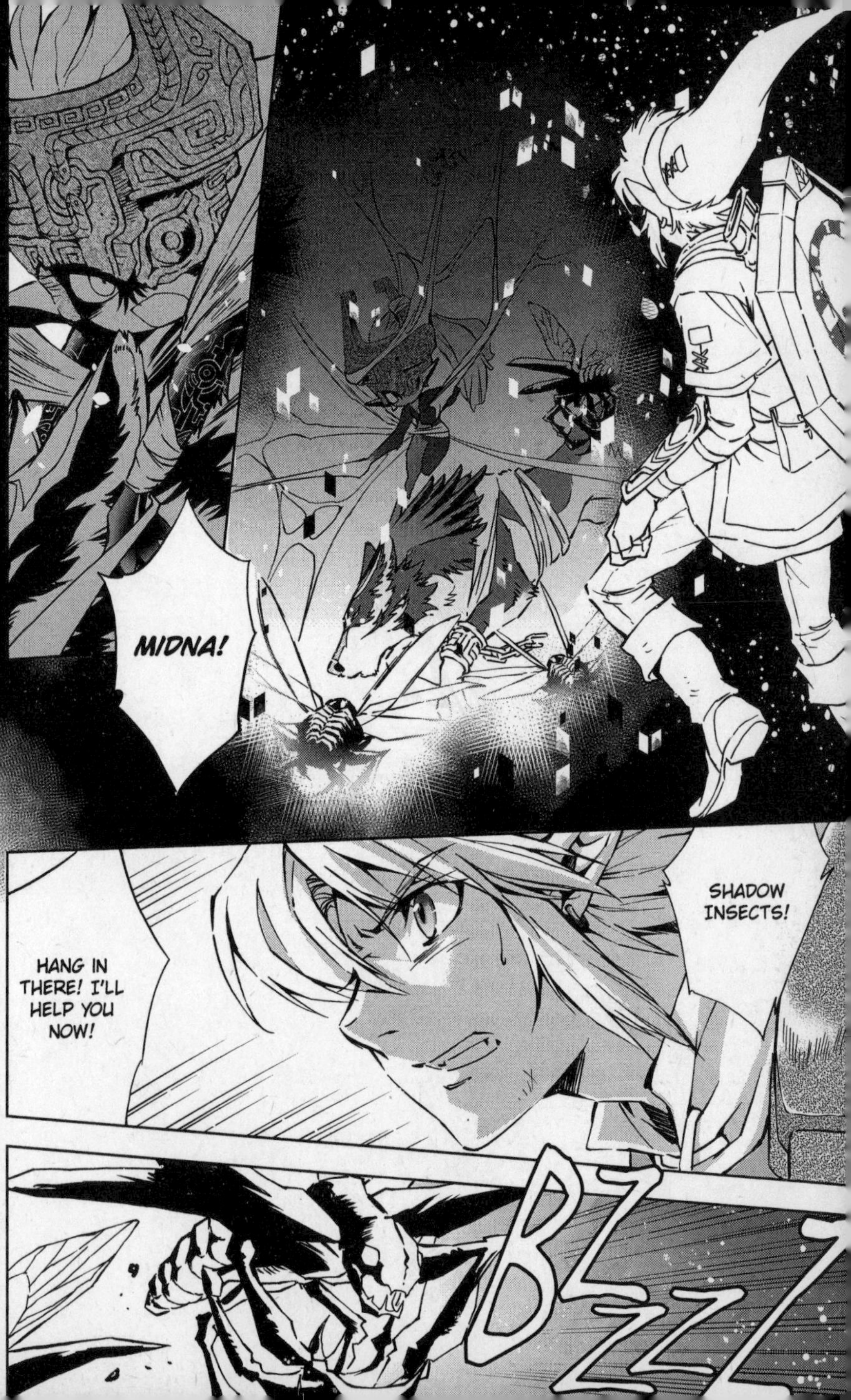
MIDNA!
SHADOW INSECTS!
HANG IN THERE! I'LL HELP YOU NOW!
BZZZ

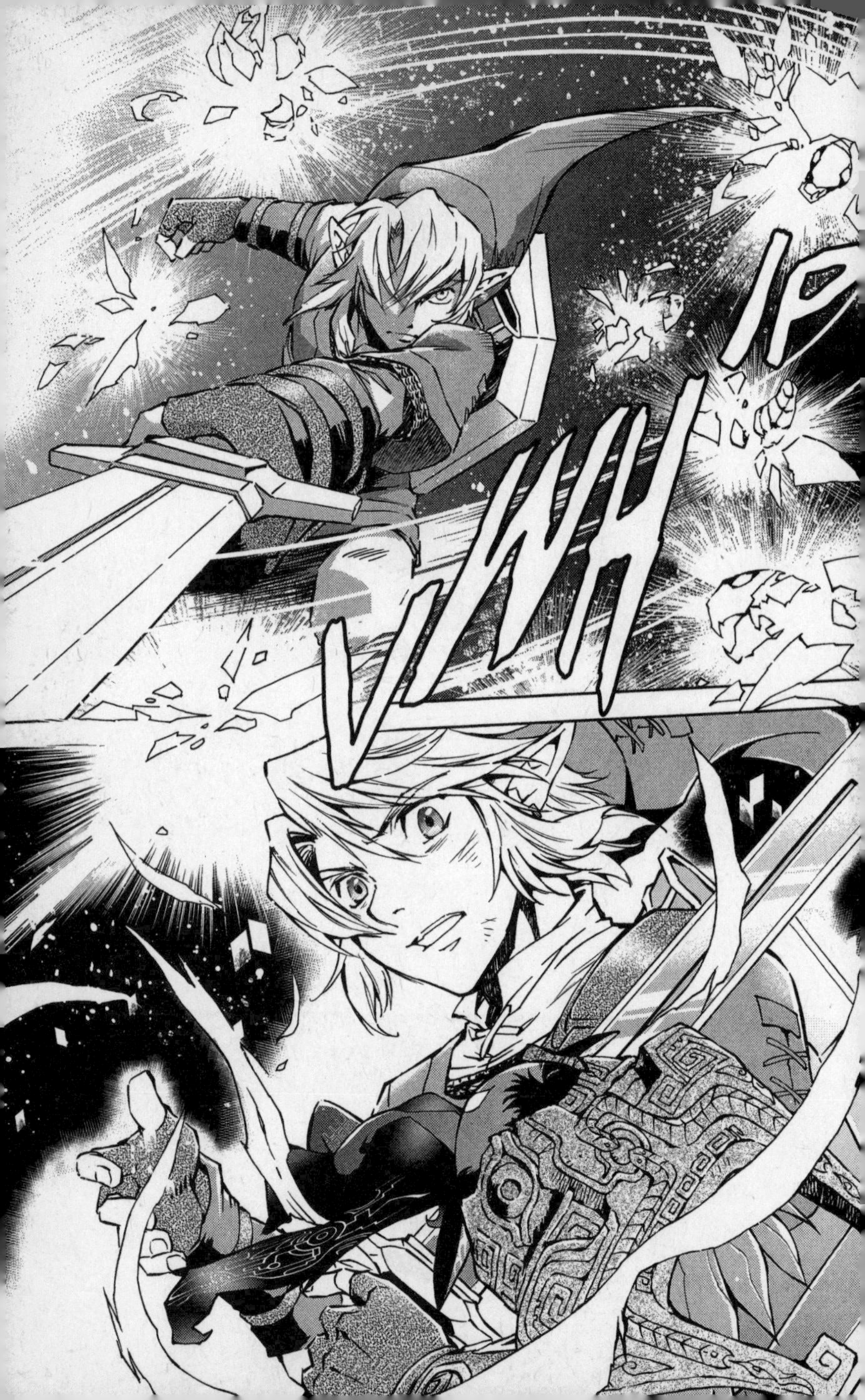
WHIP

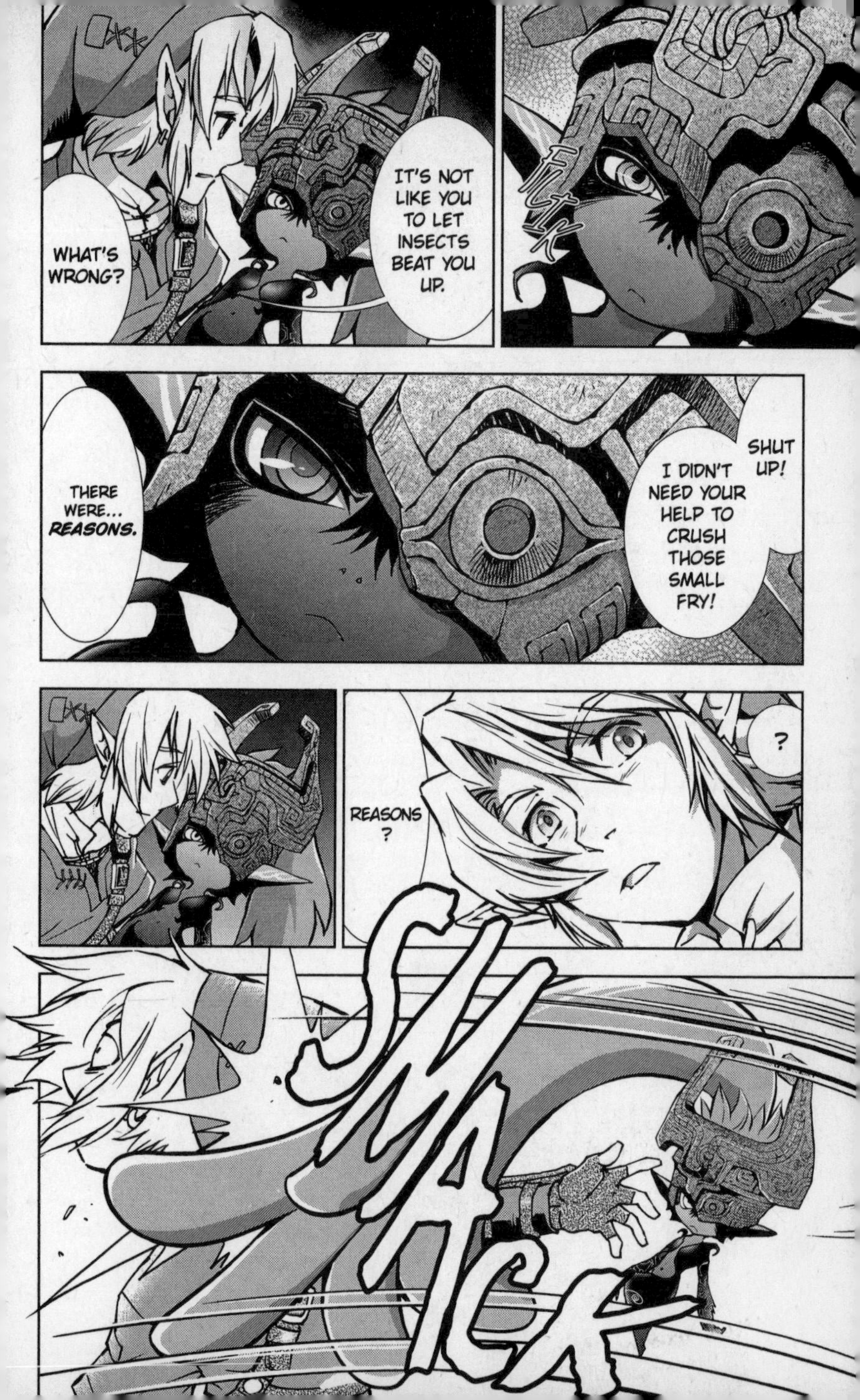
FLIK
IT'S NOT LIKE YOU TO LET INSECTS BEAT YOU UP.
WHAT'S WRONG?
SHUT UP!
I DIDN'T NEED YOUR HELP TO CRUSH THOSE SMALL FRY!
THERE WERE... *REASONS.*
?
REASONS?
SMACK

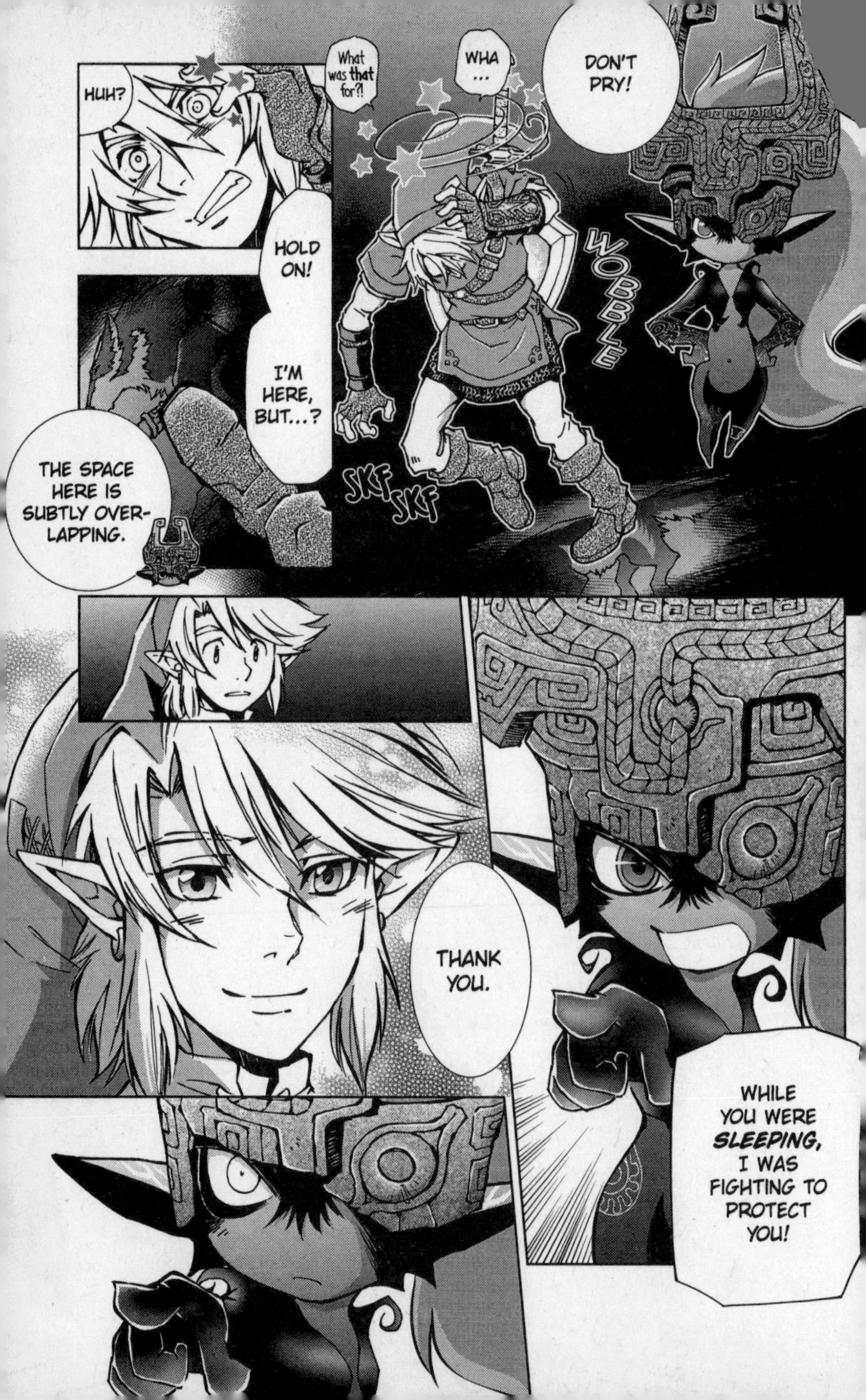
DON'T PRY!
WHA ...
What was that for?!
WOBBLE
SKF SKF
HUH?
HOLD ON!
I'M HERE, BUT...?
THE SPACE HERE IS SUBTLY OVER-LAPPING.
THANK YOU.
WHILE YOU WERE SLEEPING, I WAS FIGHTING TO PROTECT YOU!

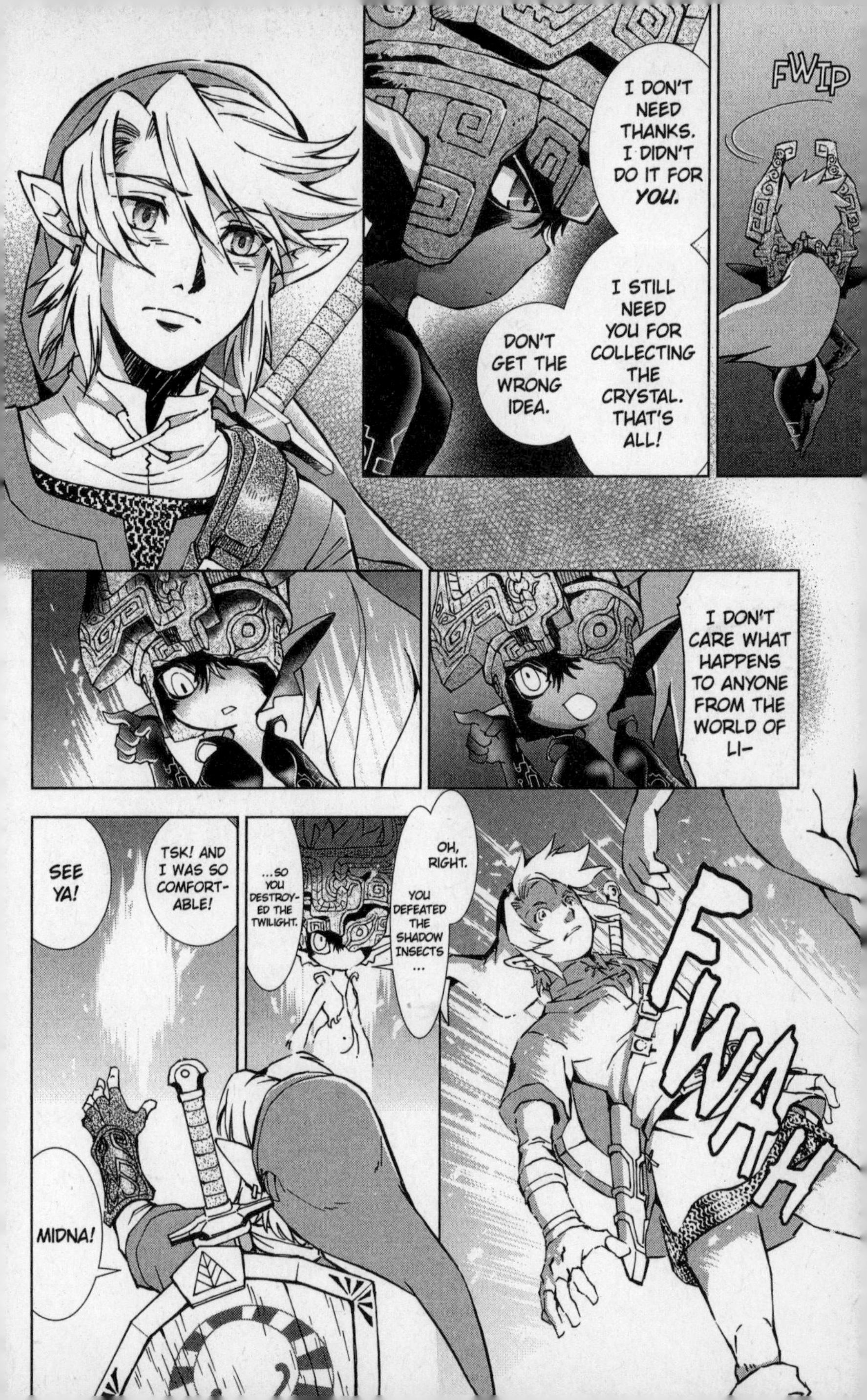
FWIP
I DON'T NEED THANKS. I DIDN'T DO IT FOR *YOU.*
I STILL NEED YOU FOR COLLECTING THE CRYSTAL. THAT'S ALL!
DON'T GET THE WRONG IDEA.
I DON'T CARE WHAT HAPPENS TO ANYONE FROM THE WORLD OF LI-
OH, RIGHT.
YOU DEFEATED THE SHADOW INSECTS...
FWAH
...SO YOU DESTROY-ED THE TWILIGHT.
TSK! AND I WAS SO COMFORT-ABLE!
SEE YA!
MIDNA!

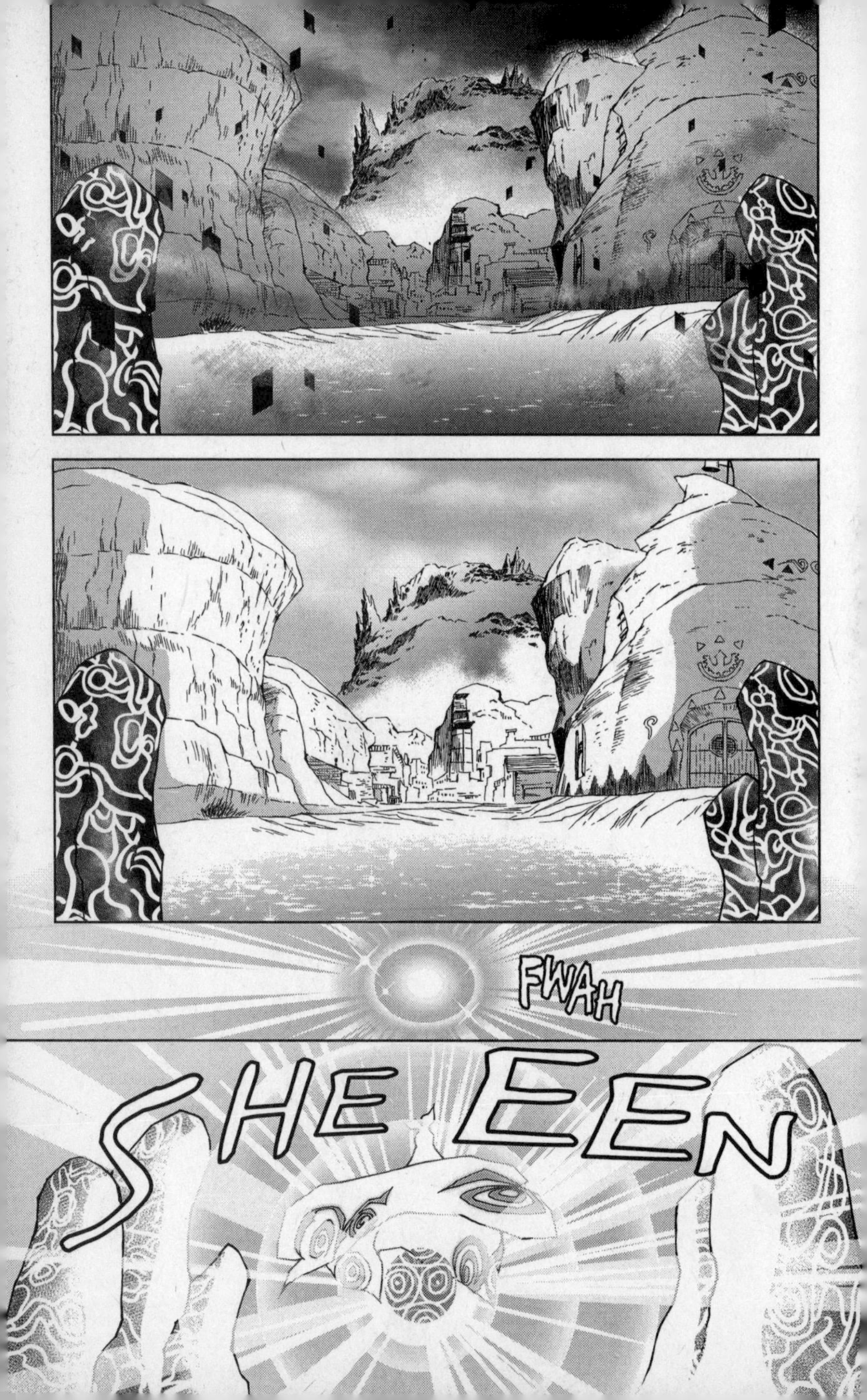
FWAH
SHEEEN

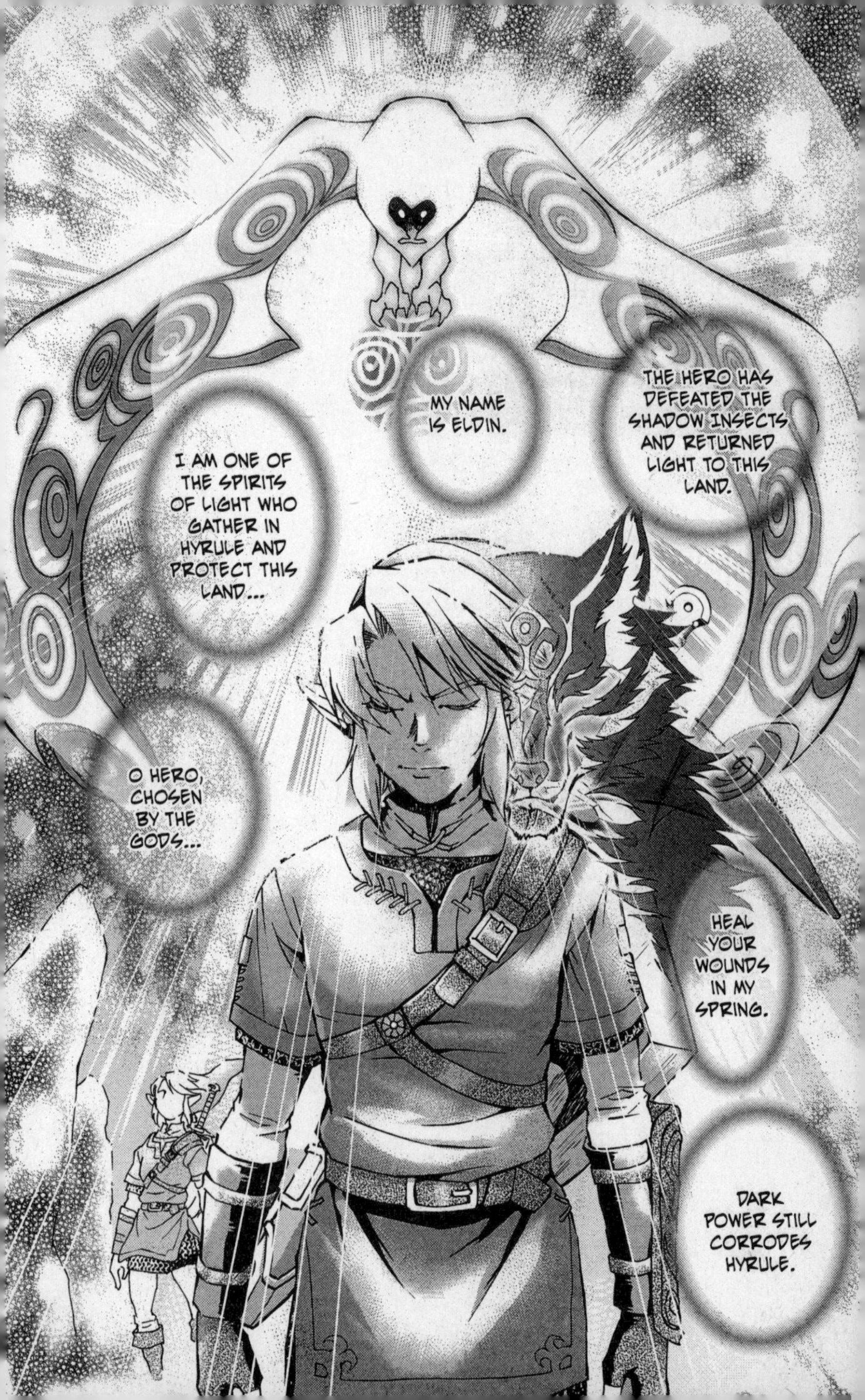
THE HERO HAS DEFEATED THE SHADOW INSECTS AND RETURNED LIGHT TO THIS LAND.
MY NAME IS ELDIN.
I AM ONE OF THE SPIRITS OF LIGHT WHO GATHER IN HYRULE AND PROTECT THIS LAND...
HEAL YOUR WOUNDS IN MY SPRING.
O HERO, CHOSEN BY THE GODS...
DARK POWER STILL CORRODES HYRULE.

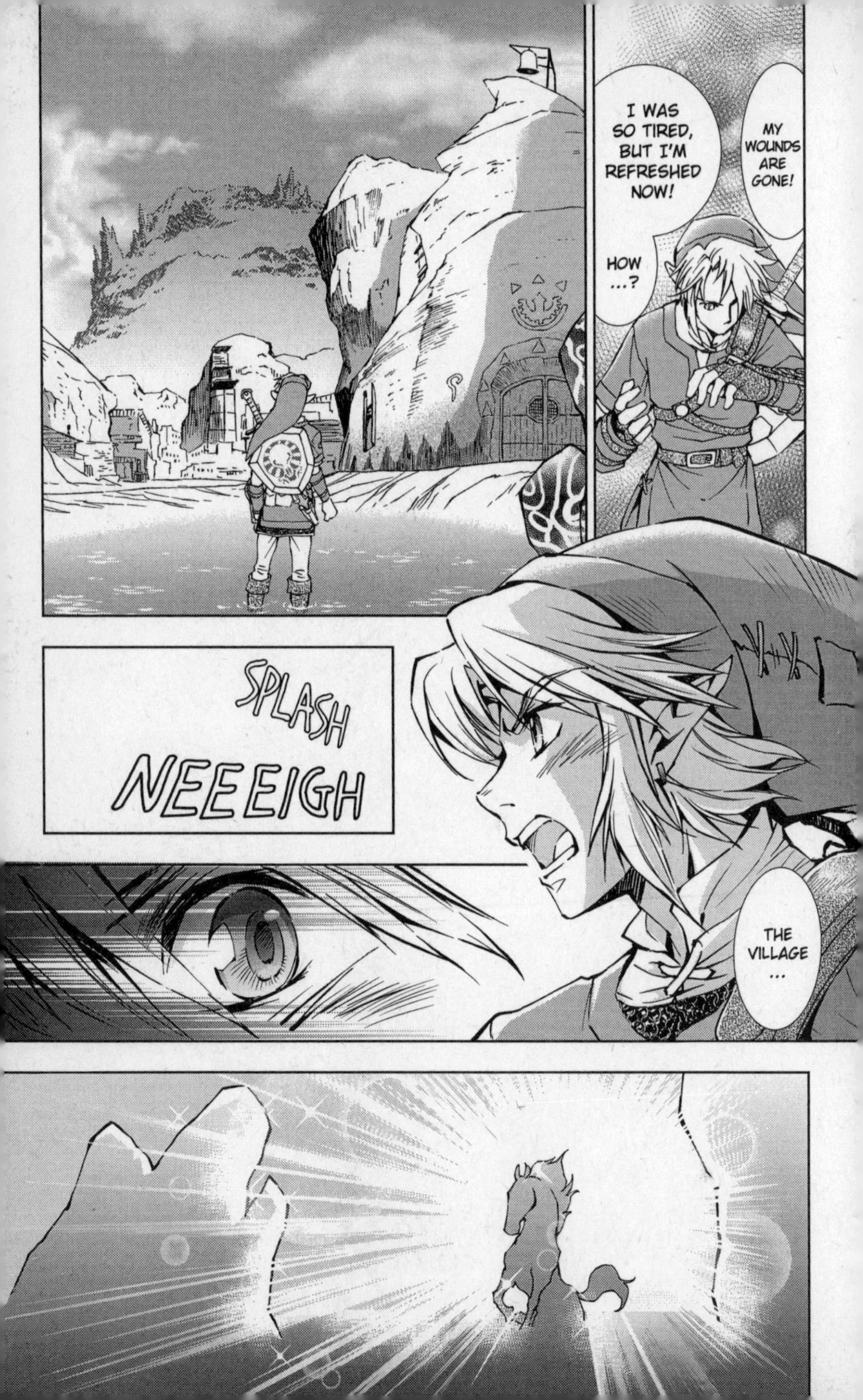
MY WOUNDS ARE GONE!
I WAS SO TIRED, BUT I'M REFRESHED NOW!
HOW ...?
THE VILLAGE ...
SPLASH
NEEEIGH

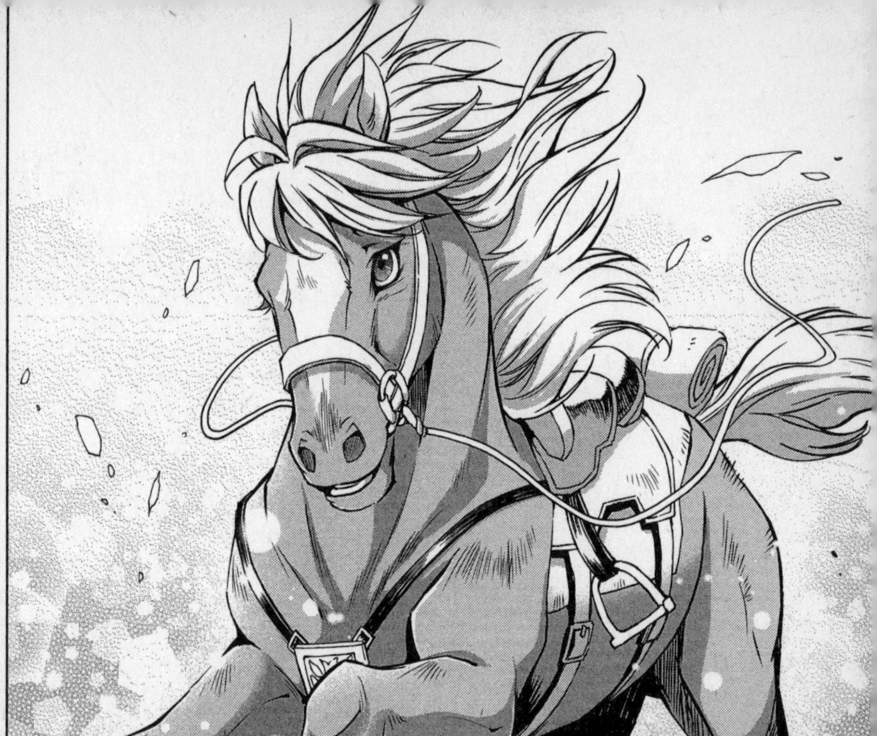
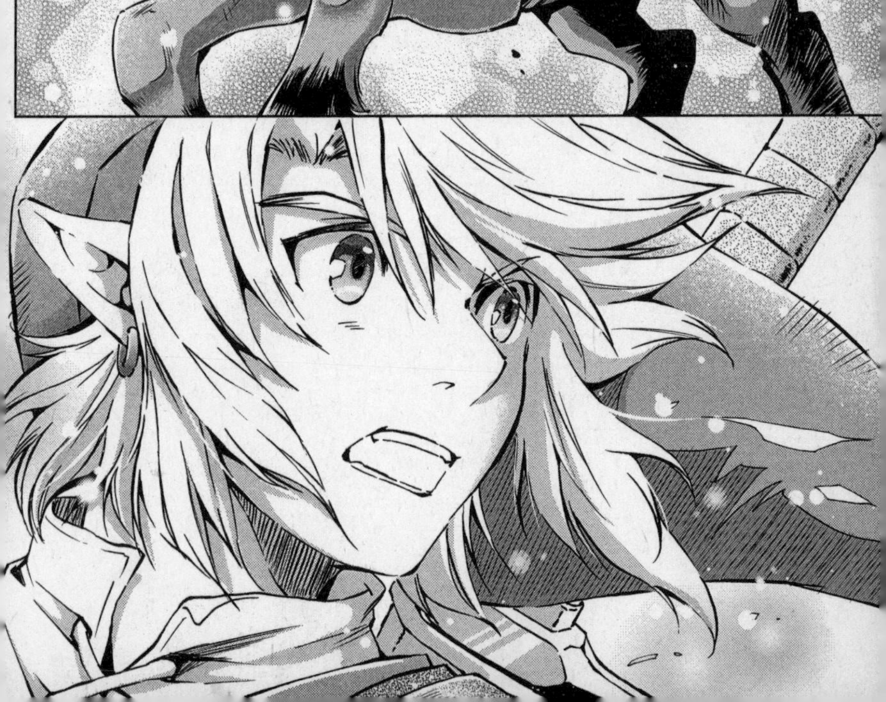

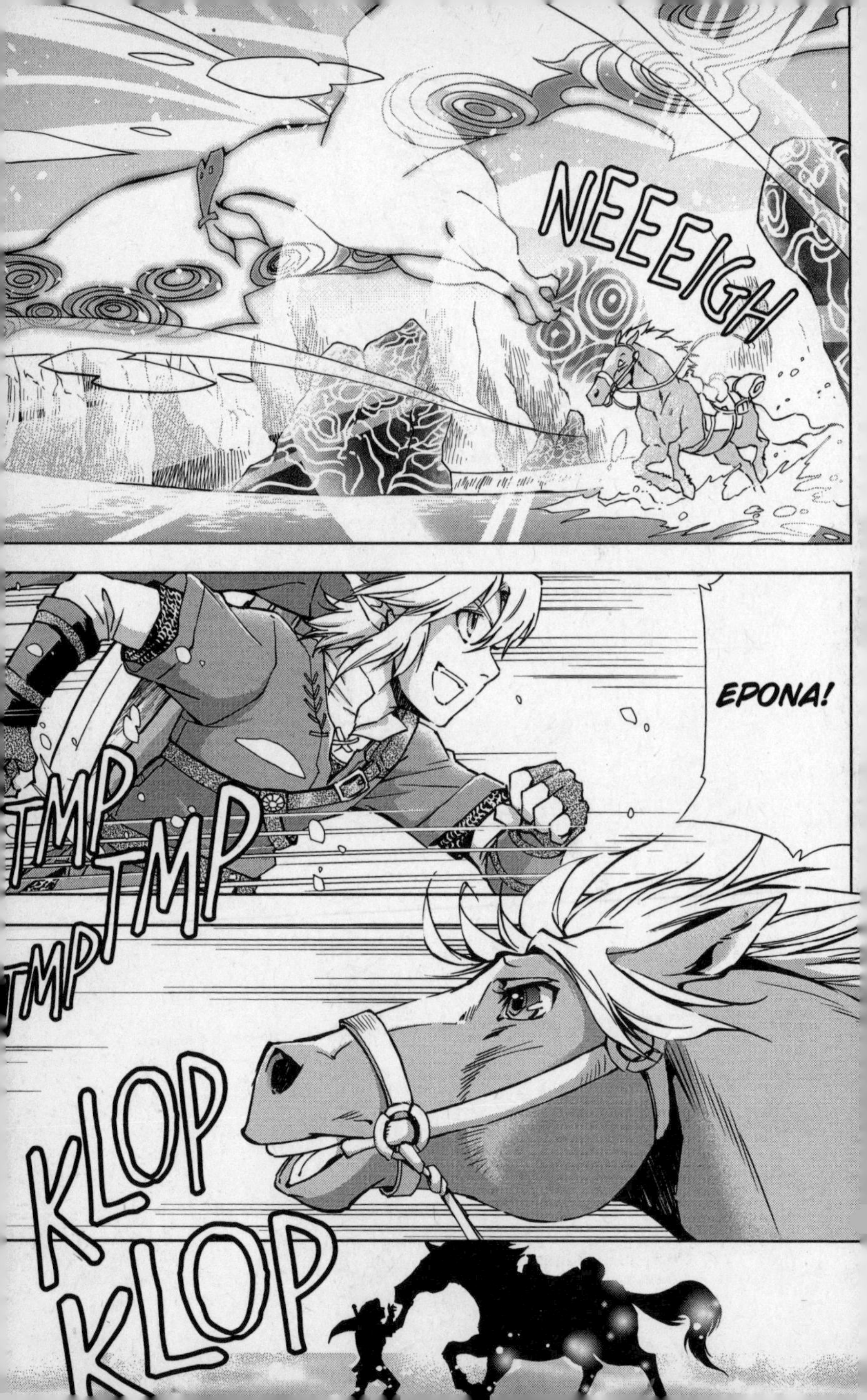
NEEEIGH
EPONA!
TMP TMP
TMP TMP
KLOP
KLOP

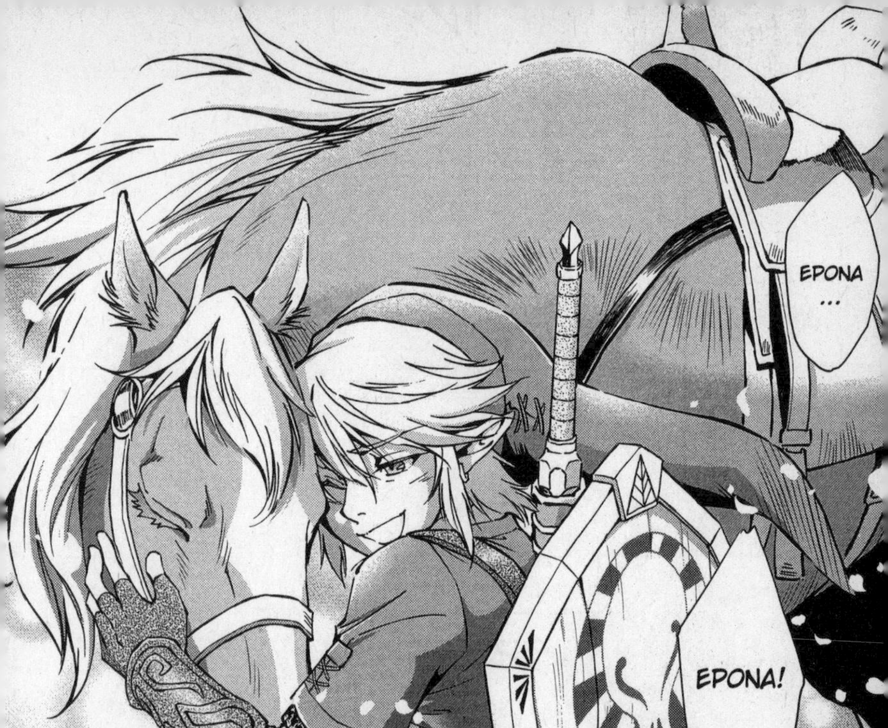
EPONA ...
EPONA!
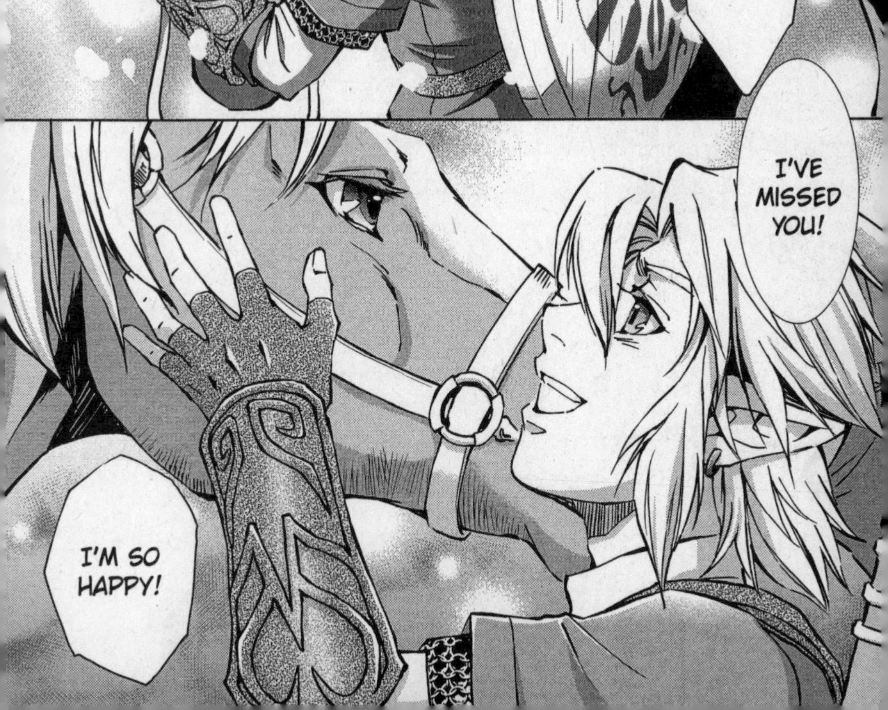
I'VE MISSED YOU!
I'M SO HAPPY!

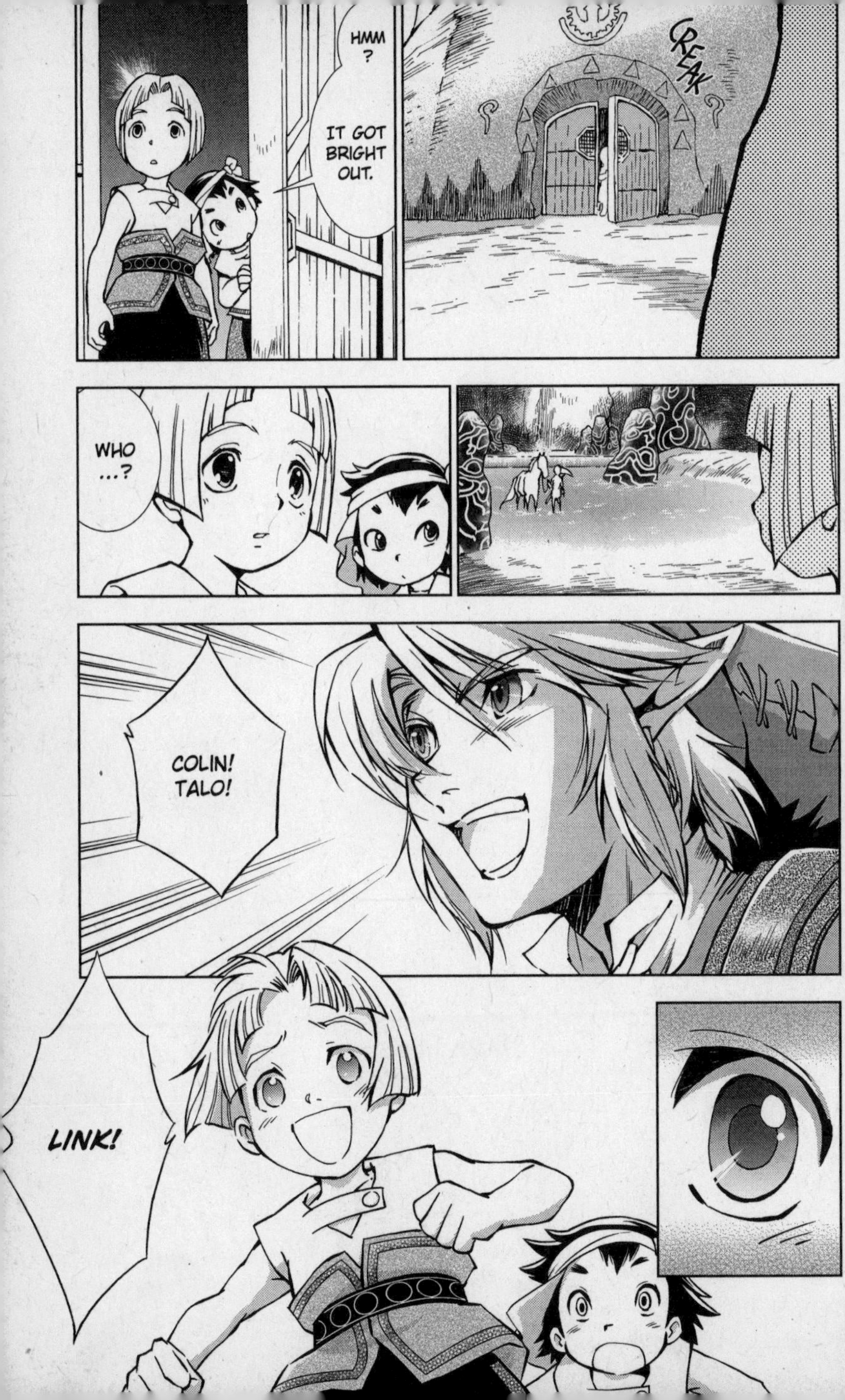
CREAK
HMM ?
IT GOT BRIGHT OUT.
WHO ...?
COLIN! TALO!
LINK!

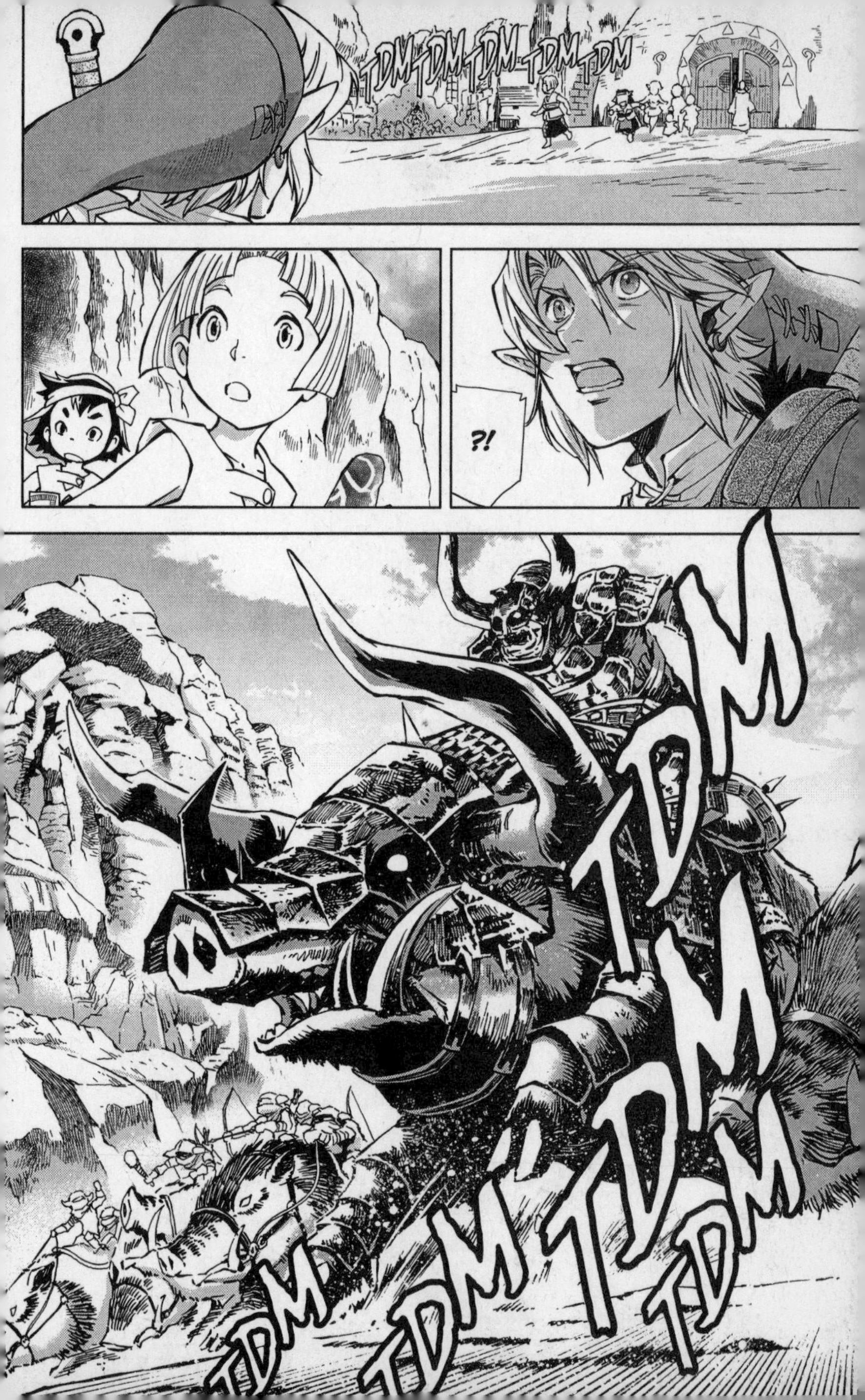

TDM TDM TDM TDM TDM
?
?
?!
TDM
TDM
TDM
TDM
TDM
TDM

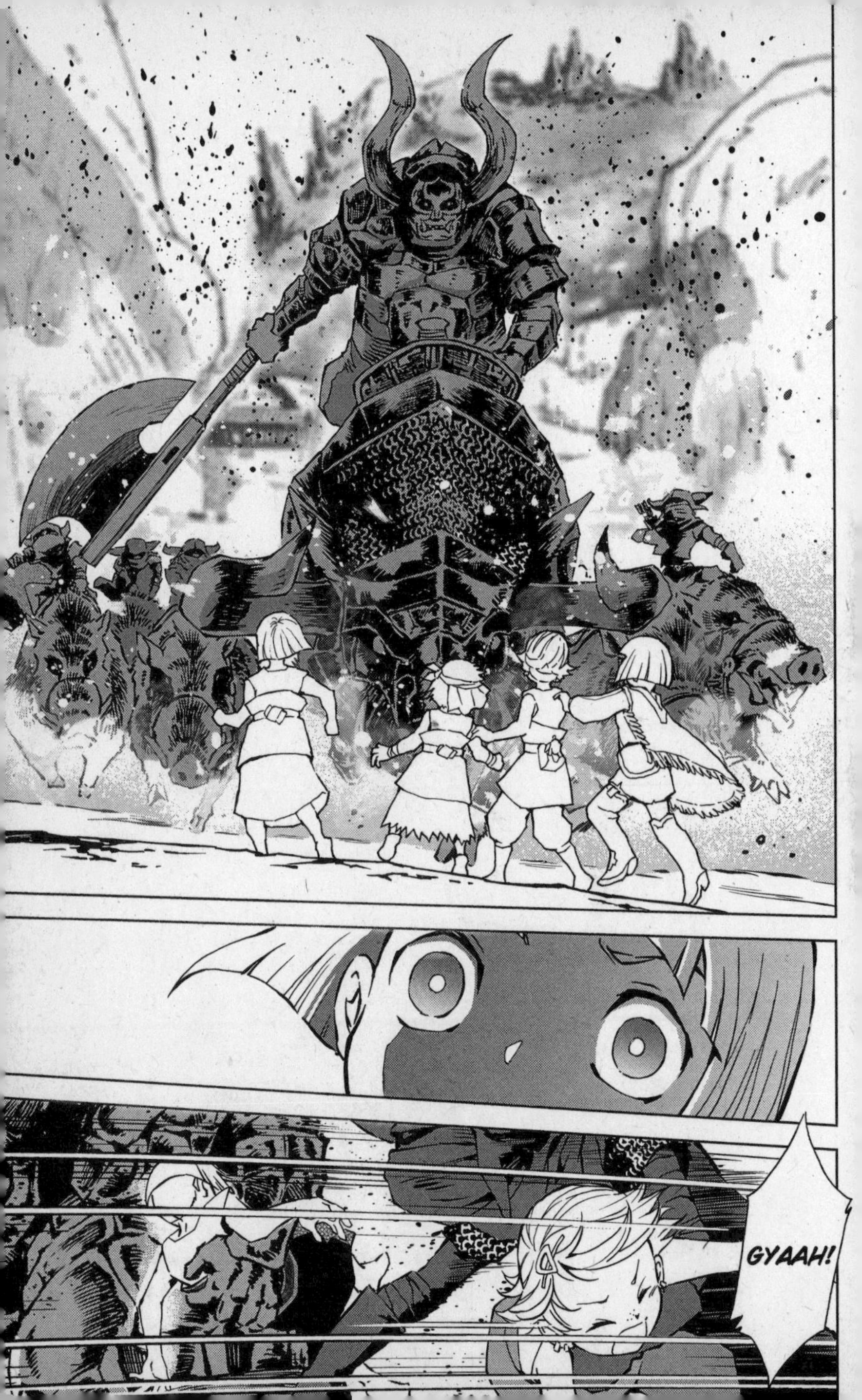
GYAAH!

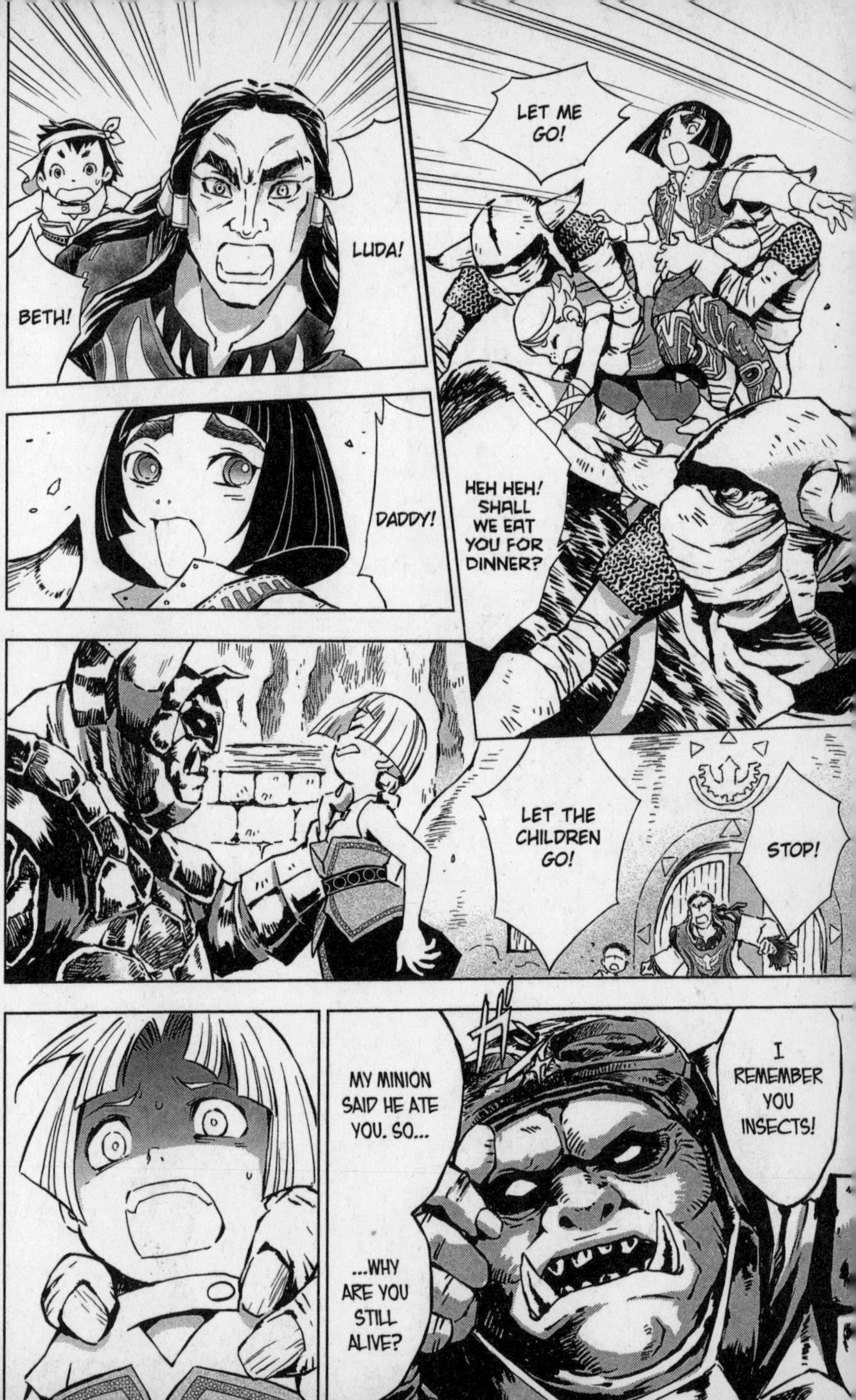
LET ME GO!
HEH HEH! SHALL WE EAT YOU FOR DINNER?
LUDA!
BETH!
DADDY!
STOP!
LET THE CHILDREN GO!
I REMEMBER YOU INSECTS!
MY MINION SAID HE ATE YOU. SO...
...WHY ARE YOU STILL ALIVE?

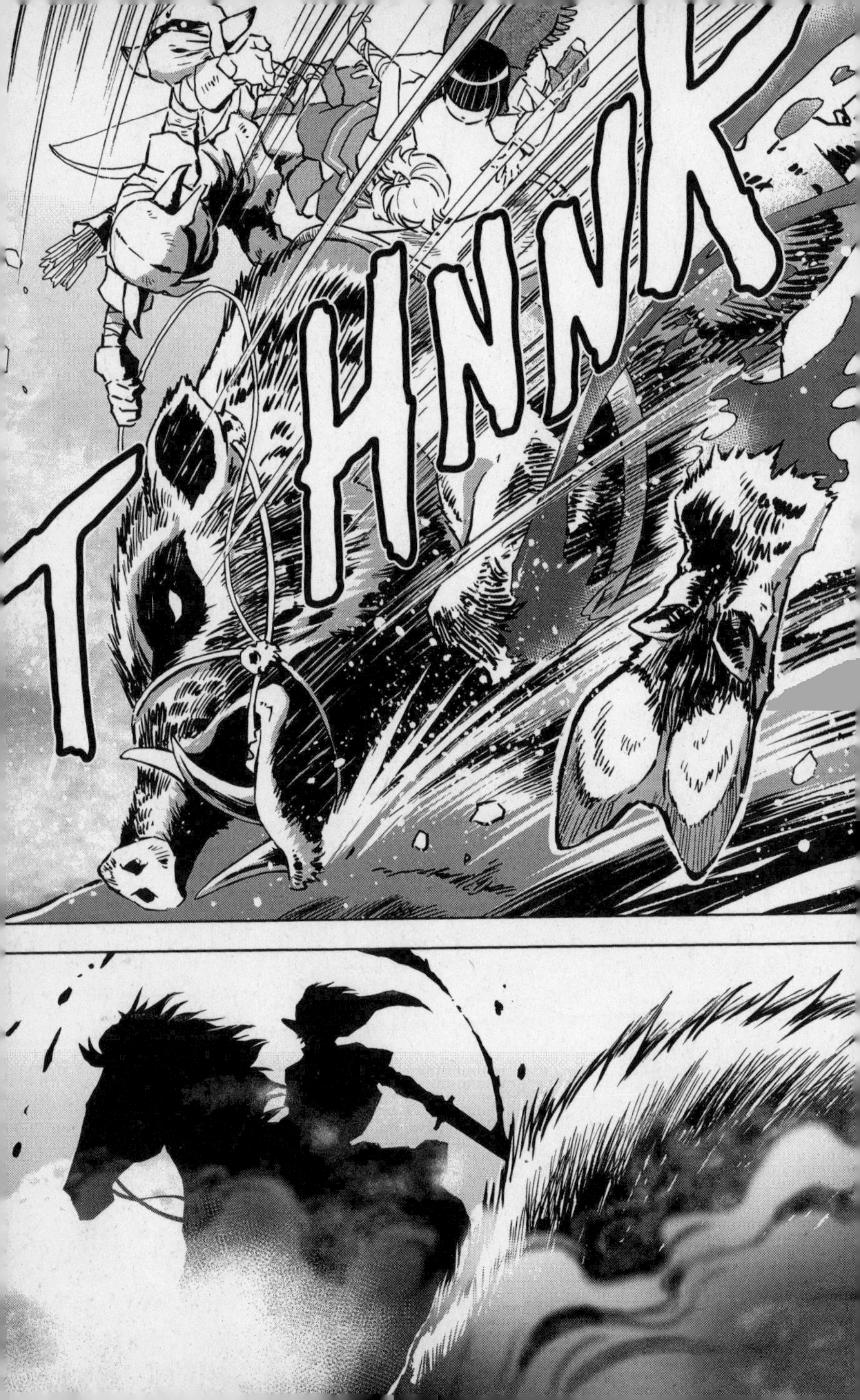
THHNNK

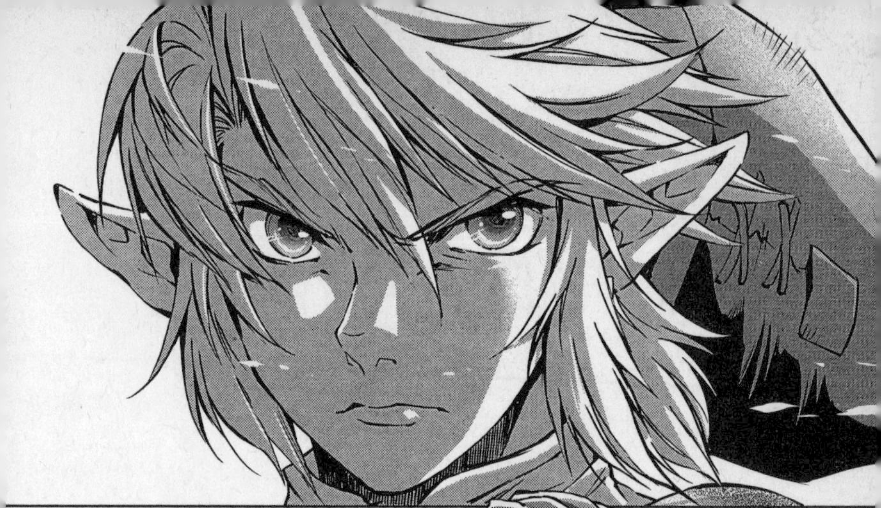
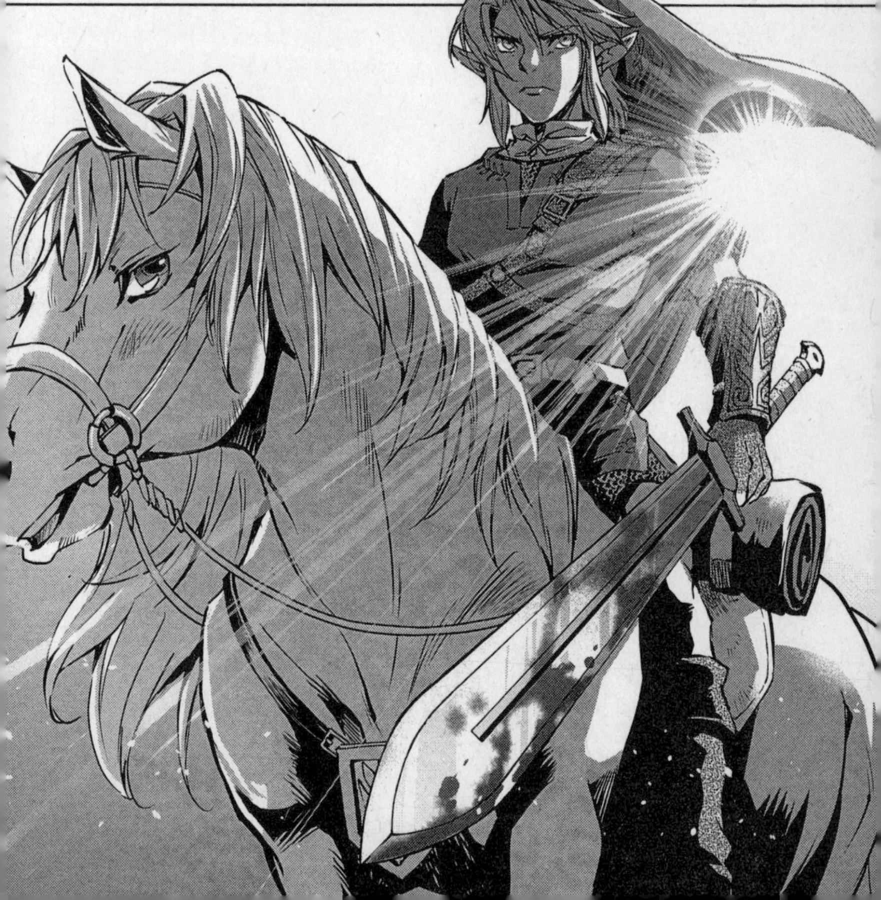

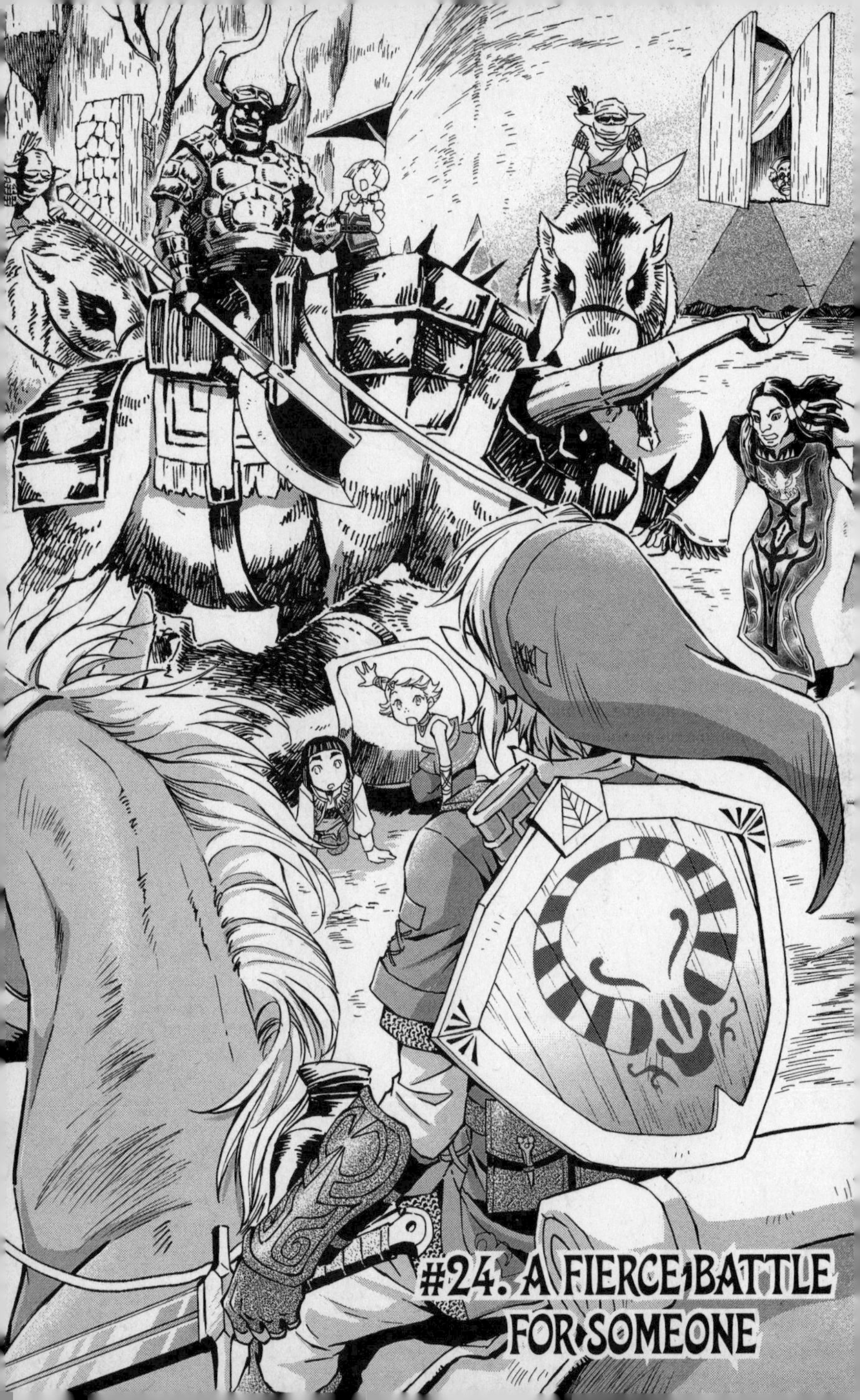
#24. A FIERCE BATTLE
FOR SOMEONE

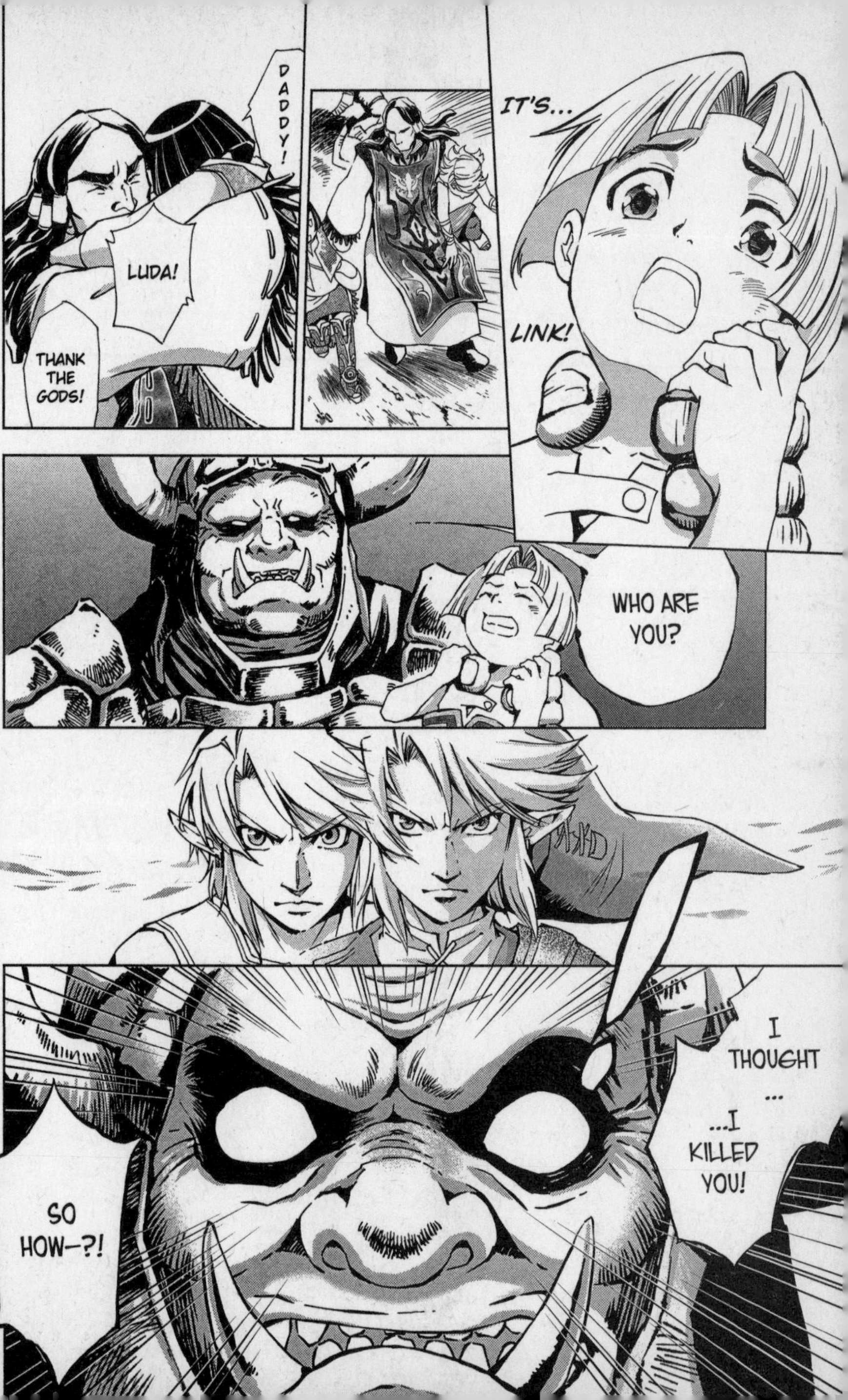
IT'S...
LINK!
DADDY!
LUDA!
THANK THE GODS!
WHO ARE YOU?
I THOUGHT...
...I KILLED YOU!
SO HOW—?!

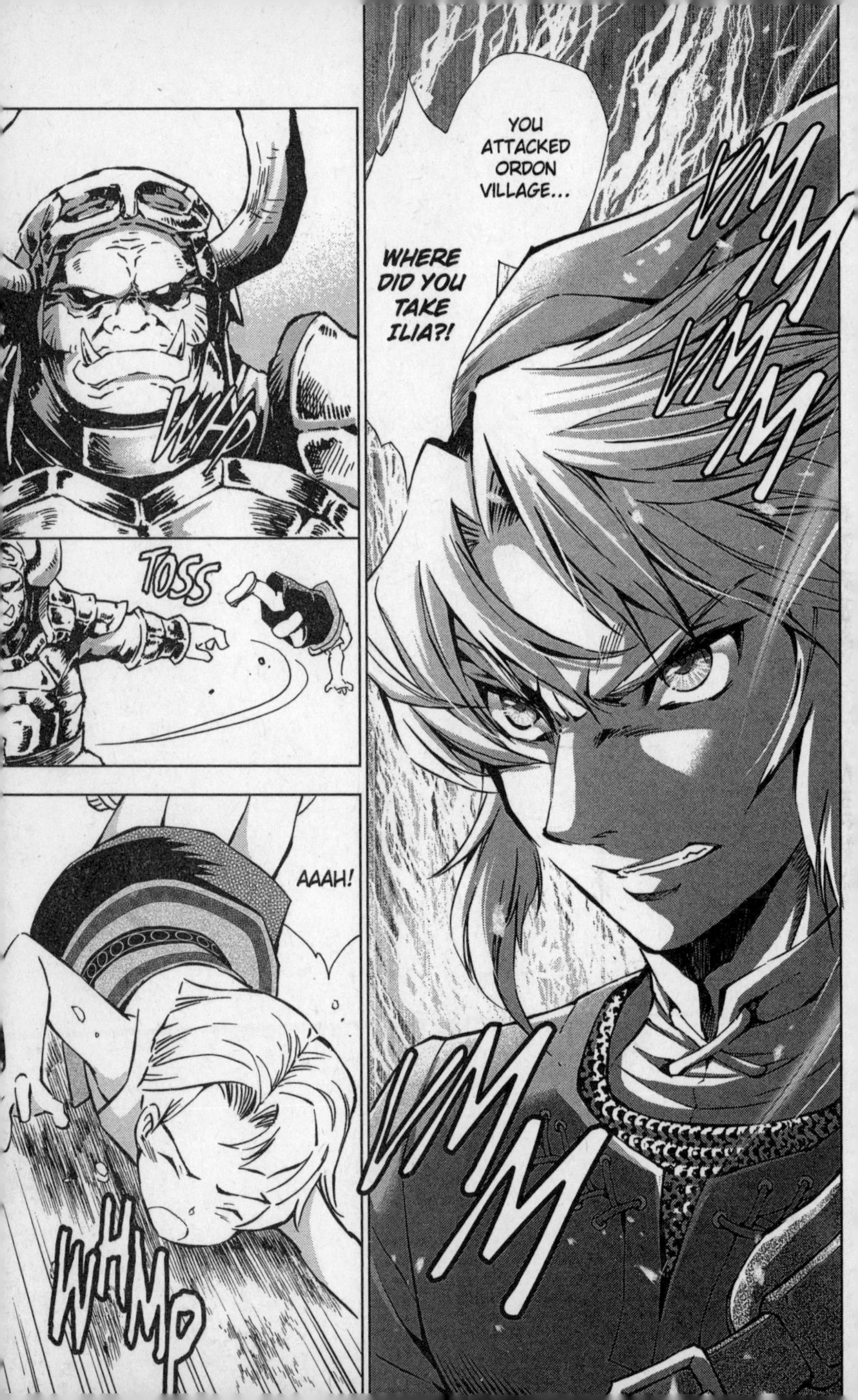
YOU ATTACKED ORDON VILLAGE...
WHERE DID YOU TAKE ILIA?!
VMMM
VMMM
VMMM
WHP
TOSS
AAAH!
WHMP

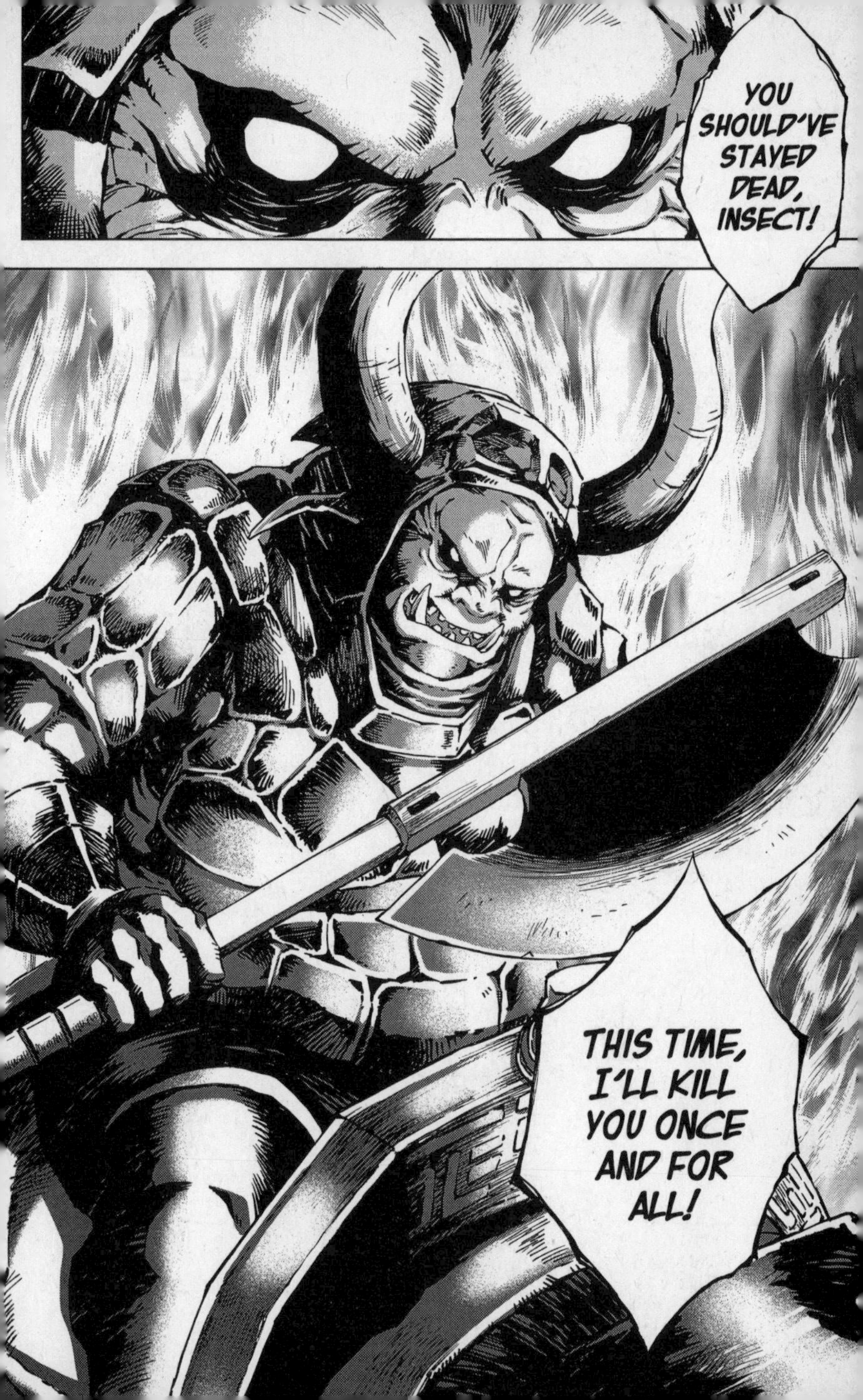
YOU SHOULD'VE STAYED DEAD, INSECT!
THIS TIME, I'LL KILL YOU ONCE AND FOR ALL!

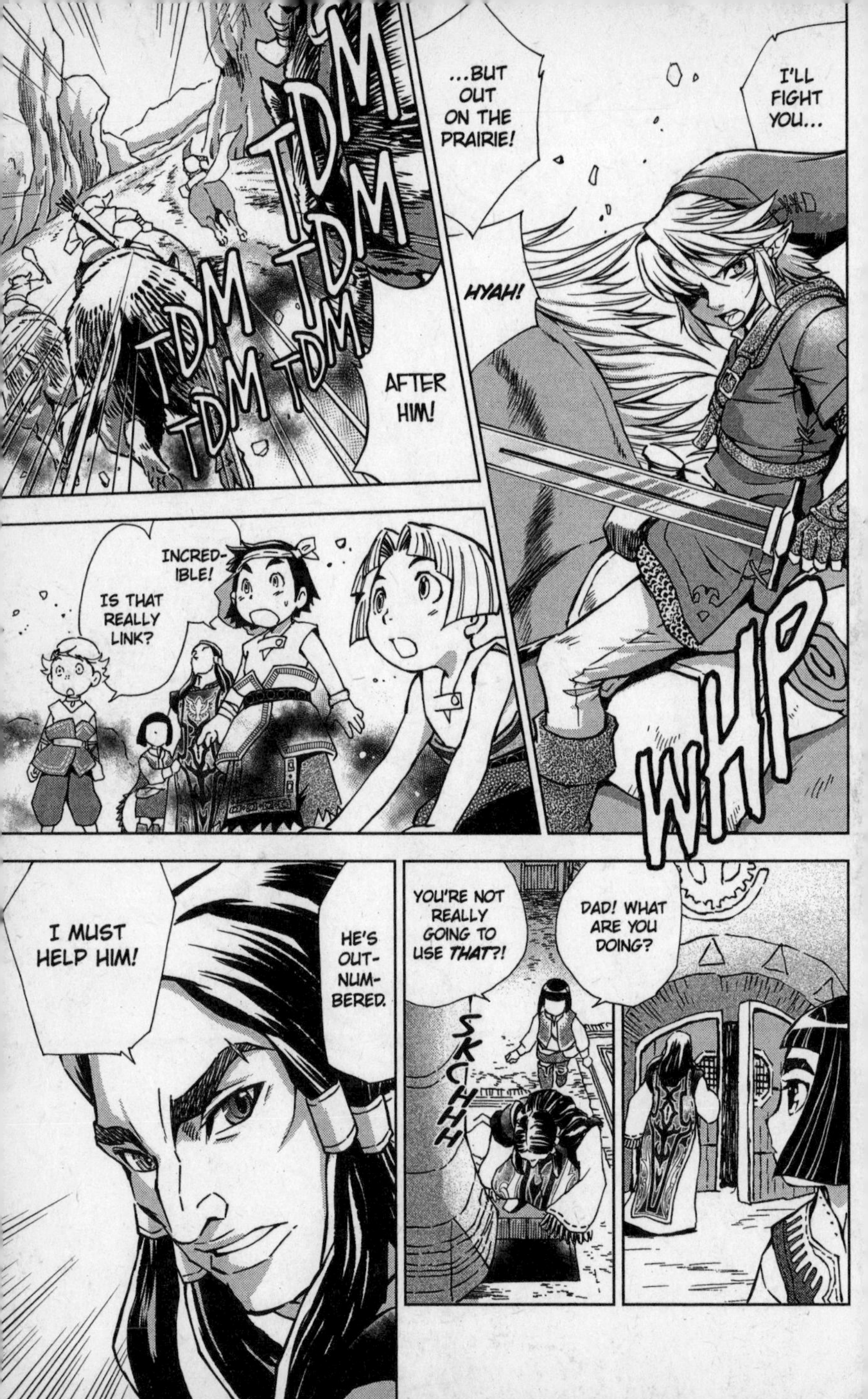
I'LL FIGHT YOU...
...BUT OUT ON THE PRAIRIE!
HYAH!
WHP
AFTER HIM!
TDM TDM TDM TDM TDM TDM TDM
INCRED-IBLE!
IS THAT REALLY LINK?
DAD! WHAT ARE YOU DOING?
YOU'RE NOT REALLY GOING TO USE *THAT*?!
SKCHHH
HE'S OUT-NUM-BERED.
I MUST HELP HIM!

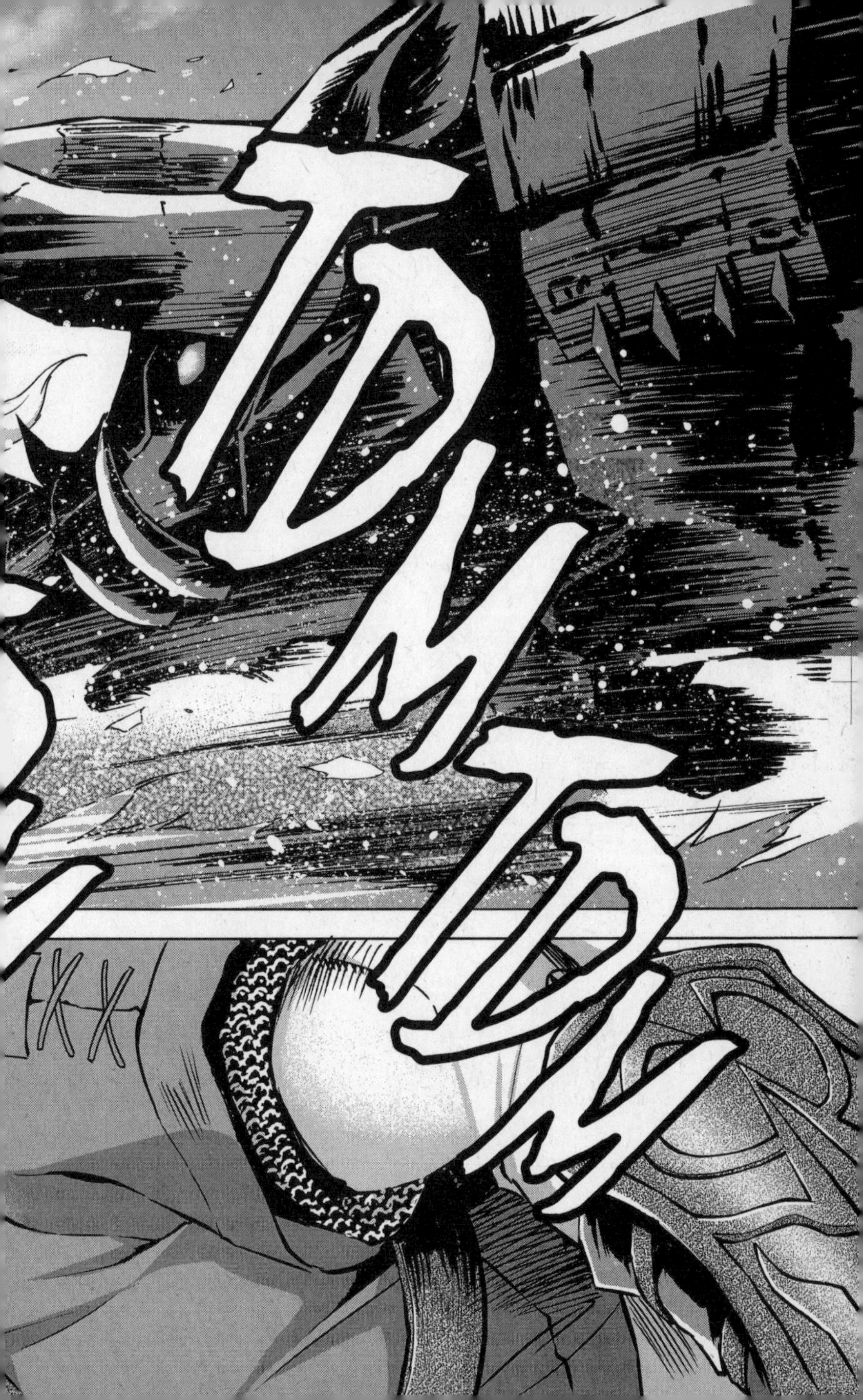

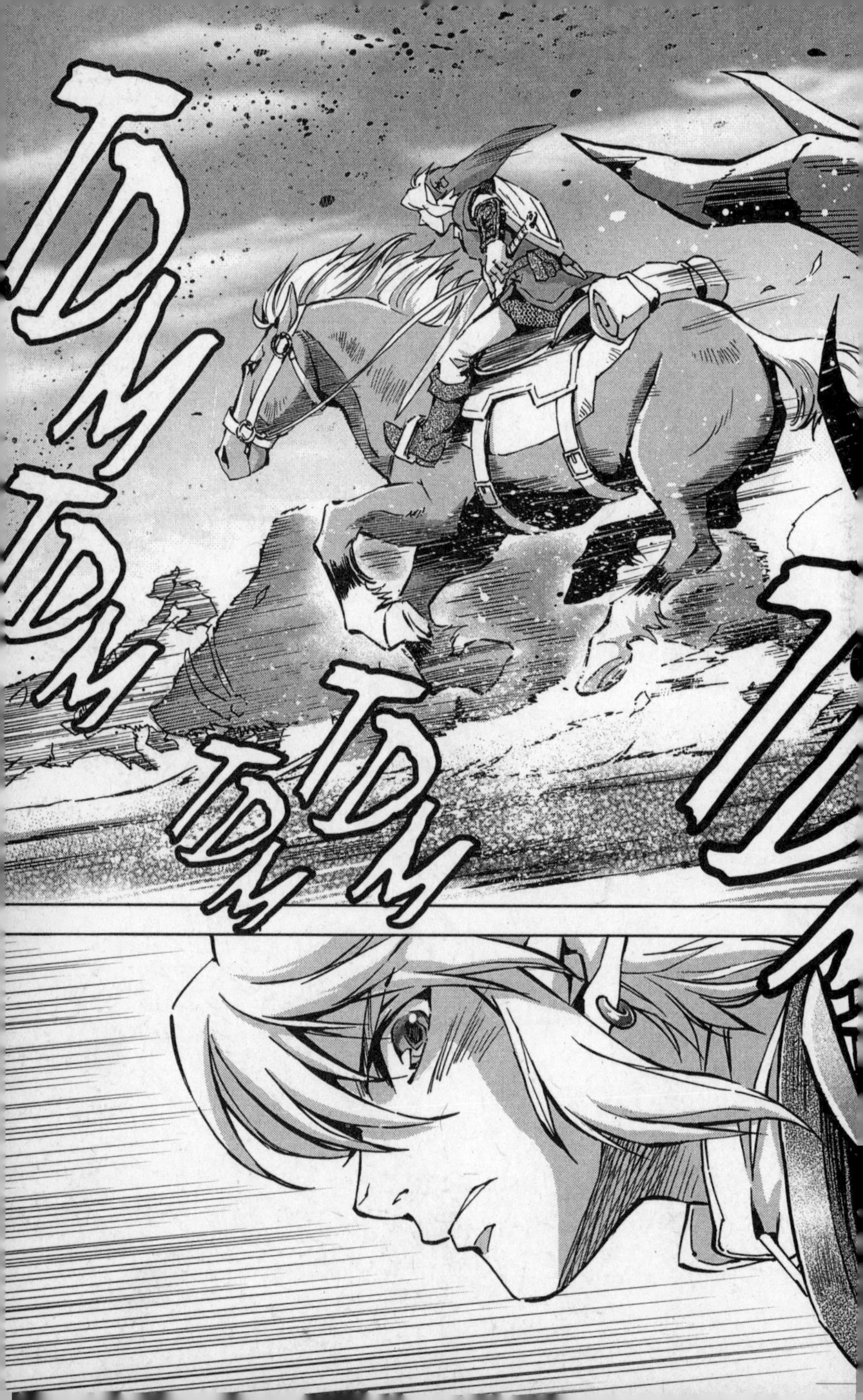
TDM
TDM
TDM
TDM

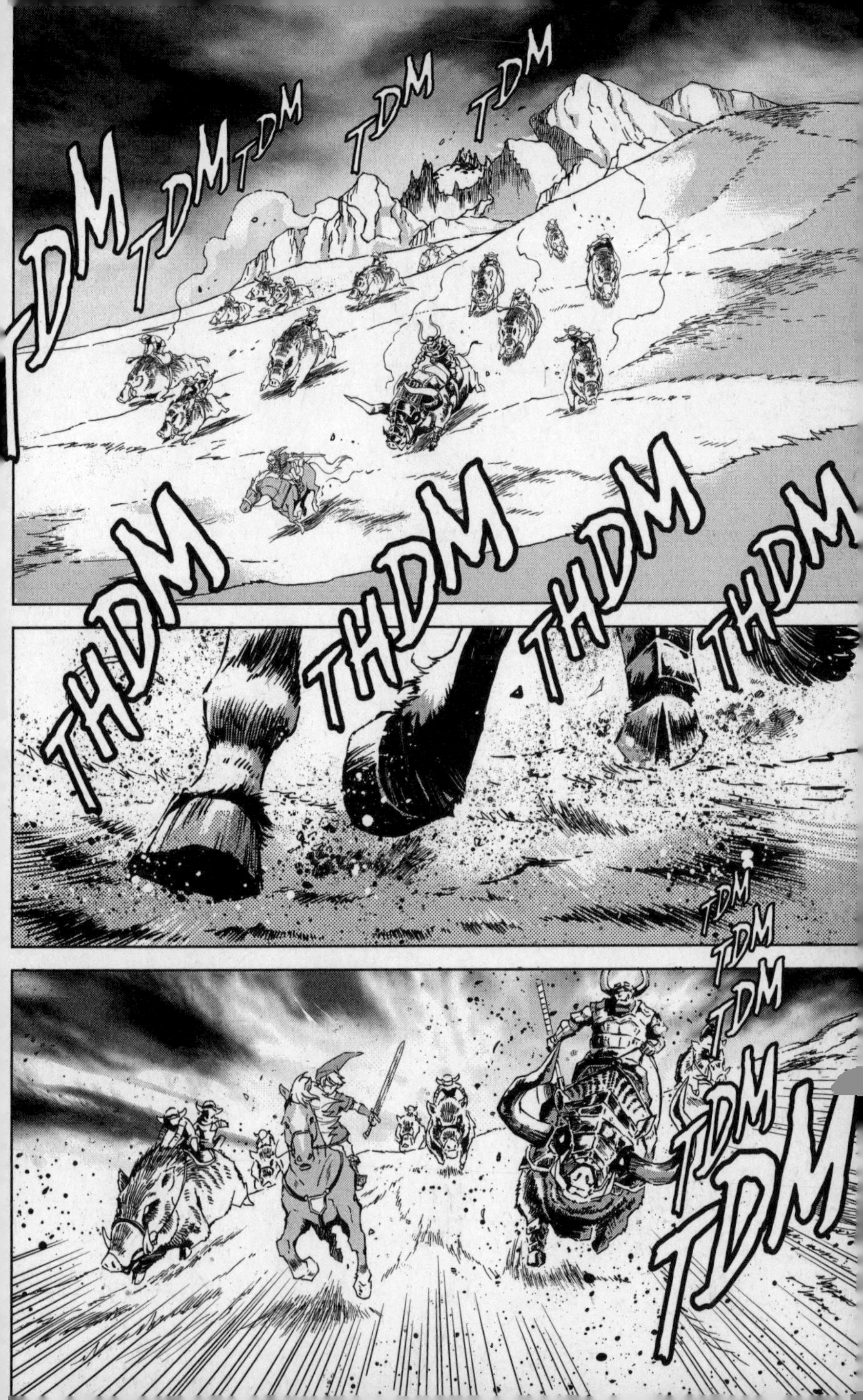
TDM
TDM
TDM
TDM
TDM
THDM
THDM
THDM
THDM
TDM
TDM
TDM
TDM
TDM

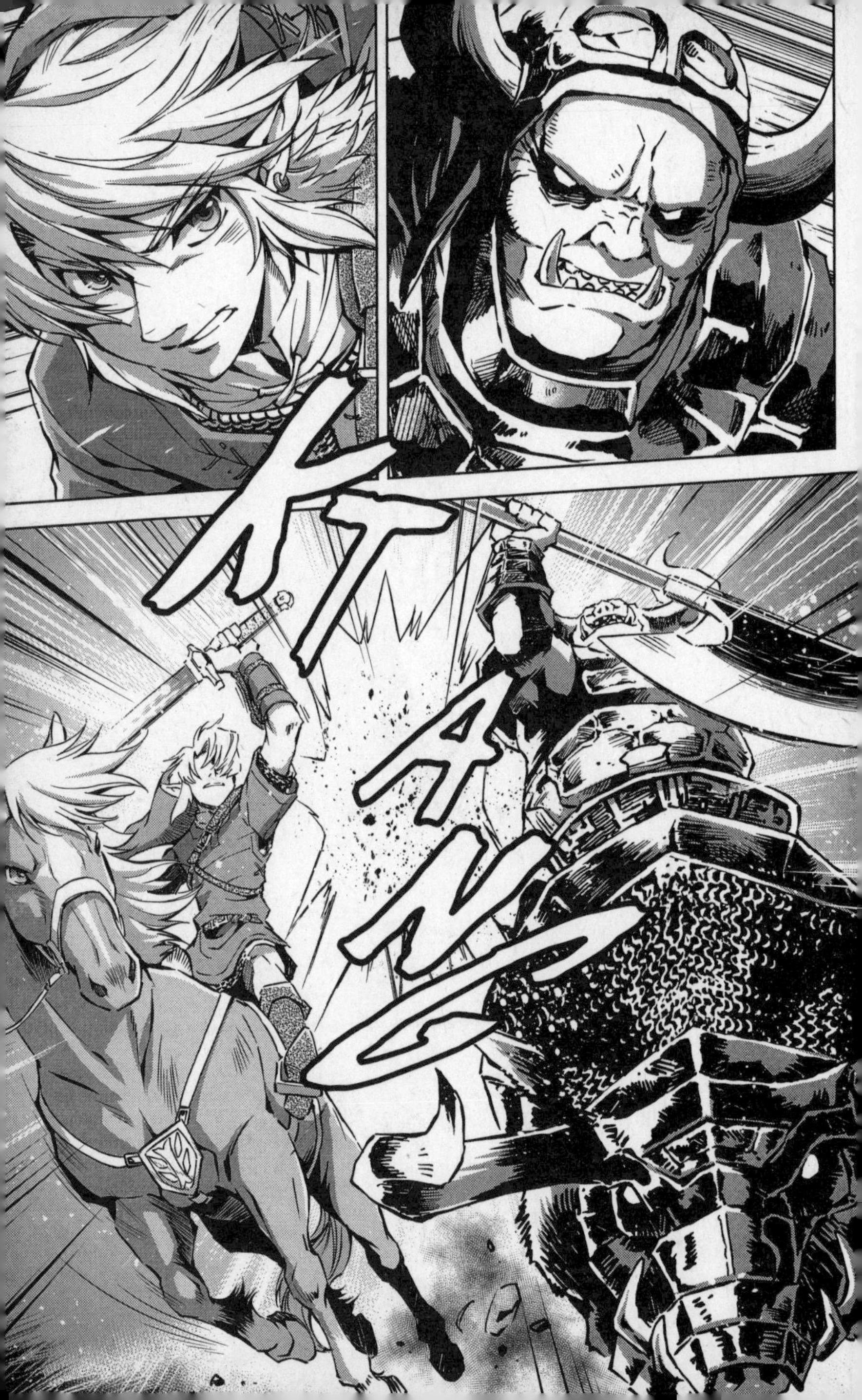
KTANG

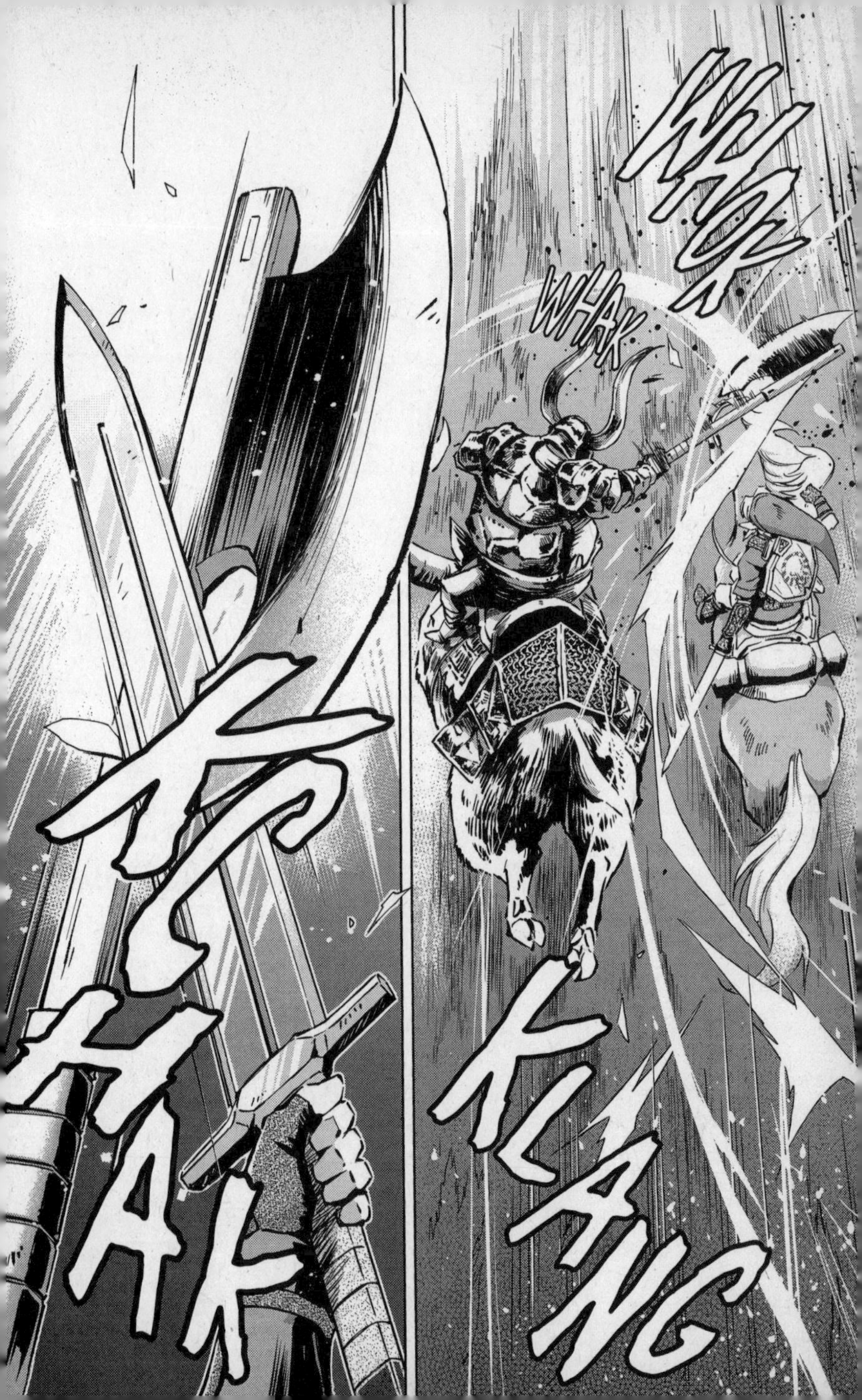
WHOK
WHAK
KLANG
KCHAK

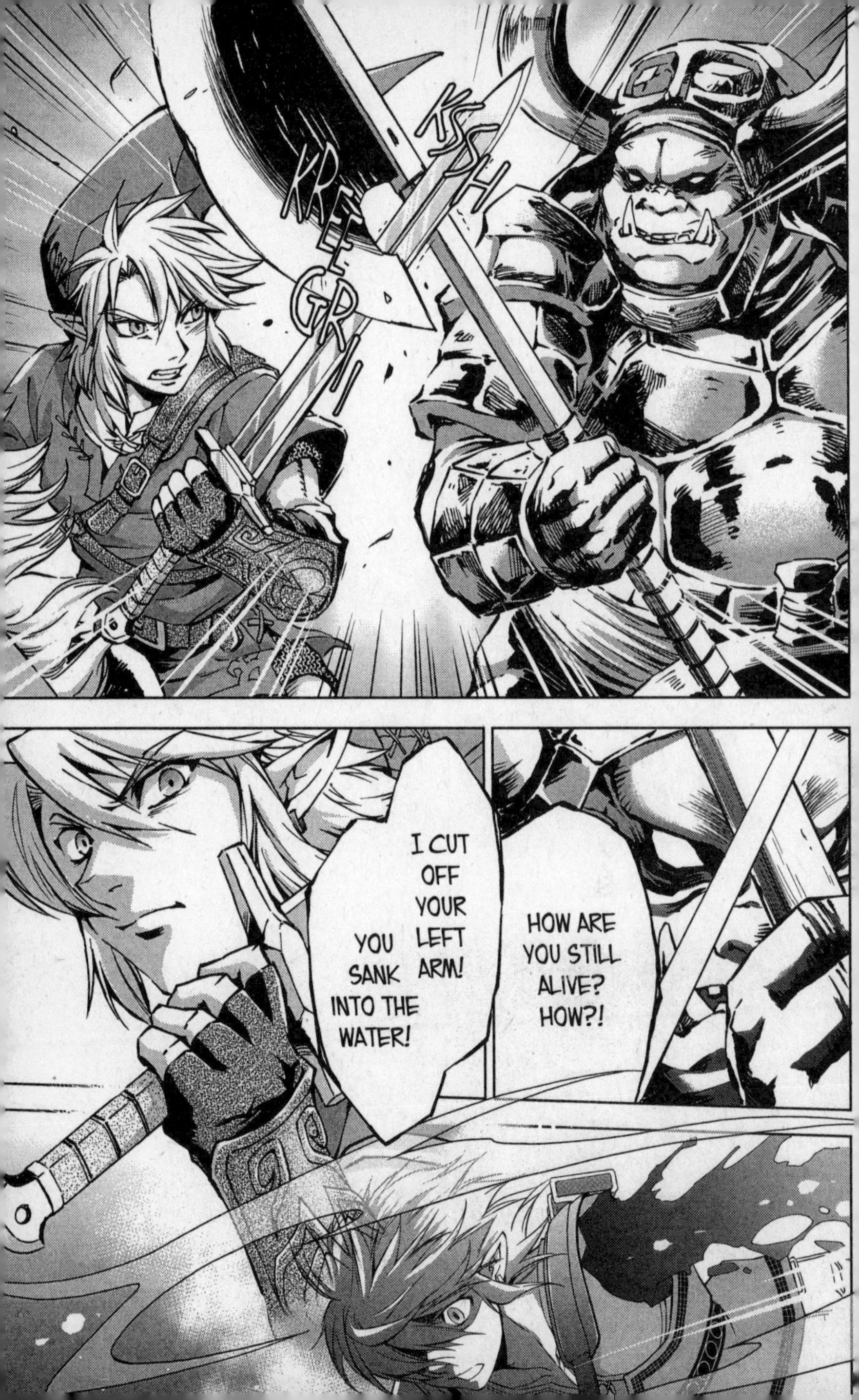
KSSH
KREE
GRII
I CUT OFF YOUR LEFT ARM!
YOU SANK INTO THE WATER!
HOW ARE YOU STILL ALIVE? HOW?!

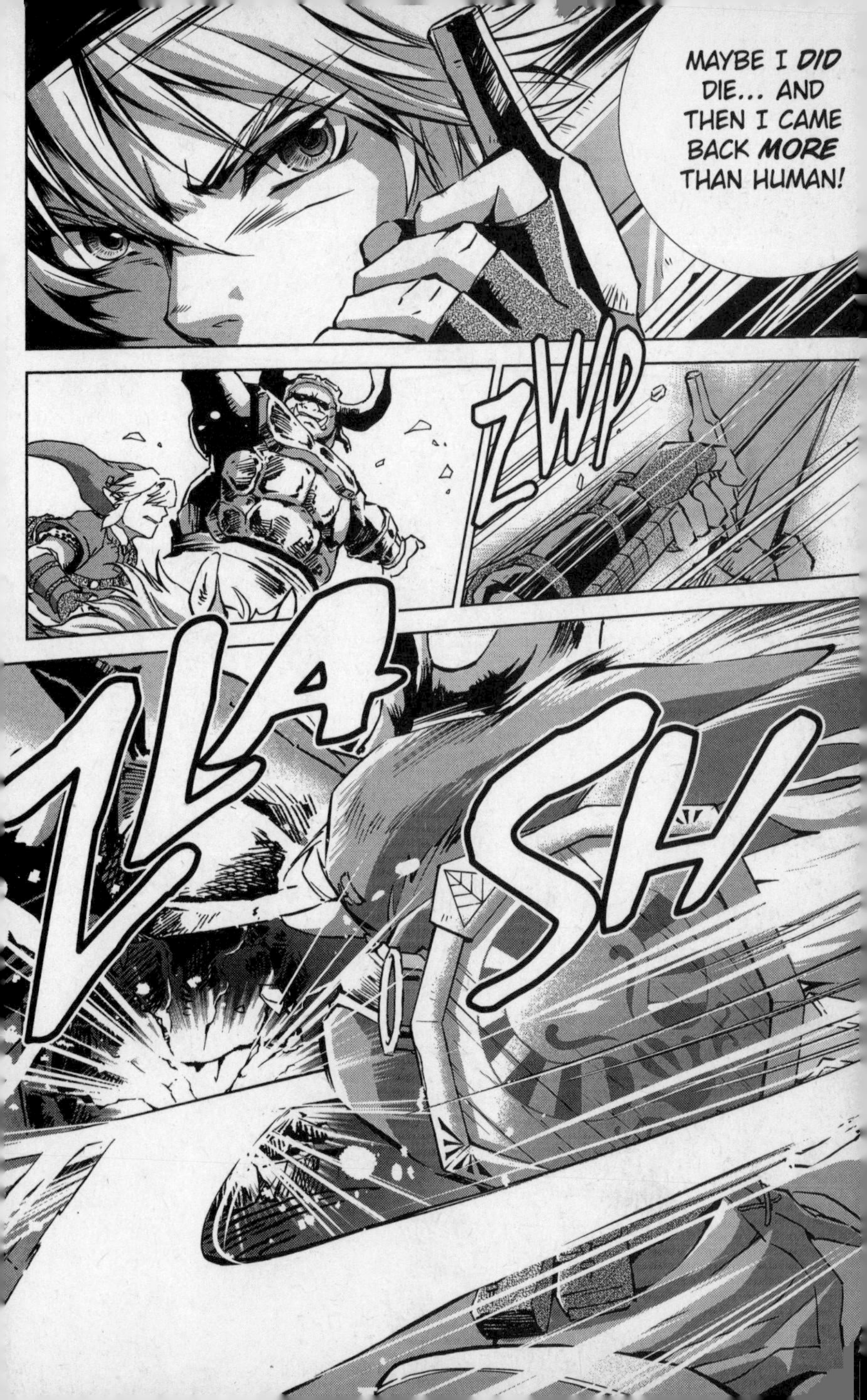
MAYBE I *DID* DIE... AND THEN I CAME BACK *MORE* THAN HUMAN!
ZWIP
ZLASH

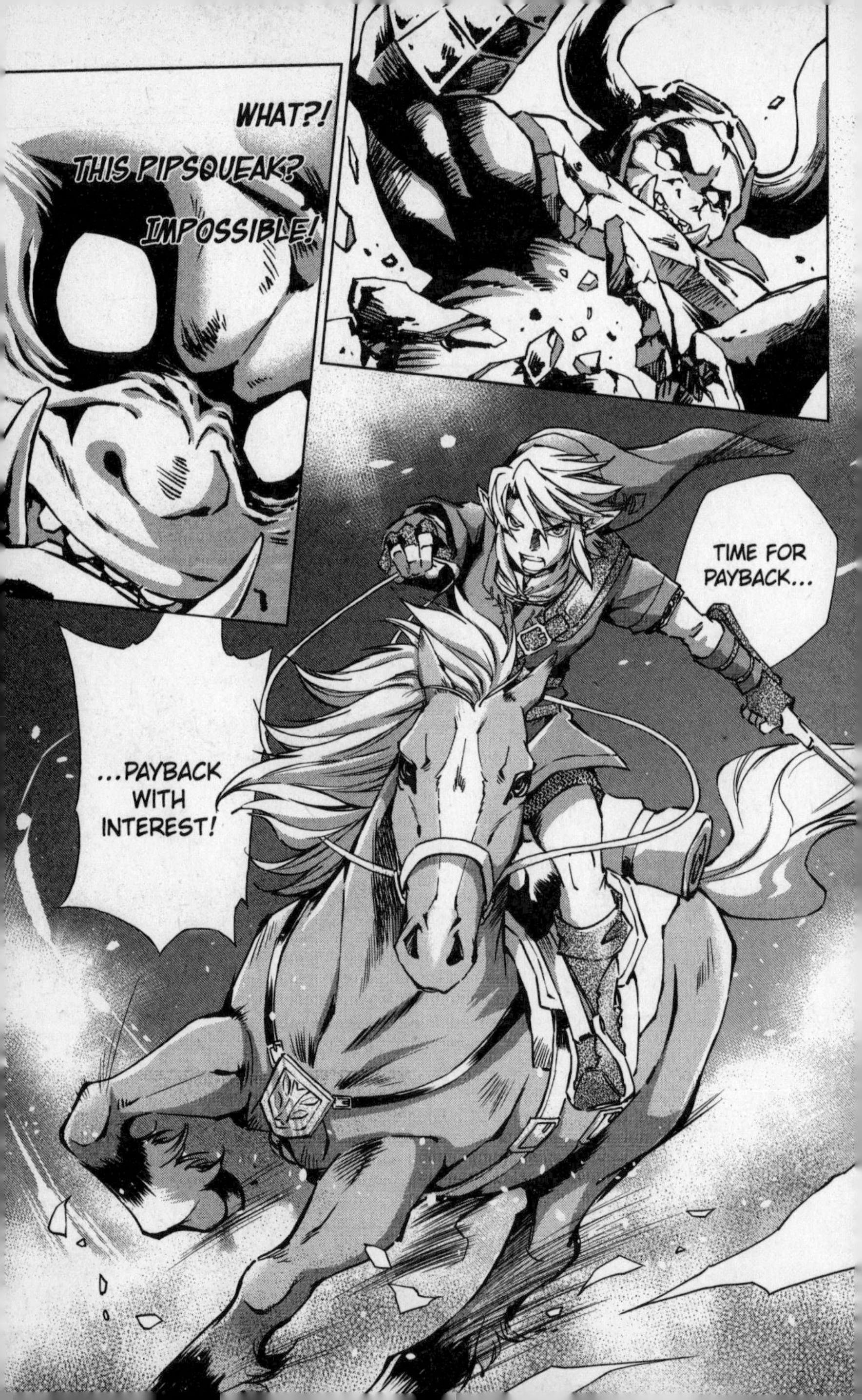
WHAT?!
THIS PIPSQUEAK?
IMPOSSIBLE!
TIME FOR PAYBACK...
...PAYBACK WITH INTEREST!

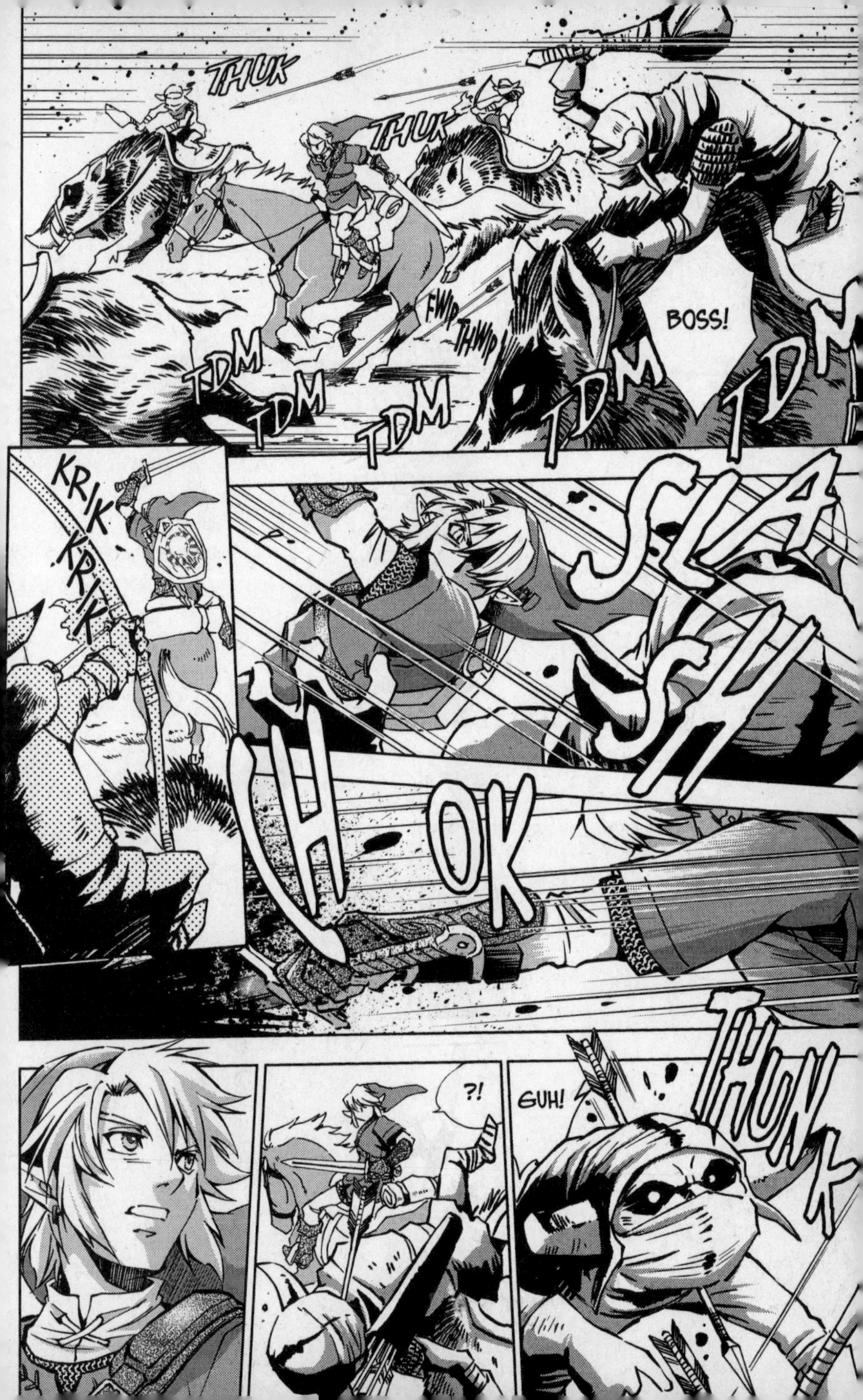
THUK
THUK
FWIP
THWIP
BOSS!
TDM
TDM
TDM
TDM
TDM
SLASH
H OK
KRIK
KRIK
KRIK
THUNK
GUH!
?!

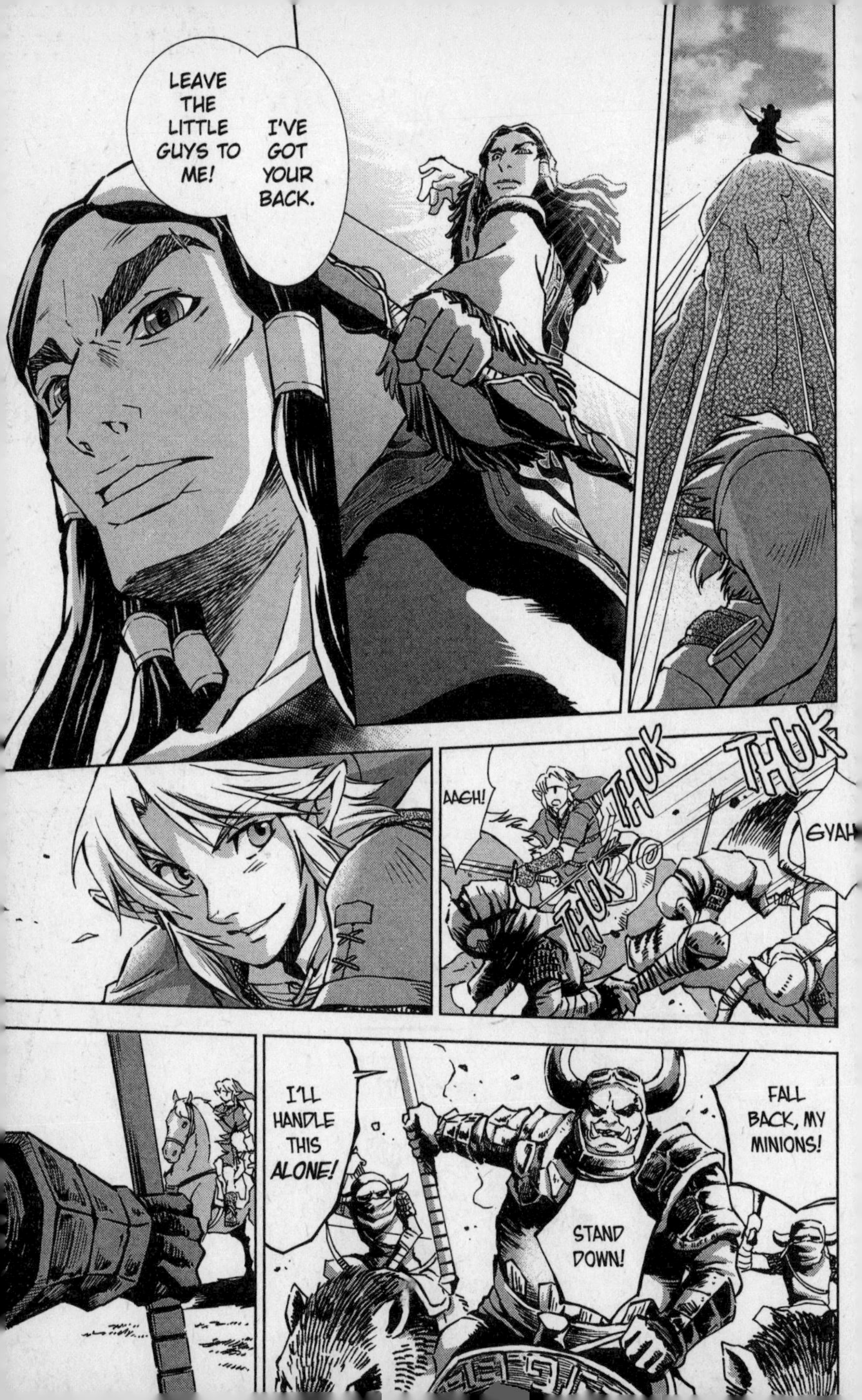
I'VE GOT YOUR BACK.
LEAVE THE LITTLE GUYS TO ME!
THUK
GYAH
THUK
AAGH!
THUK
FALL BACK, MY MINIONS!
STAND DOWN!
I'LL HANDLE THIS ALONE!

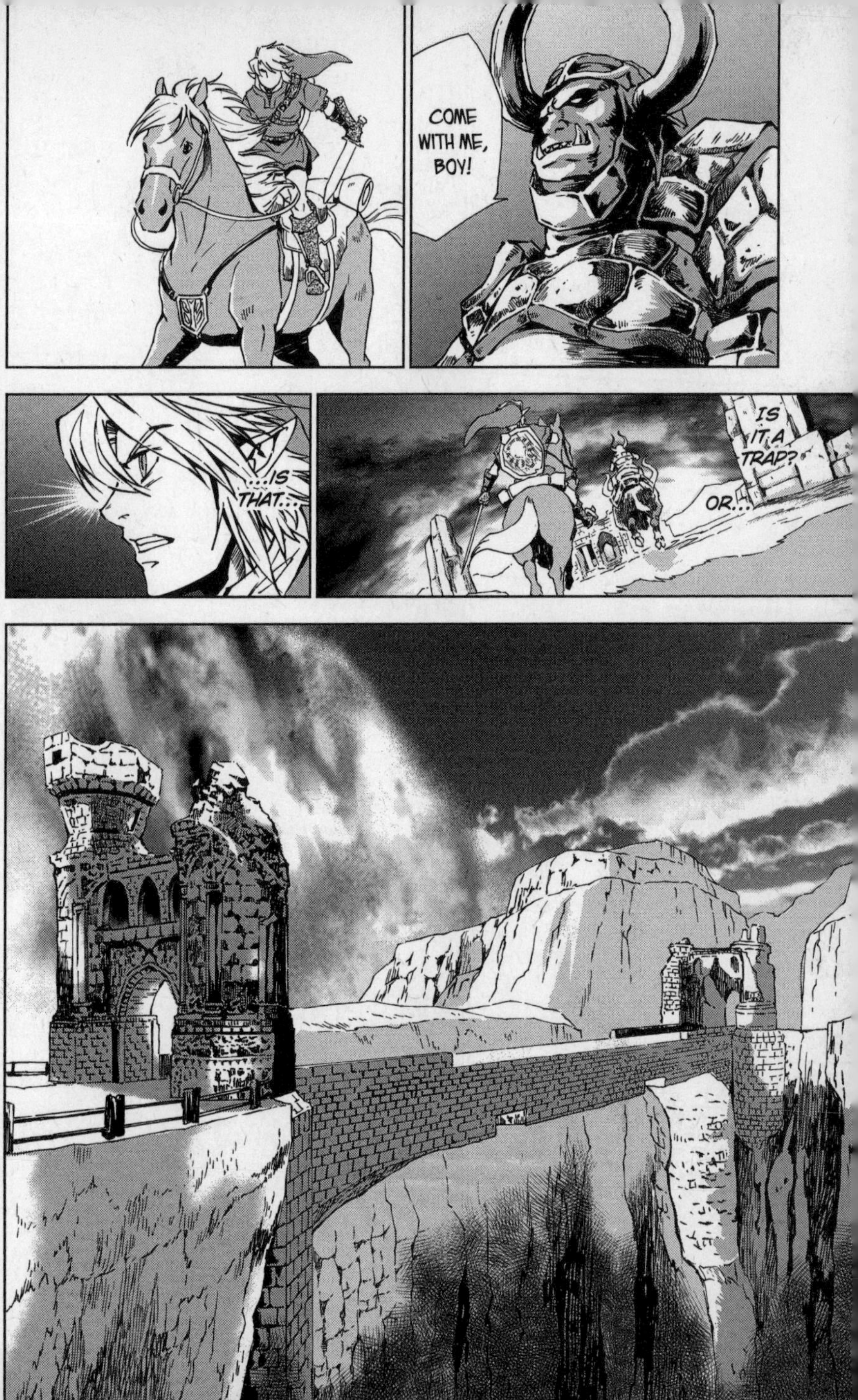
COME WITH ME, BOY!
IS IT A TRAP?
OR...
...IS THAT...

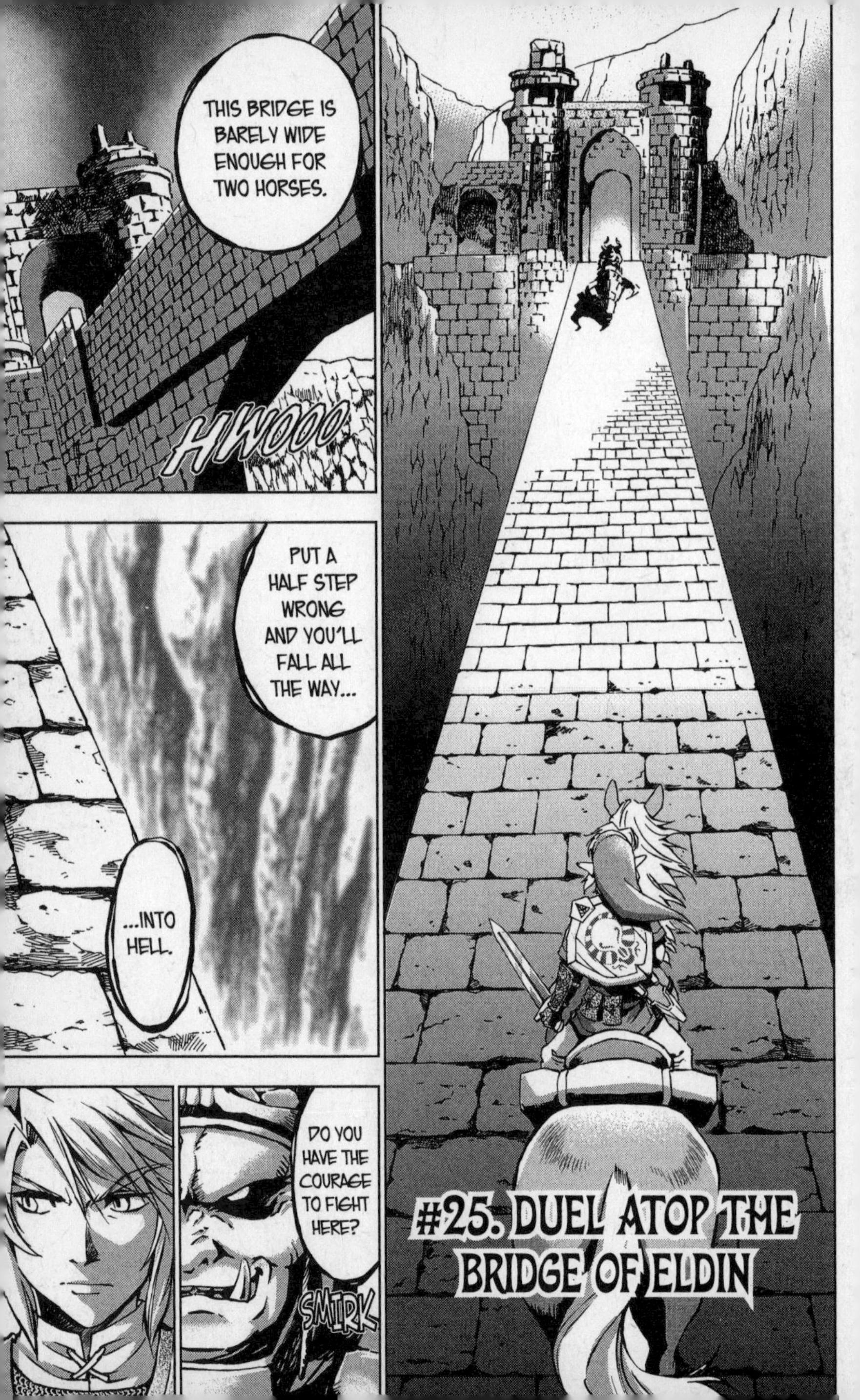
#25. DUEL ATOP THE BRIDGE OF ELDIN
THIS BRIDGE IS BARELY WIDE ENOUGH FOR TWO HORSES.
HWOOO
PUT A HALF STEP WRONG AND YOU'LL FALL ALL THE WAY...
...INTO HELL.
DO YOU HAVE THE COURAGE TO FIGHT HERE?
SMIRK

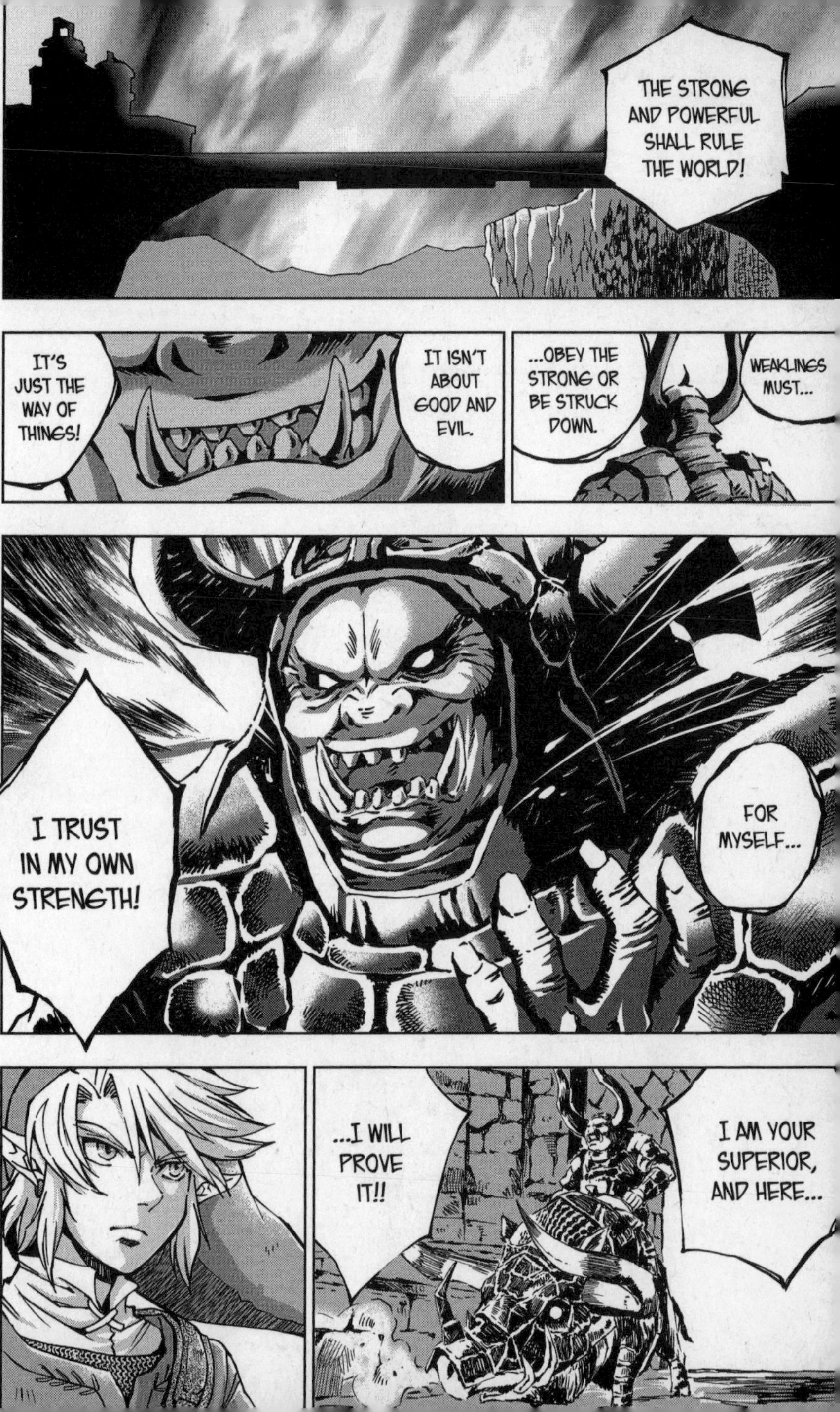
THE STRONG AND POWERFUL SHALL RULE THE WORLD!
WEAKLINGS MUST...
...OBEY THE STRONG OR BE STRUCK DOWN.
IT ISN'T ABOUT GOOD AND EVIL.
IT'S JUST THE WAY OF THINGS!
FOR MYSELF...
I TRUST IN MY OWN STRENGTH!
I AM YOUR SUPERIOR, AND HERE...
...I WILL PROVE IT!!

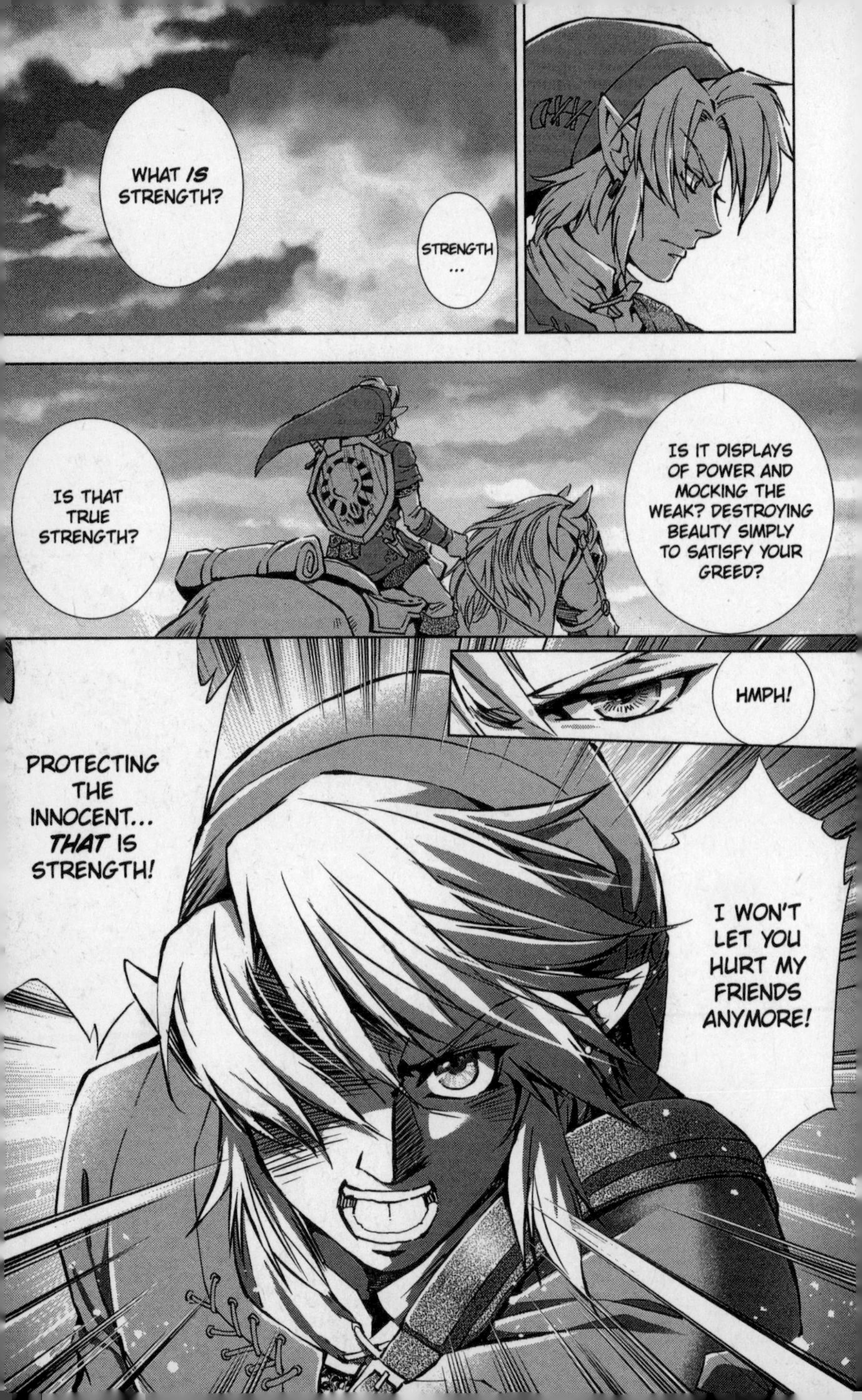
STRENGTH ...
WHAT IS STRENGTH?
IS IT DISPLAYS OF POWER AND MOCKING THE WEAK? DESTROYING BEAUTY SIMPLY TO SATISFY YOUR GREED?
IS THAT TRUE STRENGTH?
HMPH!
PROTECTING THE INNOCENT... THAT IS STRENGTH!
I WON'T LET YOU HURT MY FRIENDS ANYMORE!

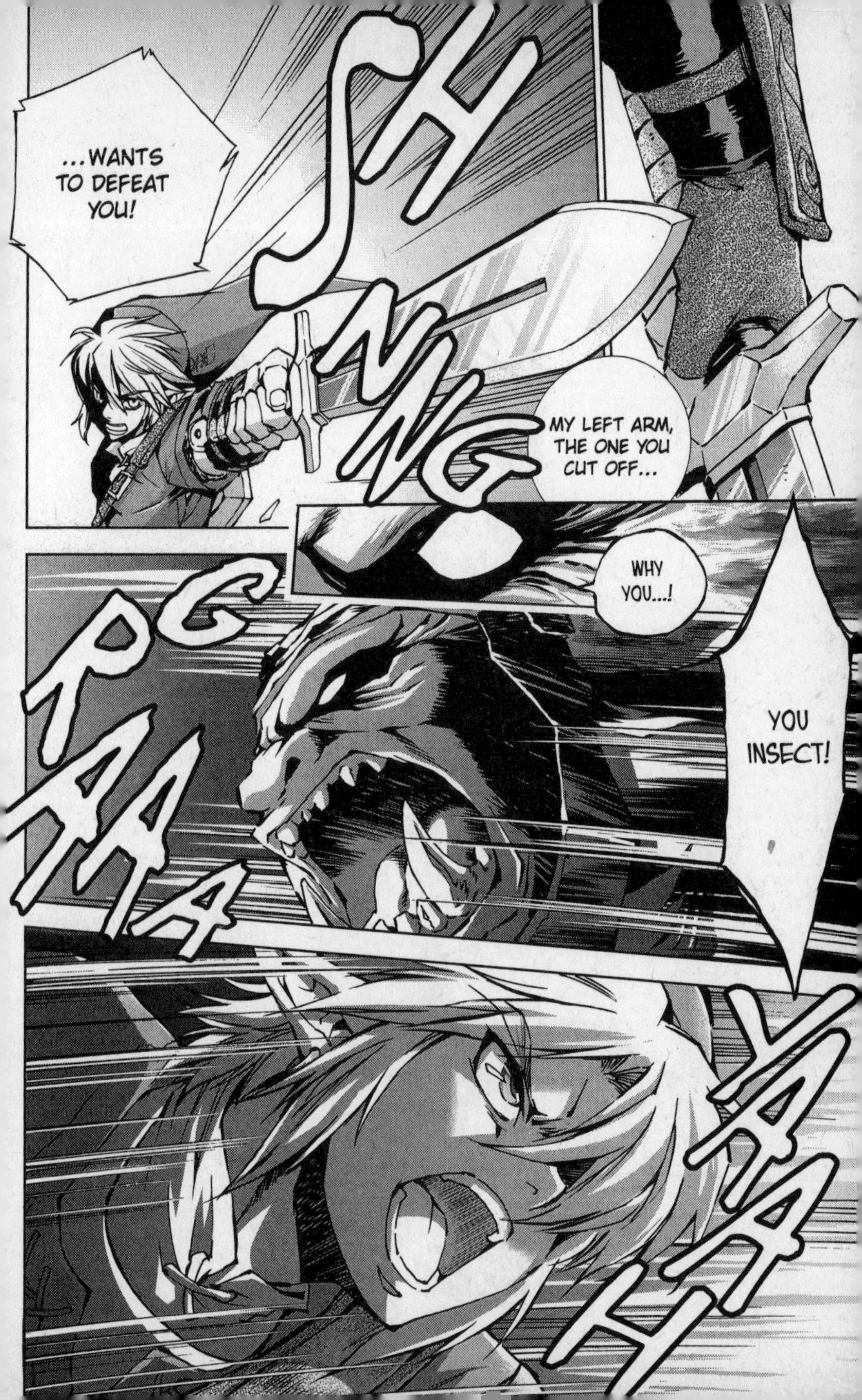
MY LEFT ARM, THE ONE YOU CUT OFF...
SHNG
...WANTS TO DEFEAT YOU!
WHY YOU...!
YOU INSECT!
GRAAAAA
YAAAH

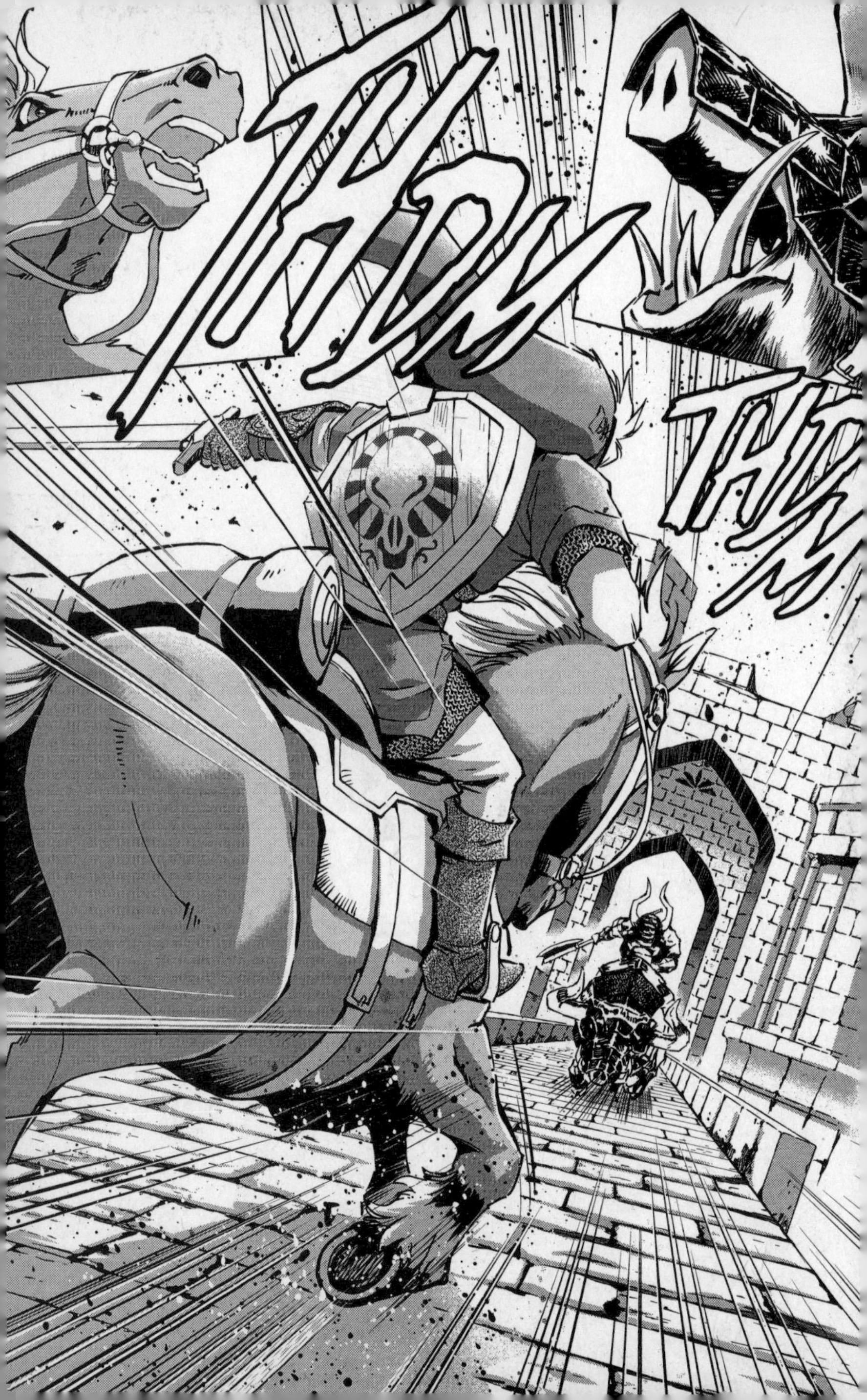

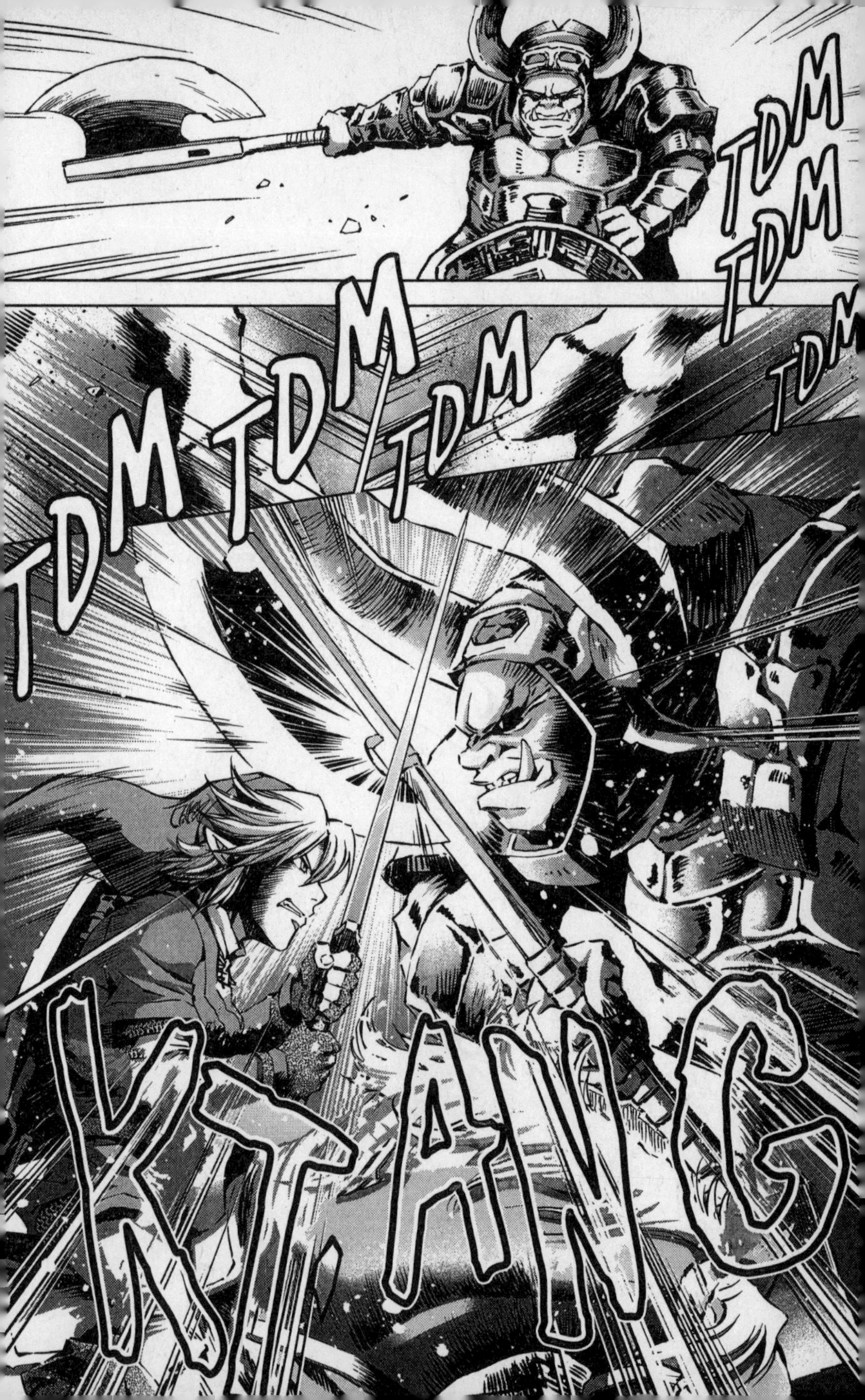
TDM
TDM
TDM
TDM TDM TDM TDM
KTANG

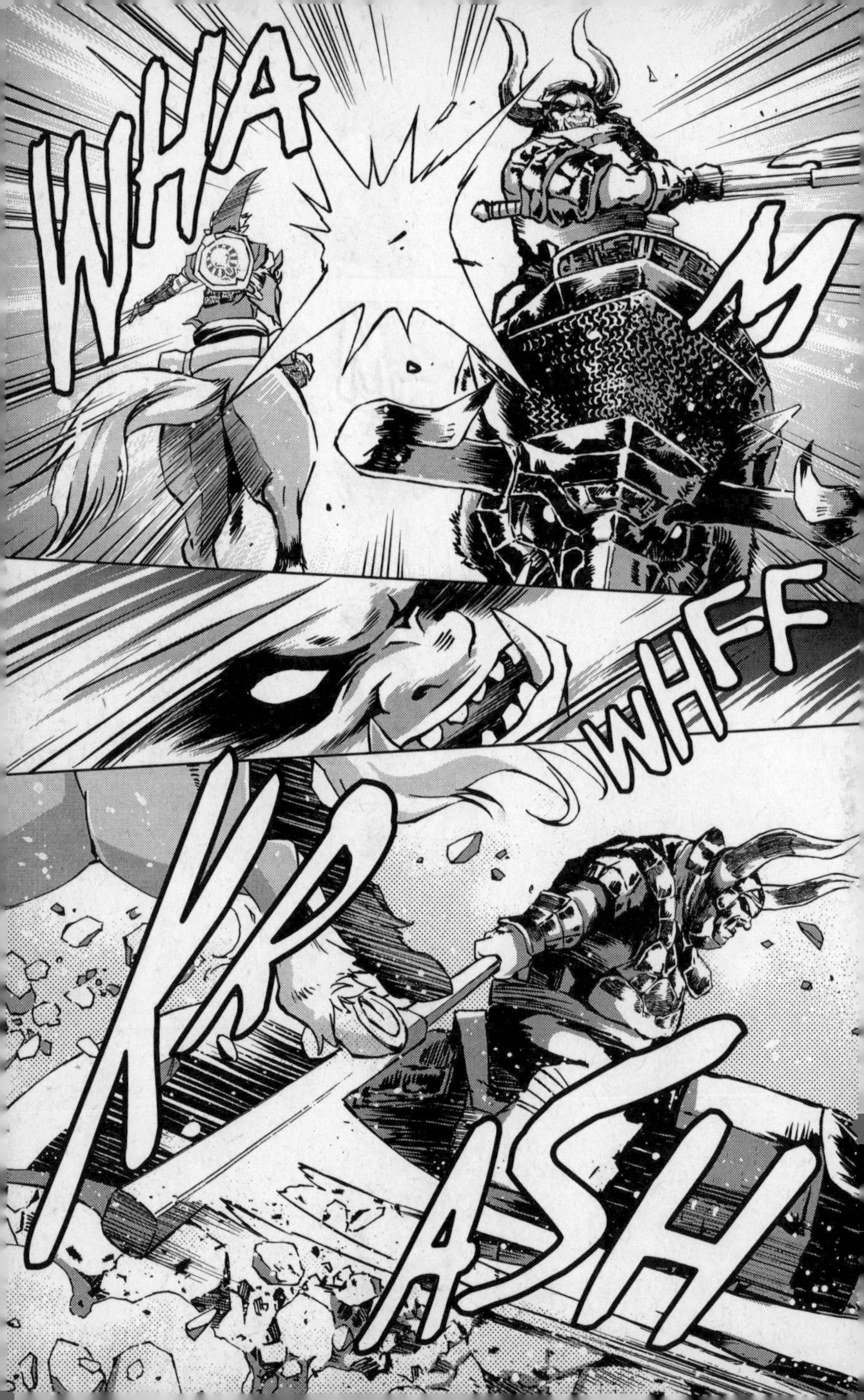
WHAM
WHFF
KRASH

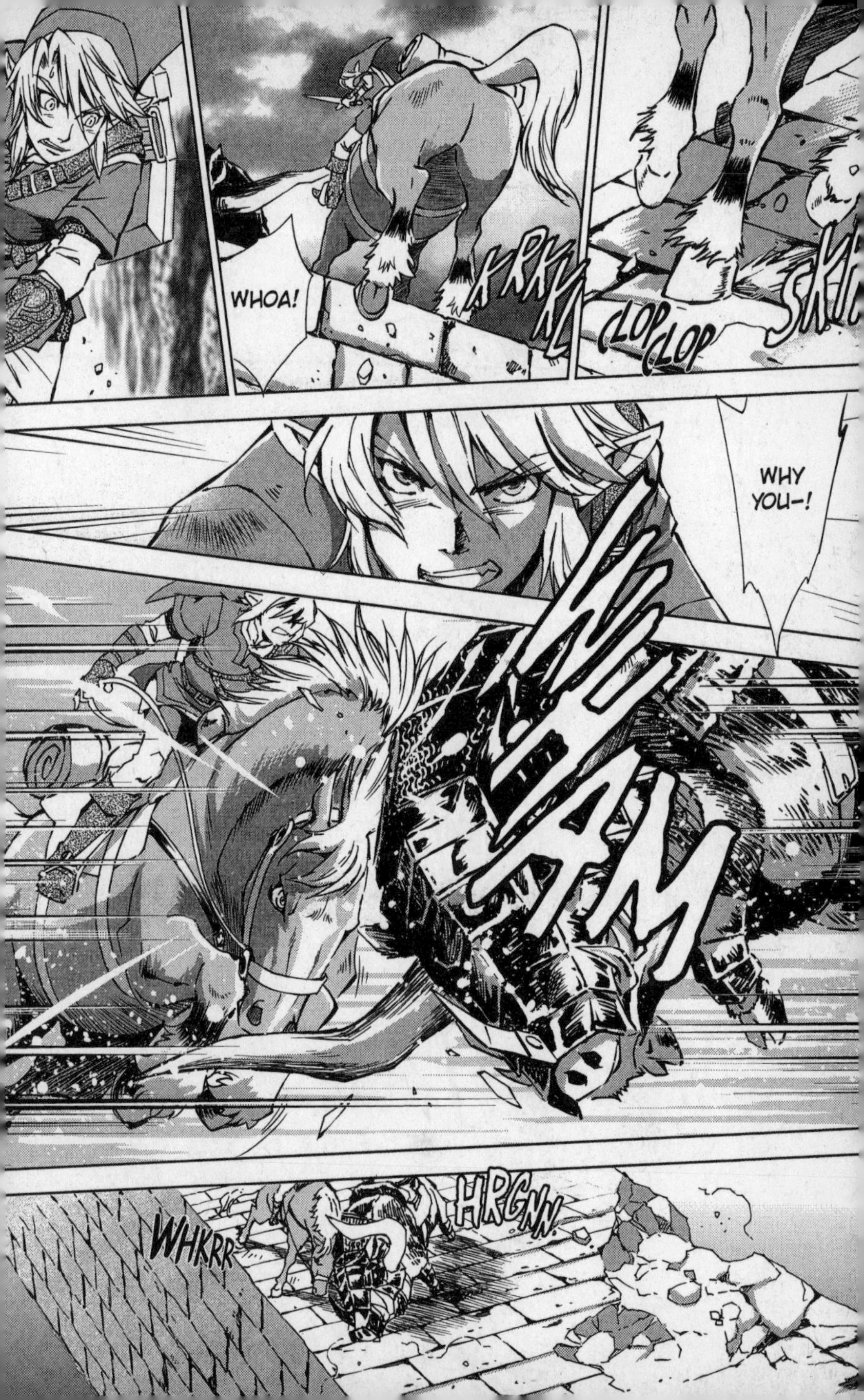
CLOP CLOP
KRKKL
WHOA!
WHY YOU-!
WHAM
HRGNN
WHKRR

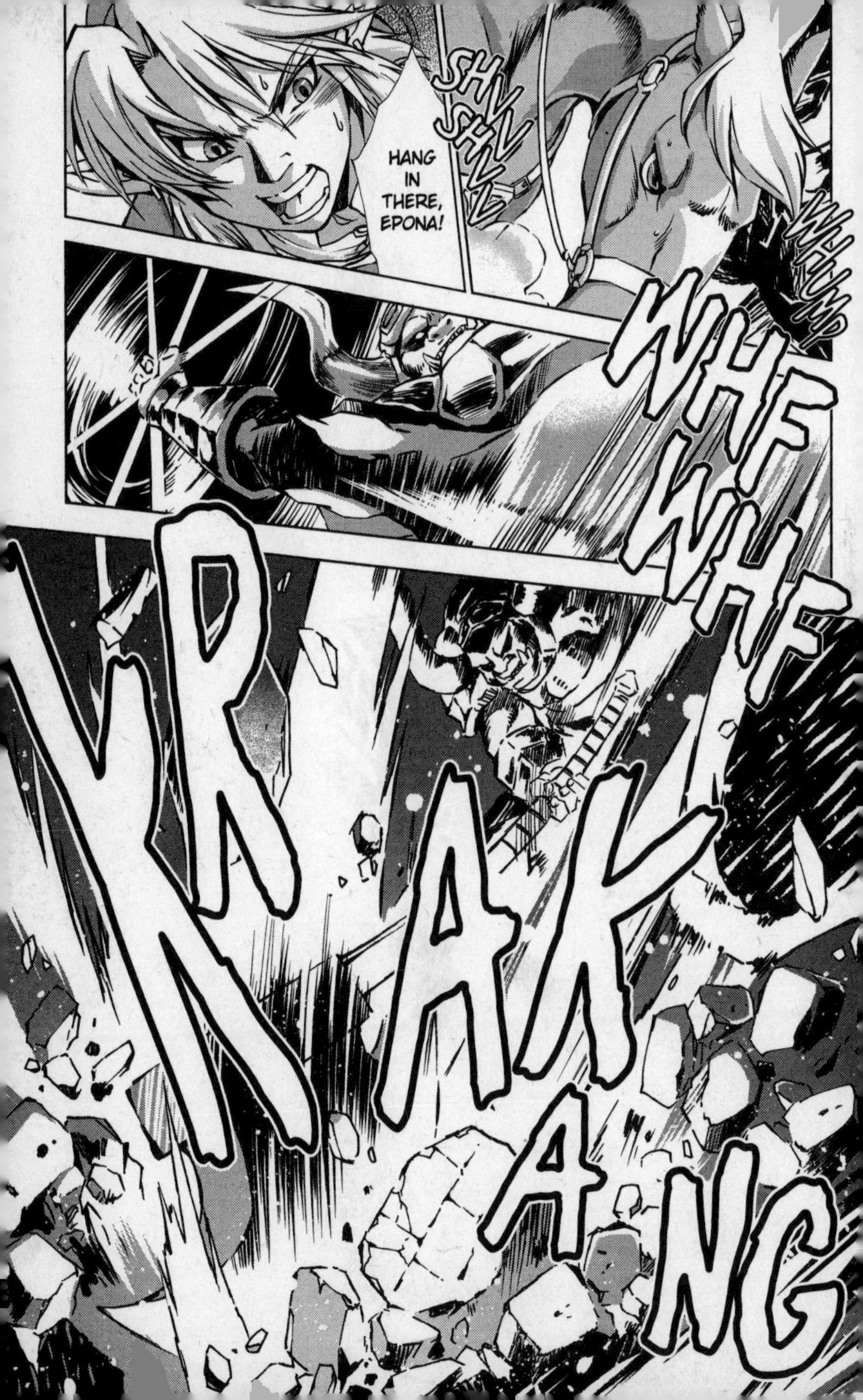
SHV SHV SHV
HANG IN THERE, EPONA!
WHUMP
WHF WHF WHF
KRAKAANG

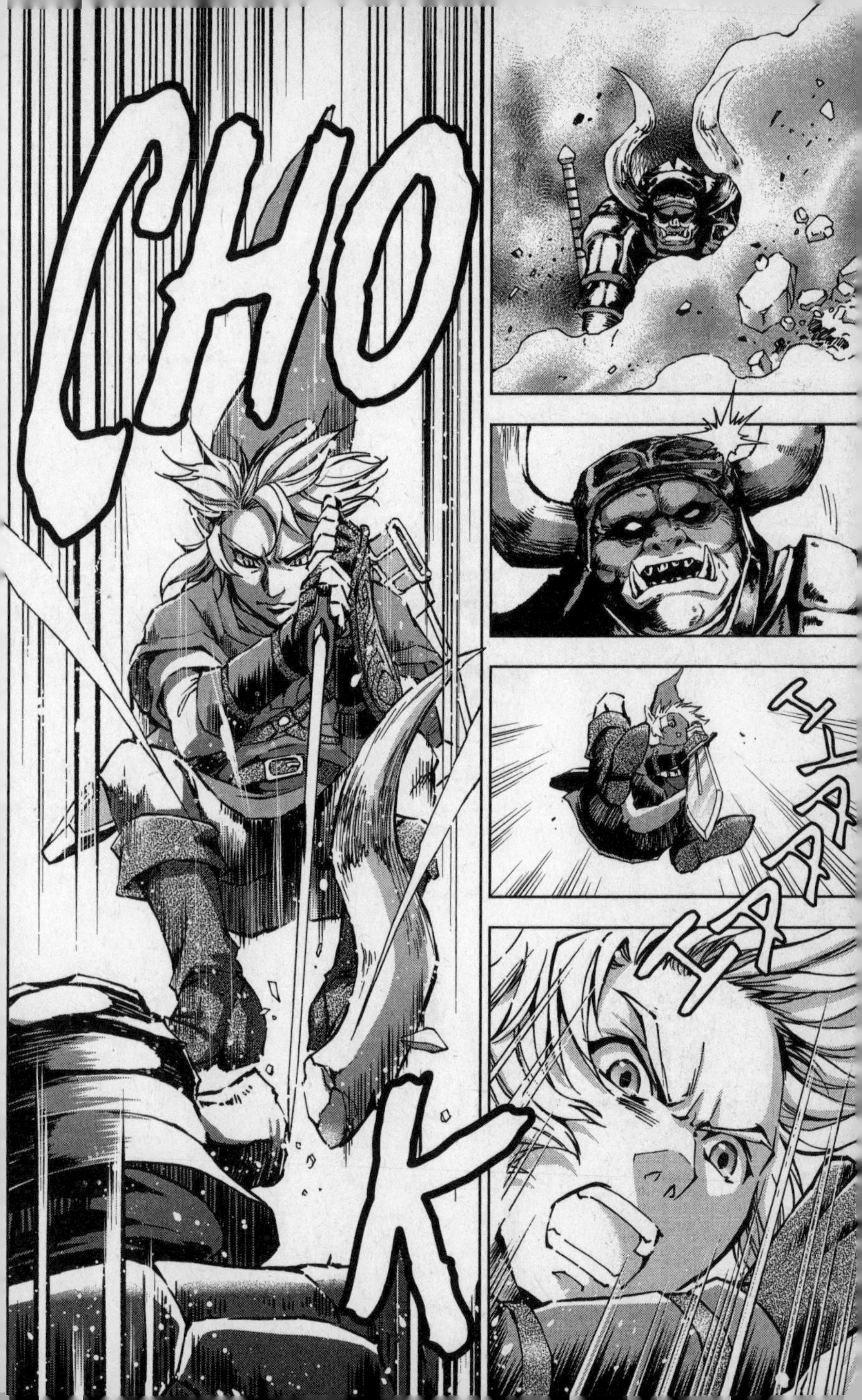
HIYAAAH
CHOK

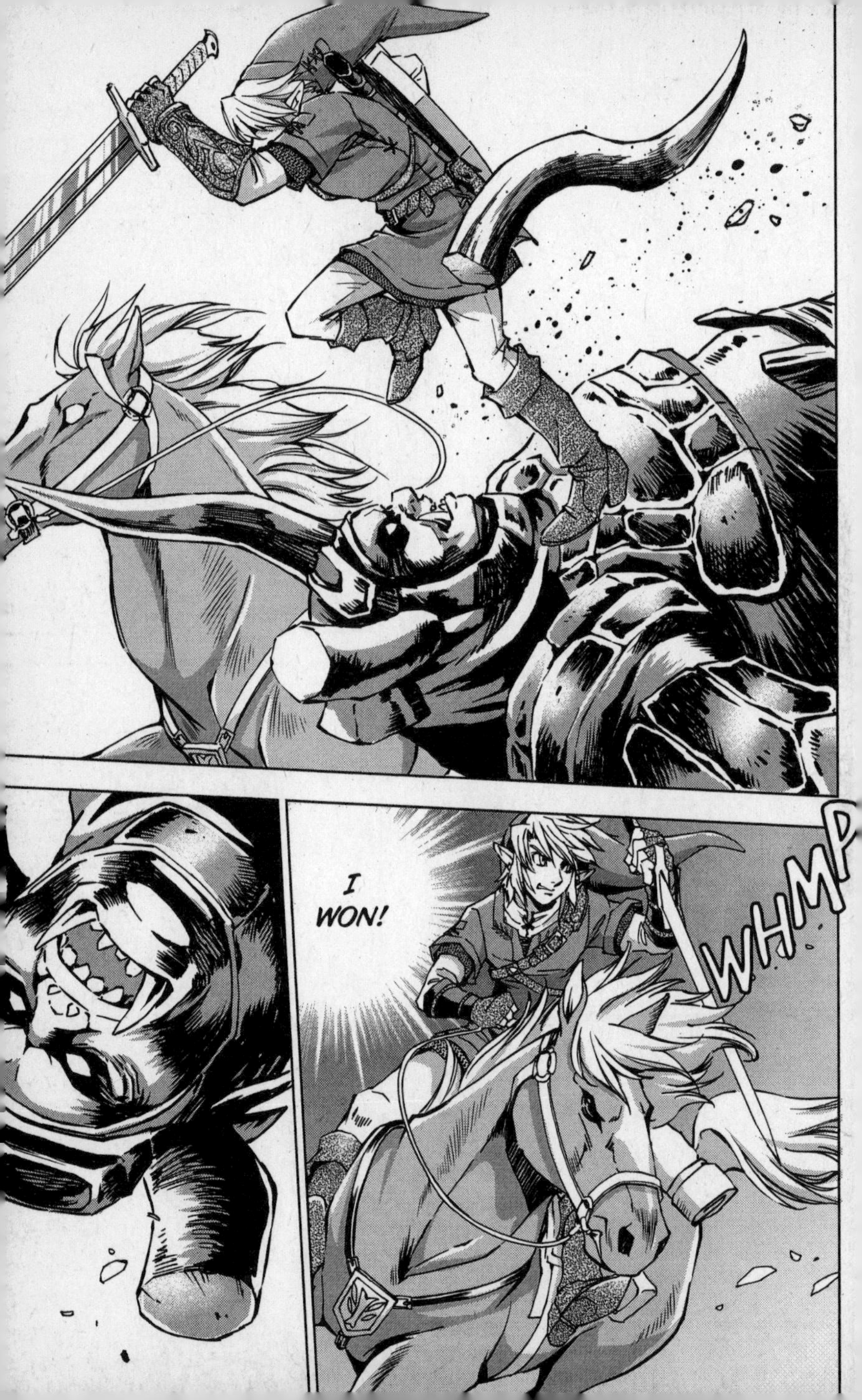
WHMP
I WON!

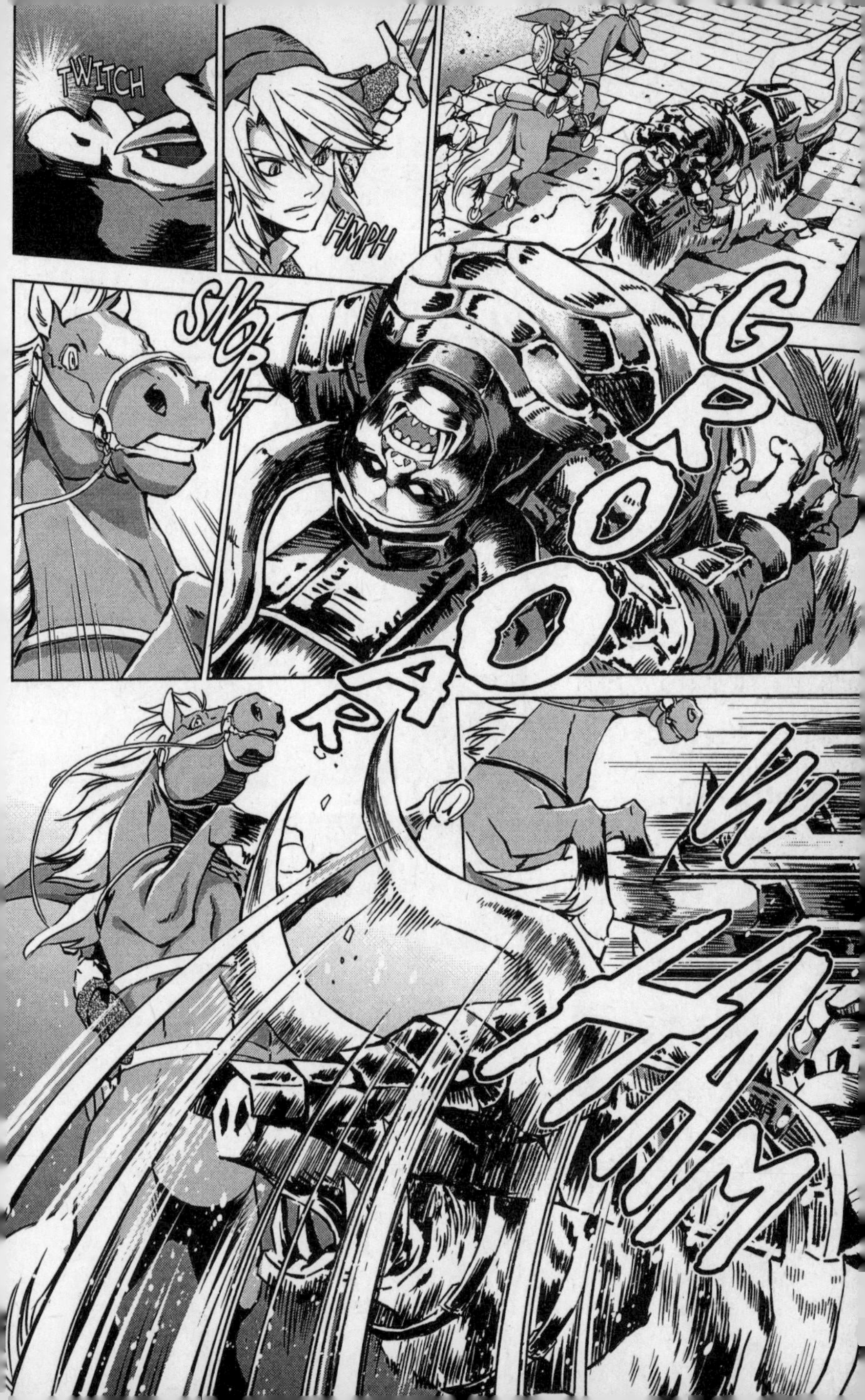
HMPH
TWITCH
GROOOAR
SNORT
WHAM

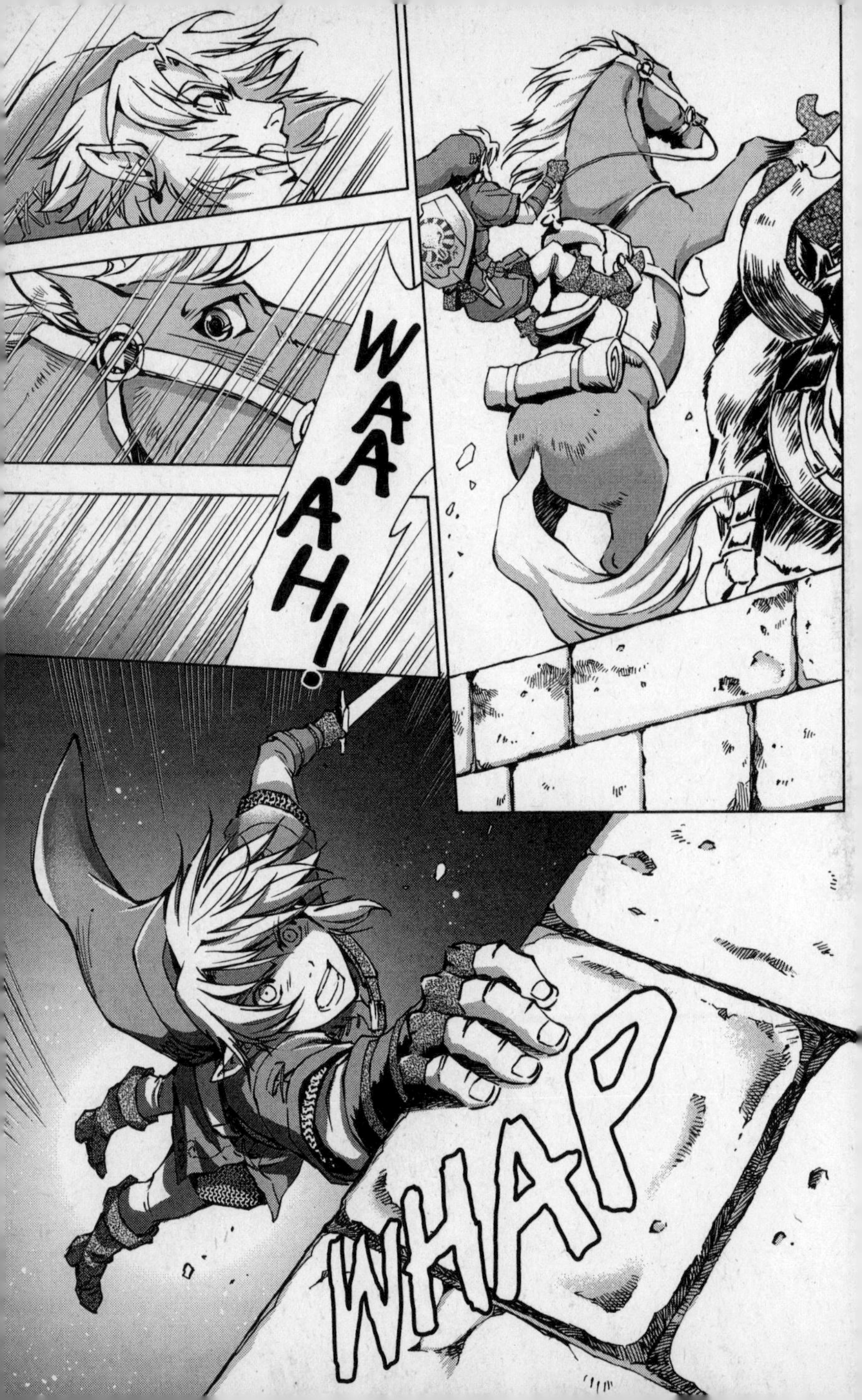
WAAAHI!
WHAP

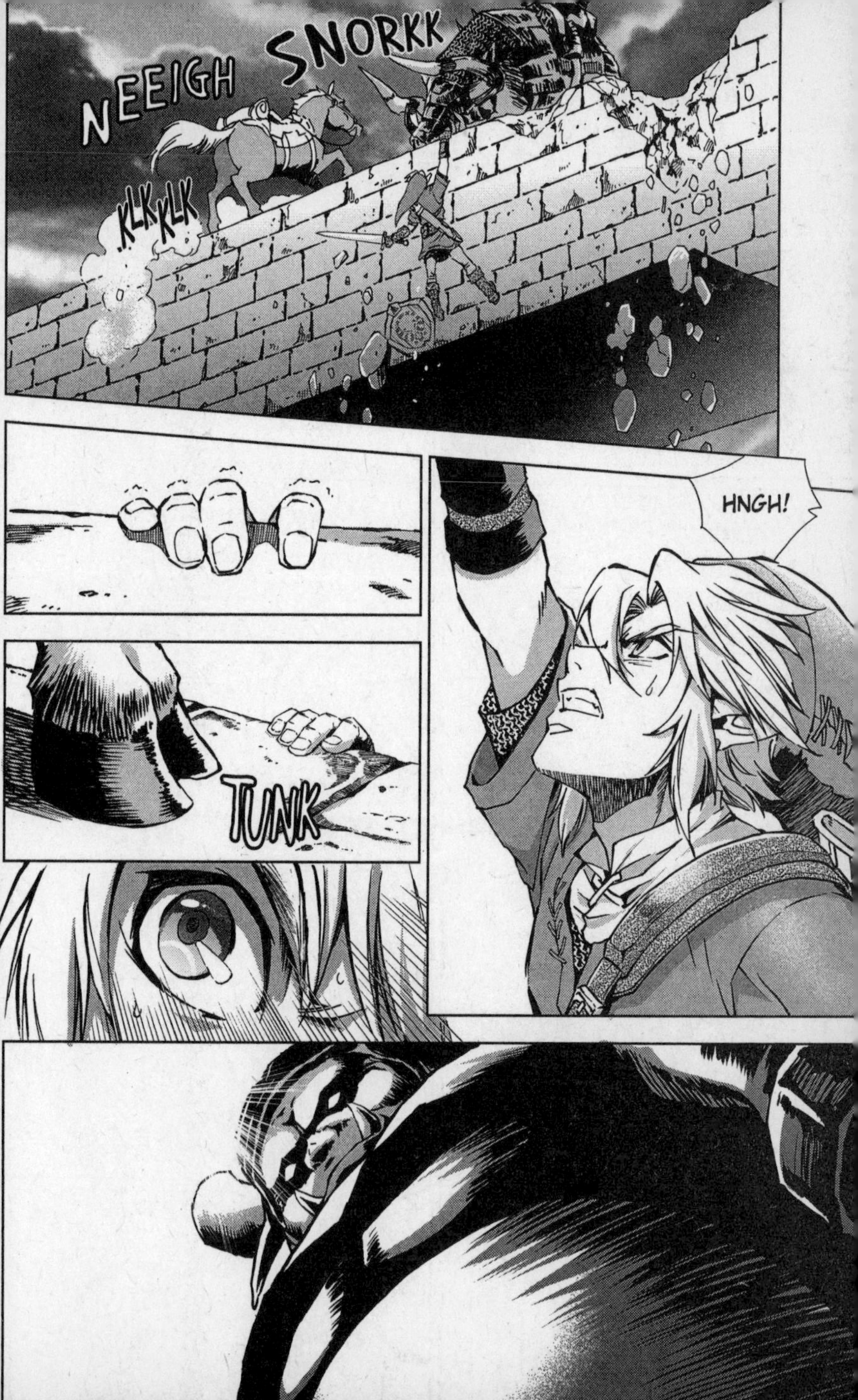
SNORKK
NEEIGH
KLK KLK
HNGH!
TUNK

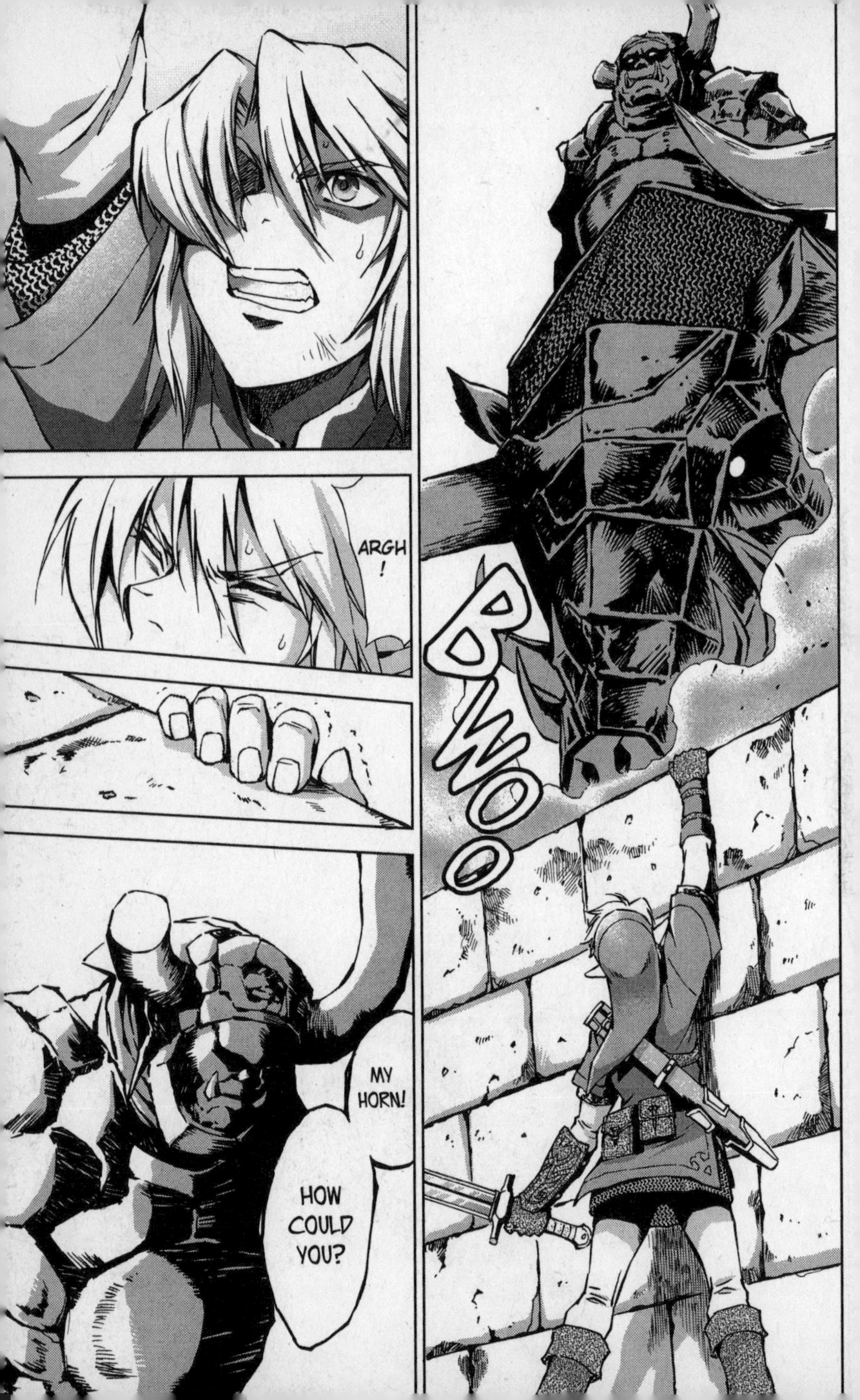
BWOOO
ARGH!
MY HORN!
HOW COULD YOU?

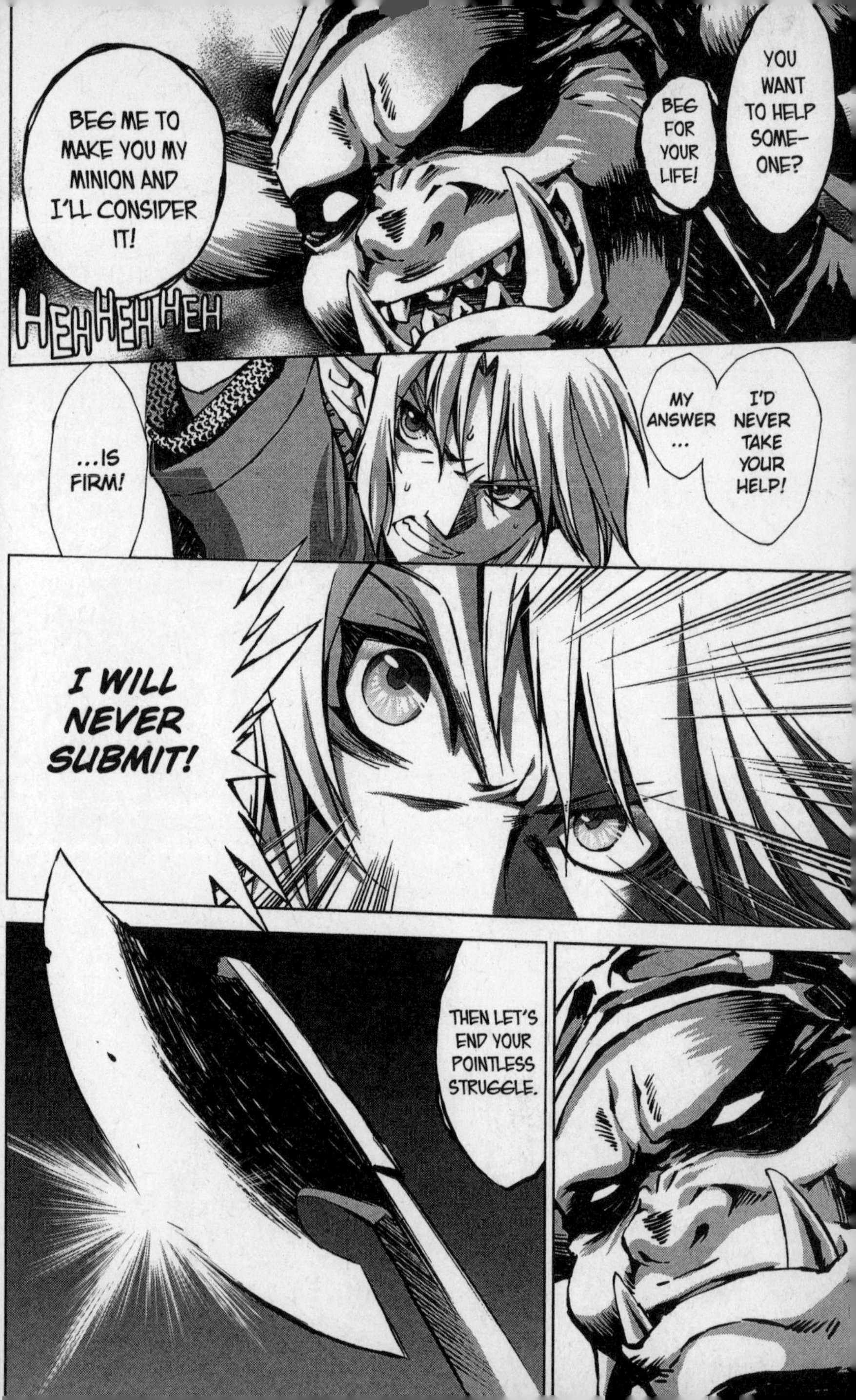
YOU WANT TO HELP SOME-ONE?
BEG FOR YOUR LIFE!
BEG ME TO MAKE YOU MY MINION AND I'LL CONSIDER IT!
HEHHEHHEH
I'D NEVER TAKE YOUR HELP!
MY ANSWER ...
...IS FIRM!
I WILL NEVER SUBMIT!
THEN LET'S END YOUR POINTLESS STRUGGLE.

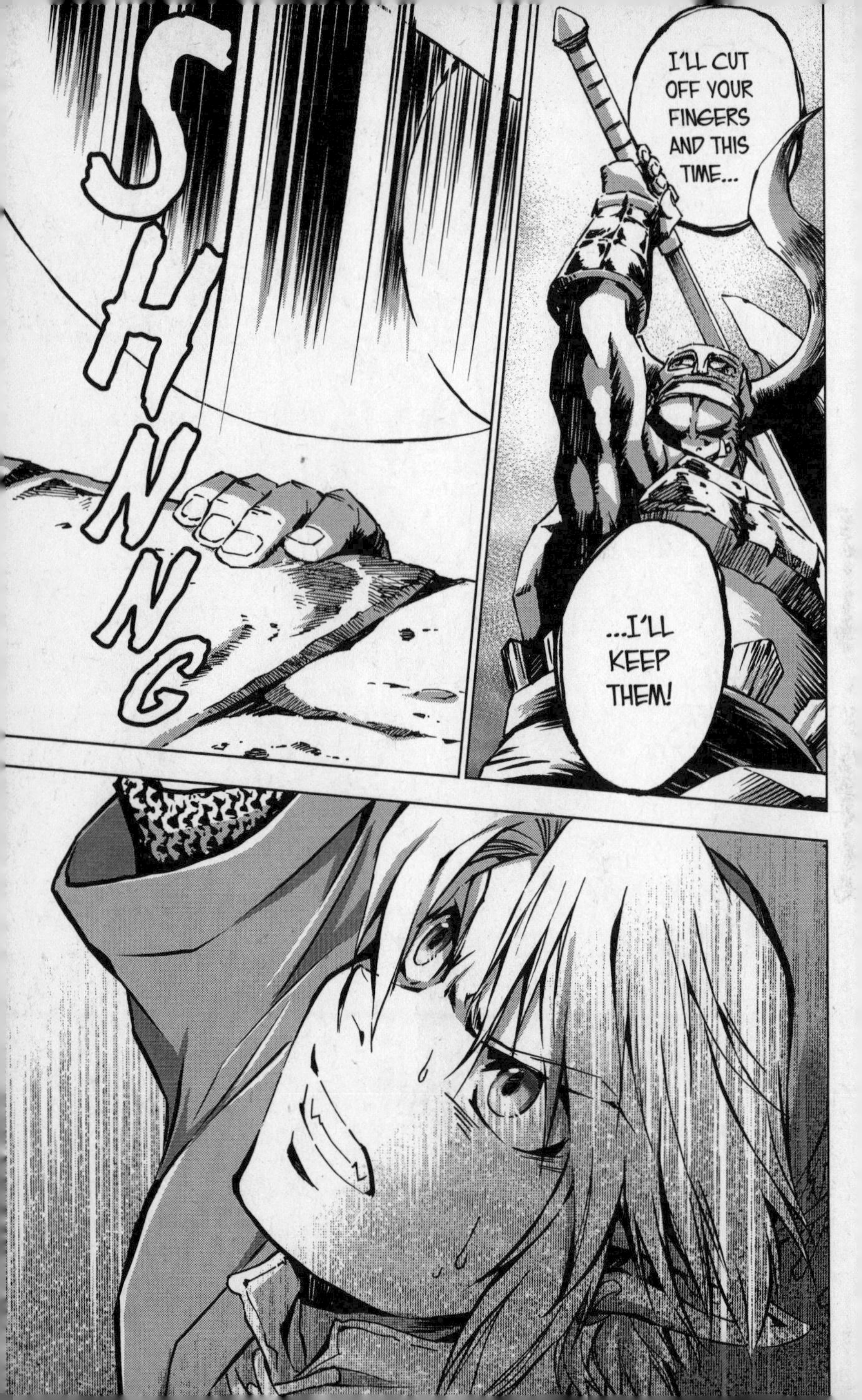
I'LL CUT OFF YOUR FINGERS AND THIS TIME...
...I'LL KEEP THEM!
SHNNG

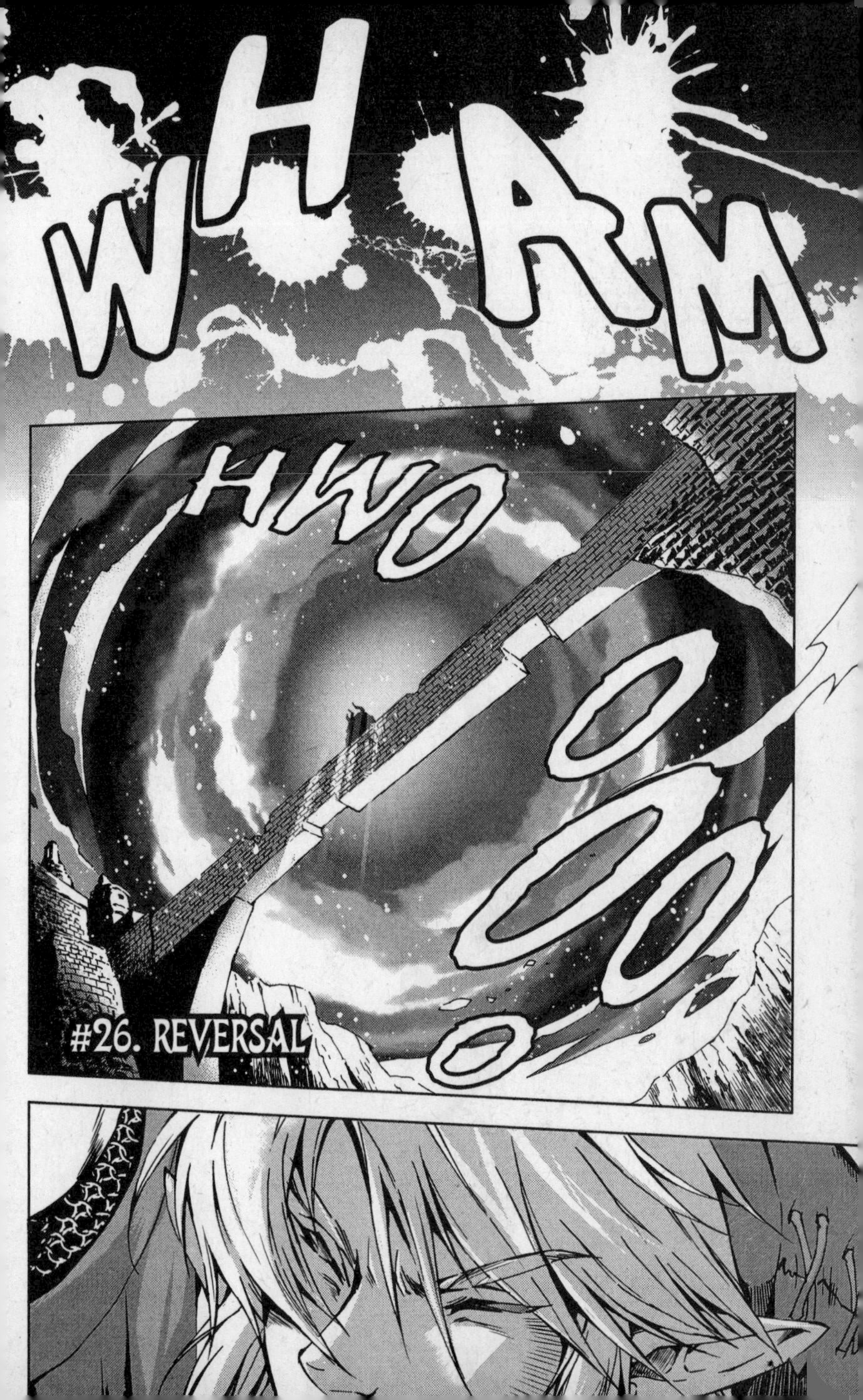
WHAM
HWOOOOO
#26. REVERSAL

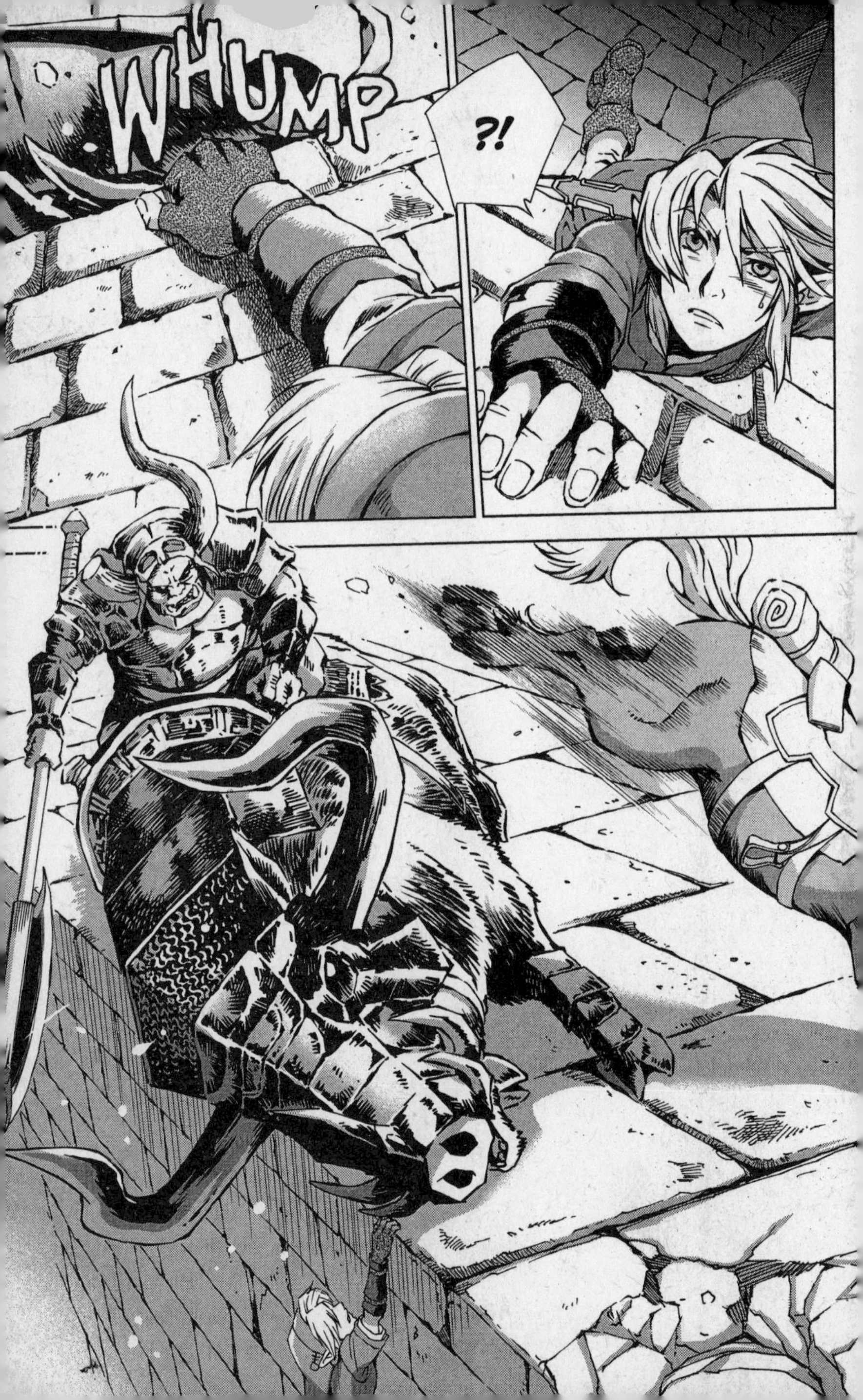
WHUMP
?!

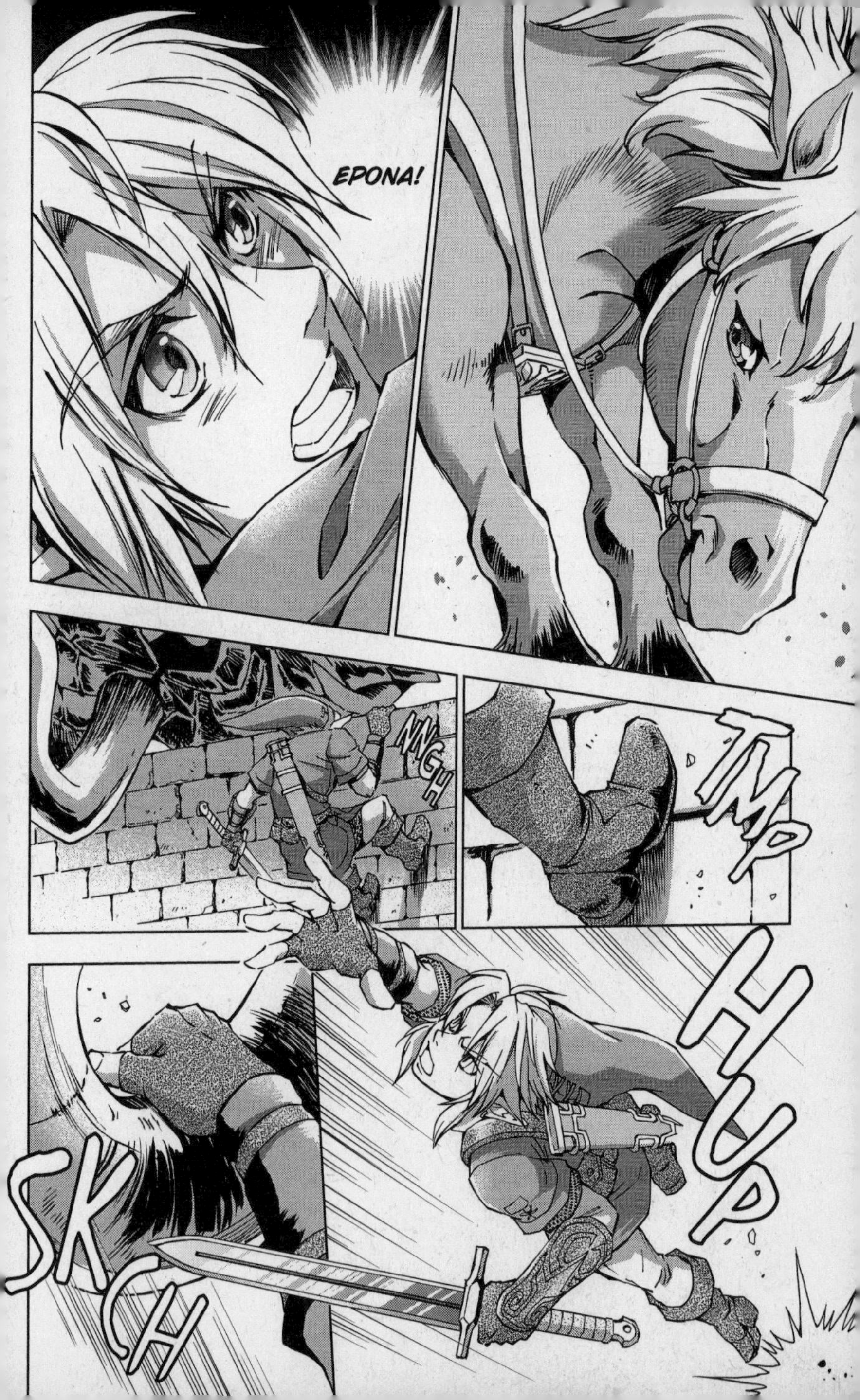
EPONA!
TMP
NNGH
HUP.
SKCH

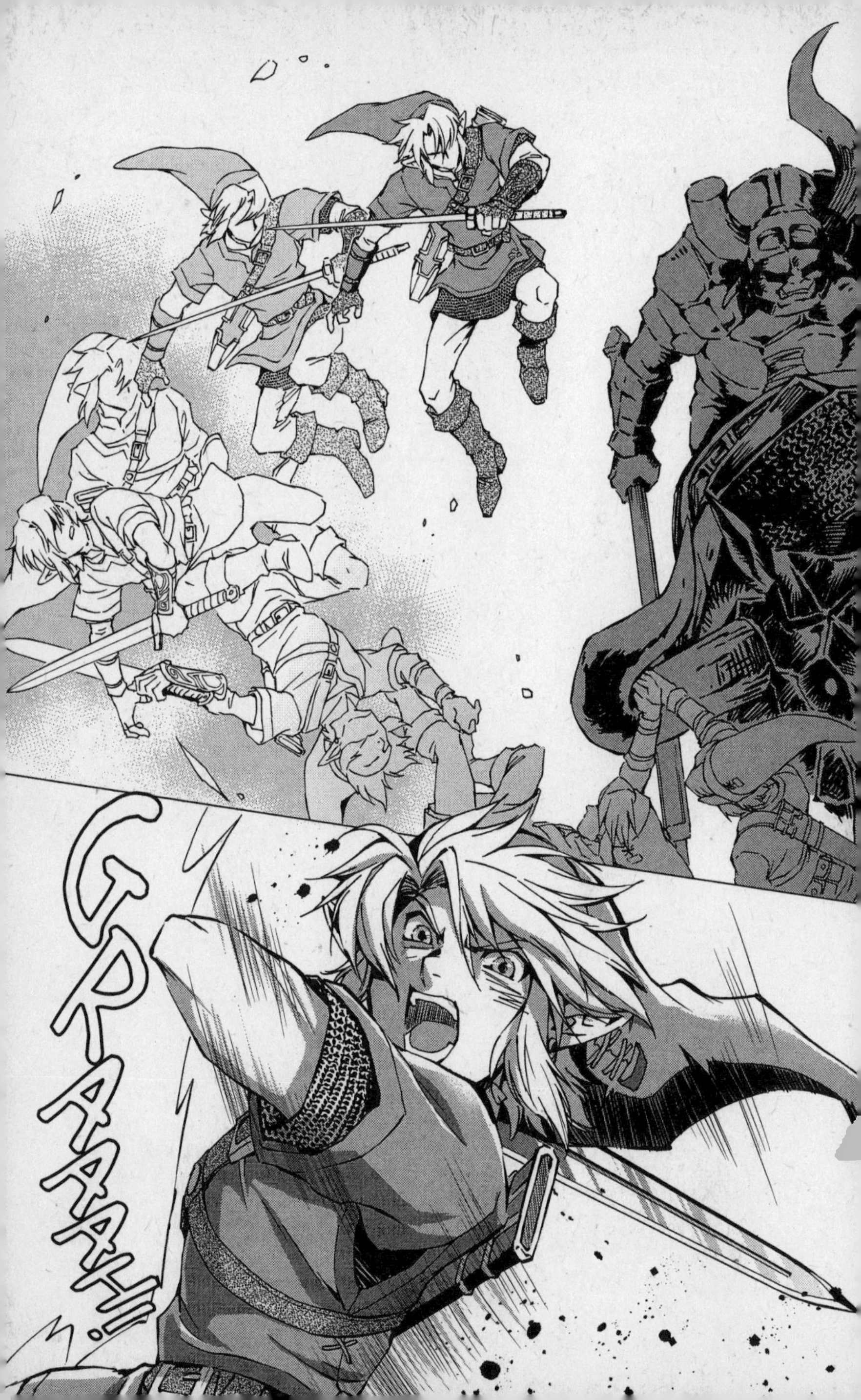
GRAAAH!!

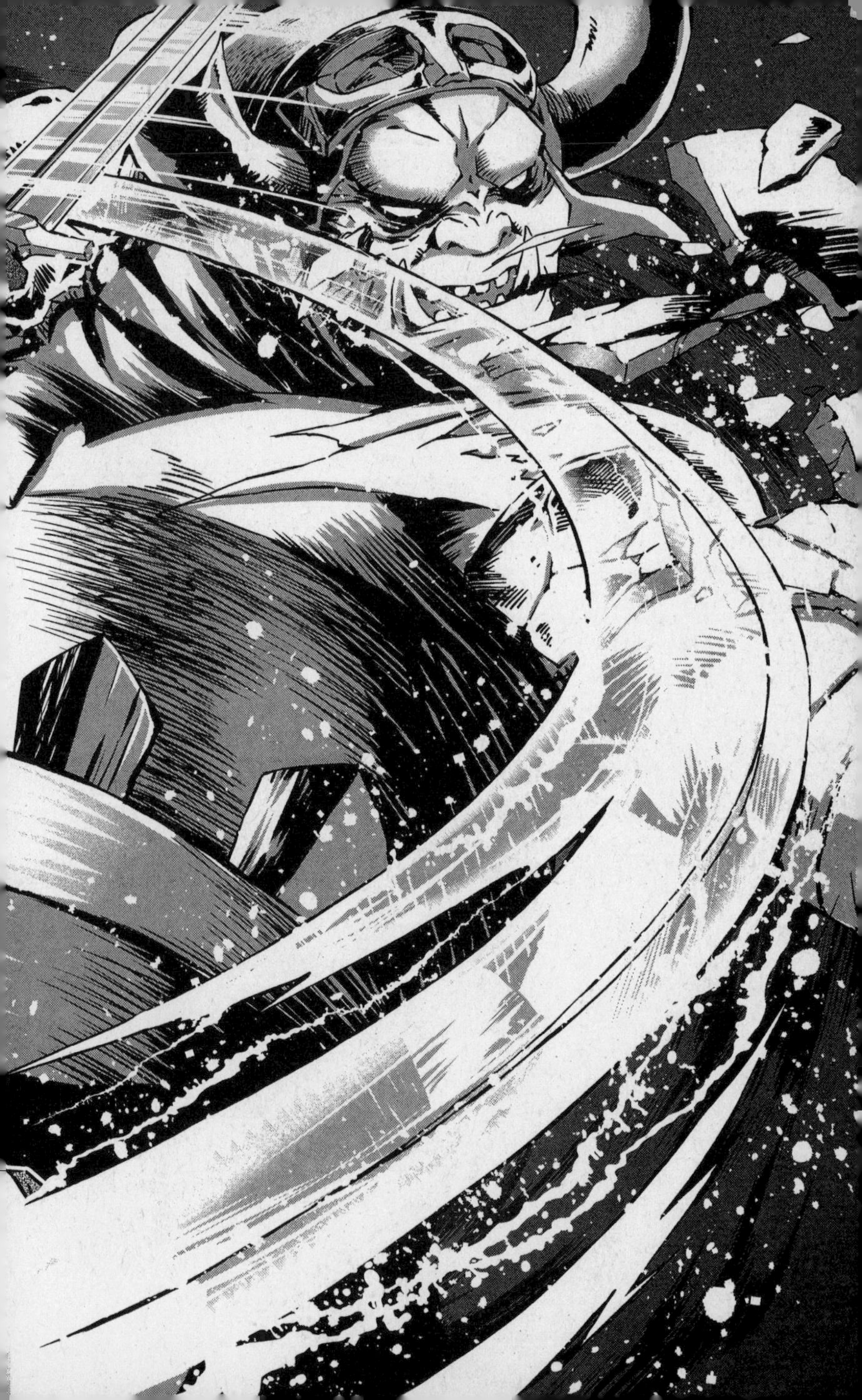

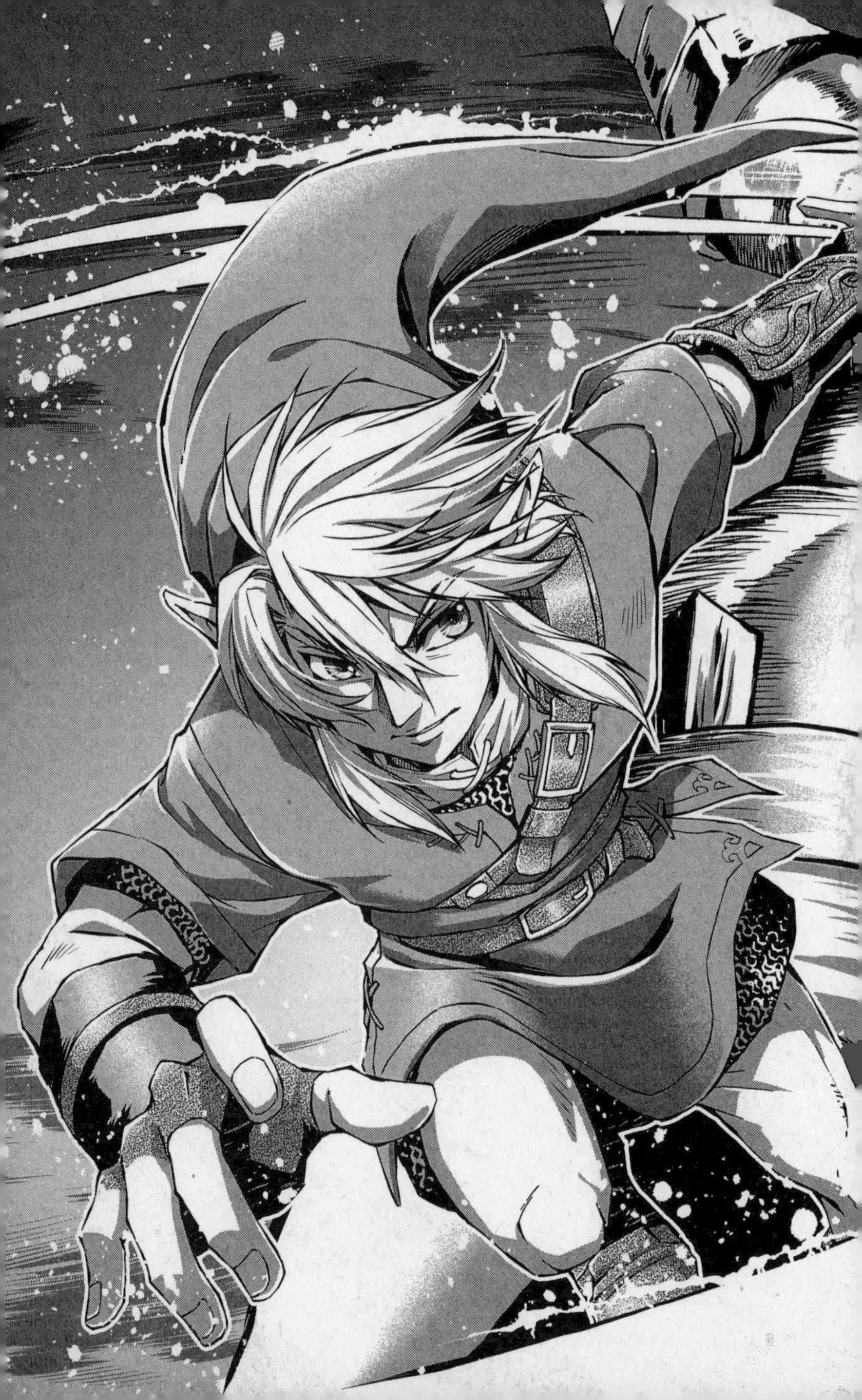

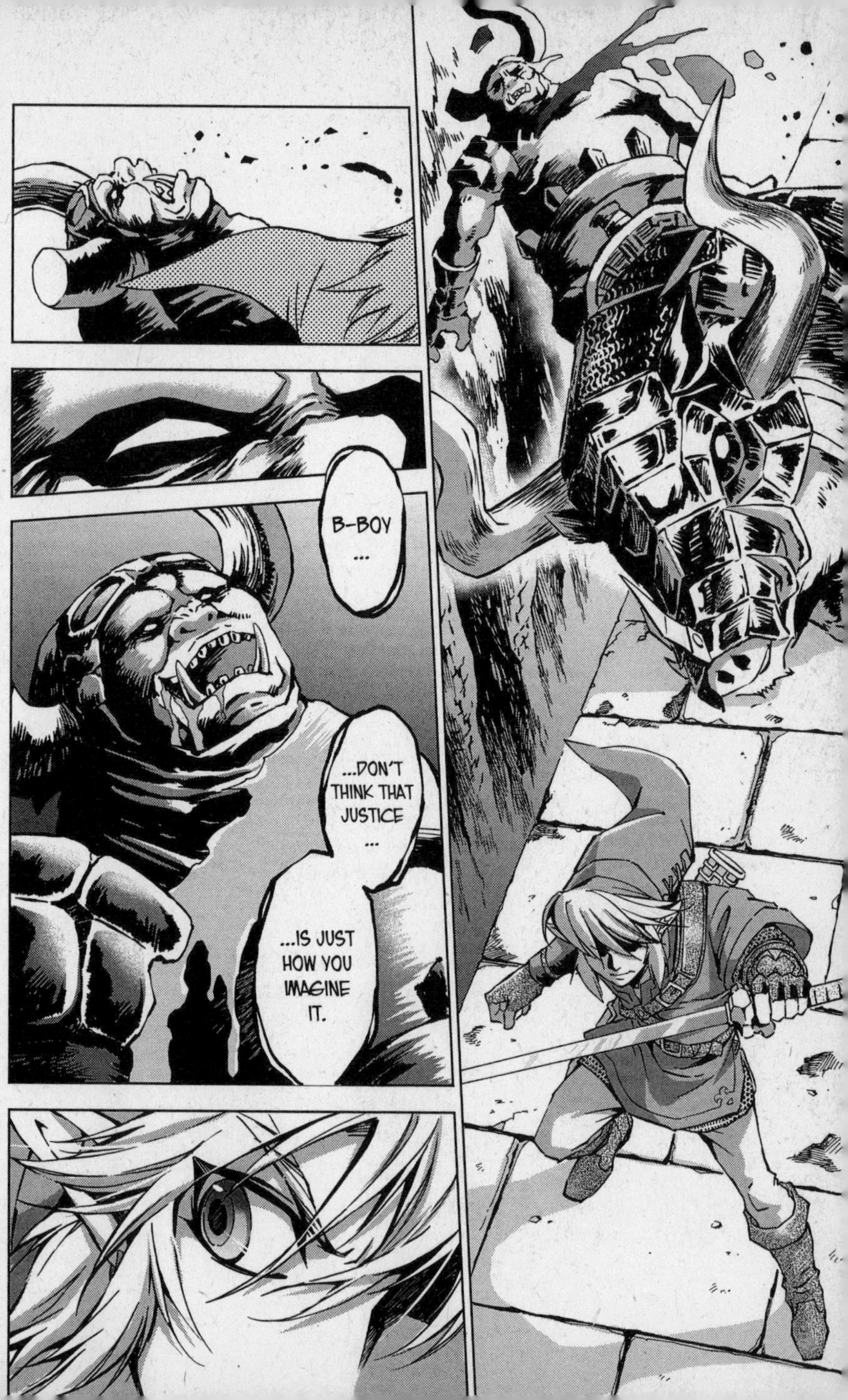
B-BOY ...
...DON'T THINK THAT JUSTICE ...
...IS JUST HOW YOU IMAGINE IT.

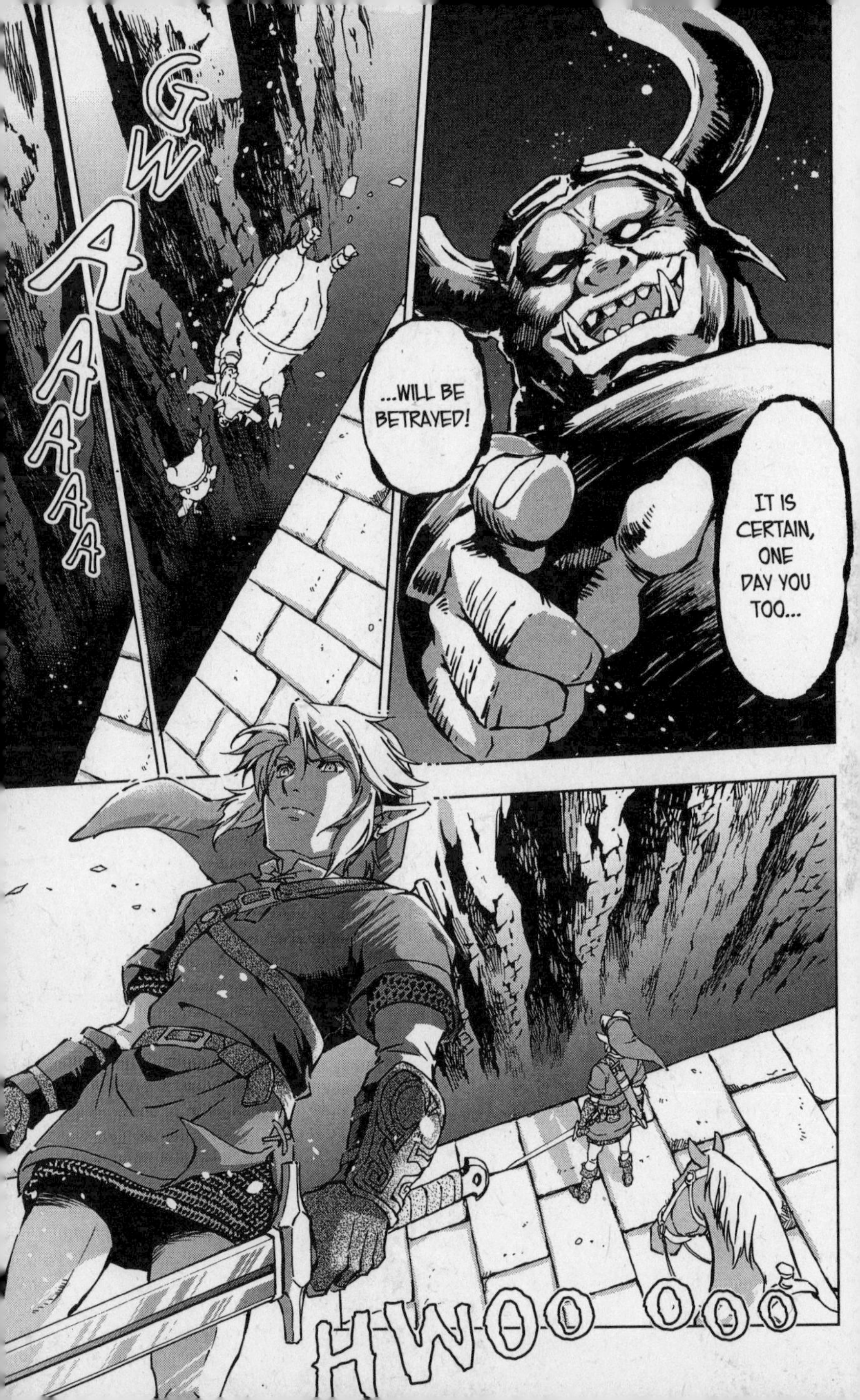
IT IS CERTAIN, ONE DAY YOU TOO...
...WILL BE BETRAYED!
GWAAAAAAA
HWOO OOO

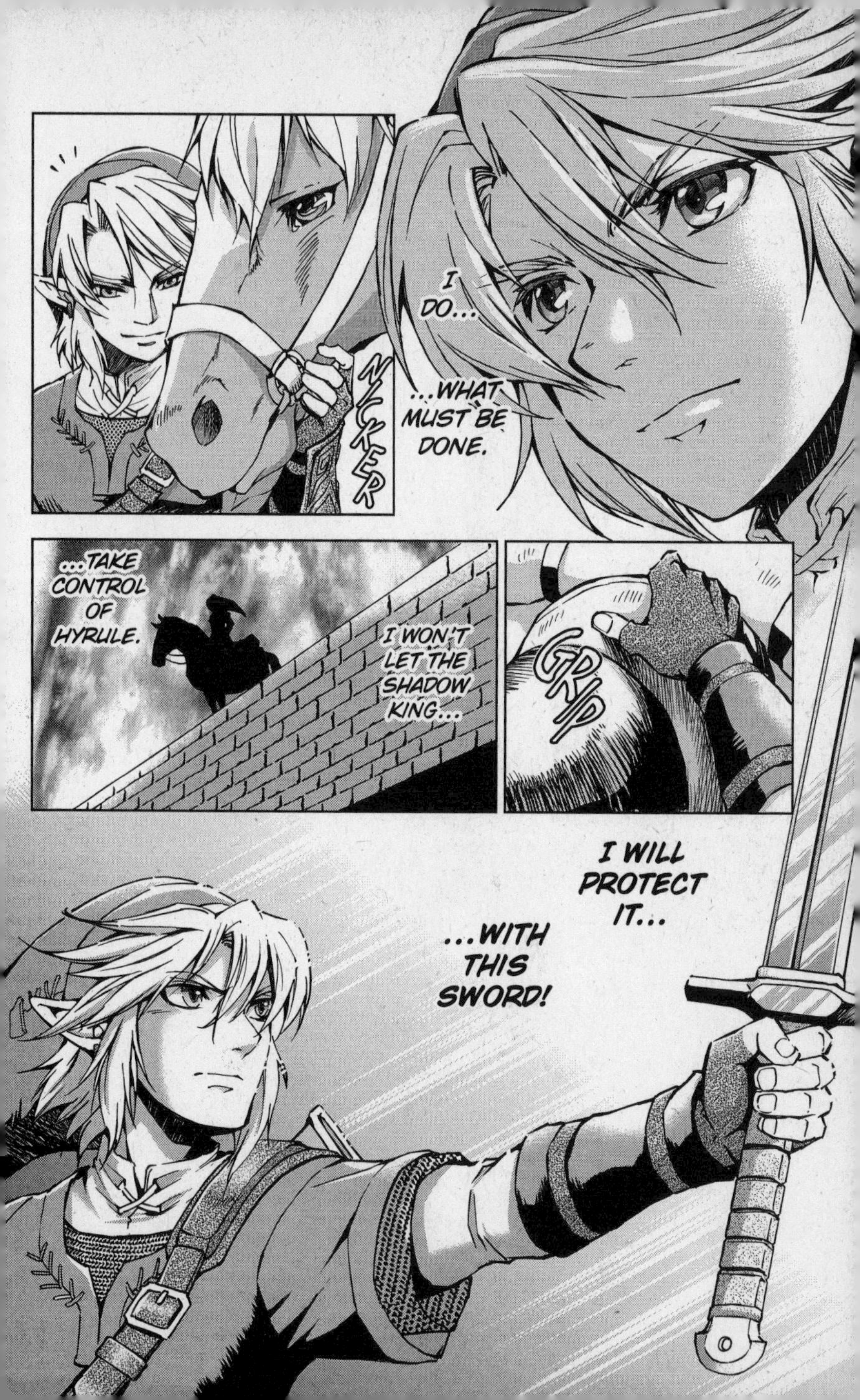
I DO...
...WHAT MUST BE DONE.
NICKER
GRIP
I WON'T LET THE SHADOW KING...
...TAKE CONTROL OF HYRULE.
I WILL PROTECT IT...
...WITH THIS SWORD!

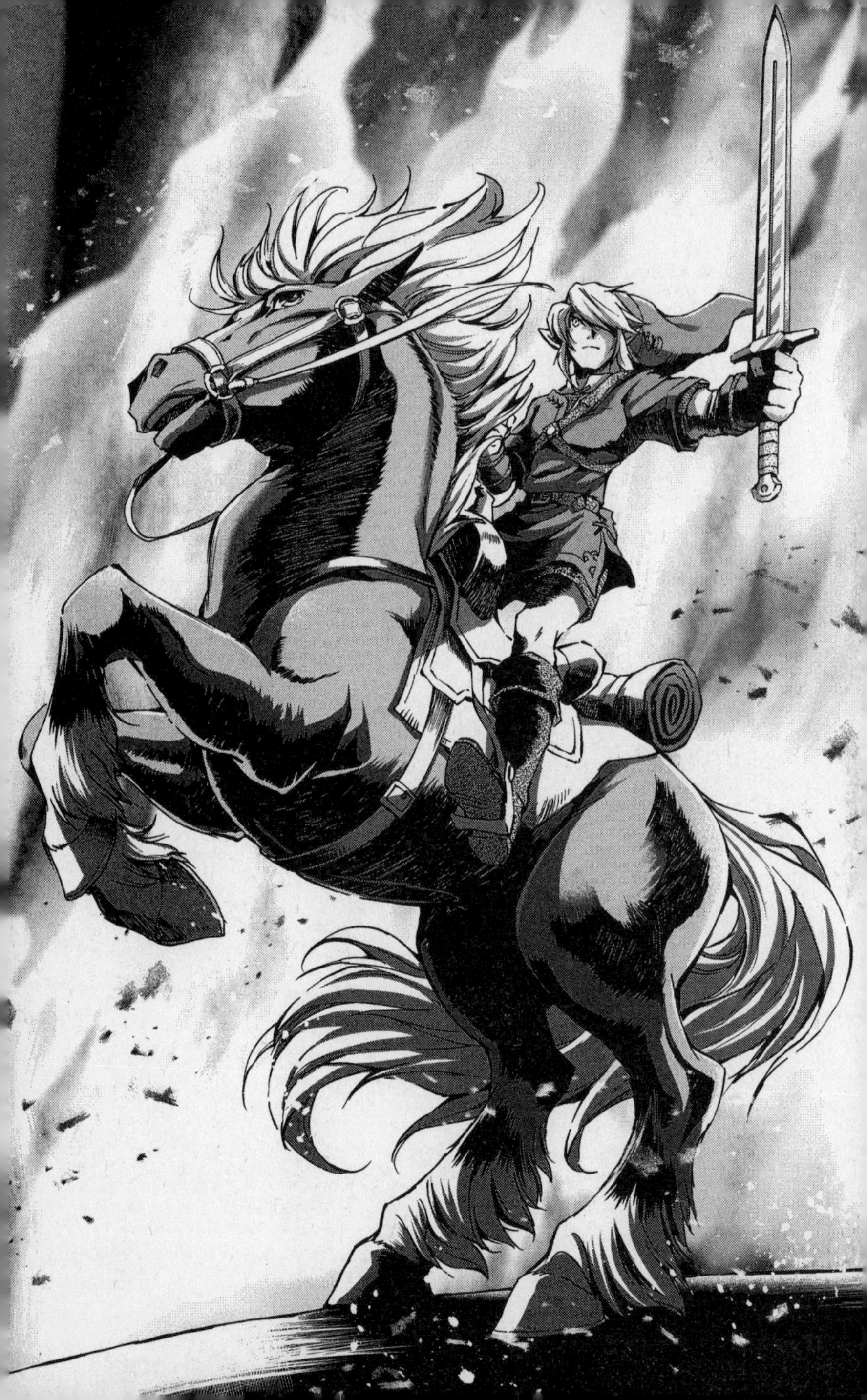

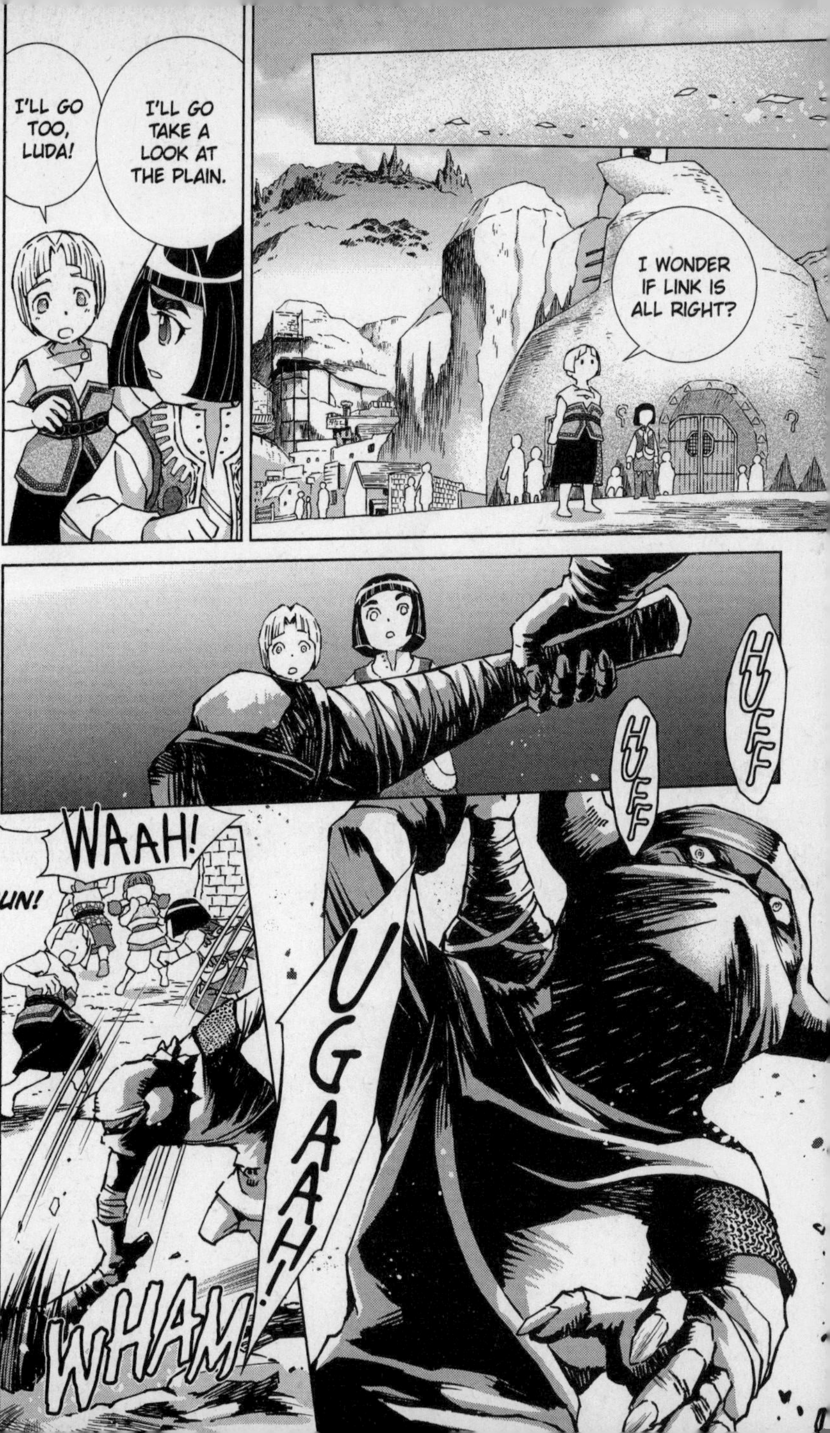
I WONDER IF LINK IS ALL RIGHT?
I'LL GO TAKE A LOOK AT THE PLAIN.
I'LL GO TOO, LUDA!
HUFF
HUFF
UGAAH!
WAAH!
RUN!
WHAM

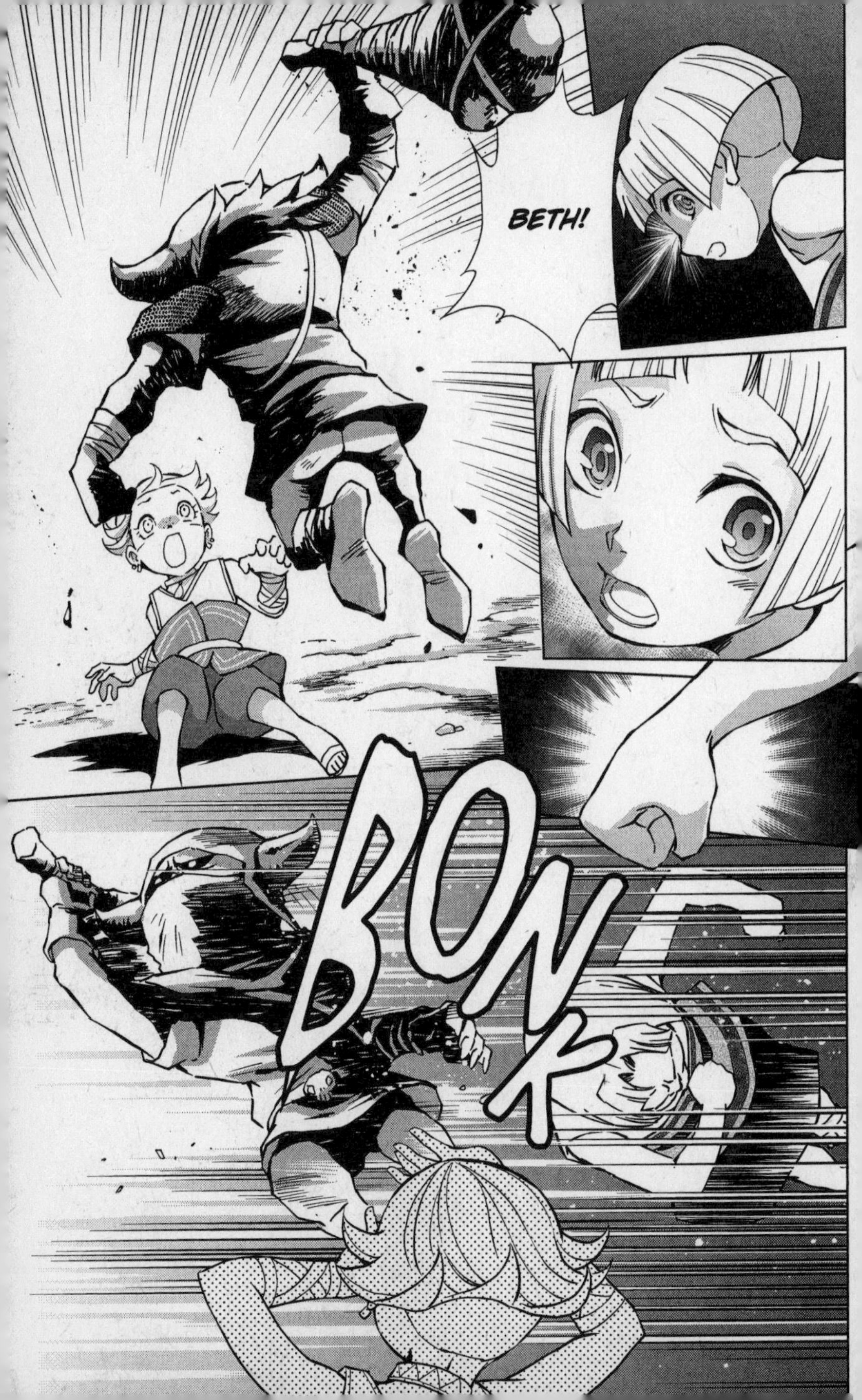
BETH!
BONK

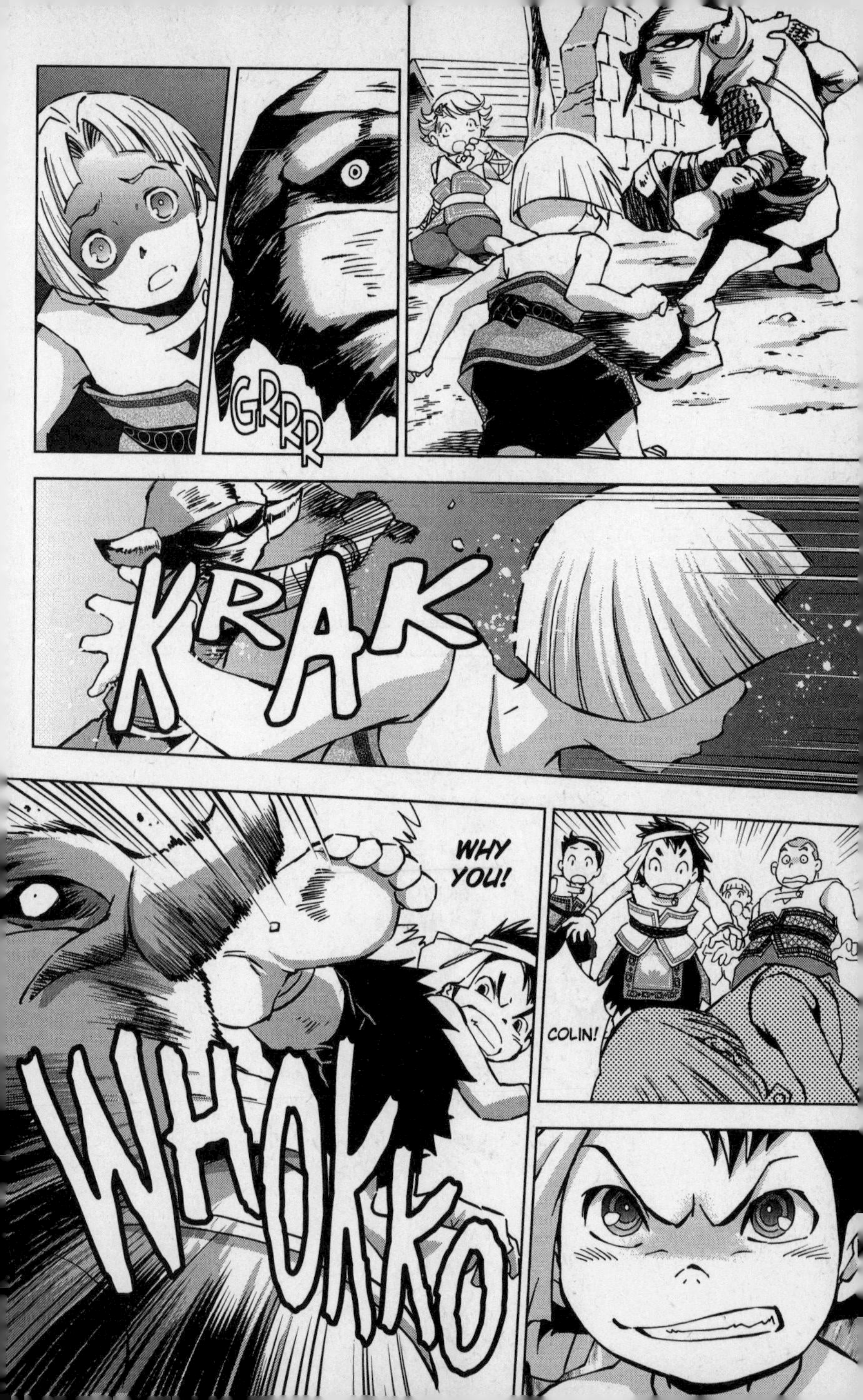
GRRRR
KRAK
COLIN!
WHY YOU!
WHOKKO

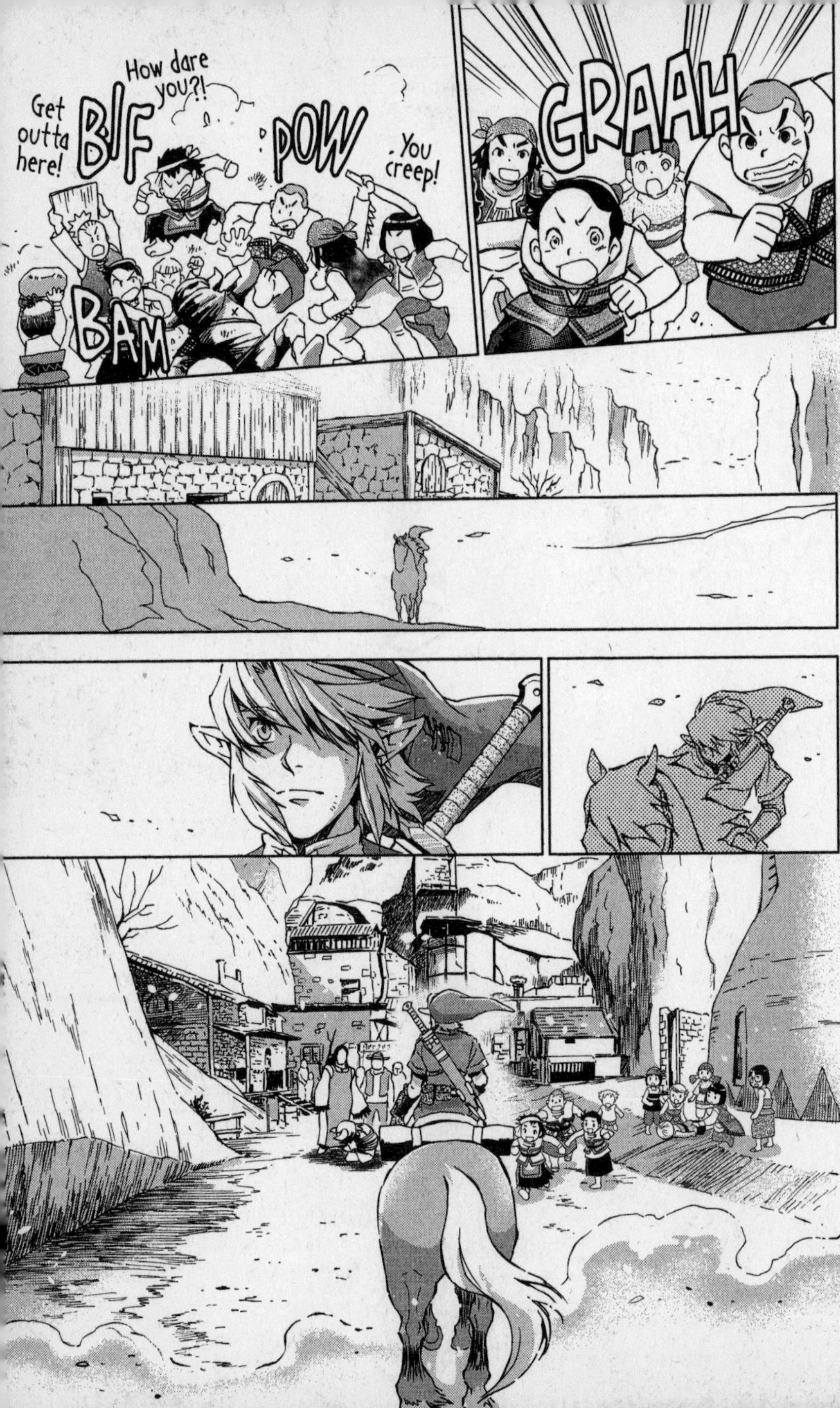
GRAAH
You creep!
POW
How dare you?!
BIF
Get outta here!
BAM

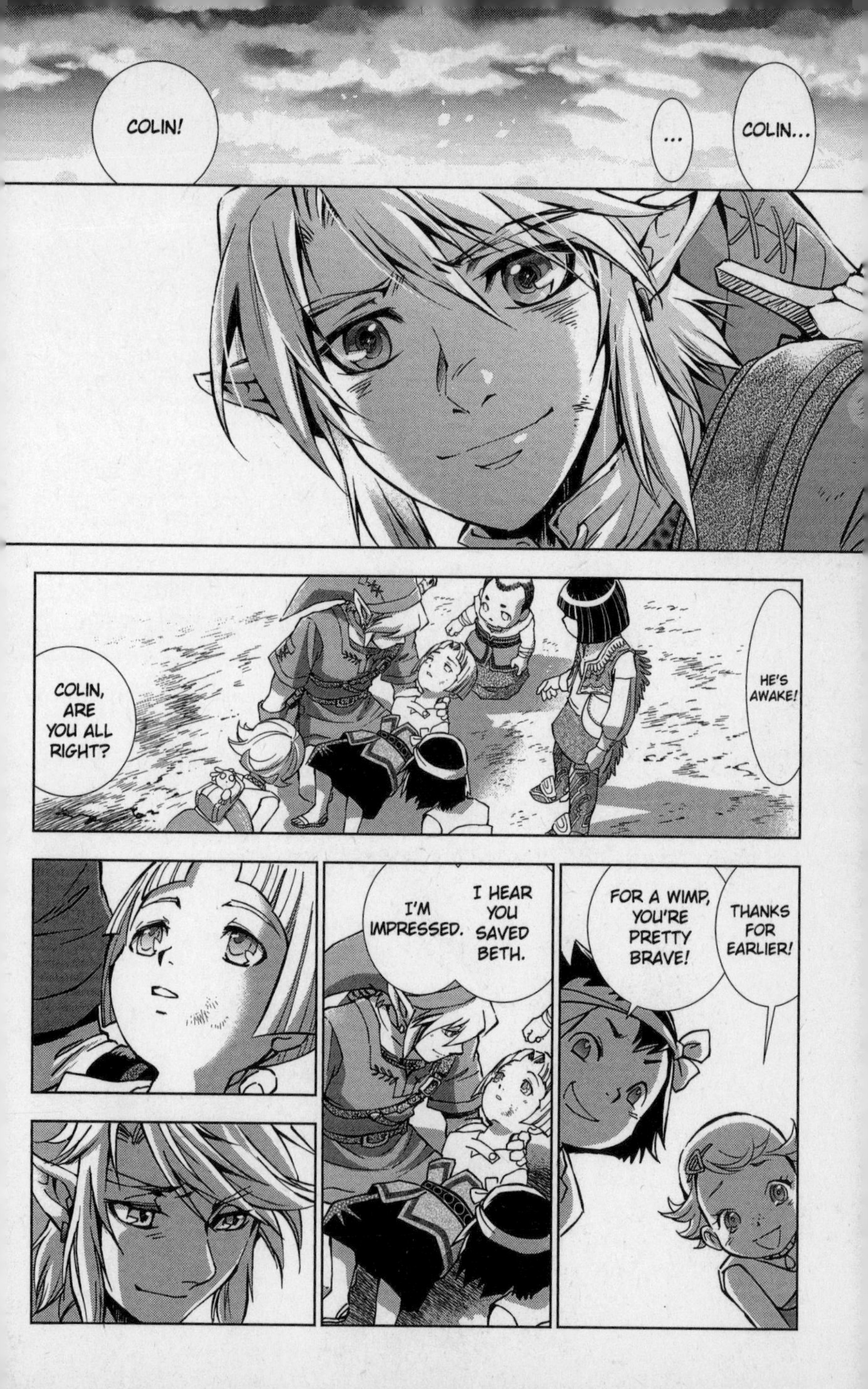
COLIN...
...
COLIN!
HE'S AWAKE!
COLIN, ARE YOU ALL RIGHT?
THANKS FOR EARLIER!
FOR A WIMP, YOU'RE PRETTY BRAVE!
I HEAR YOU SAVED BETH.
I'M IMPRESSED.

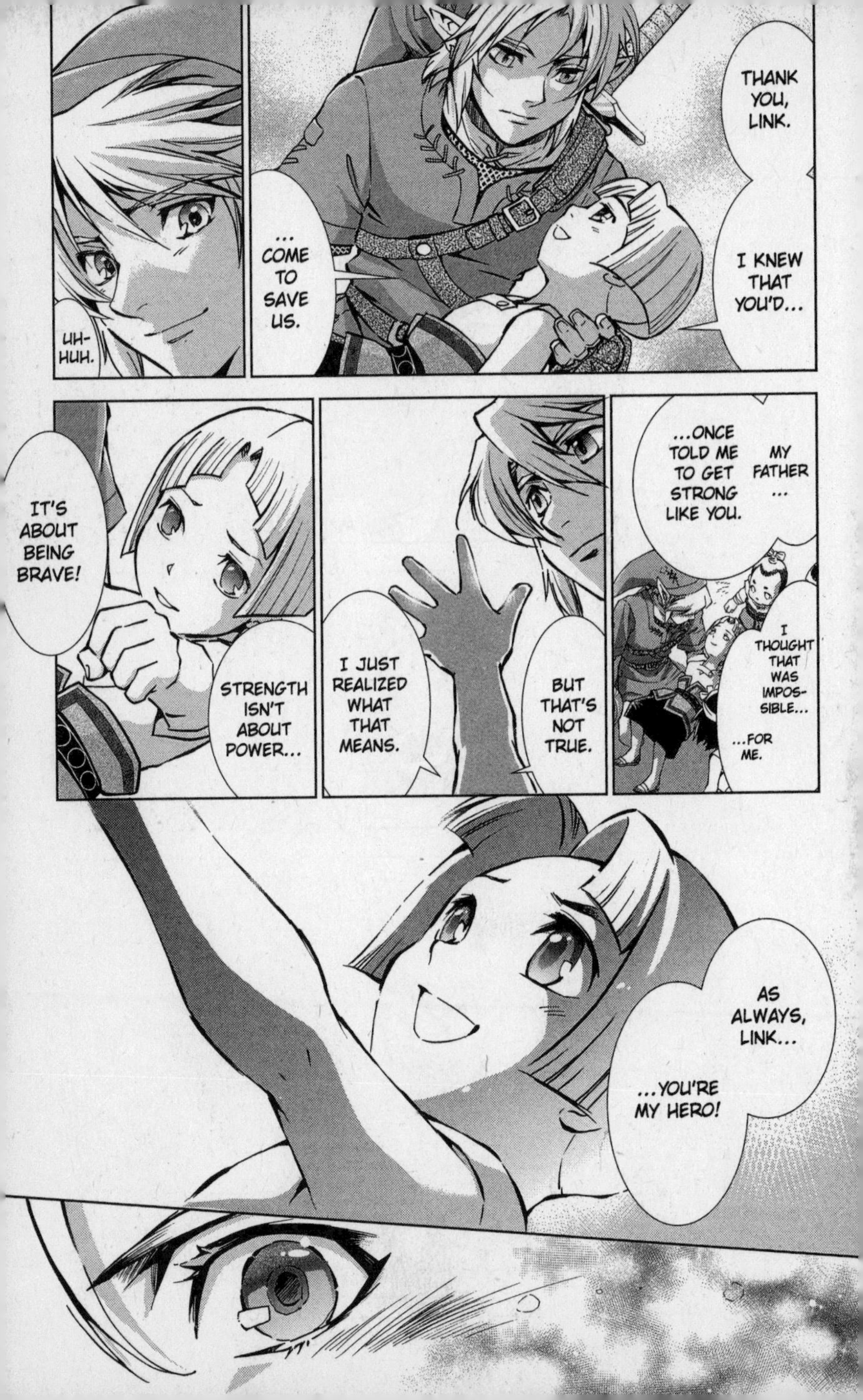
THANK YOU, LINK.
I KNEW THAT YOU'D...
...COME TO SAVE US.
UH-HUH.
MY FATHER...
...ONCE TOLD ME TO GET STRONG LIKE YOU.
I THOUGHT THAT WAS IMPOS-SIBLE...
...FOR ME.
BUT THAT'S NOT TRUE.
I JUST REALIZED WHAT THAT MEANS.
STRENGTH ISN'T ABOUT POWER...
IT'S ABOUT BEING BRAVE!
AS ALWAYS, LINK...
...YOU'RE MY HERO!

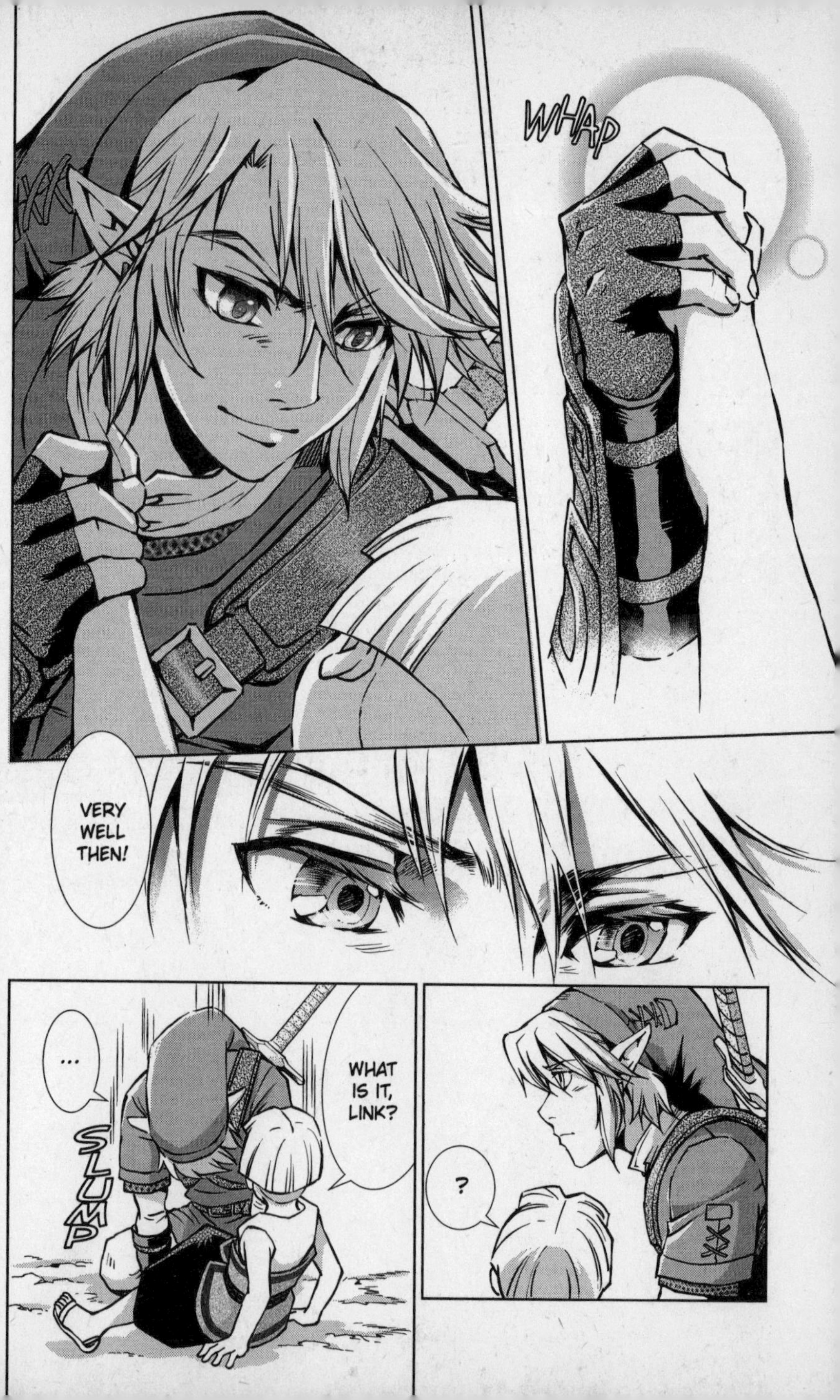
WHAP
VERY WELL THEN!
?
WHAT IS IT, LINK?
...
SLUMP

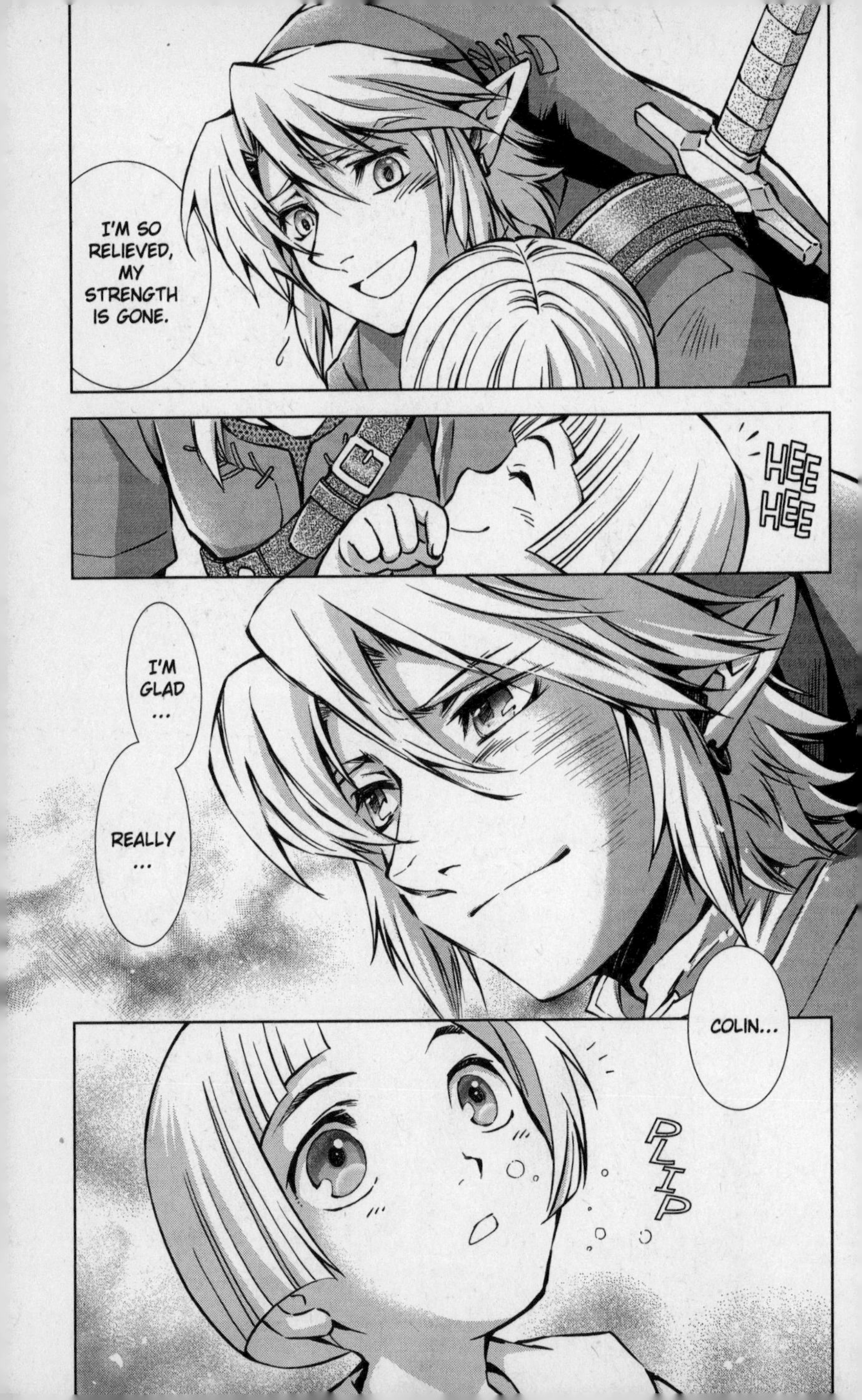
I'M SO RELIEVED, MY STRENGTH IS GONE.
HEE HEE
I'M GLAD ...
REALLY ...
COLIN...
PLIP

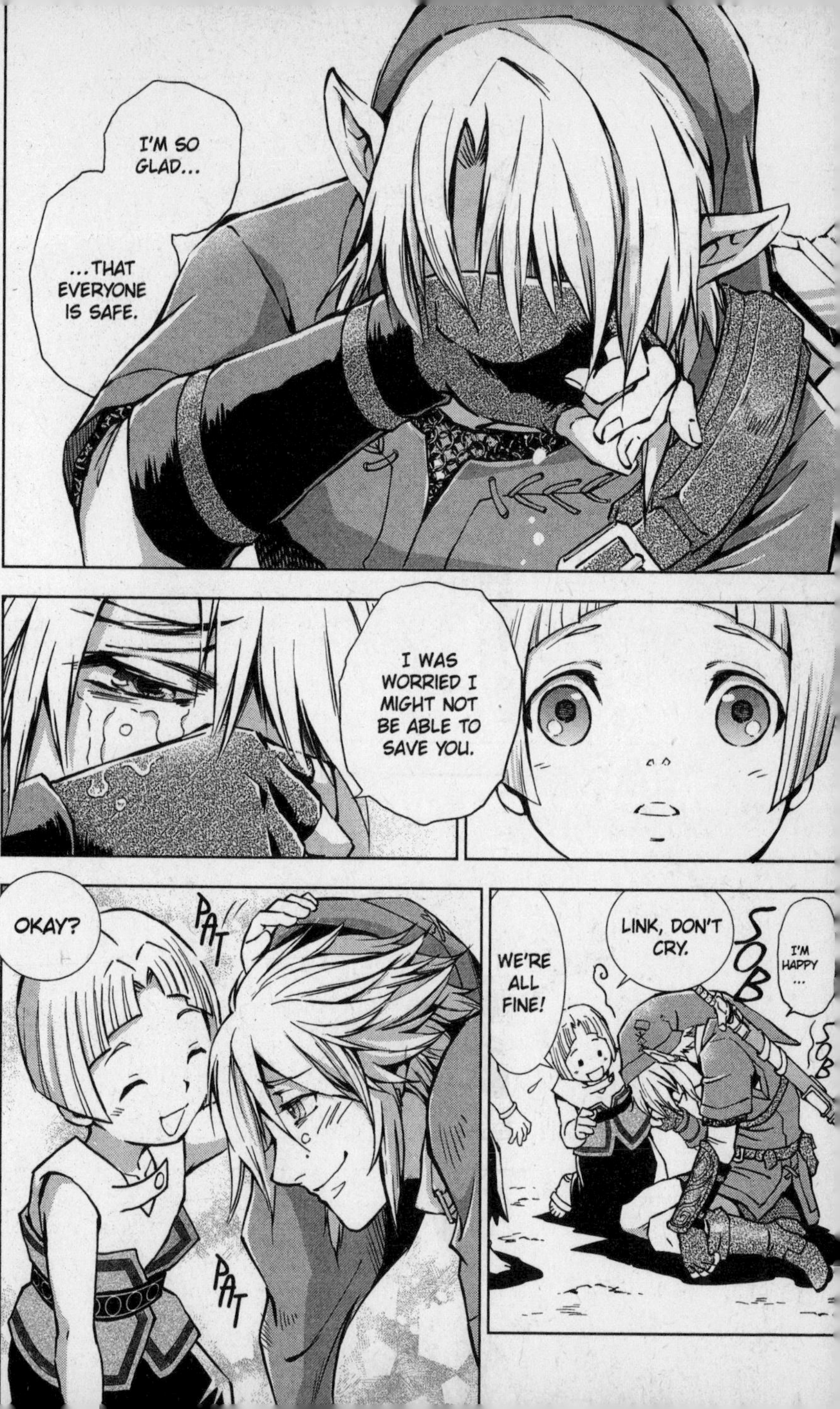
I'M SO GLAD...
...THAT EVERYONE IS SAFE.
I WAS WORRIED I MIGHT NOT BE ABLE TO SAVE YOU.
I'M HAPPY ...
SOB
SOB
LINK, DON'T CRY.
WE'RE ALL FINE!
PAT
OKAY?
PAT

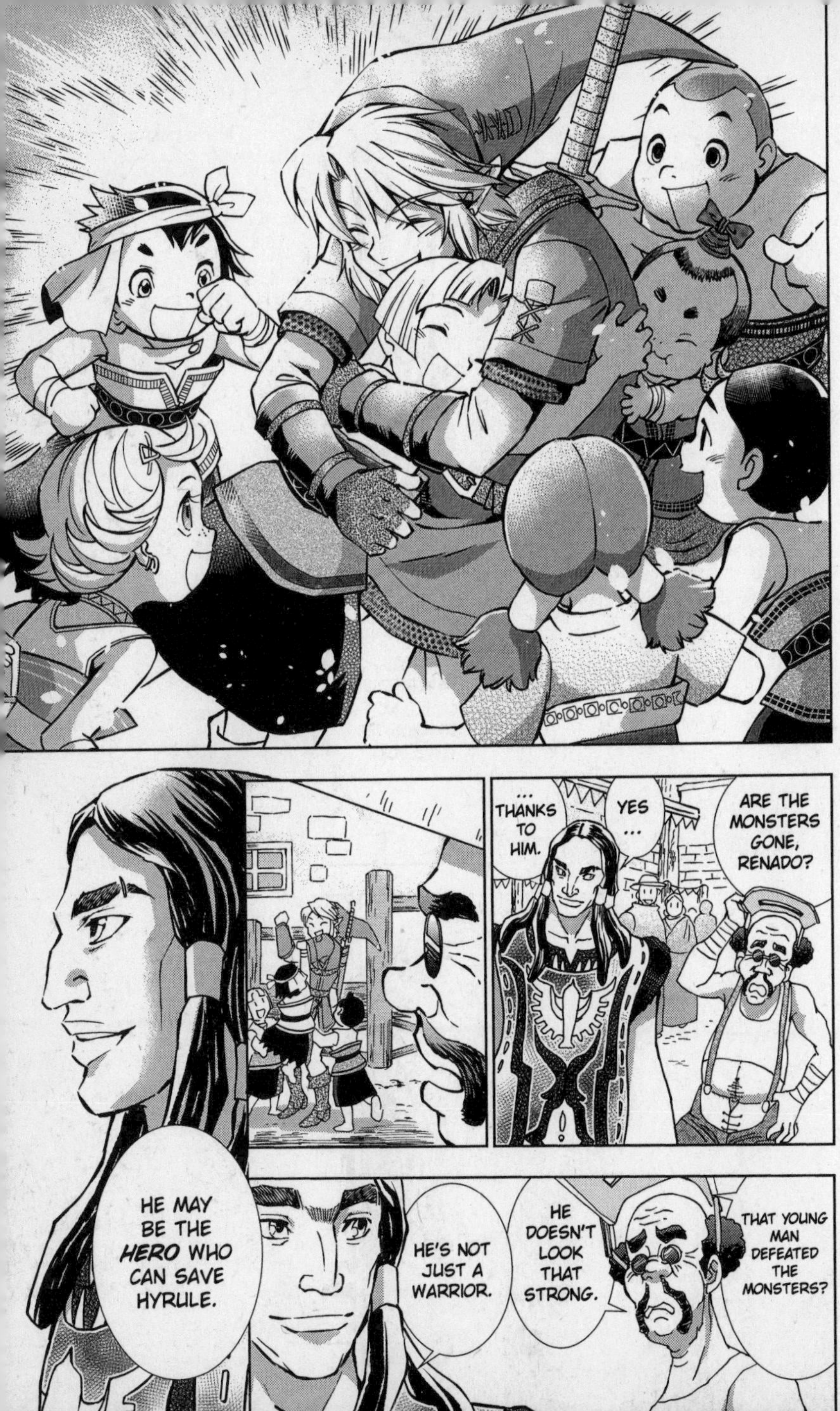
ARE THE MONSTERS GONE, RENADO?
YES ...
... THANKS TO HIM.
THAT YOUNG MAN DEFEATED THE MONSTERS?
HE DOESN'T LOOK THAT STRONG.
HE'S NOT JUST A WARRIOR.
HE MAY BE THE *HERO* WHO CAN SAVE HYRULE.

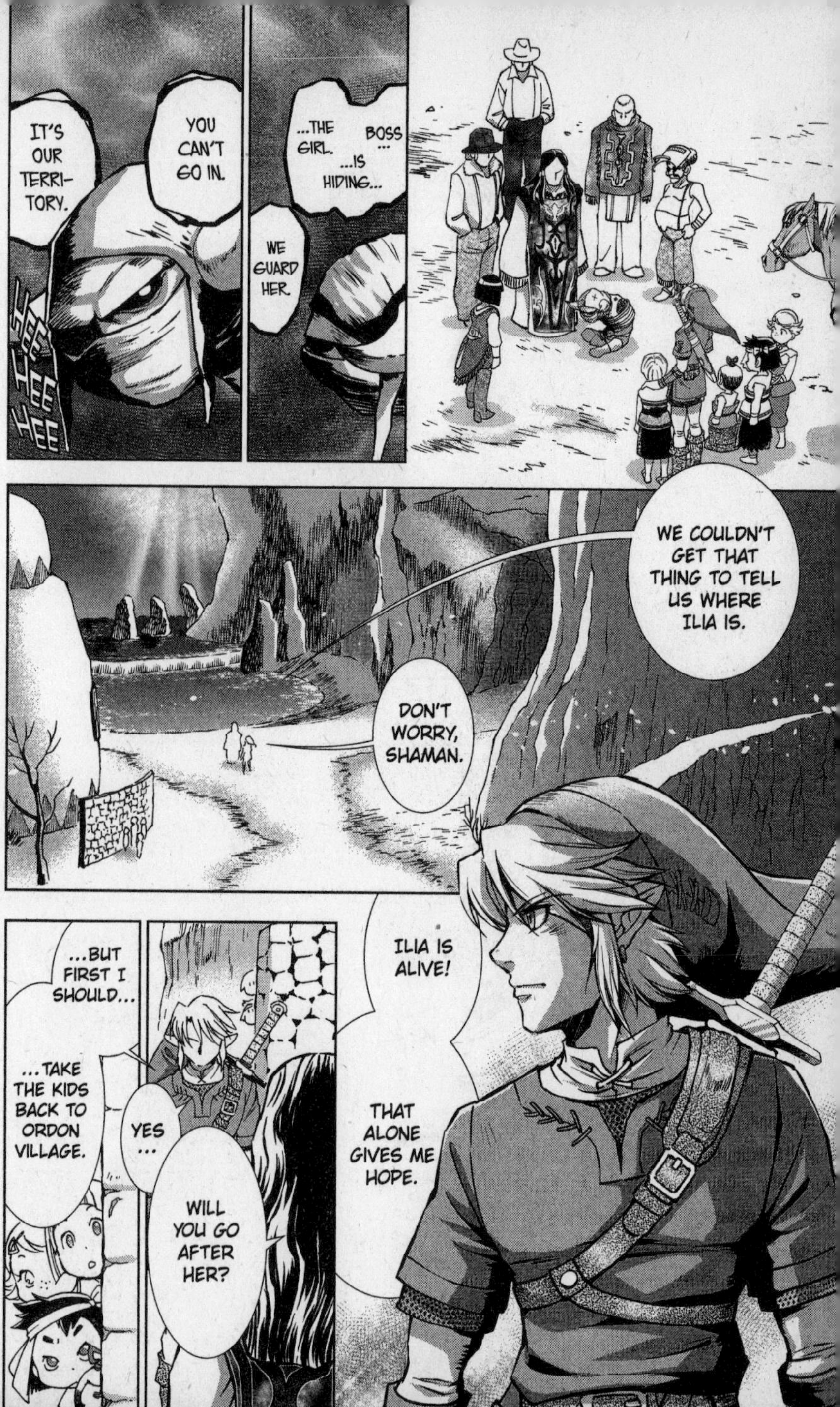
BOSS... ...THE GIRL. ...IS HIDING...
WE GUARD HER.
YOU CAN'T GO IN.
IT'S OUR TERRITORY.
HEE HEE HEE HEE
WE COULDN'T GET THAT THING TO TELL US WHERE ILIA IS.
DON'T WORRY, SHAMAN.
ILIA IS ALIVE!
THAT ALONE GIVES ME HOPE.
WILL YOU GO AFTER HER?
YES...
...BUT FIRST I SHOULD...
...TAKE THE KIDS BACK TO ORDON VILLAGE.

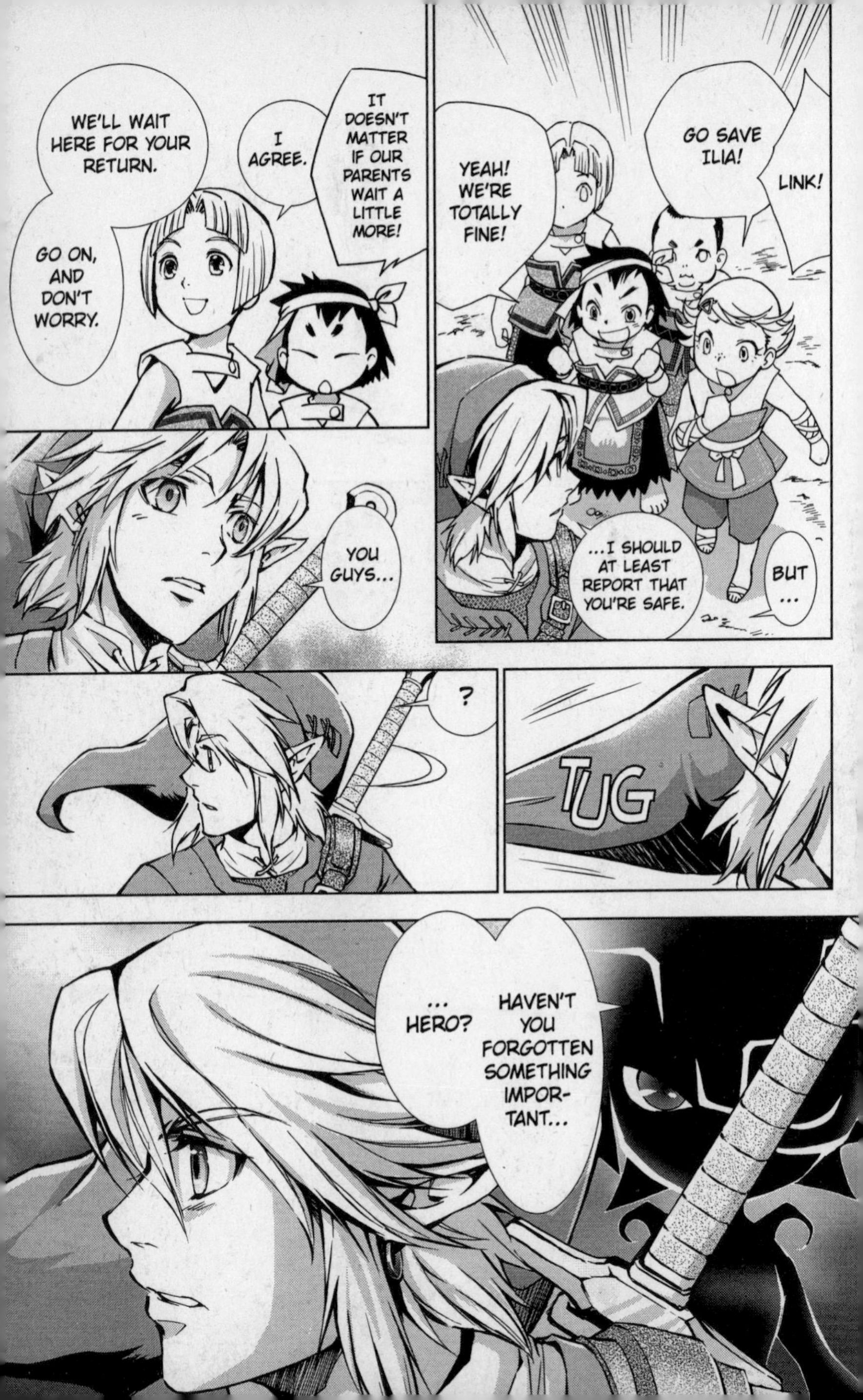
LINK!
GO SAVE ILIA!
YEAH! WE'RE TOTALLY FINE!
IT DOESN'T MATTER IF OUR PARENTS WAIT A LITTLE MORE!
I AGREE.
WE'LL WAIT HERE FOR YOUR RETURN.
GO ON, AND DON'T WORRY.
YOU GUYS...
BUT ...
...I SHOULD AT LEAST REPORT THAT YOU'RE SAFE.
TUG
?
HAVEN'T YOU FORGOTTEN SOMETHING IMPOR-TANT...
... HERO?

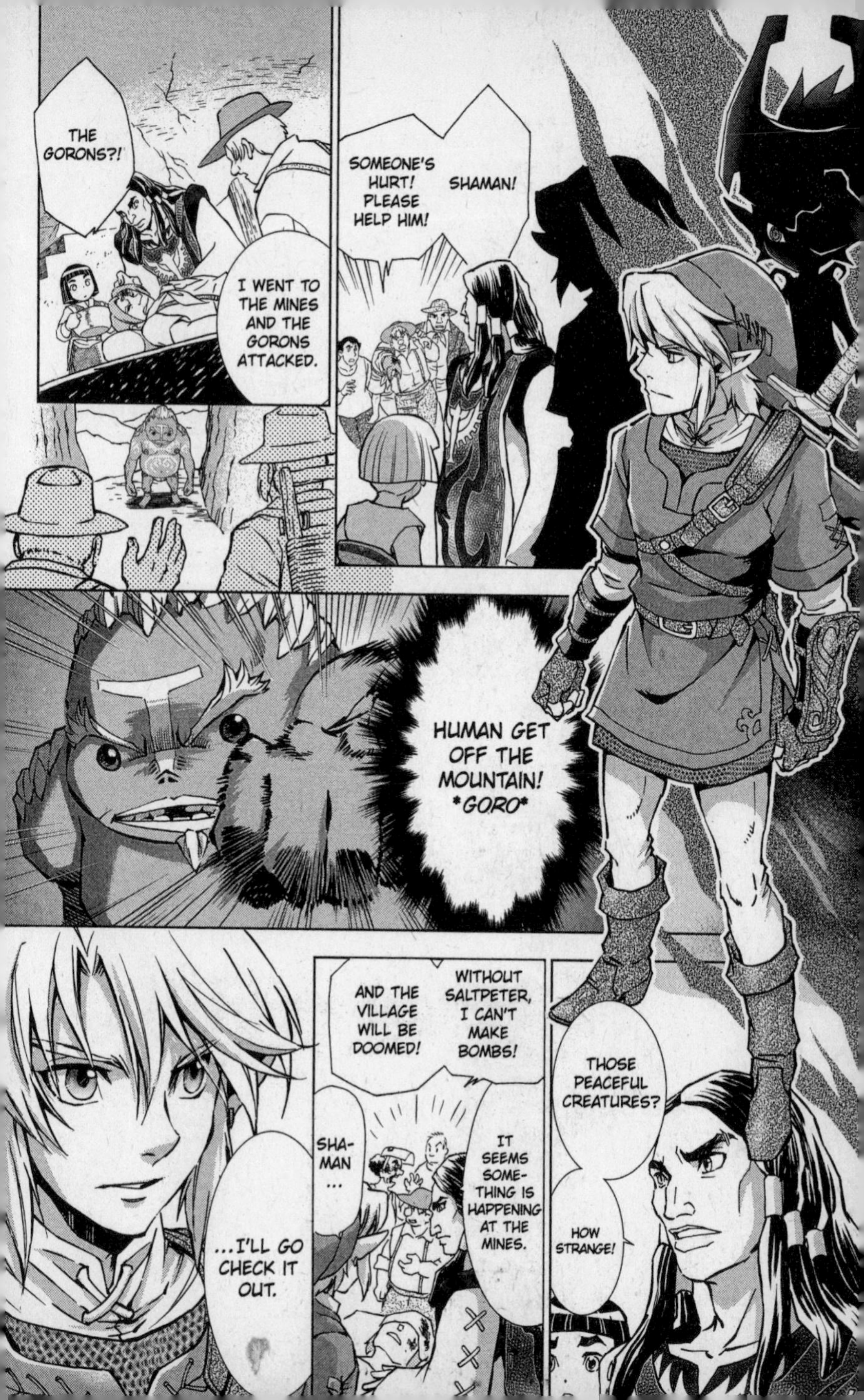
SHAMAN!
SOMEONE'S HURT! PLEASE HELP HIM!
I WENT TO THE MINES AND THE GORONS ATTACKED.
THE GORONS?!
HUMAN GET OFF THE MOUNTAIN! *GORO*
THOSE PEACEFUL CREATURES?
HOW STRANGE!
WITHOUT SALTPETER, I CAN'T MAKE BOMBS!
AND THE VILLAGE WILL BE DOOMED!
IT SEEMS SOMETHING IS HAPPENING AT THE MINES.
SHA-MAN ...
...I'LL GO CHECK IT OUT.

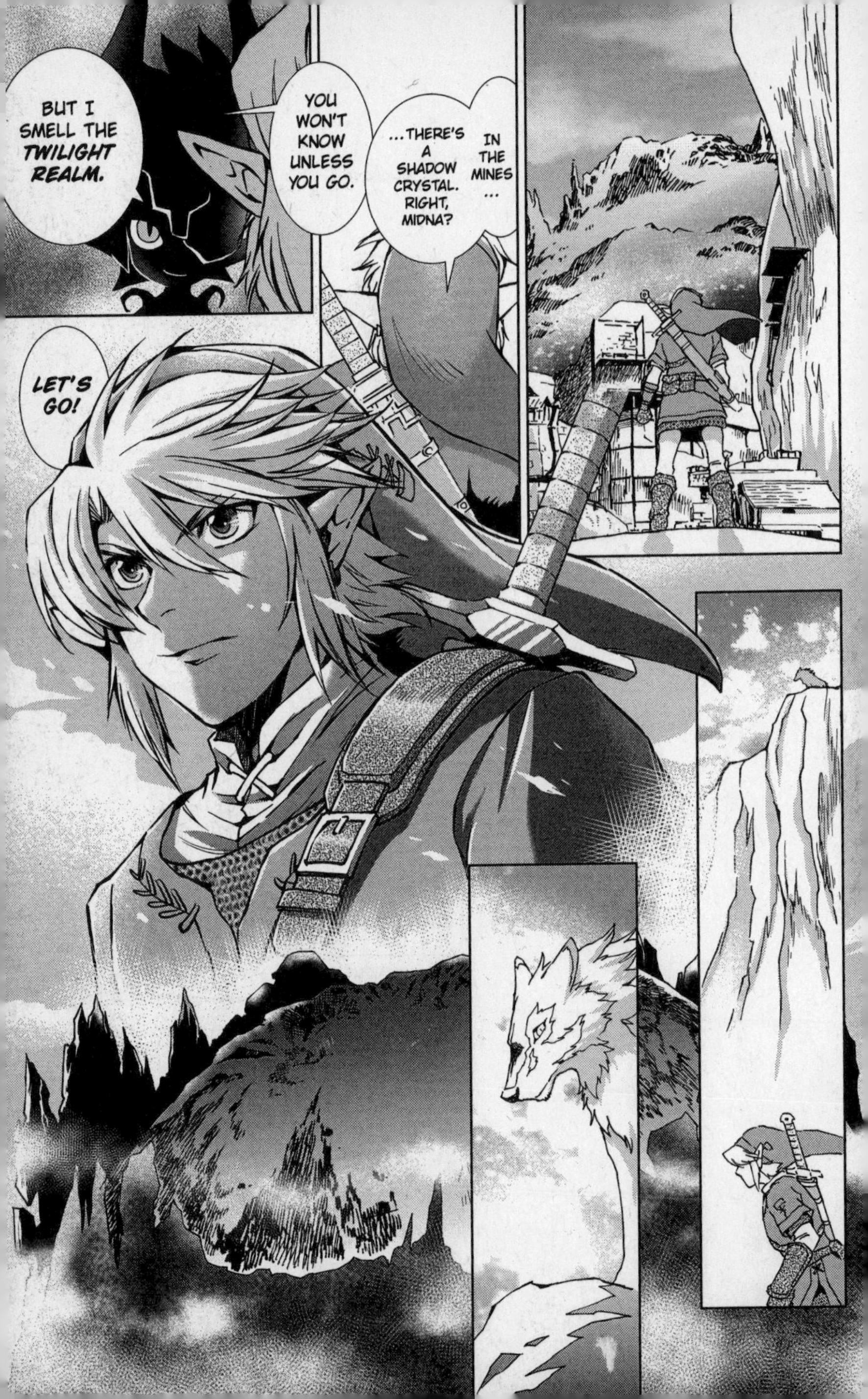
IN THE MINES...
...THERE'S A SHADOW CRYSTAL. RIGHT, MIDNA?
YOU WON'T KNOW UNLESS YOU GO.
BUT I SMELL THE *TWILIGHT REALM.*
LET'S GO!

AUTHOR'S NOTE

In March this year, it has been 3o years since we teamed up and began life as manga creators. There have been a lot of highs and lows, but we've finally reached a turning point. We'd like to take this occasion to make a fresh start and continue on with more enthusiasm than ever! Also, we recently resumed Western horseback riding. We are just beginners so, without asking too much of ourselves, we're taking it easy and enjoying life that way too. We will develop a bond to rival the one between Link and Epona!! ^^

Akira Himekawa is the collaboration of two women, A. Honda and S. Nagano. Together they have created ten manga adventures featuring Link and the popular video game world of *The Legend of Zelda*™. Their most recent work, *The Legend of Zelda*™: *Twilight Princess*, is serialized digitally on Shogakukan's MangaONE app in Japan.

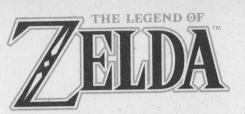

THE LEGEND OF ZELDA™

TWILIGHT PRINCESS

Volume 3—VIZ Media Edition

STORY AND ART BY
Akira Himekawa

TRANSLATION John Werry
ENGLISH ADAPTATION Stan!
TOUCH-UP ART & LETTERING Evan Waldinger
DESIGNER Shawn Carrico
EDITOR Mike Montesa

Printed in the U.S.A.

Published by VIZ Media, LLC
P.O. Box 77010
San Francisco, CA 94107

10 9 8 7 6 5 4 3 2 1
First printing, March 2018

viz media
www.viz.com

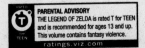

POCKET COMICS

STORY & ART BY **SANTA HARUKAZE**

BLACK & WHITE

LEGENDARY POKÉMON

X•Y

A Pokémon pocket-sized book chock-full of four-panel gags, Pokémon trivia and fun quizzes based on the characters you know and love!

viz media
www.viz.com

Begin your Pokémon Adventure here in the Kanto region!

POKÉMON™ ADVENTURES

RED & BLUE BOX SET

Story by HIDENORI KUSAKA Art by MATO

POKÉMON
ADVENTURES
Bonus Poster Inside!
RED & BLUE BOX SET:
POKÉMON ADVENTURES VOLUMES 1-7

Includes POKÉMON ADVENTURES Vols. 1-7 and a collectible poster!

All your favorite Pokémon game characters jump out of the screen into the pages of this action-packed manga!

Red doesn't just want to train Pokémon, he wants to be their friend too. Bulbasaur and Poliwhirl seem game. But independent Pikachu won't be so easy to win over!

And watch out for Team Rocket, Red... They only want to be your enemy!

Start the adventure today!

RATED A FOR ALL AGES ratings.viz.com

PERFECT SQUARE

VIZ media www.viz.com

The adventure continues in the Johto region!

POKÉMON™

ADVENTURES

GOLD & SILVER BOX SET

Story by
**HIDENORI
KUSAKA**

Art by
MATO,

**SATOSHI
YAMAMOTO**

More exciting Pokémon adventures starring Gold and his rival Silver! First someone steals Gold's backpack full of Poké Balls (and Pokémon!). Then someone steals Prof. Elm's Totodile. Can Gold catch the thief—or thieves?!

Keep an eye on Team Rocket, Gold... Could they be behind this crime wave?

POKÉMON
ΩRUBY • αSAPPHIRE
OMEGA • ALPHA

STORY BY
HIDENORI KUSAKA

ART BY
SATOSHI YAMAMOTO

Awesome adventures inspired by the best-selling
Pokémon Omega Ruby and Pokémon Alpha Sapphire
video games that pick up where the *Pokémon Adventures*
Ruby & Sapphire saga left off!

viz media
viz.com

RATED
A
ALL AGES

Hey! You're Reading in the Wrong Direction!

This is the **end** of this graphic novel!

To properly enjoy this VIZ graphic novel, please turn it around and begin reading from **right to left.** Unlike English, Japanese is read right to left, so Japanese comics are read in reverse order from the way English comics are typically read.

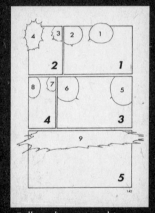

Follow the action this way

This book has been printed in the original Japanese format in order to preserve the orientation of the original artwork. Have fun with it!